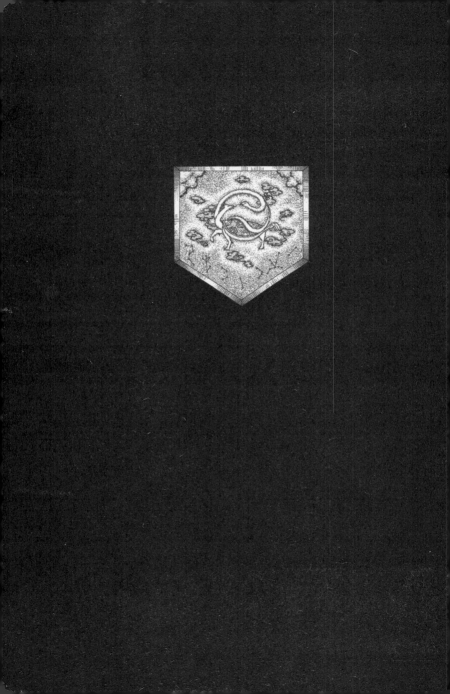

Shojo Beat

Fushigi Yûgi
Genbu Kaiden

四神天地之書
召喚神獸時
巫女和七星士必須調氣
使之進入「無」的狀態
ふしぎ遊戯
玄武開伝
渡瀬悠宇

story and art by **YUU WATASE** Vol. 8

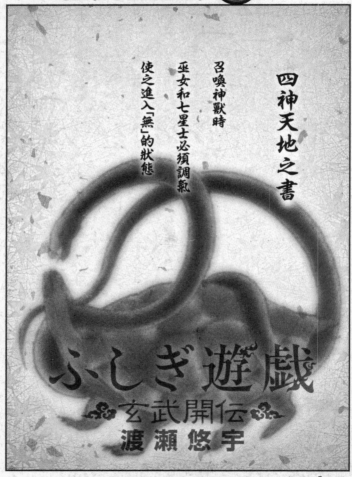

CONTENTS

TRANSLATION OF "THE UNIVERSE OF
THE FOUR GODS"

At the summoning of the Sacred Beast, the Priestess
and the seven Celestial Warriors must compose their
chis and empty their minds.

Cast of **Characters**

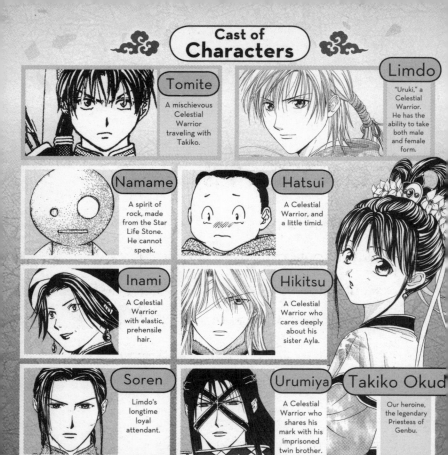

Tomite
A mischievous Celestial Warrior traveling with Takiko.

Limdo
"Uruki," a Celestial Warrior. He has the ability to take both male and female form.

Namame
A spirit of rock, made from the Star Life Stone. He cannot speak.

Hatsui
A Celestial Warrior, and a little timid.

Inami
A Celestial Warrior with elastic, prehensile hair.

Hikitsu
A Celestial Warrior who cares deeply about his sister Ayla.

Soren
Limdo's longtime loyal attendant.

Urumiya
A Celestial Warrior who shares his mark with his imprisoned twin brother.

Takiko Okud
Our heroine, the legendary Priestess of Genbu.

The Story Thus Far

The year is 1923. Takiko is drawn into the pages of *The Universe of the Four Gods*, a book her father has translated from Chinese. There, she is told that she is the legendary Priestess of Genbu, destined to save the country of Bêi-jîa. She must find the seven Celestial Warriors who will help her on her quest.

Urumiya refuses to join the Celestial Warriors, not believing that Takiko can help him save his brother Teg. When Takiko is taken captive, Uruki's retainer, Soren, sacrifices his life to save her. Inconsolable at Soren's death, Uruki attacks Tèwulán in a blind rage. He is thwarted by Teg, who has the power to neutralize Celestial powers with his song. Badly wounded, Uruki collapses and is rescued by a mysterious girl...

FUSHIGI YÛGI:
GENBU KAIDEN

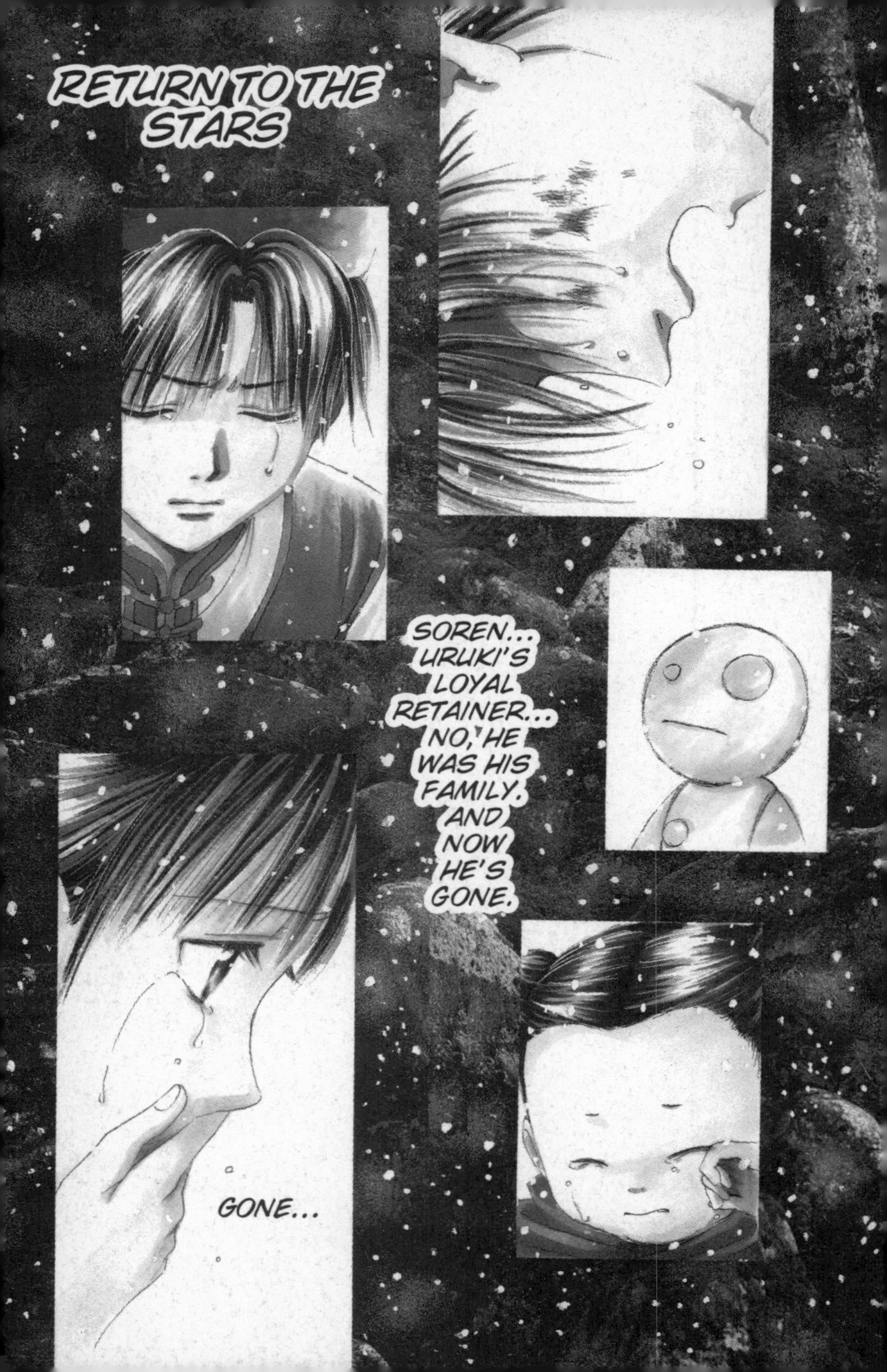
RETURN TO THE STARS
SOREN... URUKI'S LOYAL RETAINER... NO, HE WAS HIS FAMILY. AND NOW HE'S GONE.
GONE...

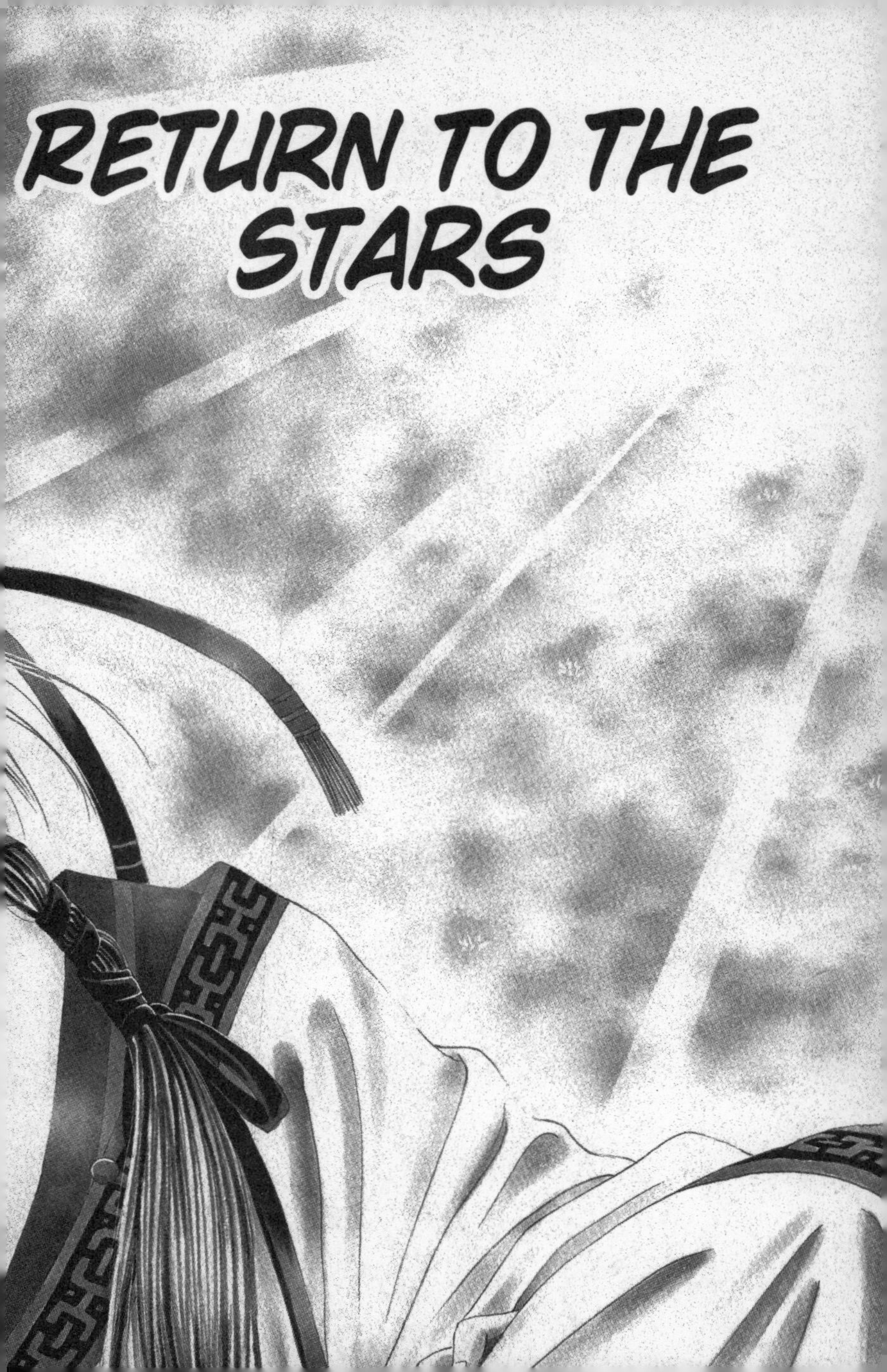
RETURN TO THE STARS

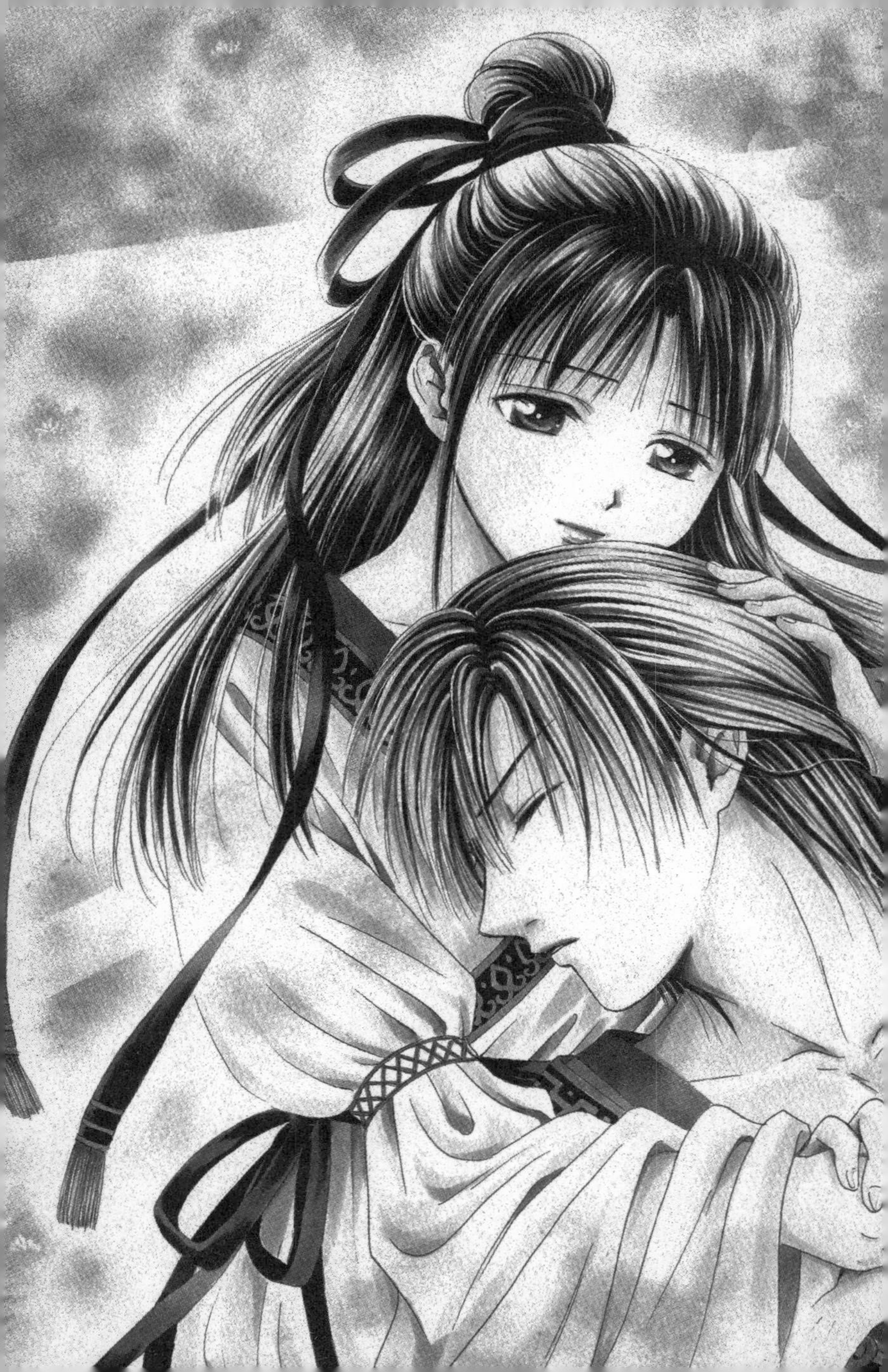

FUSHIGI YÛGI: GENBU KAIDEN

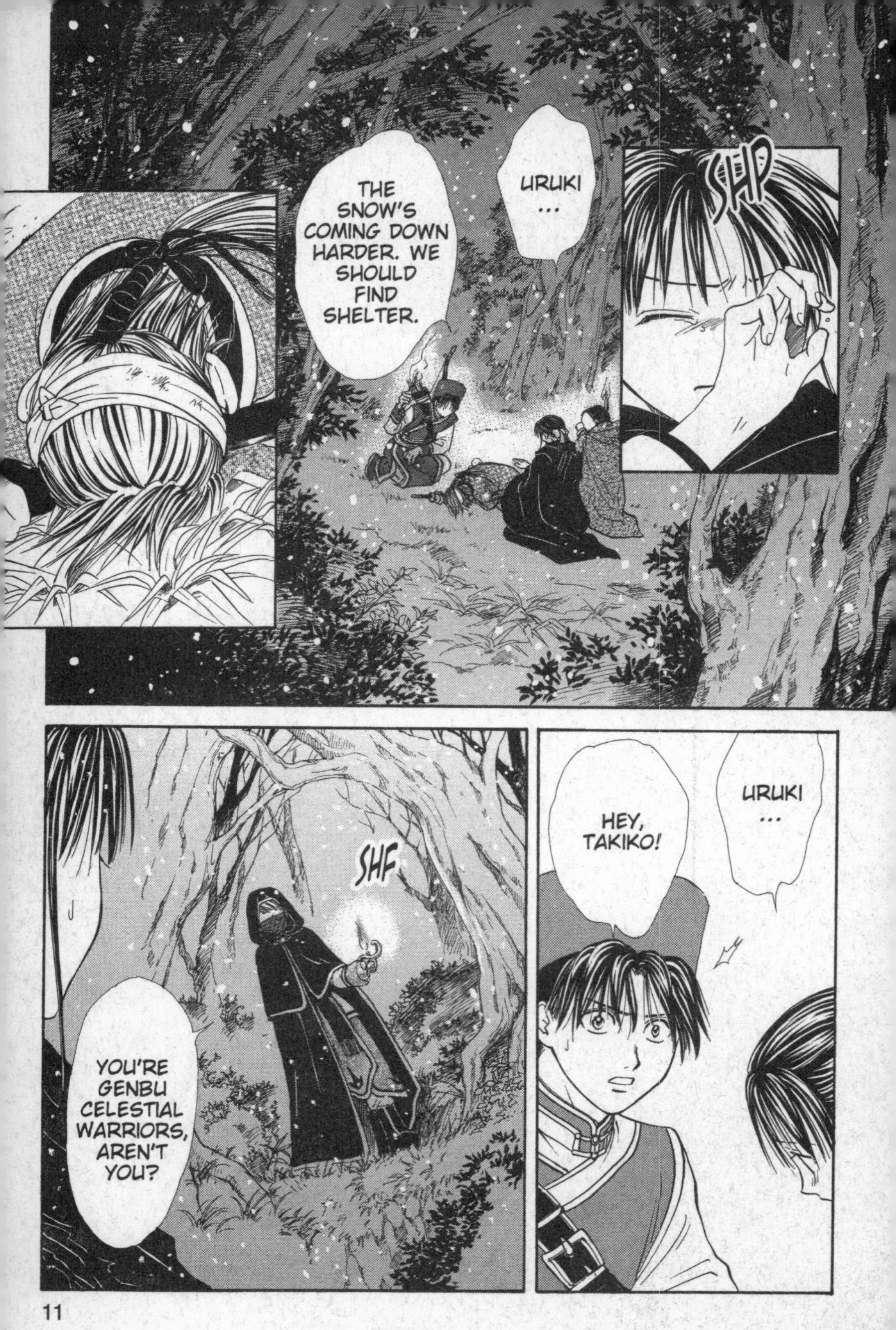
SHP
URUKI ...
THE SNOW'S COMING DOWN HARDER. WE SHOULD FIND SHELTER.
URUKI ...
HEY, TAKIKO!
SHF
YOU'RE GENBU CELESTIAL WARRIORS, AREN'T YOU?

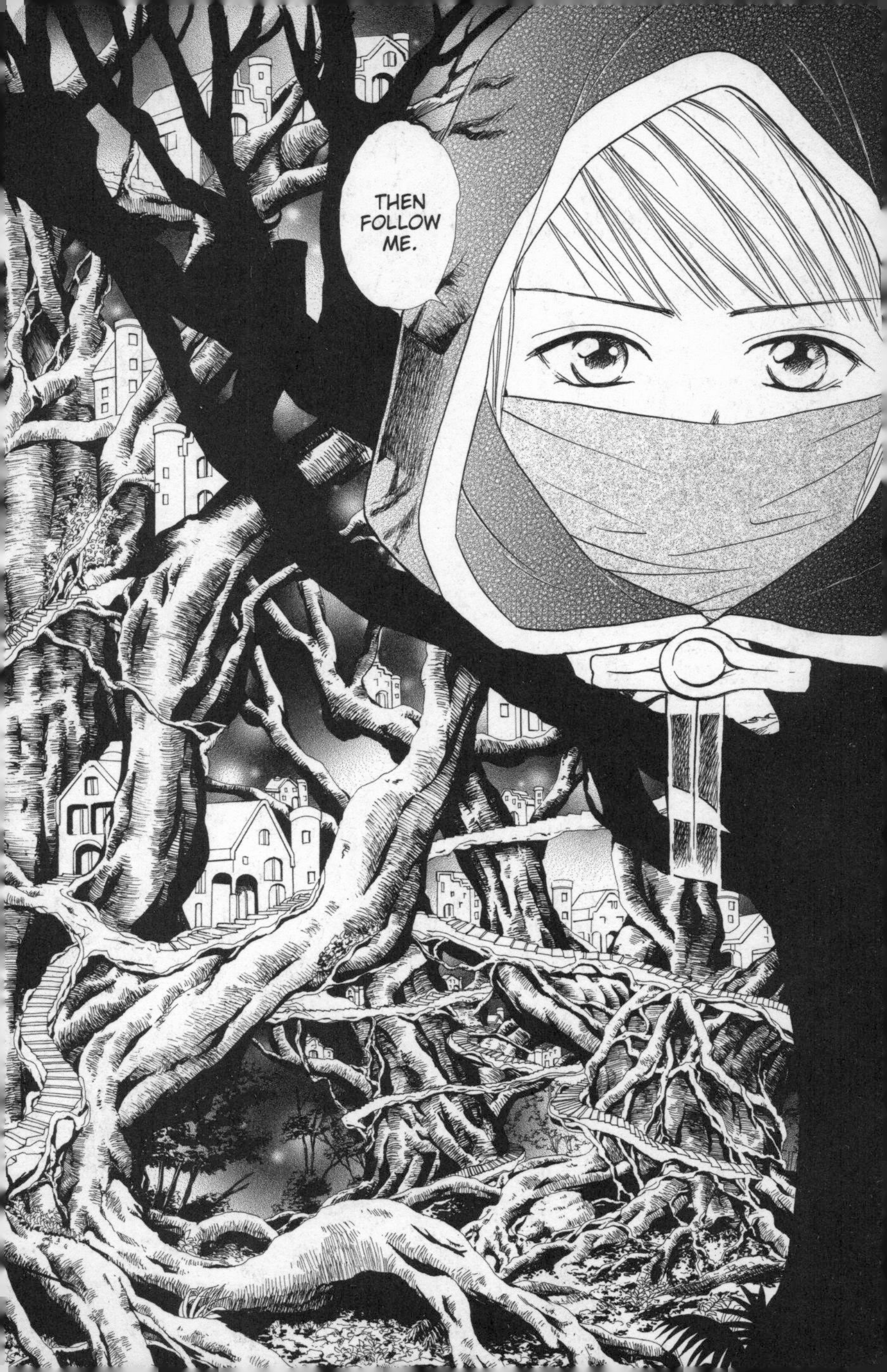
THEN FOLLOW ME.

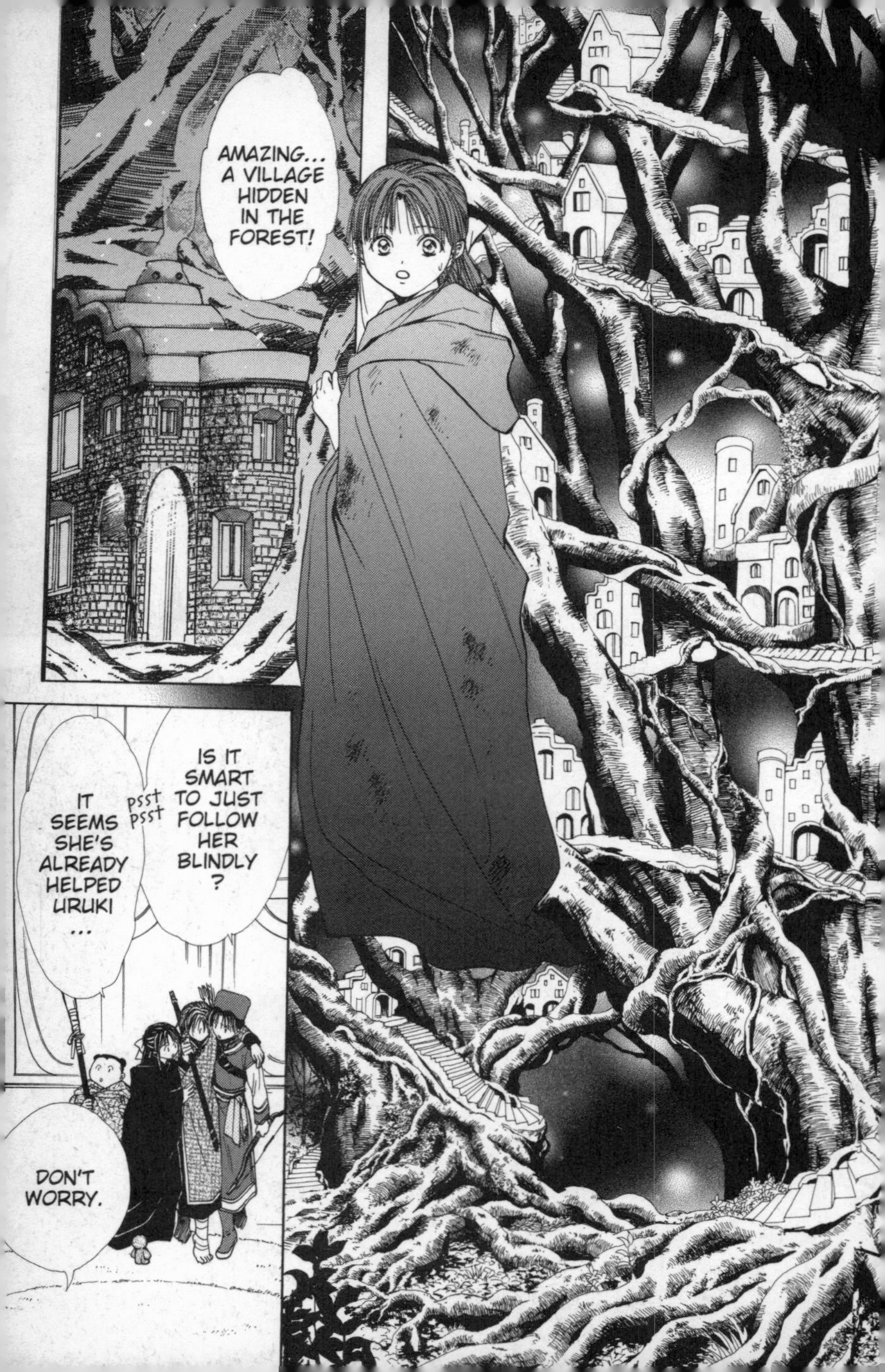
AMAZING... A VILLAGE HIDDEN IN THE FOREST!
IS IT SMART TO JUST FOLLOW HER BLINDLY?
psst psst
IT SEEMS SHE'S ALREADY HELPED URUKI...
DON'T WORRY.

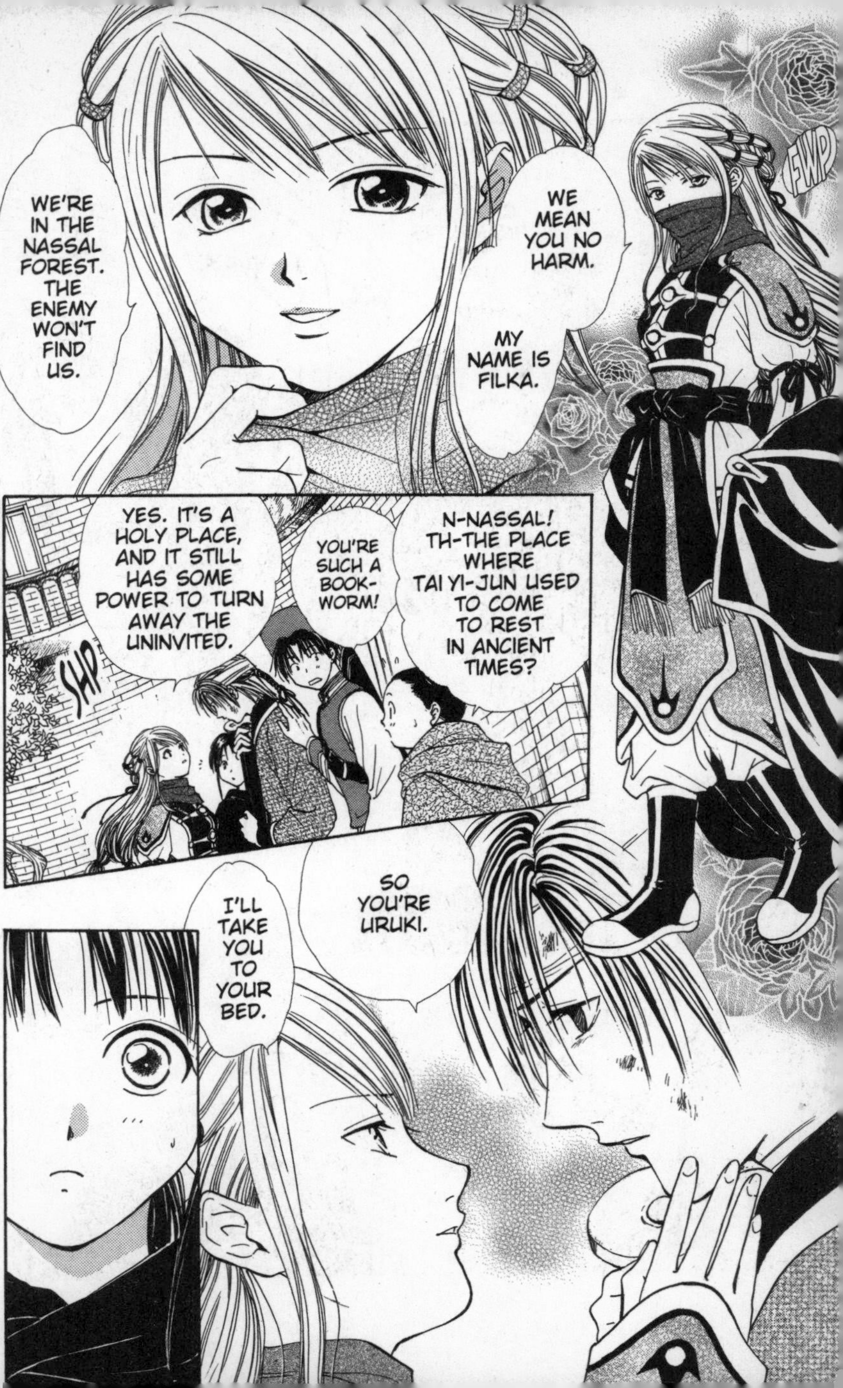
FWP
WE MEAN YOU NO HARM.
MY NAME IS FILKA.
WE'RE IN THE NASSAL FOREST. THE ENEMY WON'T FIND US.
N-NASSAL! TH-THE PLACE WHERE TAI YI-JUN USED TO COME TO REST IN ANCIENT TIMES?
YOU'RE SUCH A BOOK-WORM!
YES. IT'S A HOLY PLACE, AND IT STILL HAS SOME POWER TO TURN AWAY THE UNINVITED.
SHP
SO YOU'RE URUKI.
I'LL TAKE YOU TO YOUR BED.

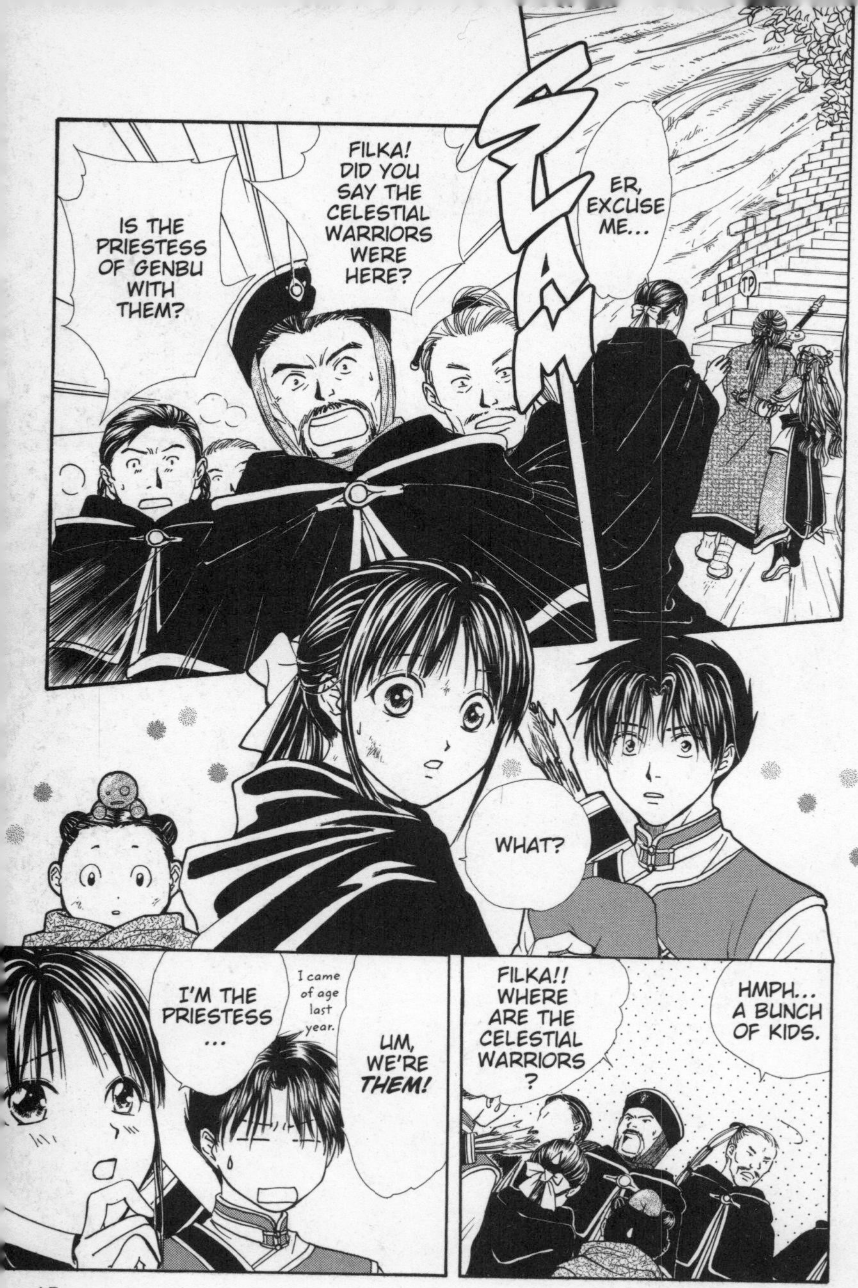
ER, EXCUSE ME...
SLAM
FILKA! DID YOU SAY THE CELESTIAL WARRIORS WERE HERE?
IS THE PRIESTESS OF GENBU WITH THEM?
WHAT?
HMPH... A BUNCH OF KIDS.
FILKA!! WHERE ARE THE CELESTIAL WARRIORS?
UM, WE'RE *THEM!*
I came of age last year.
I'M THE PRIESTESS...

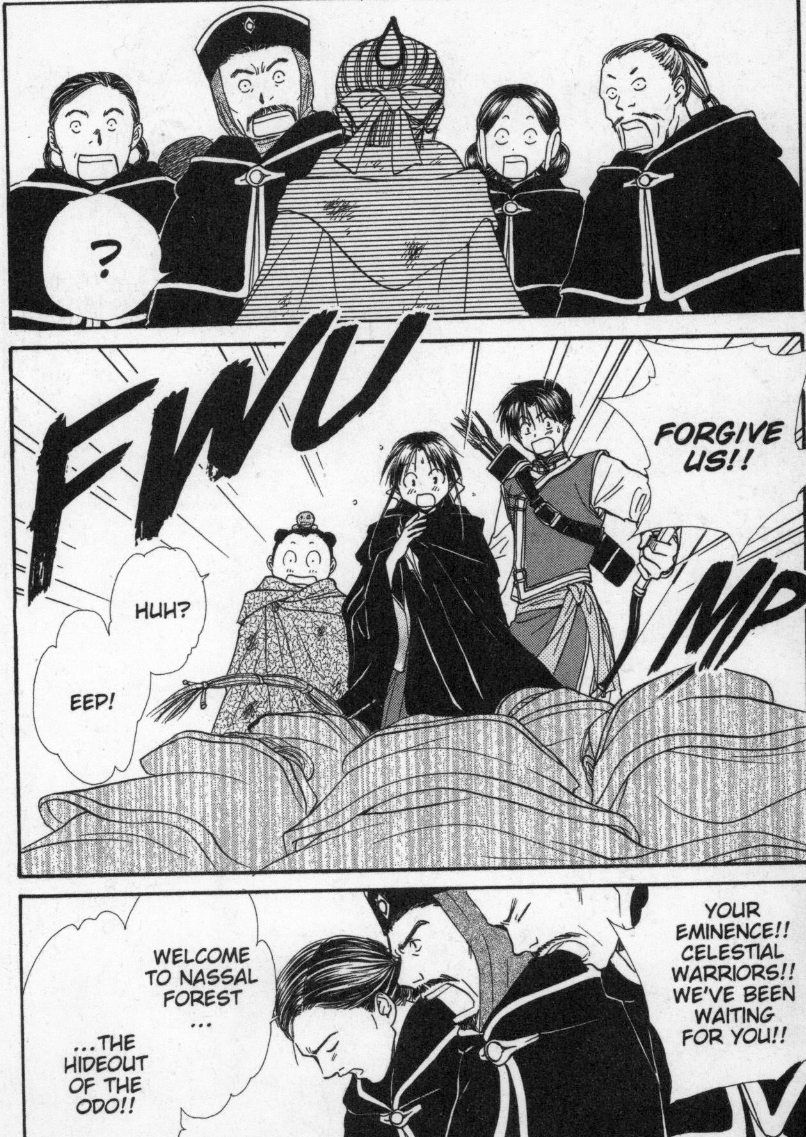
?
FORGIVE US!!
FWU
MP
HUH?
EEP!
YOUR EMINENCE!! CELESTIAL WARRIORS!! WE'VE BEEN WAITING FOR YOU!!
WELCOME TO NASSAL FOREST ...
...THE HIDEOUT OF THE ODO!!

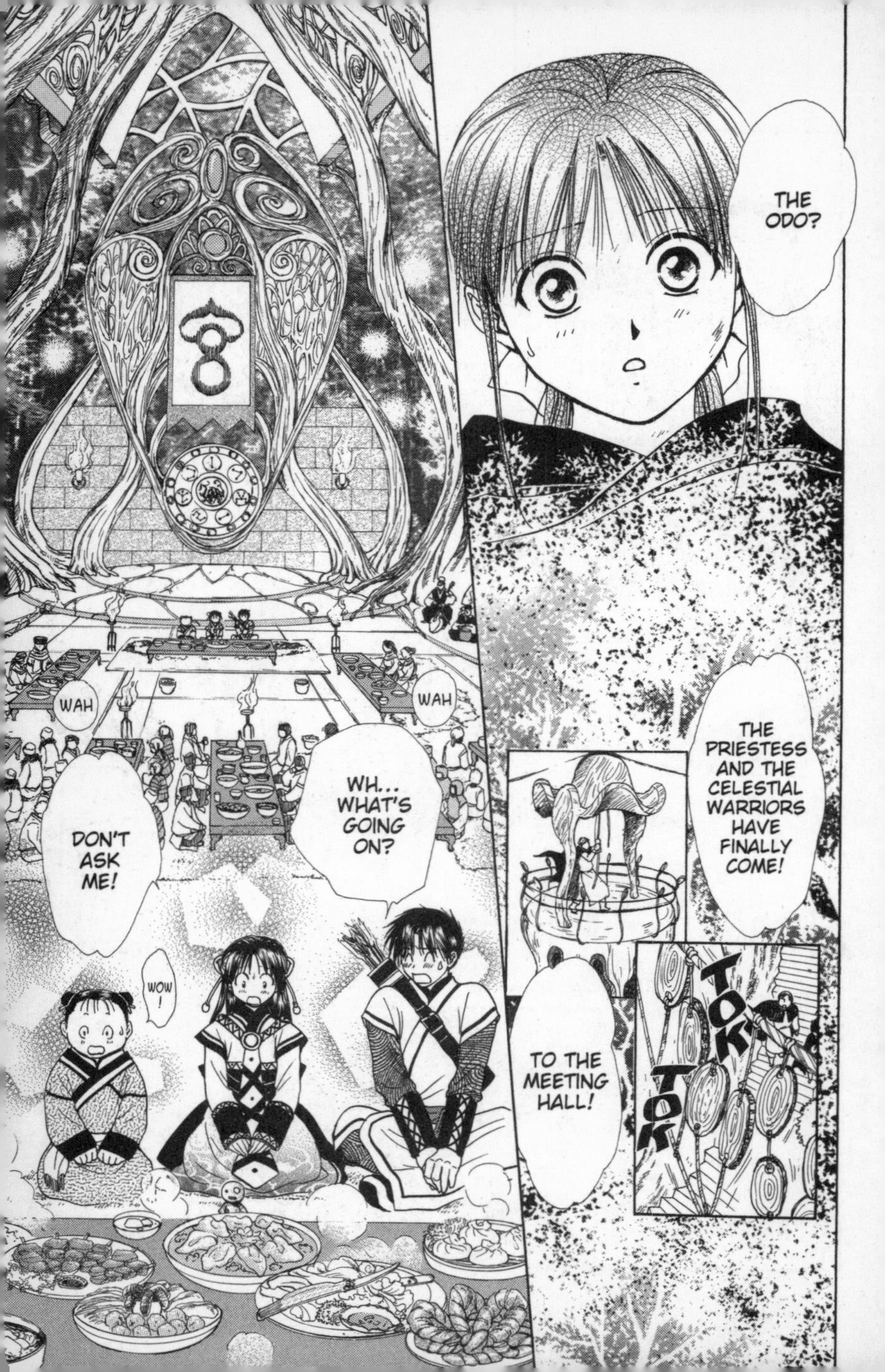
THE ODO?
THE PRIESTESS AND THE CELESTIAL WARRIORS HAVE FINALLY COME!
TOK TOK TOK
TO THE MEETING HALL!
WAH
WAH
WH... WHAT'S GOING ON?
DON'T ASK ME!
WOW!

YOUR EMINENCE! CELESTIAL WARRIORS! PLEASE HELP YOUR-SELVES.
THANK YOU, CHIEF.
YOU MUST'VE HAD A LONG, HARSH JOURNEY ...
...BUT WE CAN TALK LATER. YOU NEED YOUR REST.
FILKA IS TAKING GOOD CARE OF URUKI.
YOU STILL DON'T FEEL LIKE EATING?
YOU SHOULD LIE DOWN THEN.

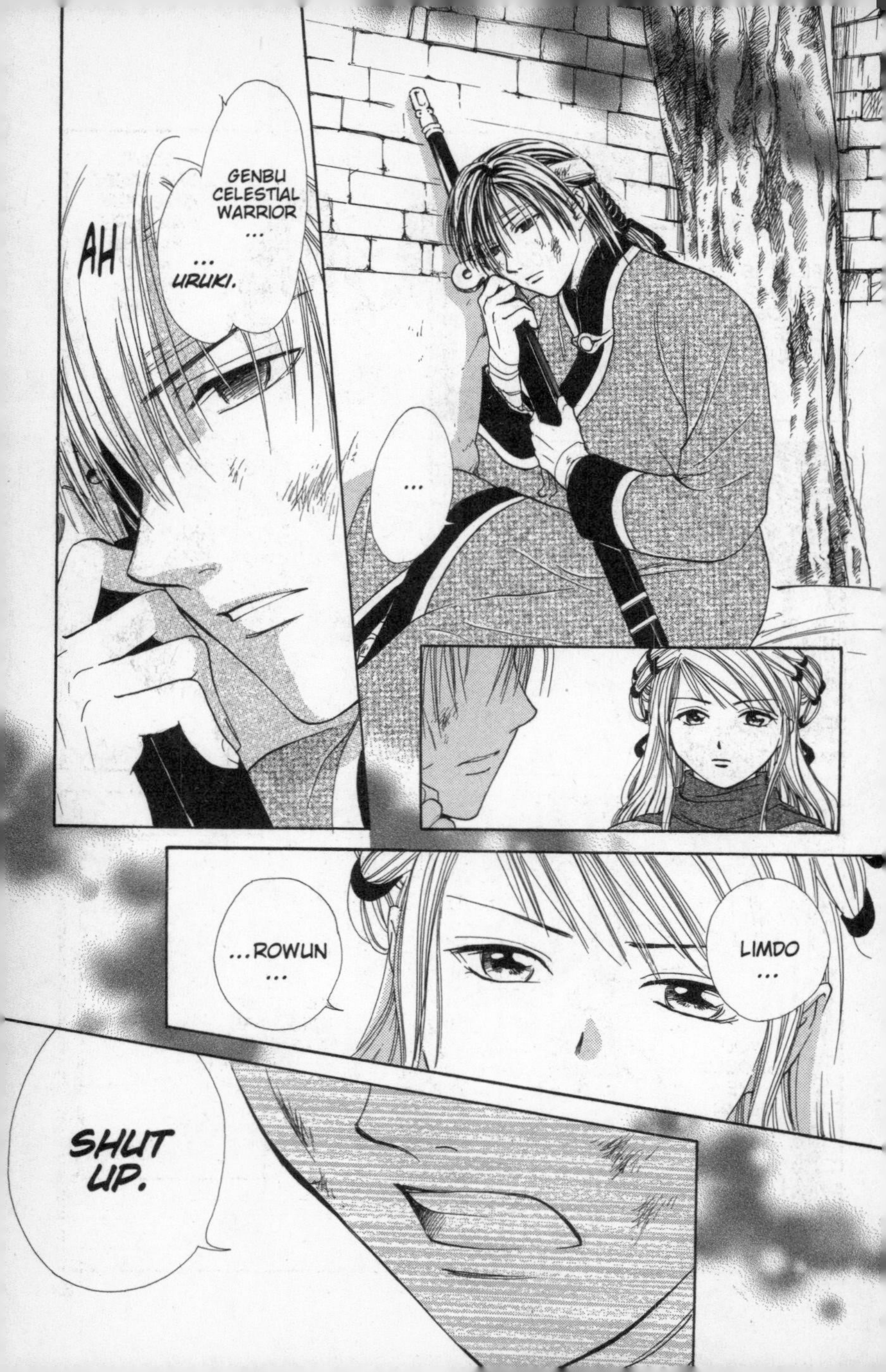
...
GENBU CELESTIAL WARRIOR ... ... URUKI.
AH
LIMDO ...
...ROWUN ...
SHUT UP.

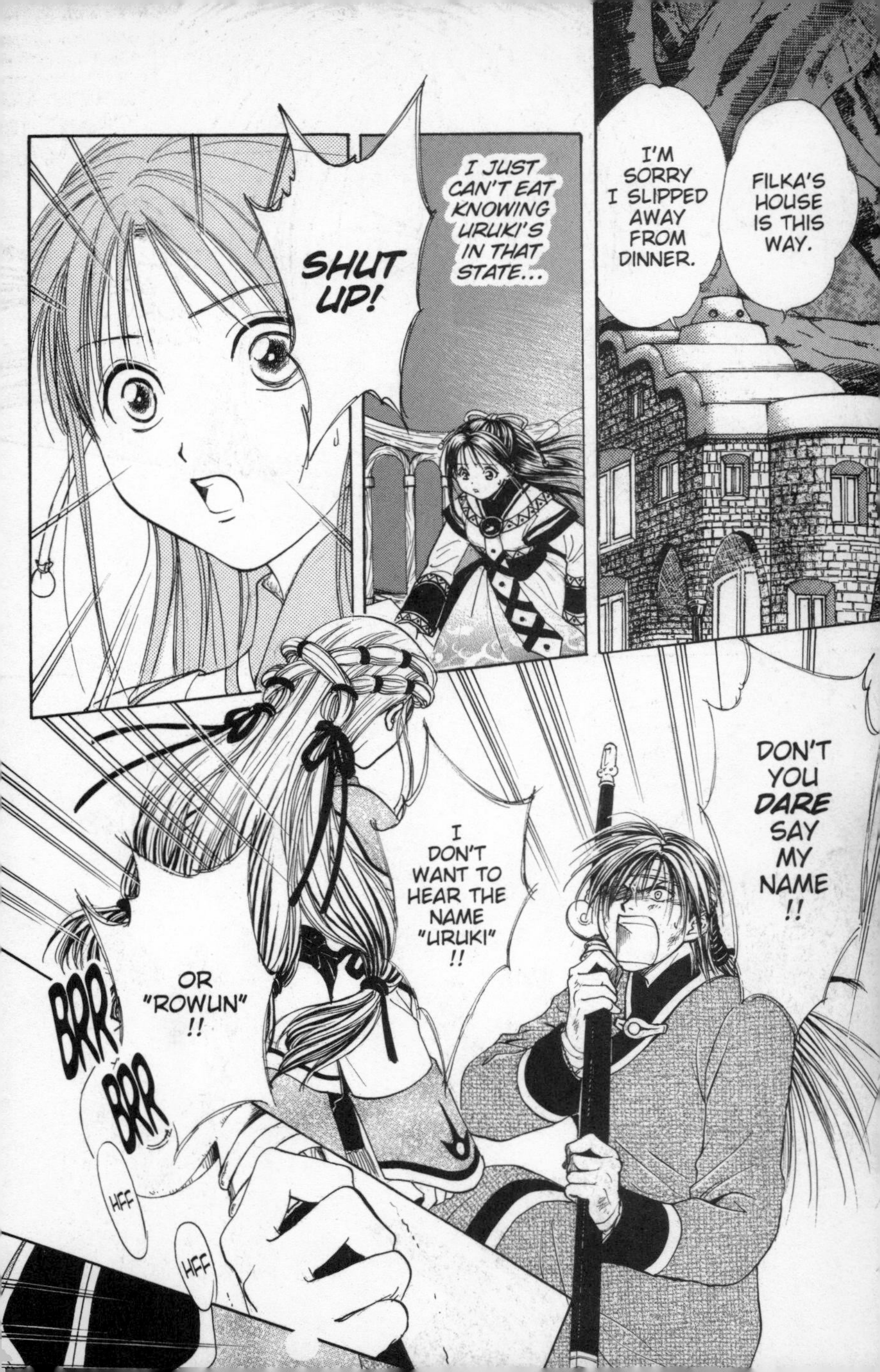
FILKA'S HOUSE IS THIS WAY.
I'M SORRY I SLIPPED AWAY FROM DINNER.
I JUST CAN'T EAT KNOWING URUKI'S IN THAT STATE...
SHUT UP!
DON'T YOU DARE SAY MY NAME!!
I DON'T WANT TO HEAR THE NAME "URUKI"!!
OR "ROWUN"!!
BRR BRR
HFF
HFF

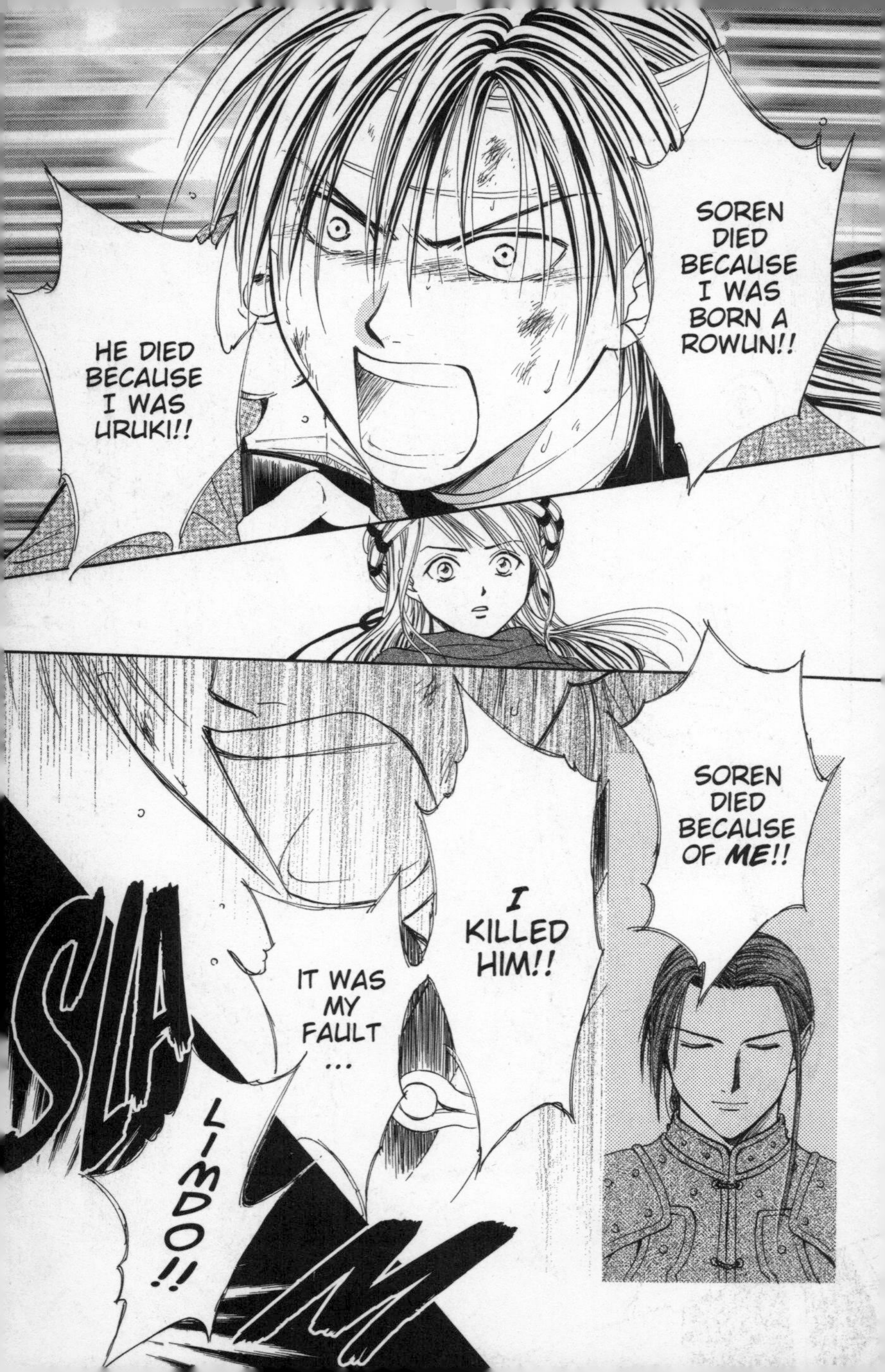
SOREN DIED BECAUSE I WAS BORN A ROWUN!!
HE DIED BECAUSE I WAS URUKI!!
SOREN DIED BECAUSE OF *ME*!!
I KILLED HIM!!
IT WAS MY FAULT ...
LIMDO!!
SLAM

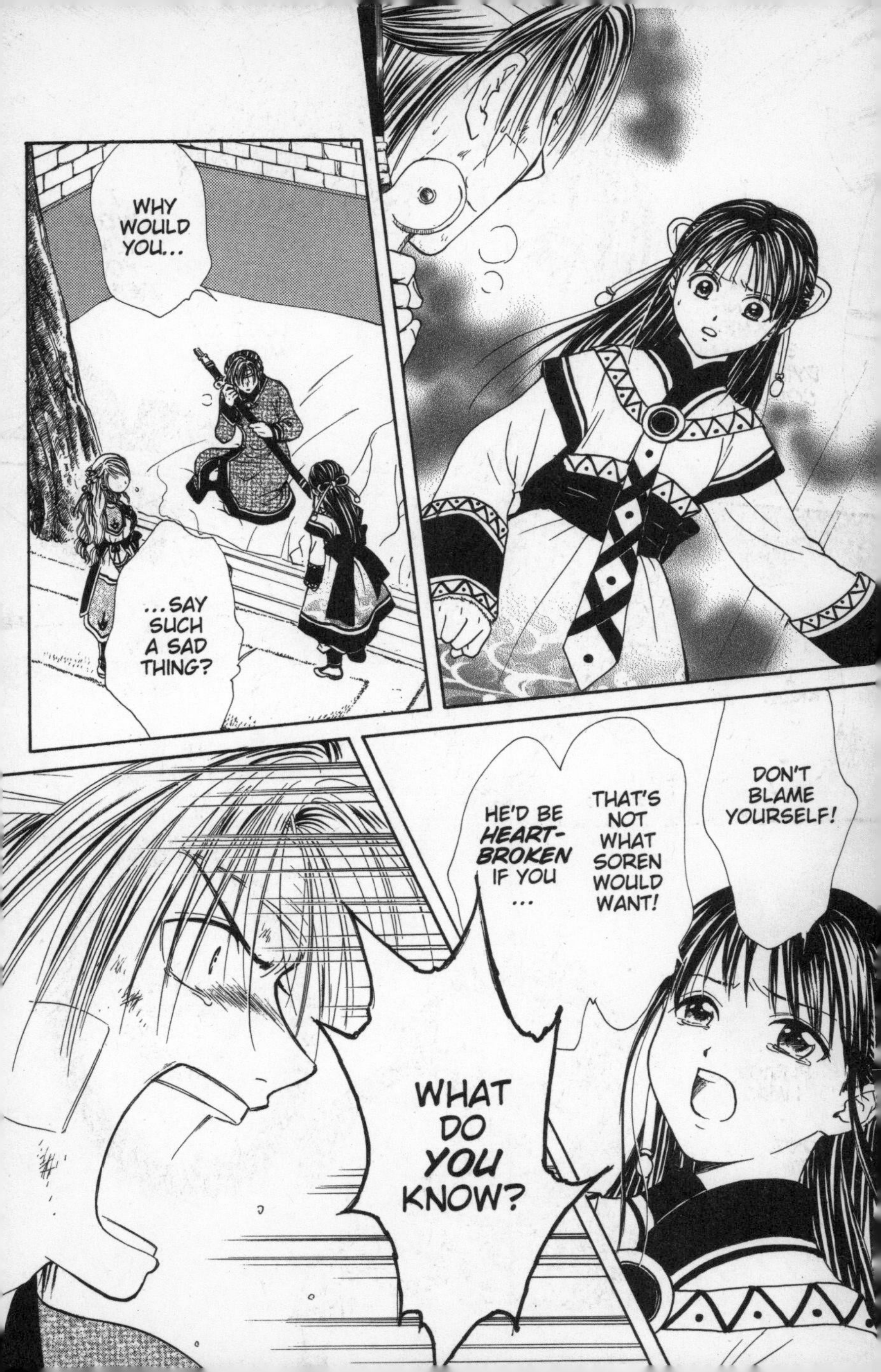
WHY WOULD YOU...
...SAY SUCH A SAD THING?
DON'T BLAME YOURSELF!
THAT'S NOT WHAT SOREN WOULD WANT!
HE'D BE *HEART-BROKEN* IF YOU...
WHAT DO *YOU* KNOW?

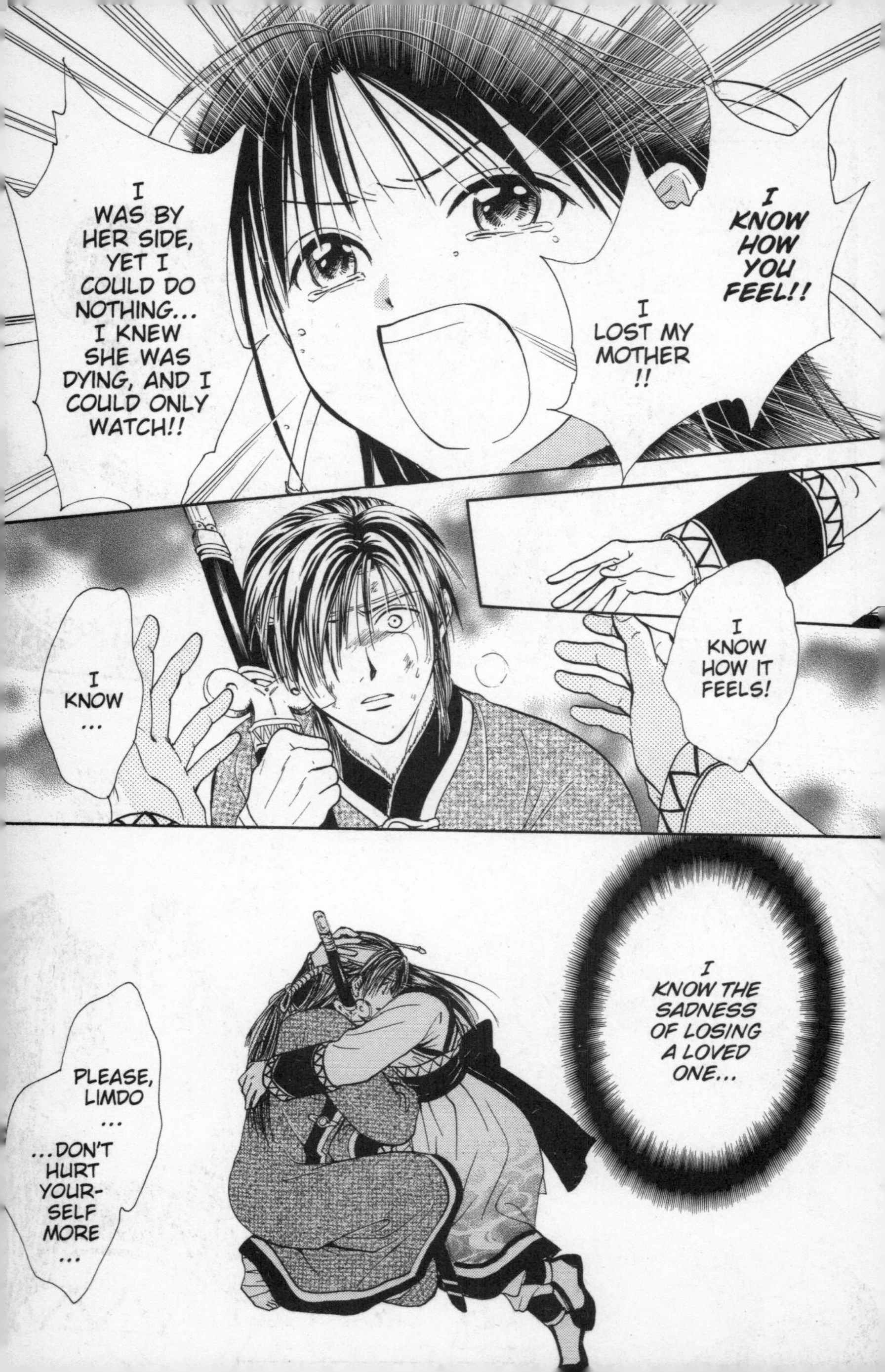
I KNOW HOW YOU FEEL!!
I LOST MY MOTHER !!
I WAS BY HER SIDE, YET I COULD DO NOTHING... I KNEW SHE WAS DYING, AND I COULD ONLY WATCH!!
I KNOW HOW IT FEELS!
I KNOW ...
I KNOW THE SADNESS OF LOSING A LOVED ONE...
PLEASE, LIMDO ...
...DON'T HURT YOUR-SELF MORE ...

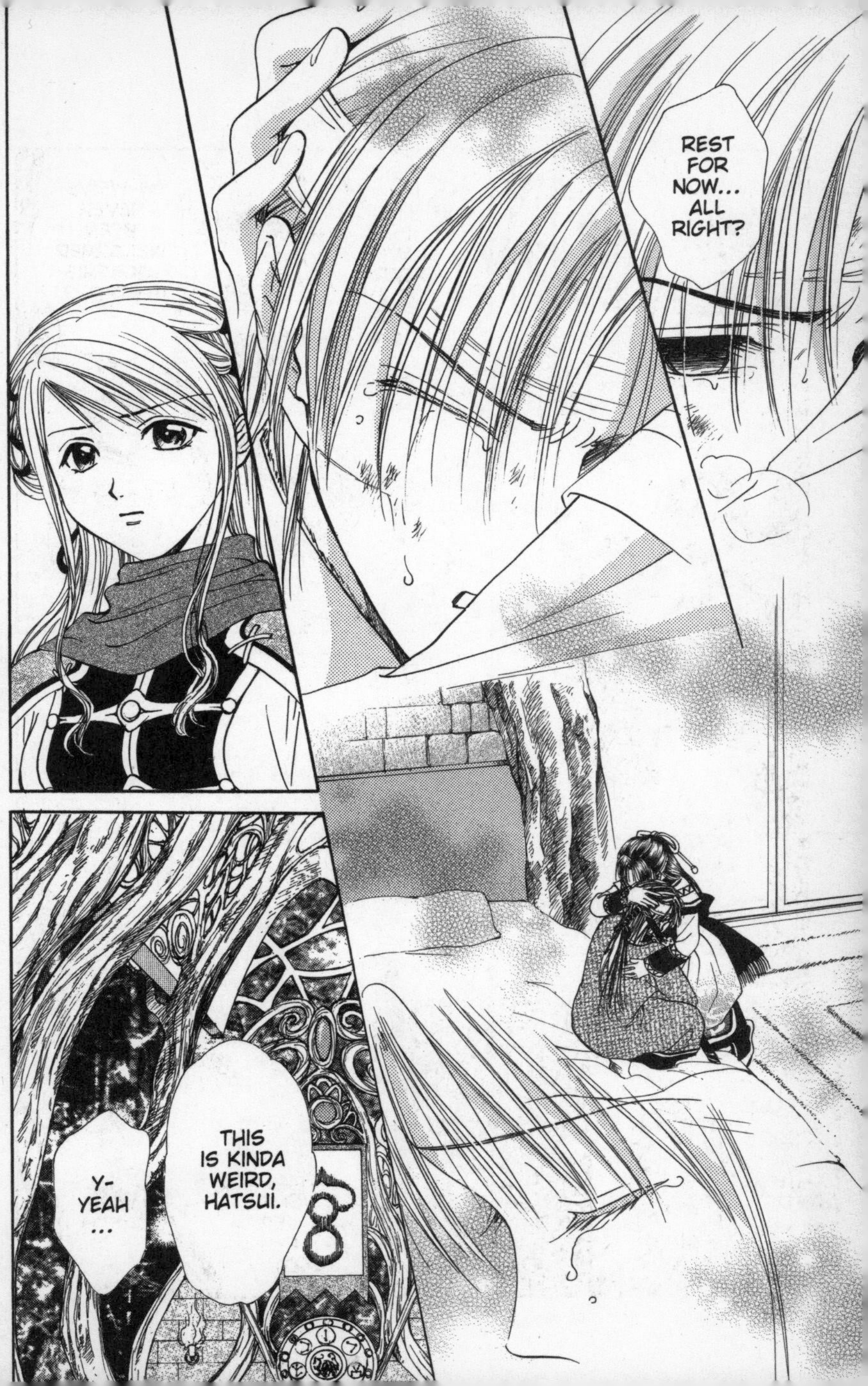
REST FOR NOW... ALL RIGHT?
THIS IS KINDA WEIRD, HATSUI.
Y-YEAH...

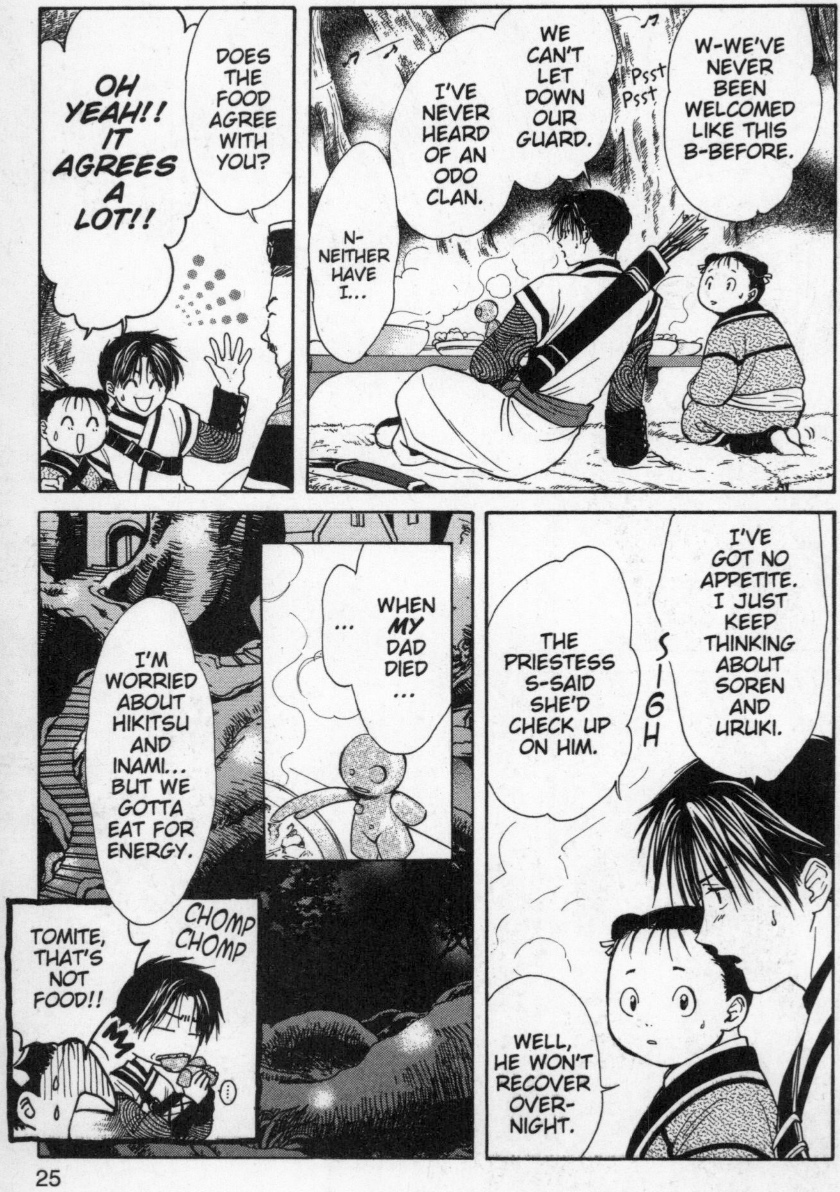
W-WE'VE NEVER BEEN WELCOMED LIKE THIS B-BEFORE.
Psst Psst
WE CAN'T LET DOWN OUR GUARD.
I'VE NEVER HEARD OF AN ODO CLAN.
N-NEITHER HAVE I...
DOES THE FOOD AGREE WITH YOU?
OH YEAH!! IT AGREES A LOT!!
I'VE GOT NO APPETITE. I JUST KEEP THINKING ABOUT SOREN AND URUKI.
SIGH
THE PRIESTESS S-SAID SHE'D CHECK UP ON HIM.
WELL, HE WON'T RECOVER OVER-NIGHT.
WHEN MY DAD DIED ...
...
I'M WORRIED ABOUT HIKITSU AND INAMI... BUT WE GOTTA EAT FOR ENERGY.
CHOMP CHOMP
TOMITE, THAT'S NOT FOOD!!
...

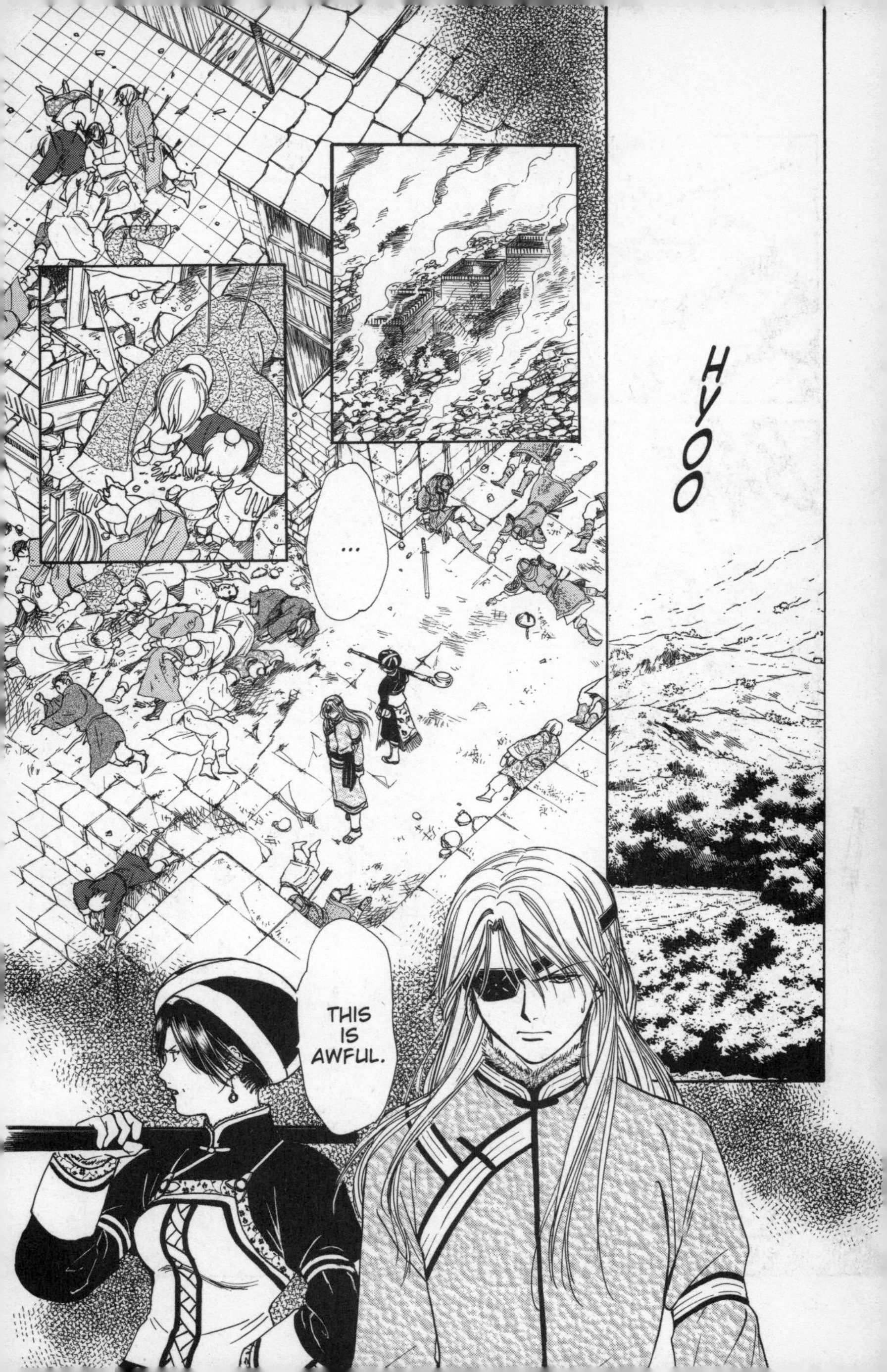
HYOO
...
THIS IS AWFUL.

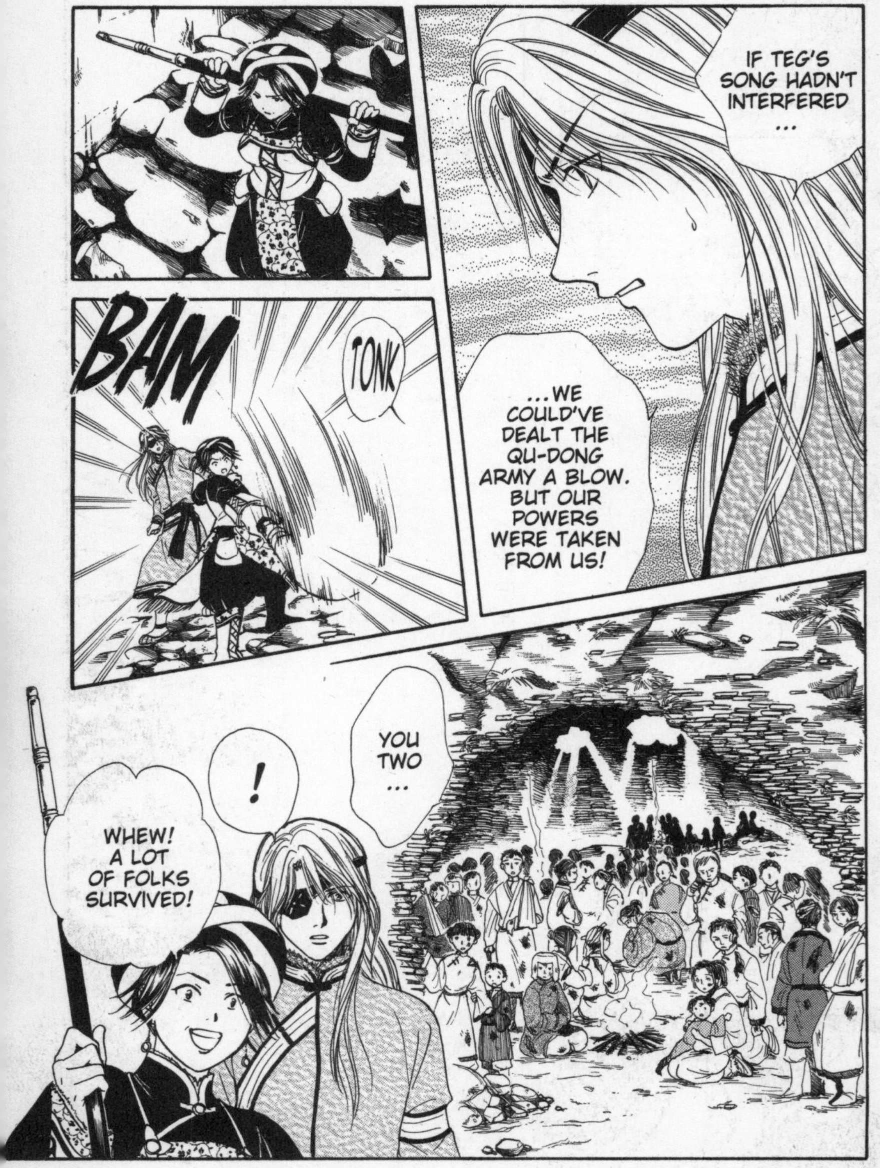
IF TEG'S SONG HADN'T INTERFERED ...
...WE COULD'VE DEALT THE QU-DONG ARMY A BLOW. BUT OUR POWERS WERE TAKEN FROM US!
TONK
BAM
YOU TWO ...
!
WHEW! A LOT OF FOLKS SURVIVED!

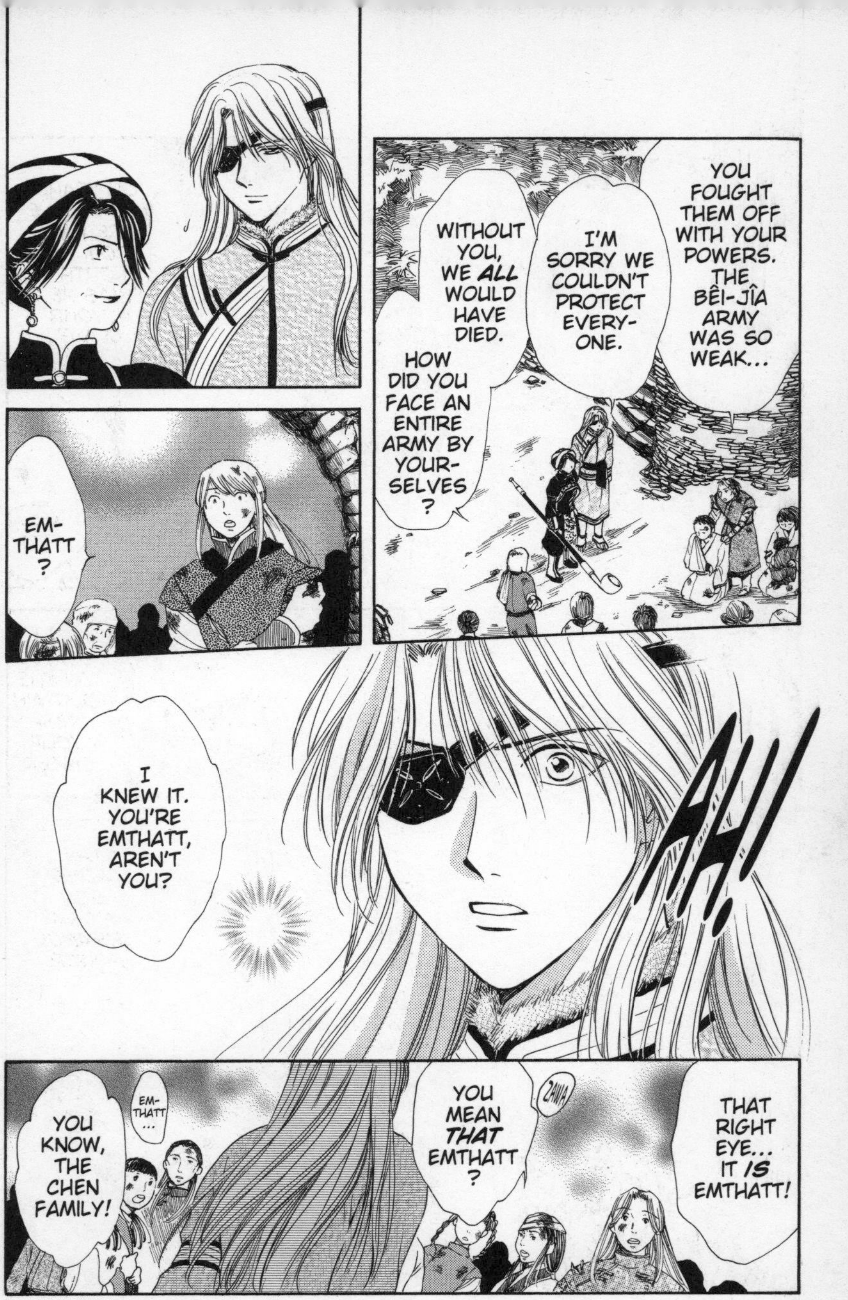
YOU FOUGHT THEM OFF WITH YOUR POWERS. THE BÊI-JÎA ARMY WAS SO WEAK...
I'M SORRY WE COULDN'T PROTECT EVERY-ONE.
WITHOUT YOU, WE ALL WOULD HAVE DIED.
HOW DID YOU FACE AN ENTIRE ARMY BY YOUR-SELVES?
EM-THATT?
AH!
I KNEW IT. YOU'RE EMTHATT, AREN'T YOU?
THAT RIGHT EYE... IT IS EMTHATT!
ZAWA
YOU MEAN THAT EMTHATT?
EM-THATT...
YOU KNOW, THE CHEN FAMILY!

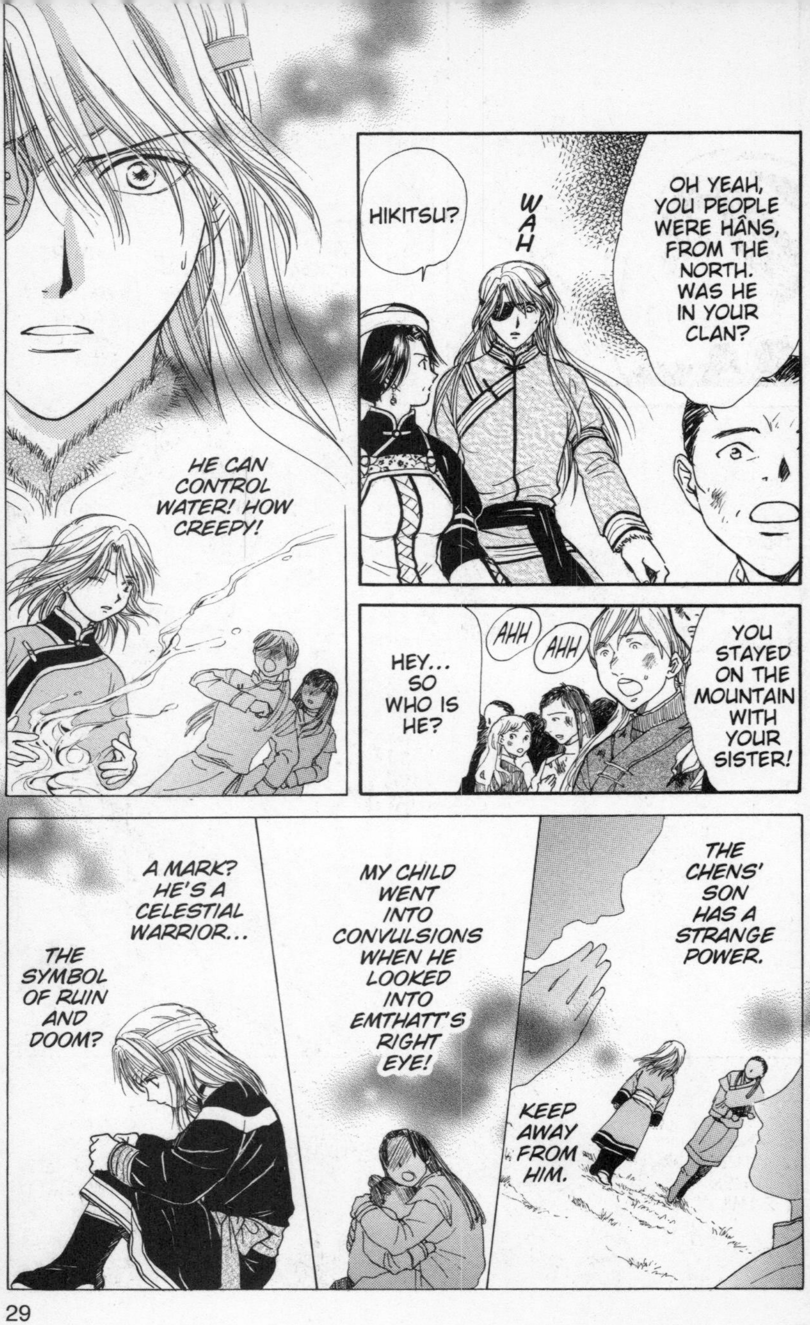
OH YEAH, YOU PEOPLE WERE HÂNS, FROM THE NORTH. WAS HE IN YOUR CLAN?
WAH
HIKITSU?
YOU STAYED ON THE MOUNTAIN WITH YOUR SISTER!
AHH
AHH
HEY... SO WHO IS HE?
HE CAN CONTROL WATER! HOW CREEPY!
THE CHENS' SON HAS A STRANGE POWER.
KEEP AWAY FROM HIM.
MY CHILD WENT INTO CONVULSIONS WHEN HE LOOKED INTO EMTHATT'S RIGHT EYE!
A MARK? HE'S A CELESTIAL WARRIOR...
THE SYMBOL OF RUIN AND DOOM?

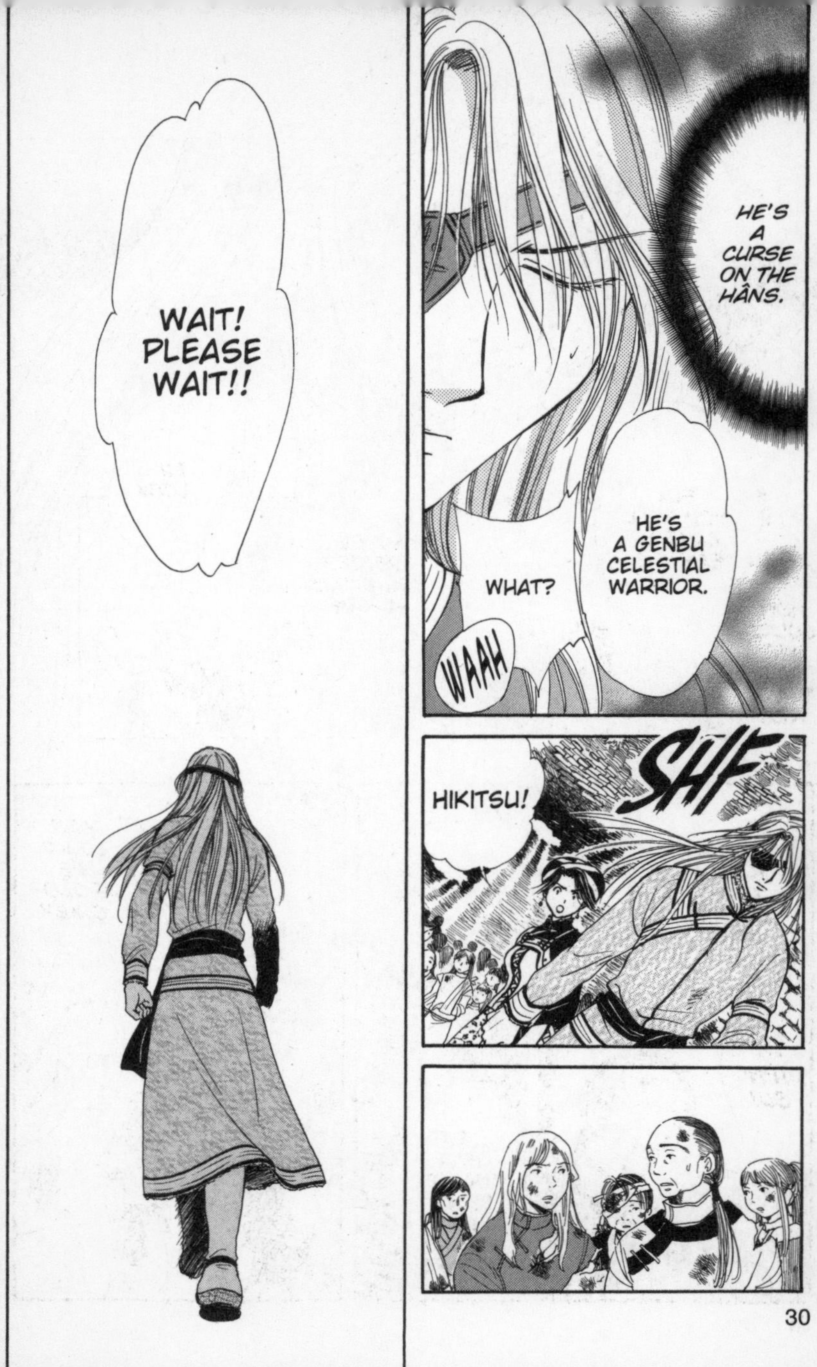
HE'S A CURSE ON THE HÂNS.
HE'S A GENBU CELESTIAL WARRIOR.
WHAT?
WAAH
SHF
HIKITSU!
WAIT! PLEASE WAIT!!

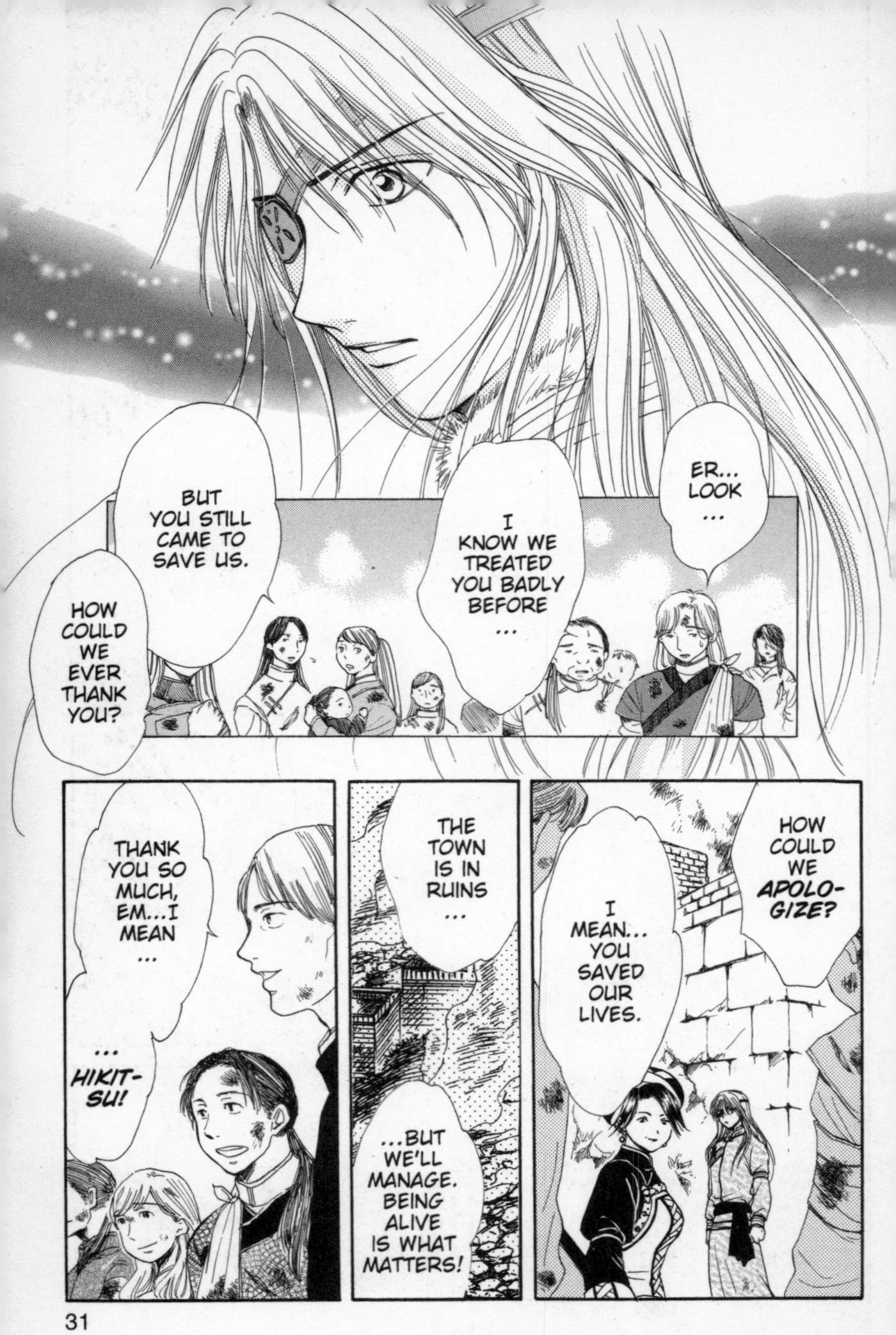
ER... LOOK ...
I KNOW WE TREATED YOU BADLY BEFORE ...
BUT YOU STILL CAME TO SAVE US.
HOW COULD WE EVER THANK YOU?
HOW COULD WE APOLO-GIZE?
I MEAN... YOU SAVED OUR LIVES.
THE TOWN IS IN RUINS ...
...BUT WE'LL MANAGE. BEING ALIVE IS WHAT MATTERS!
THANK YOU SO MUCH, EM...I MEAN ...
... HIKIT-SU!

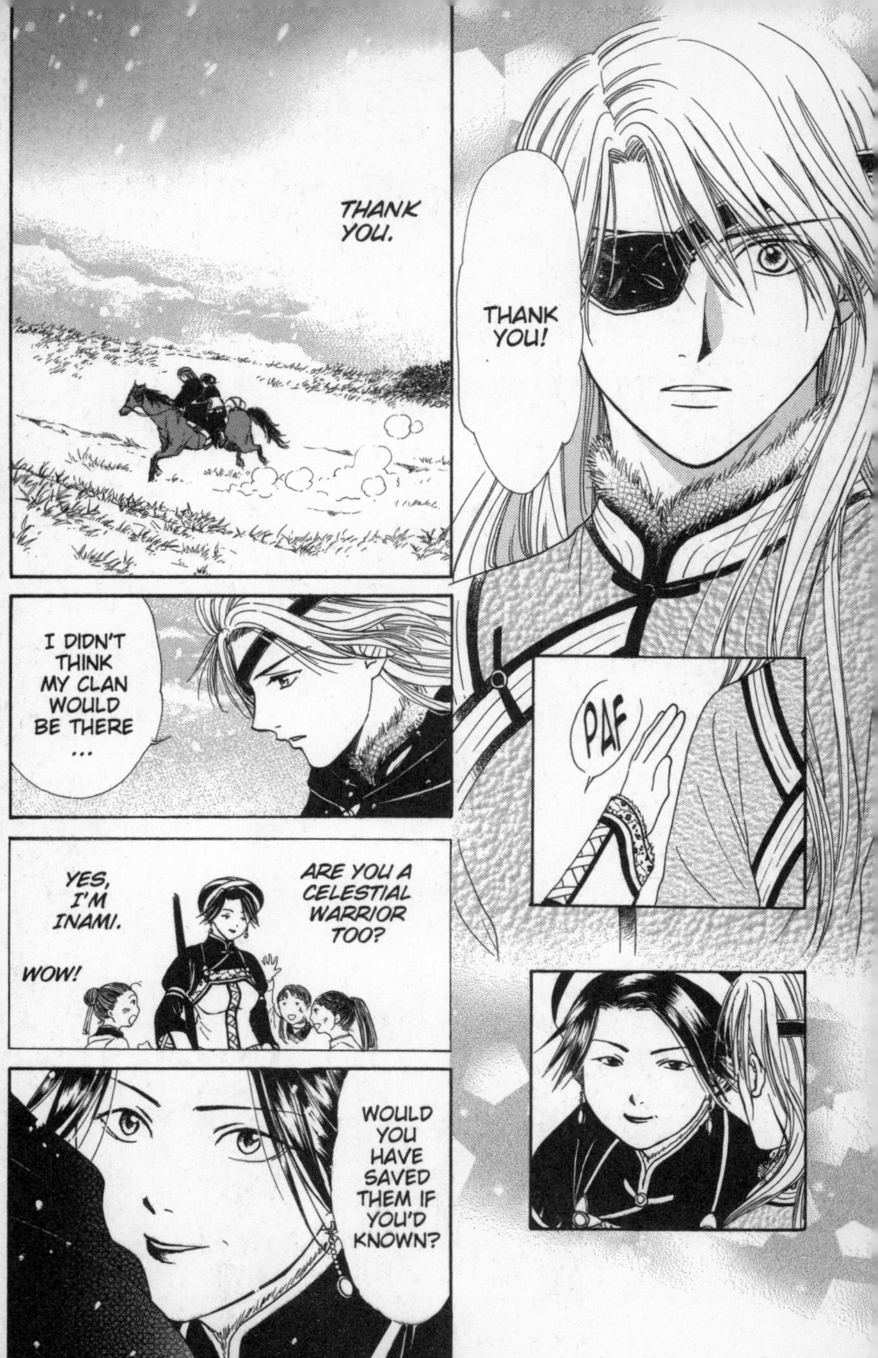
THANK YOU!
THANK YOU.
I DIDN'T THINK MY CLAN WOULD BE THERE ...
PAF
ARE YOU A CELESTIAL WARRIOR TOO?
YES, I'M INAMI.
WOW!
WOULD YOU HAVE SAVED THEM IF YOU'D KNOWN?

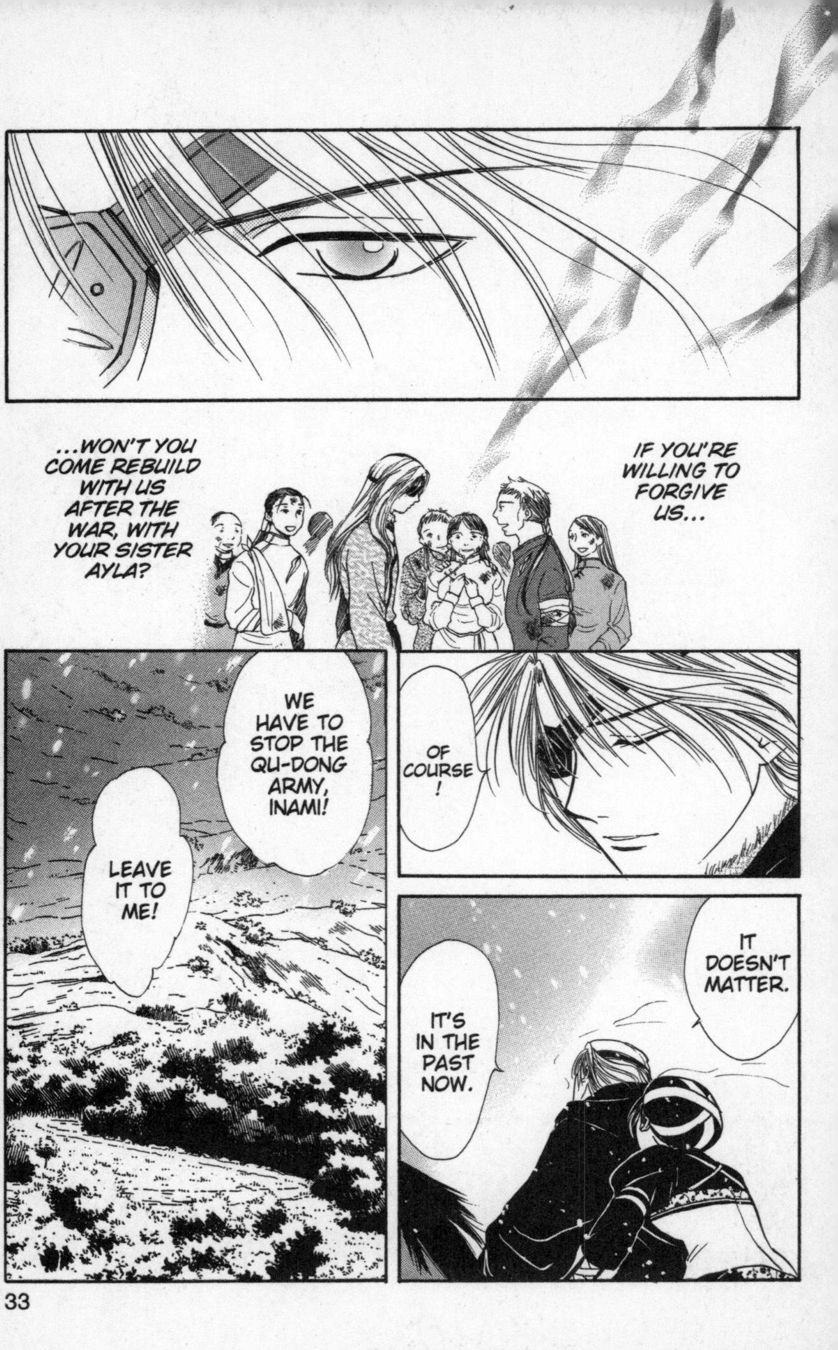
IF YOU'RE WILLING TO FORGIVE US...
...WON'T YOU COME REBUILD WITH US AFTER THE WAR, WITH YOUR SISTER AYLA?
OF COURSE!
IT DOESN'T MATTER.
IT'S IN THE PAST NOW.
WE HAVE TO STOP THE QU-DONG ARMY, INAMI!
LEAVE IT TO ME!

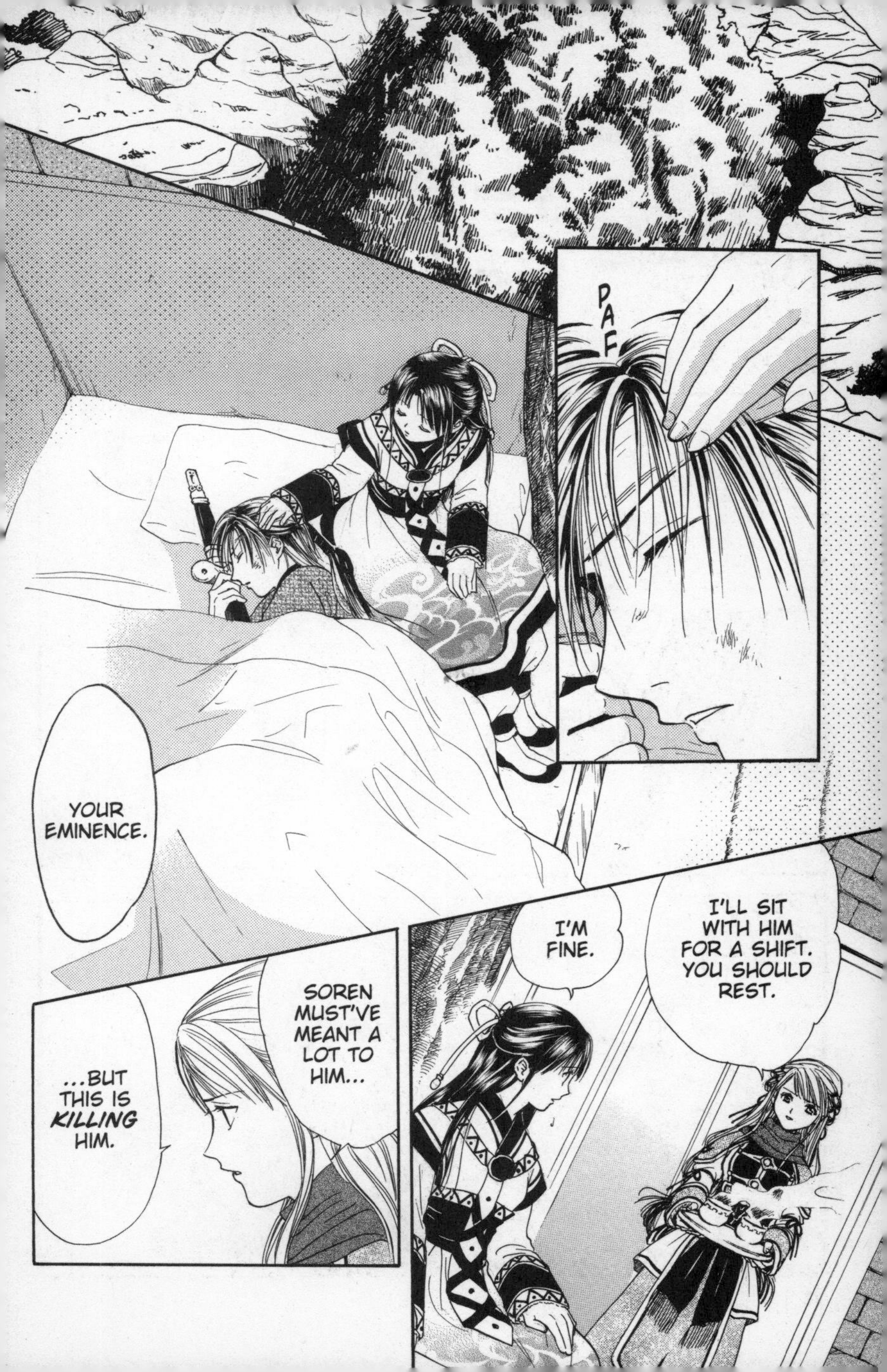
PAF
YOUR EMINENCE.
I'LL SIT WITH HIM FOR A SHIFT. YOU SHOULD REST.
I'M FINE.
SOREN MUST'VE MEANT A LOT TO HIM...
...BUT THIS IS *KILLING* HIM.

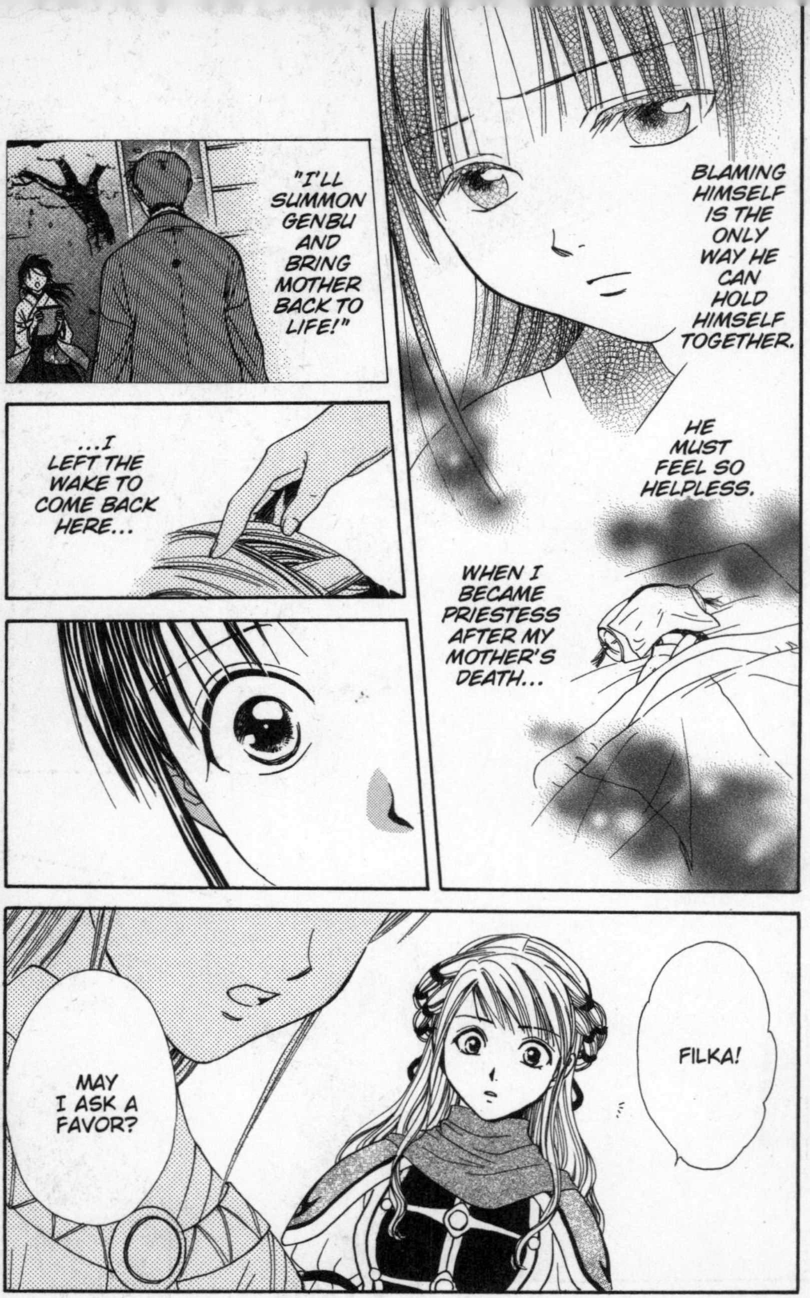

BLAMING HIMSELF IS THE ONLY WAY HE CAN HOLD HIMSELF TOGETHER.
HE MUST FEEL SO HELPLESS.
WHEN I BECAME PRIESTESS AFTER MY MOTHER'S DEATH...
"I'LL SUMMON GENBU AND BRING MOTHER BACK TO LIFE!"
...I LEFT THE WAKE TO COME BACK HERE...
FILKA!
MAY I ASK A FAVOR?

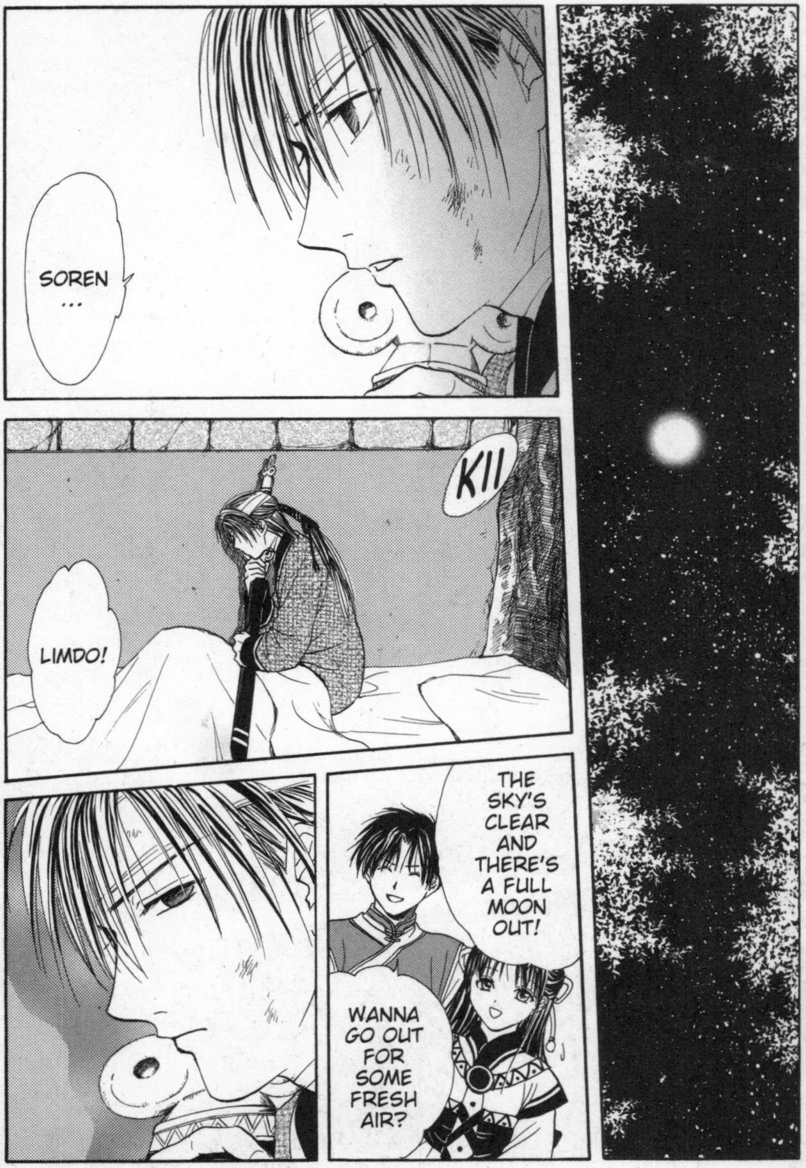
SOREN ...
KII
LIMDO!
THE SKY'S CLEAR AND THERE'S A FULL MOON OUT!
WANNA GO OUT FOR SOME FRESH AIR?

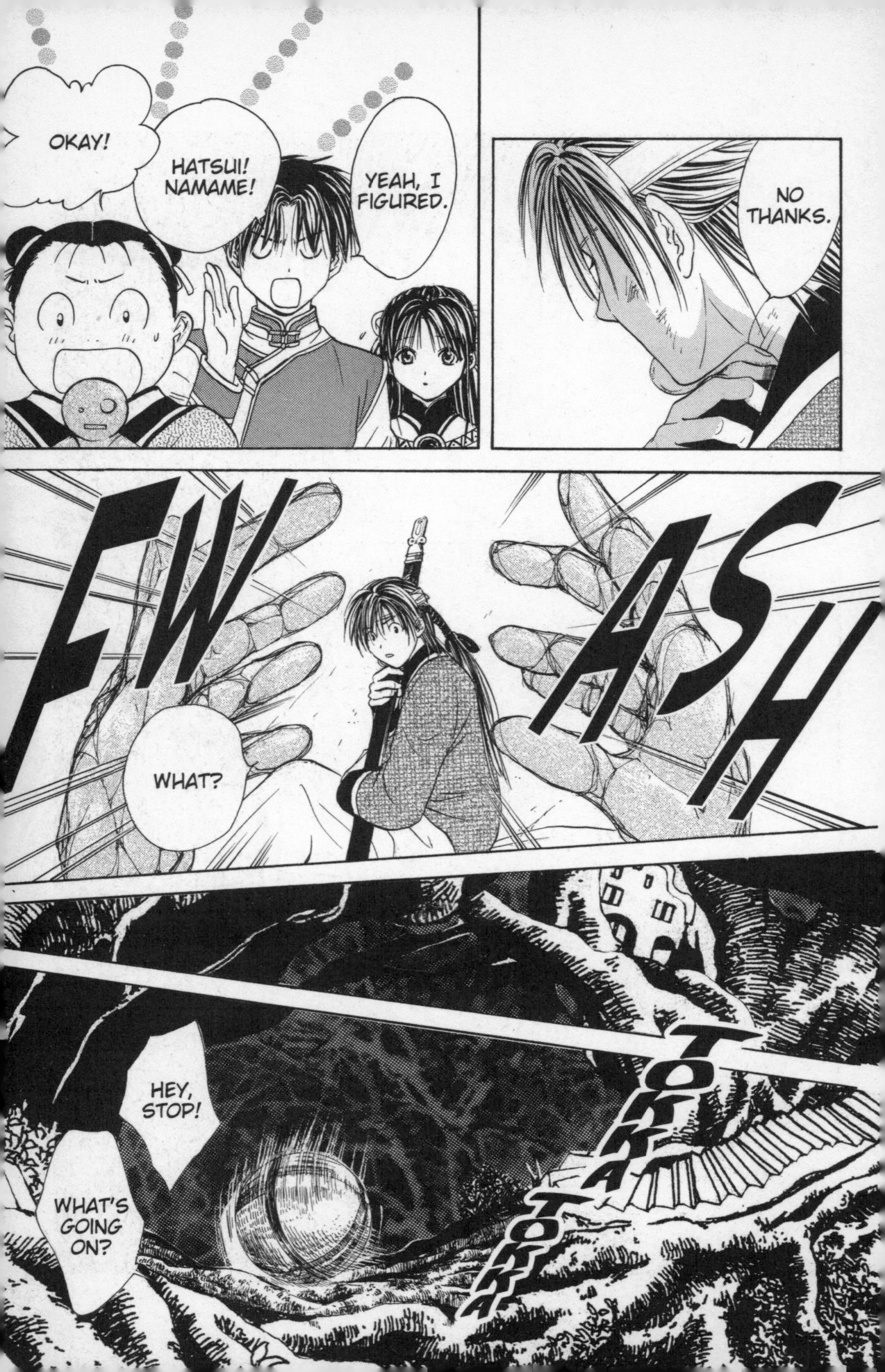
NO THANKS.
YEAH, I FIGURED.
HATSUI! NAMAME!
OKAY!
FWASH
WHAT?
TOKA TOKA TOKA
HEY, STOP!
WHAT'S GOING ON?

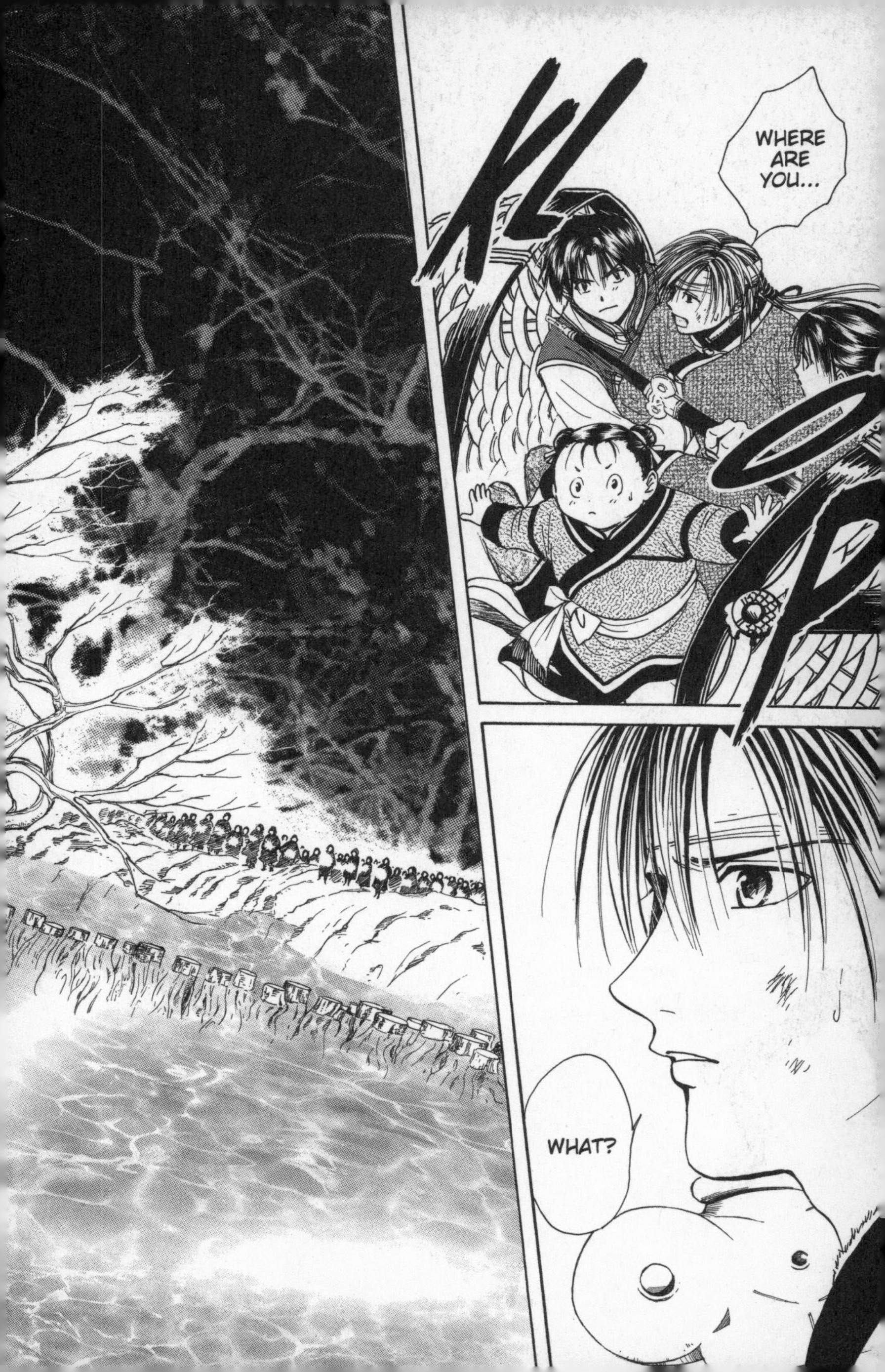
WHERE ARE YOU...
WHAT?

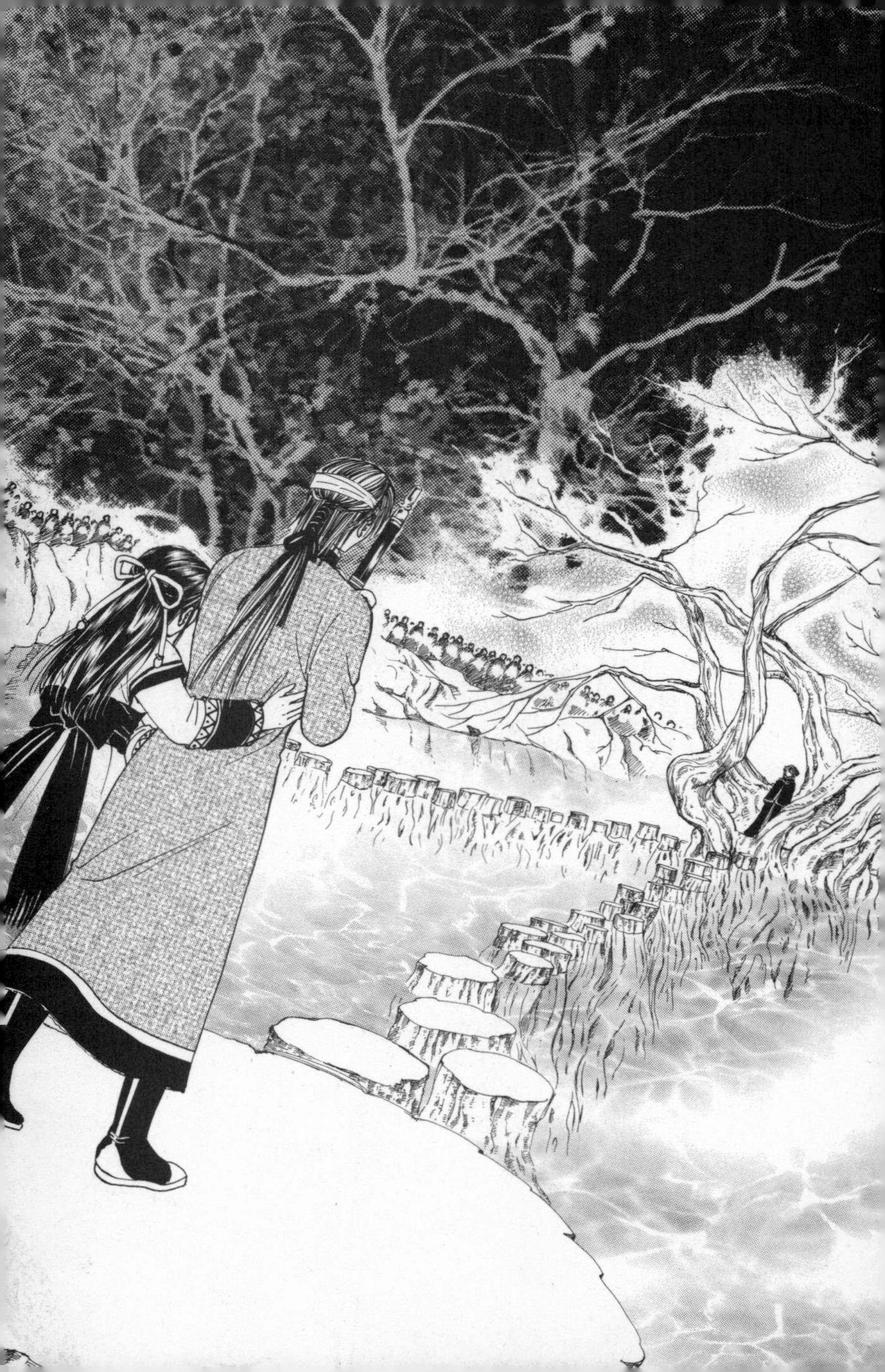

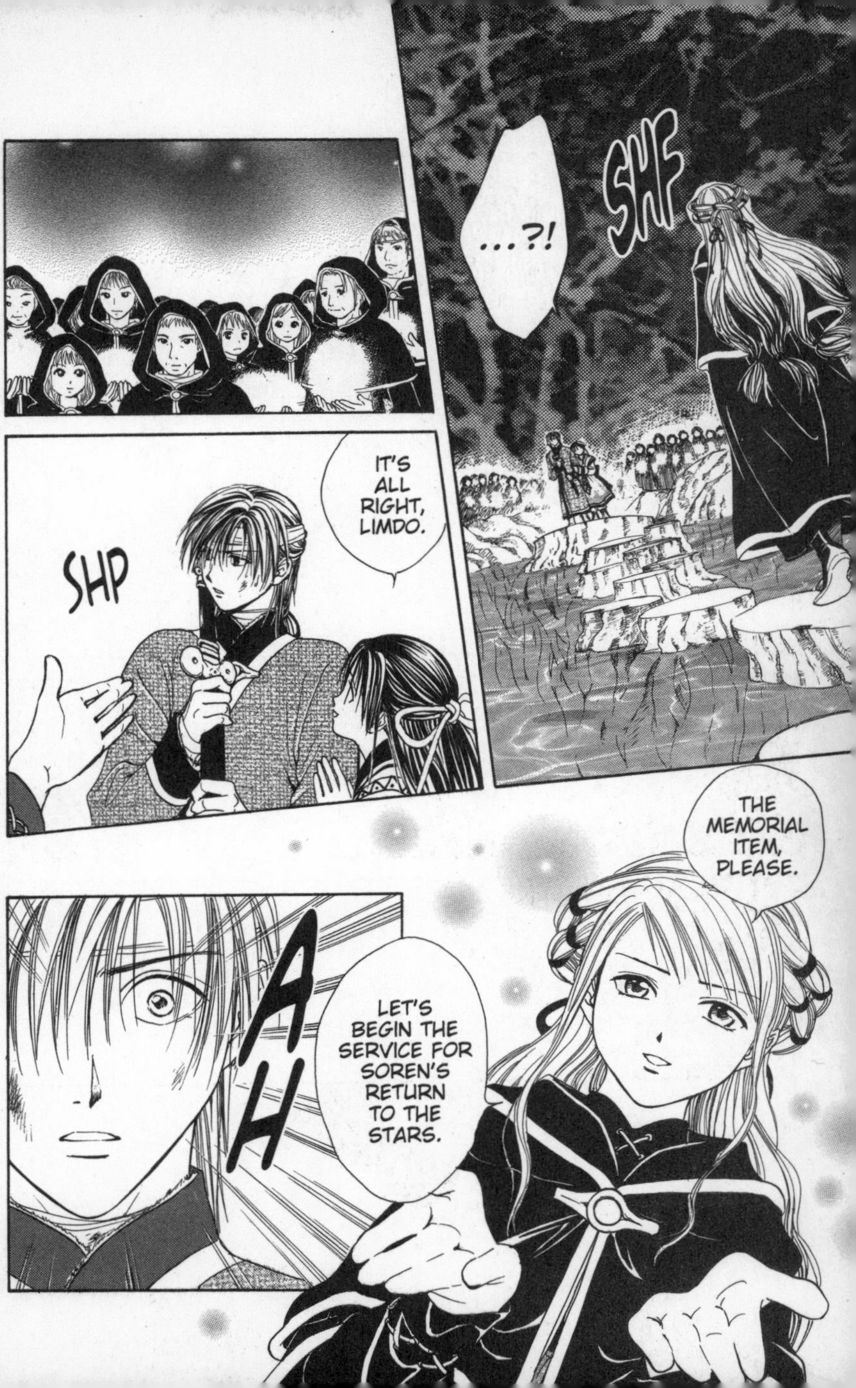
SHF
...?!
IT'S ALL RIGHT, LIMDO.
SHP
THE MEMORIAL ITEM, PLEASE.
LET'S BEGIN THE SERVICE FOR SOREN'S RETURN TO THE STARS.
AH

LIMDO
...

GRP

WE'LL
ALL DO IT
TOGETHER
...

WE
SHOULD
SEND
SOREN OFF
PROPERLY.

IT'S
ALL
RIGHT.

SOREN
...

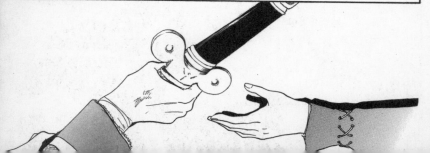

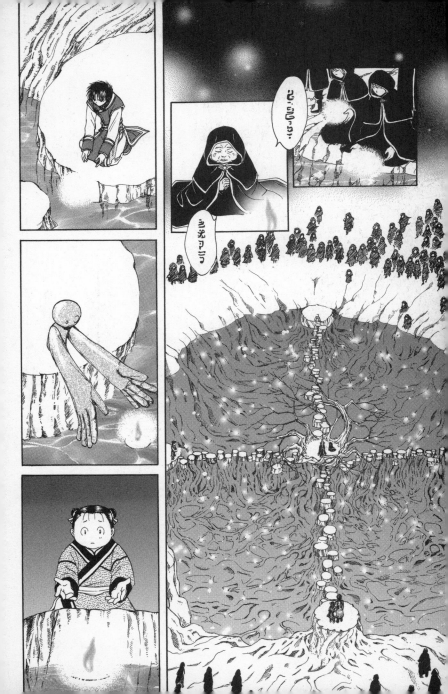

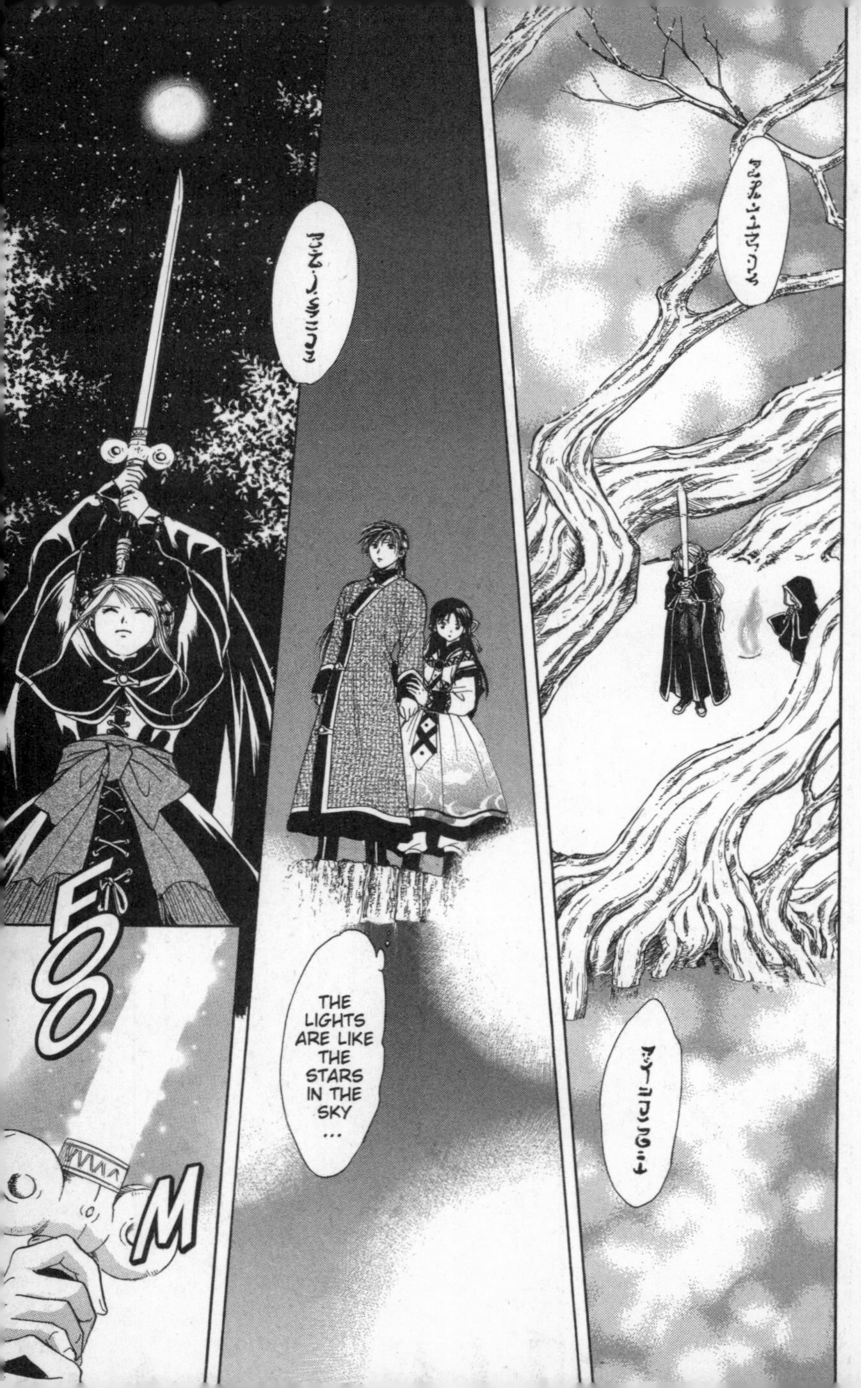
THE LIGHTS ARE LIKE THE STARS IN THE SKY...
FOOM

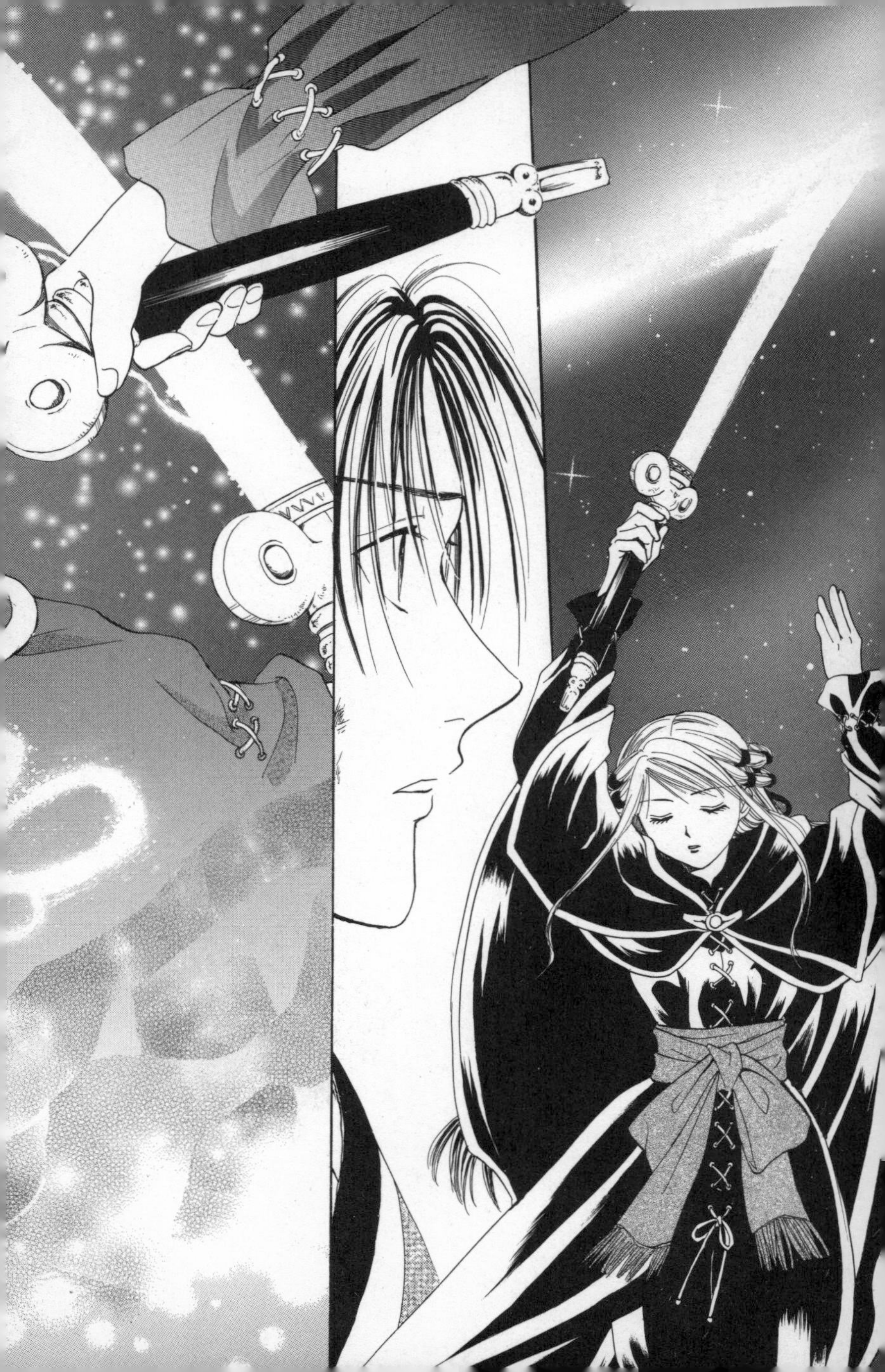

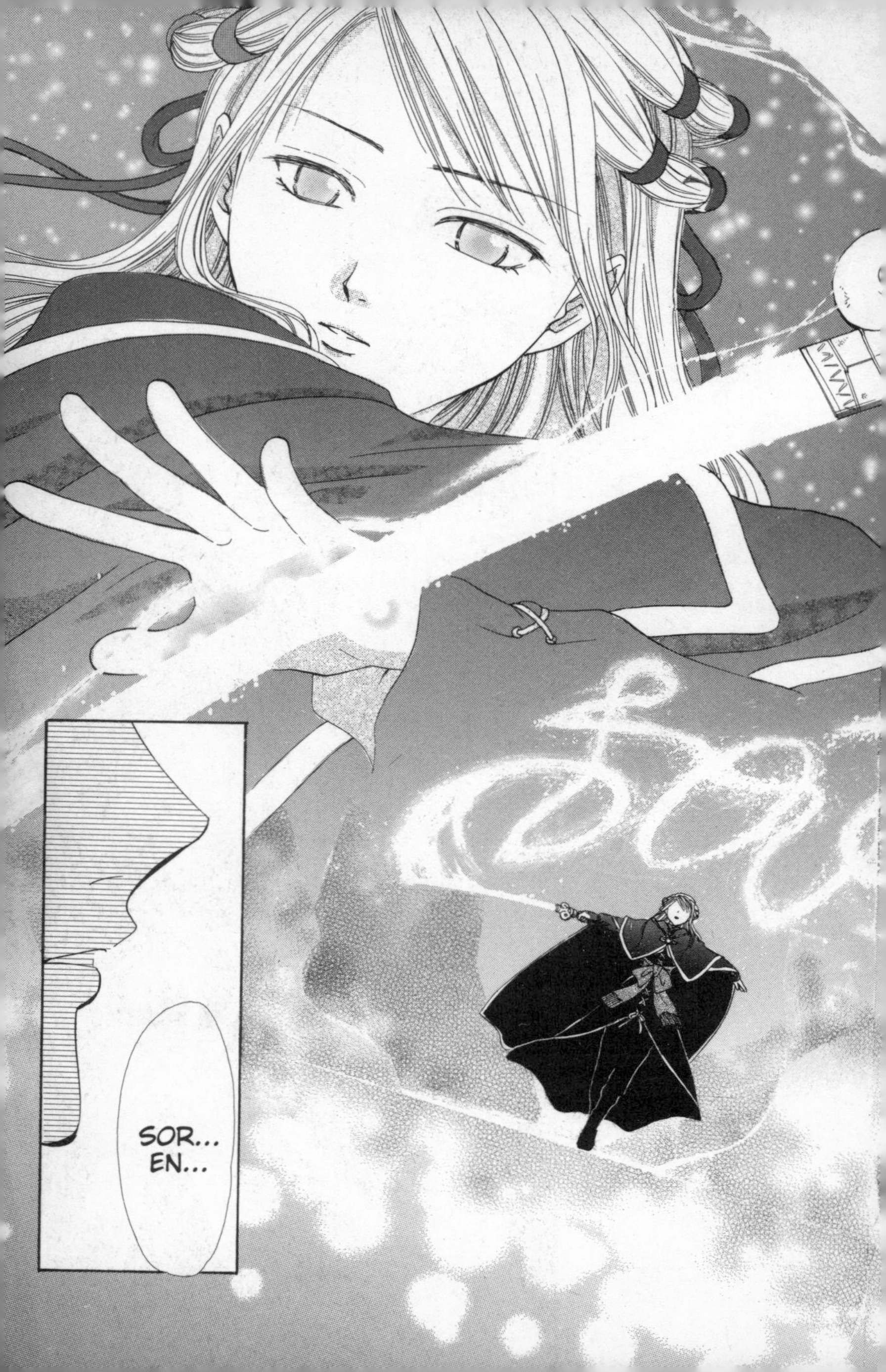
SOR... EN...

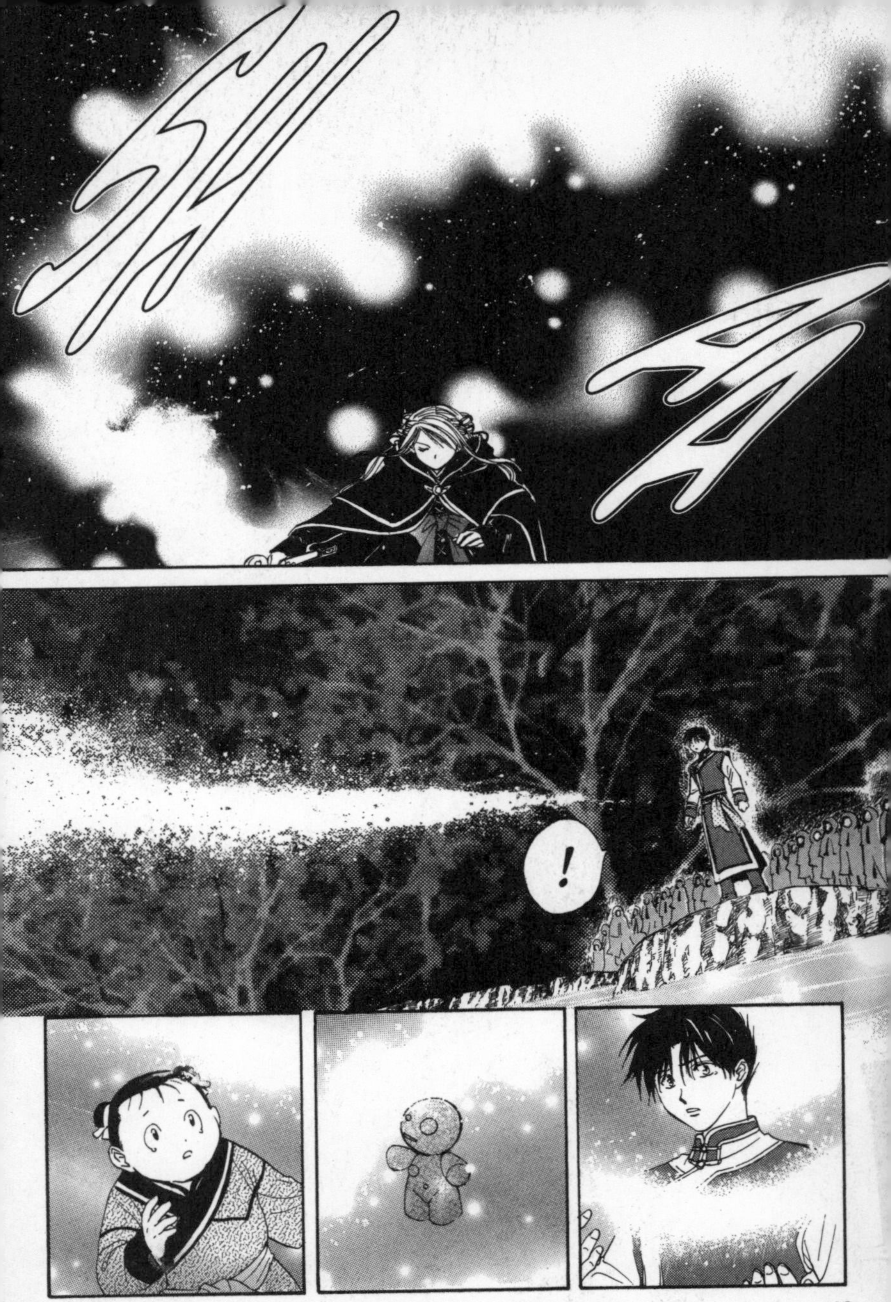
!

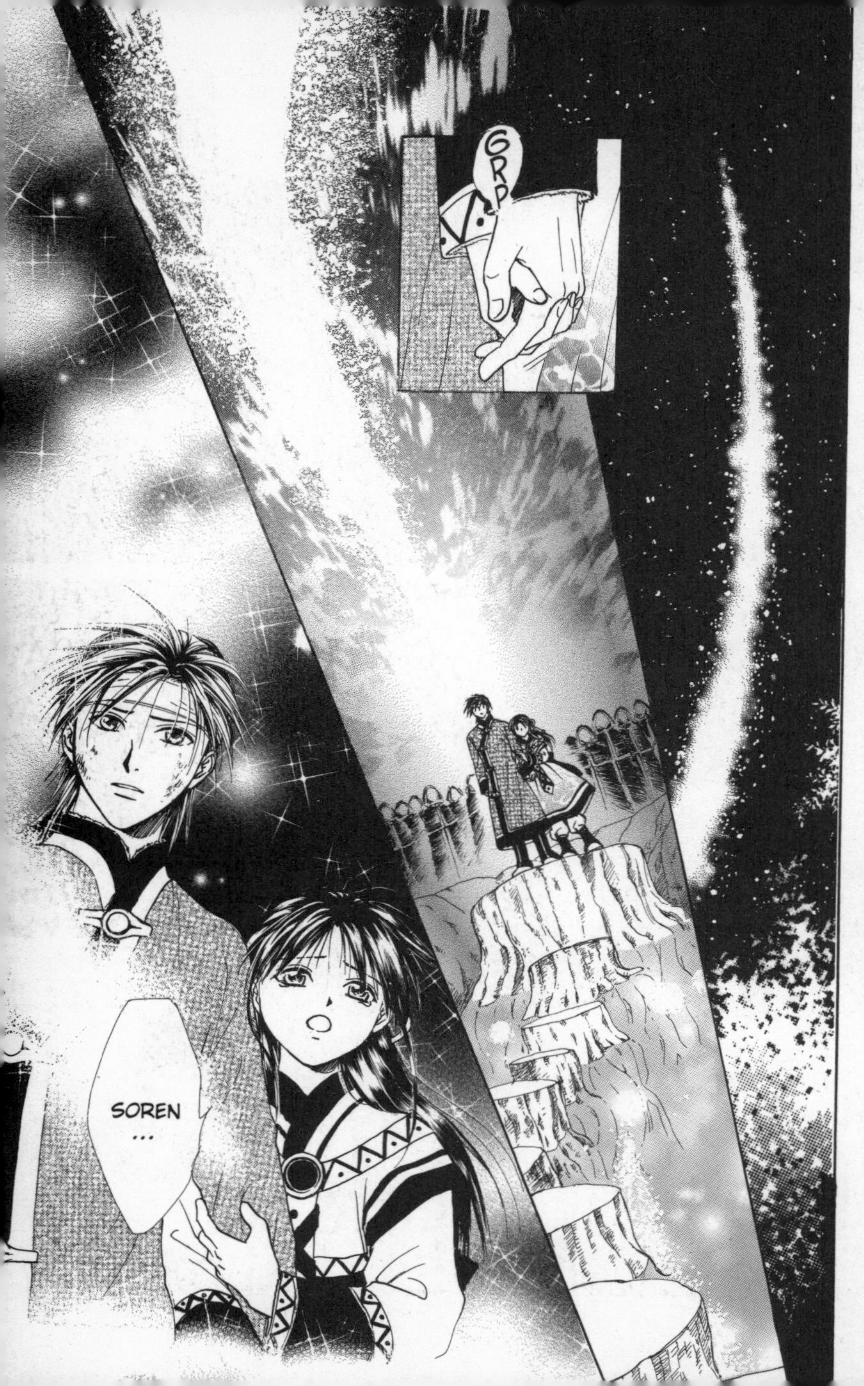
GRP
SOREN
...

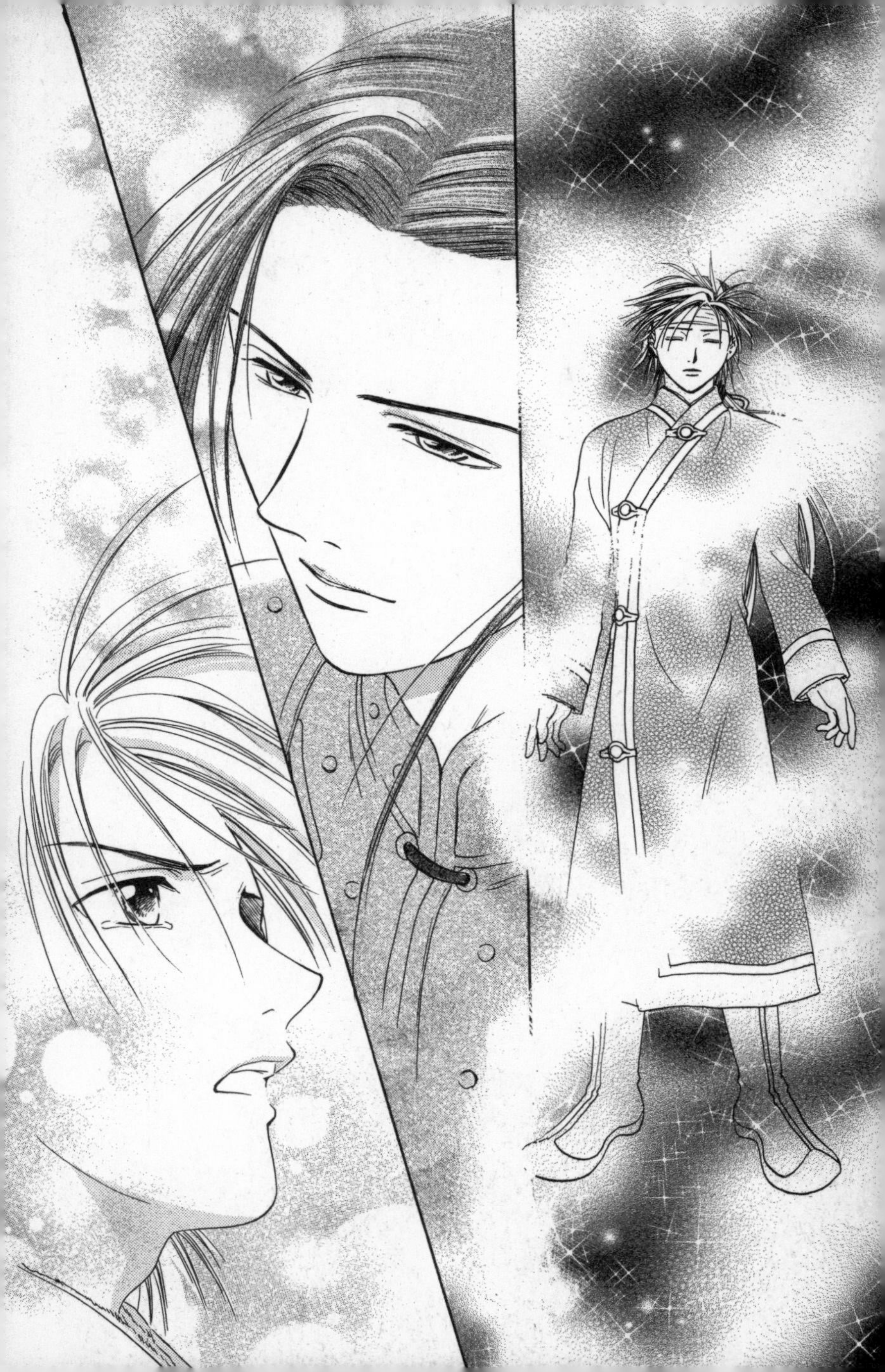

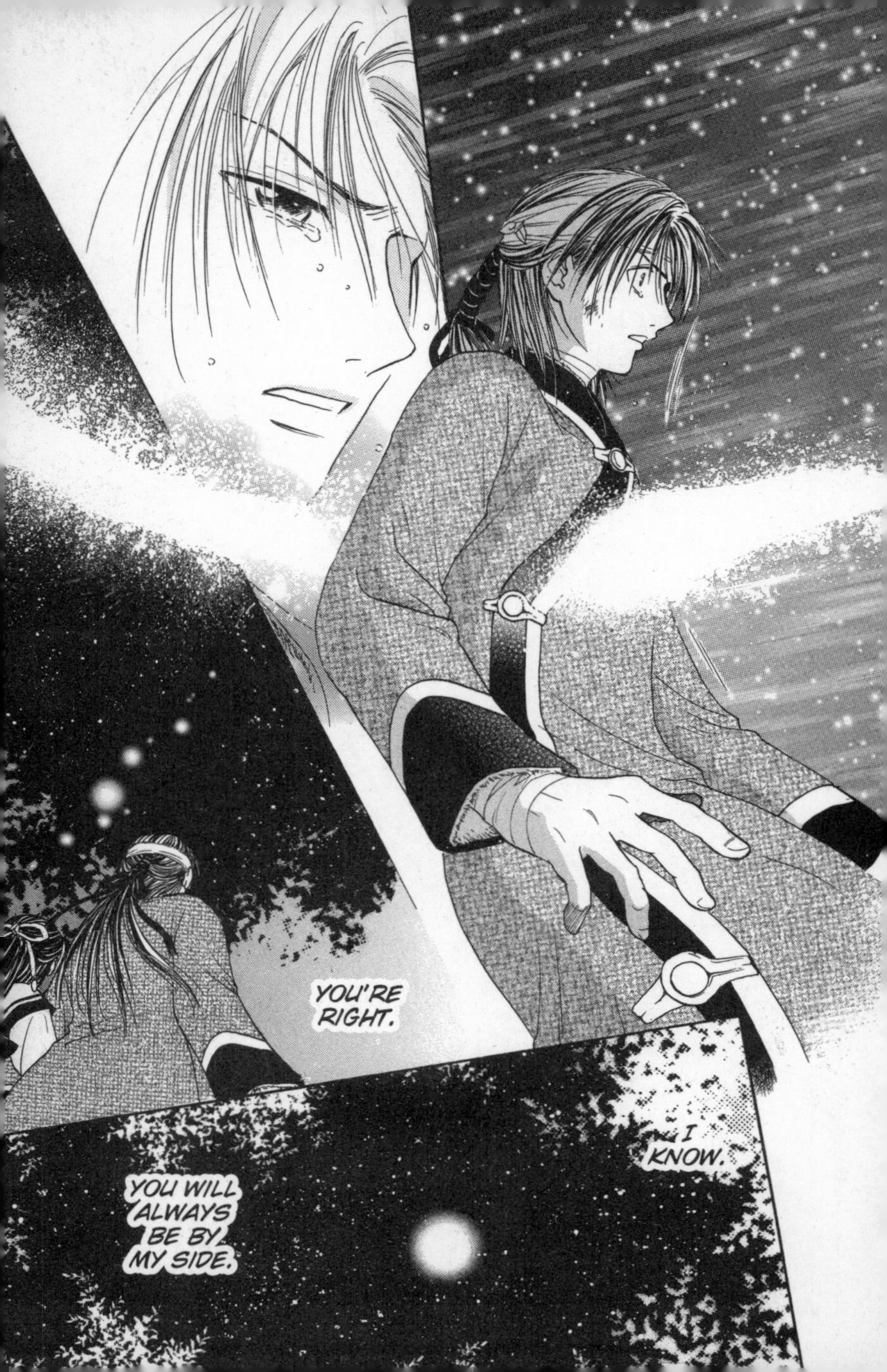
YOU'RE RIGHT.
I KNOW.
YOU WILL ALWAYS BE BY MY SIDE.

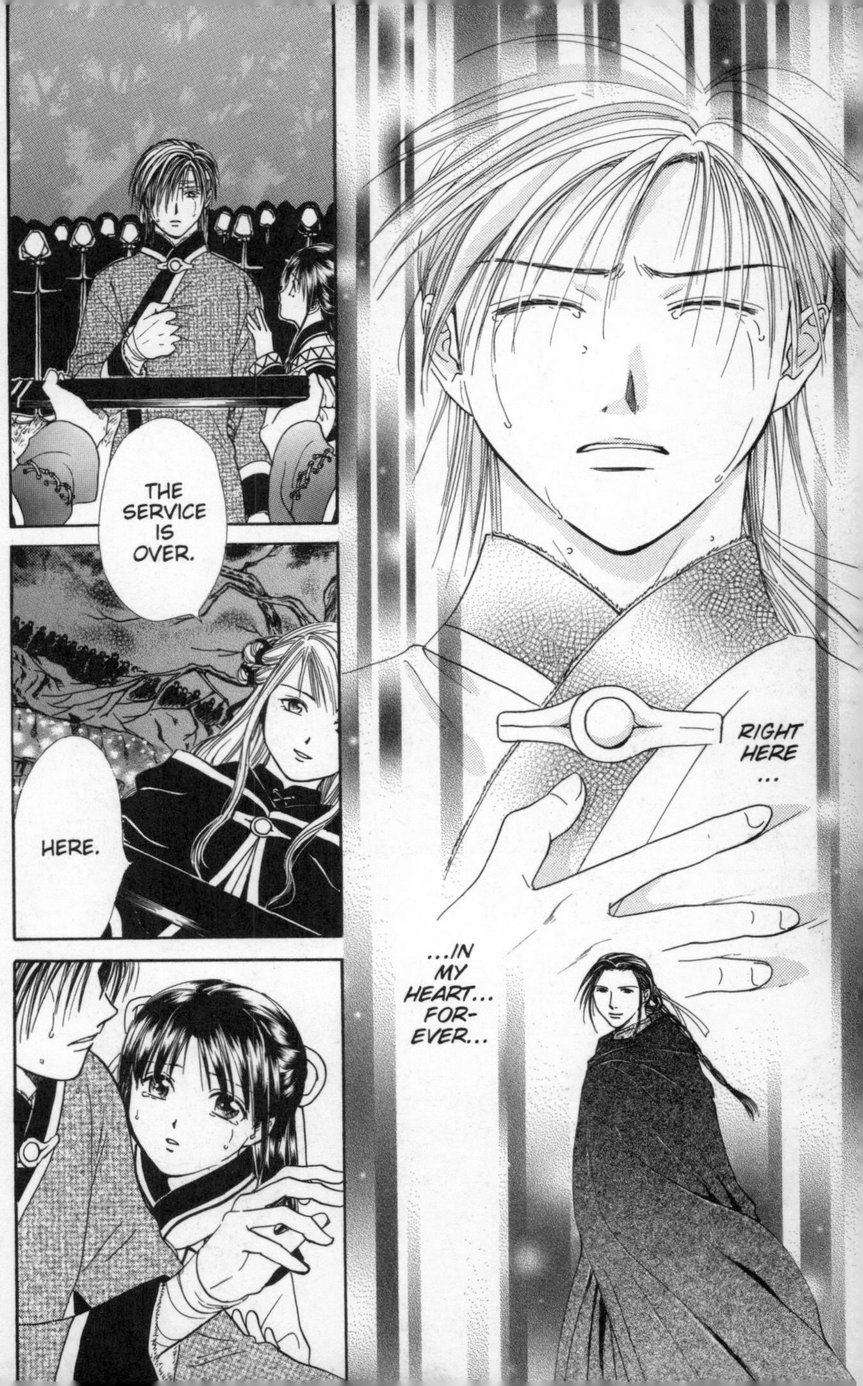
RIGHT HERE...
...IN MY HEART... FOR-EVER...
THE SERVICE IS OVER.
HERE.

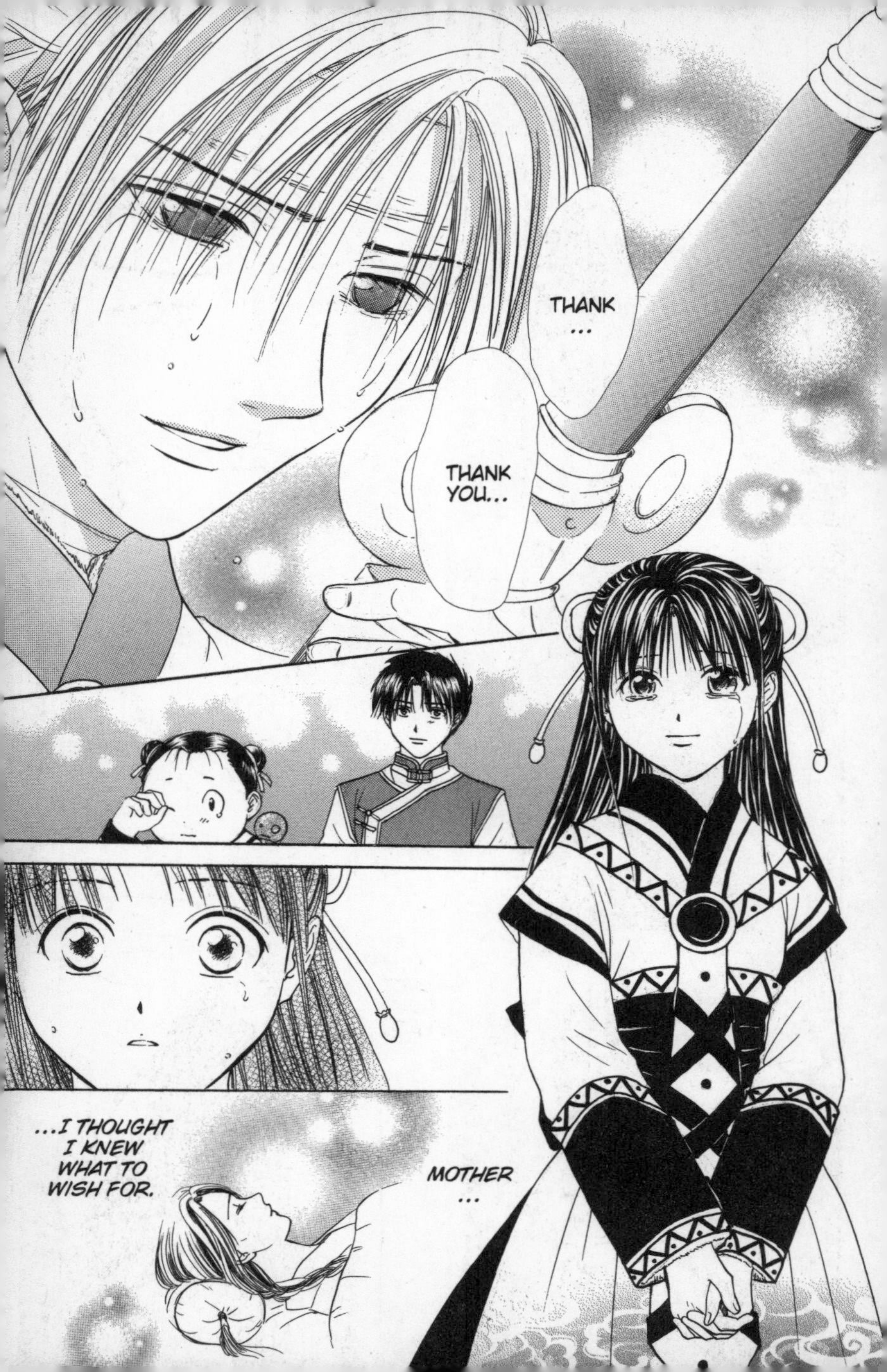
THANK ...
THANK YOU...
MOTHER ...
...I THOUGHT I KNEW WHAT TO WISH FOR.

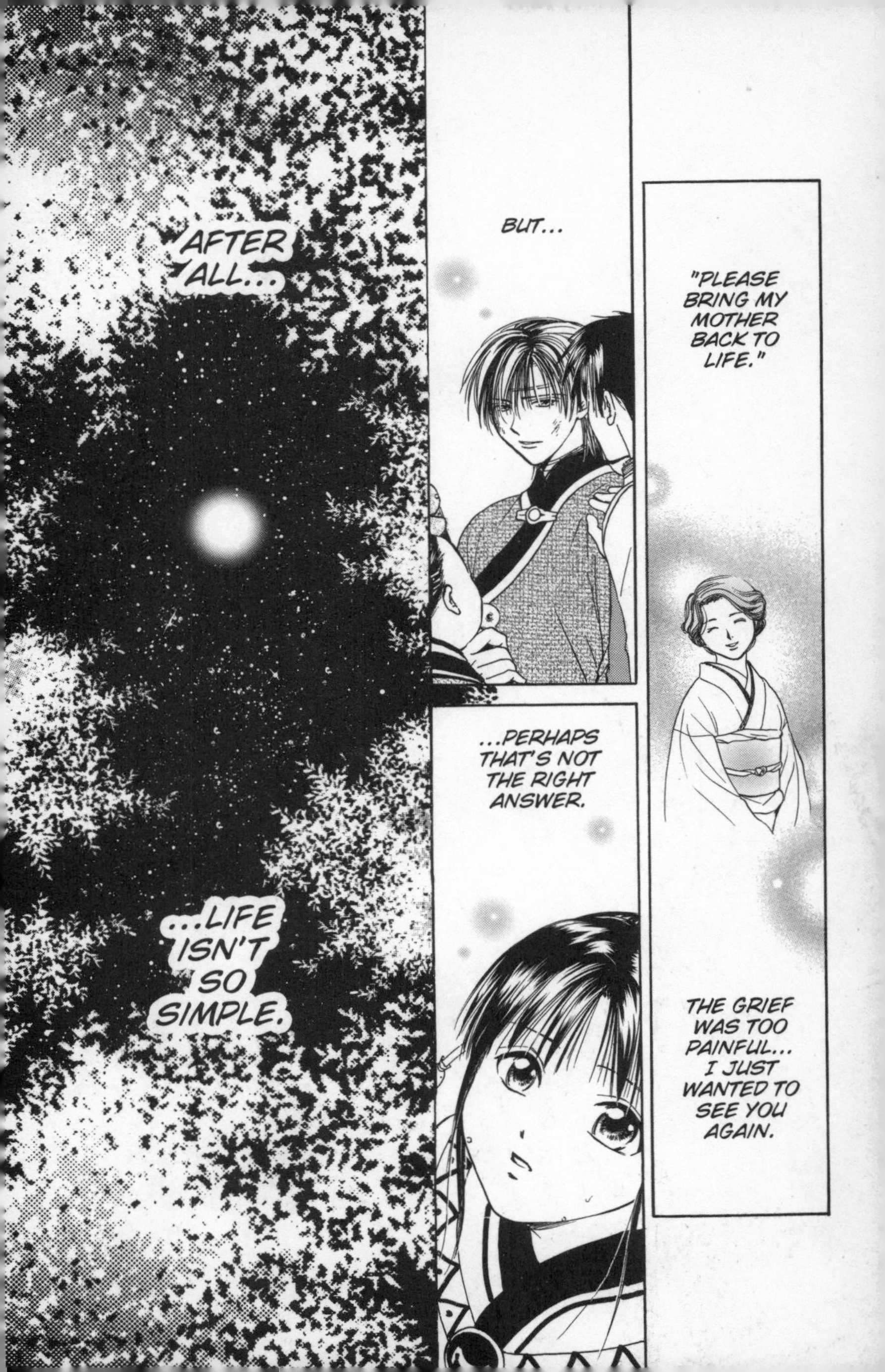
"PLEASE BRING MY MOTHER BACK TO LIFE."
THE GRIEF WAS TOO PAINFUL... I JUST WANTED TO SEE YOU AGAIN.
BUT...
...PERHAPS THAT'S NOT THE RIGHT ANSWER.
AFTER ALL...
...LIFE ISN'T SO SIMPLE.

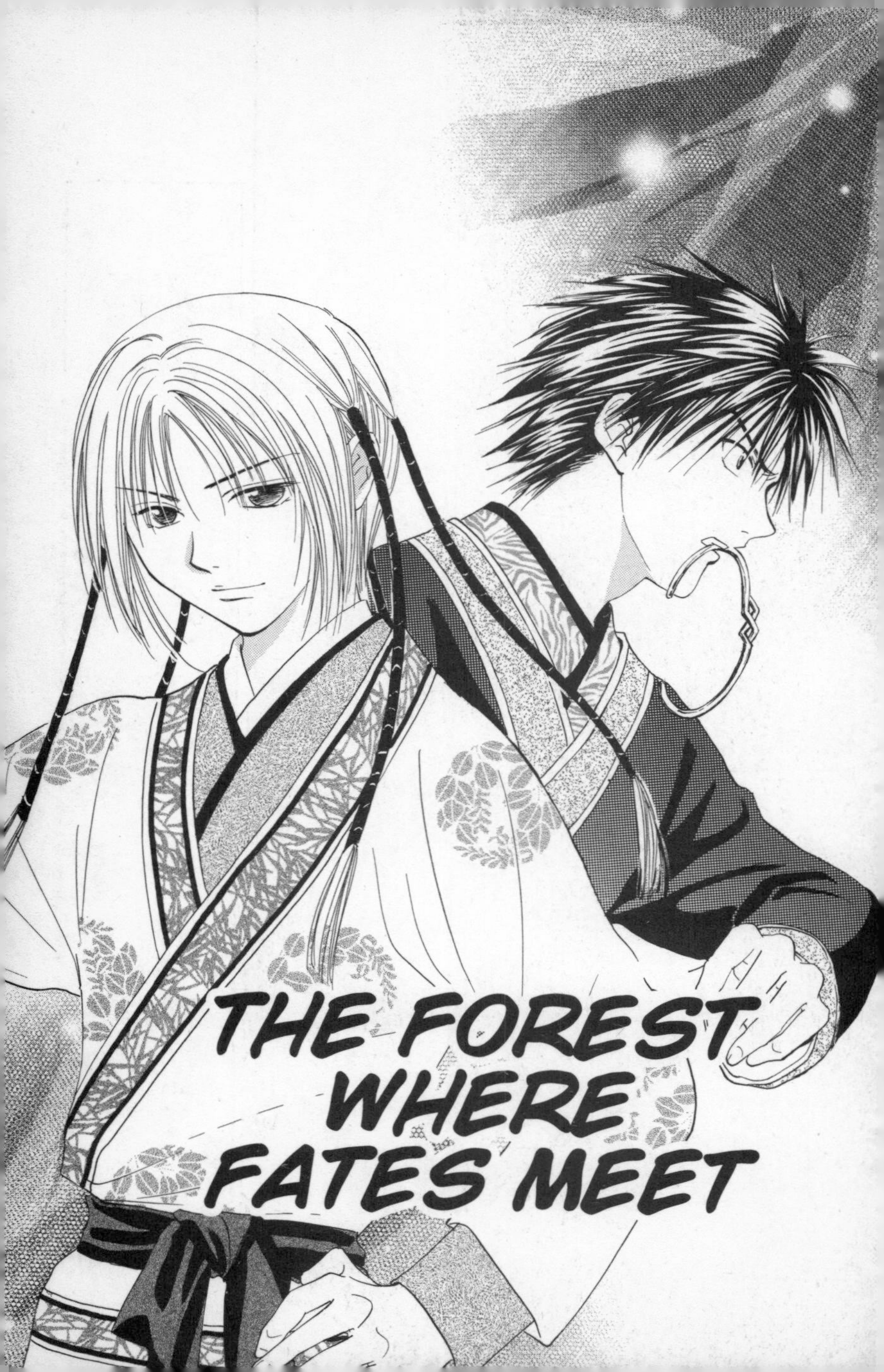
THE FOREST WHERE FATES MEET

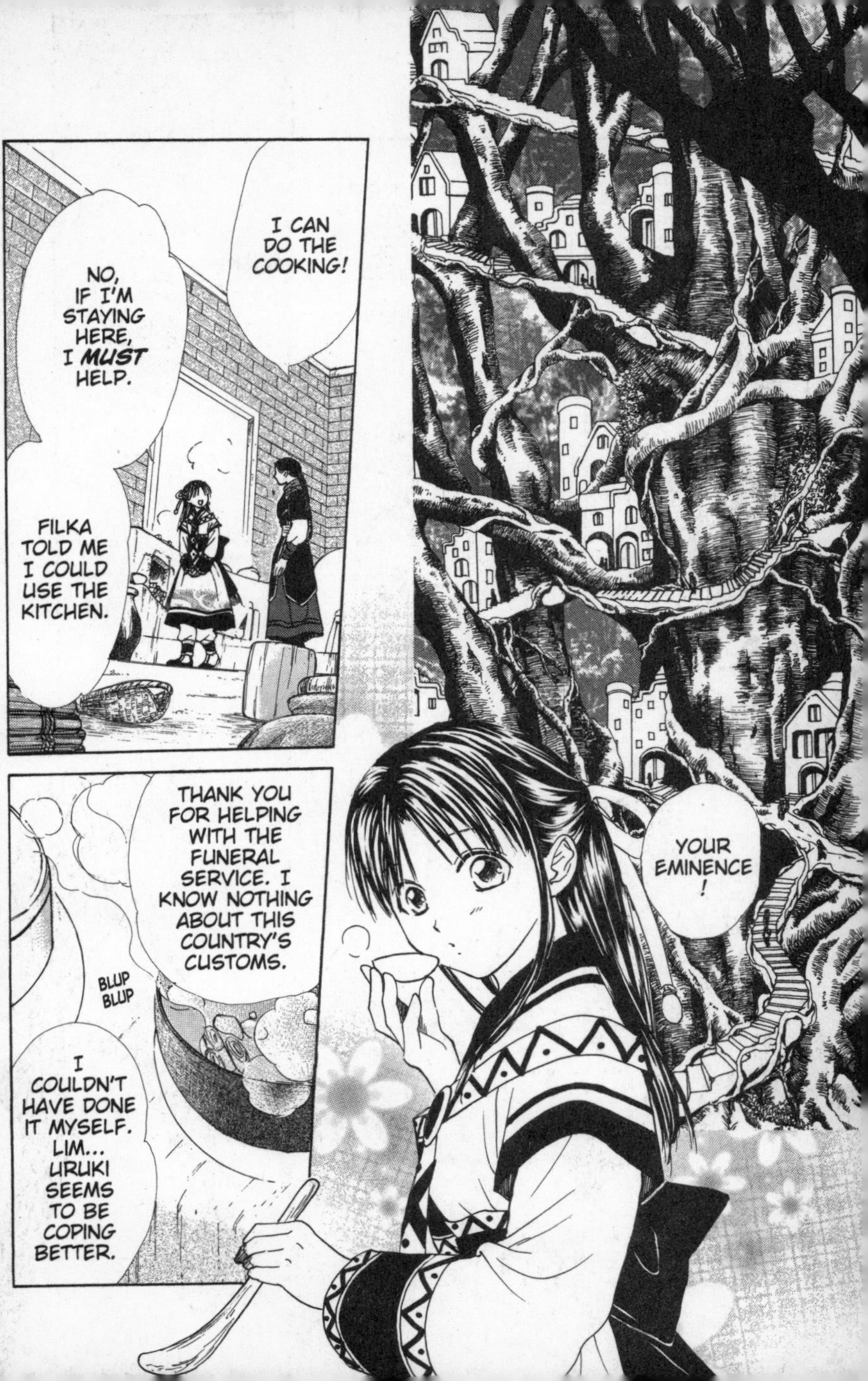
YOUR EMINENCE!
I CAN DO THE COOKING!
NO, IF I'M STAYING HERE, I *MUST* HELP.
FILKA TOLD ME I COULD USE THE KITCHEN.
THANK YOU FOR HELPING WITH THE FUNERAL SERVICE. I KNOW NOTHING ABOUT THIS COUNTRY'S CUSTOMS.
BLUP BLUP
I COULDN'T HAVE DONE IT MYSELF. LIM... URUKI SEEMS TO BE COPING BETTER.

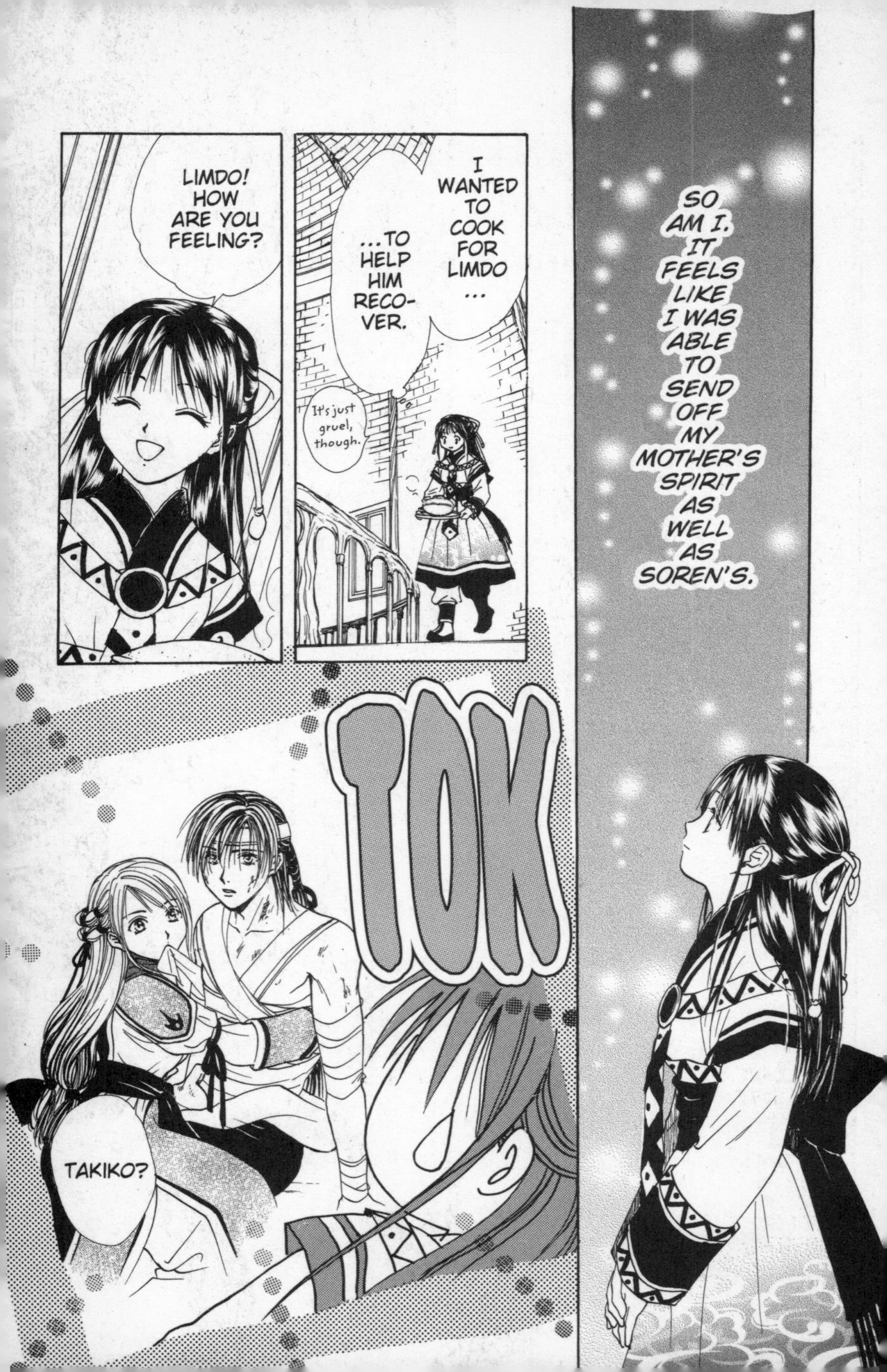
SO AM I. IT FEELS LIKE I WAS ABLE TO SEND OFF MY MOTHER'S SPIRIT AS WELL AS SOREN'S.
I WANTED TO COOK FOR LIMDO...
...TO HELP HIM RECOVER.
It's just gruel, though.
LIMDO! HOW ARE YOU FEELING?
TOK
TAKIKO?

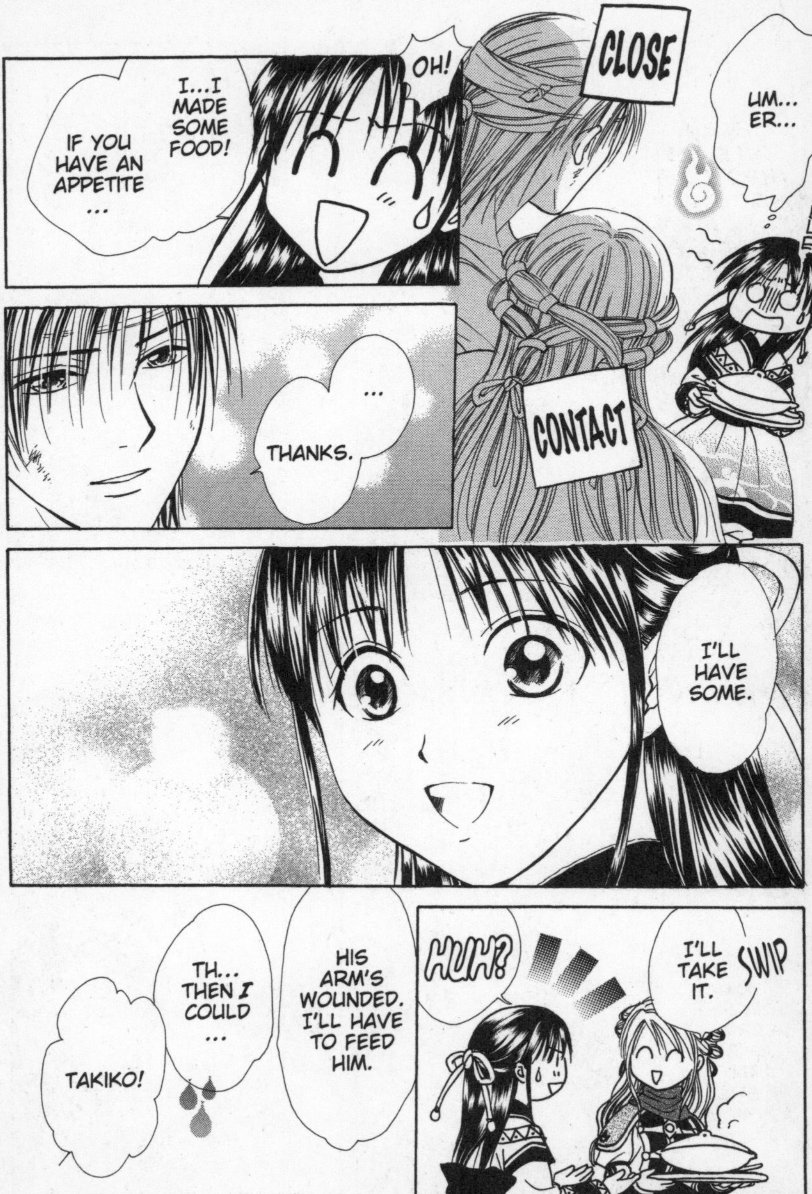
UM... ER...
WOBBLE
CLOSE
CONTACT
OH!
I...I MADE SOME FOOD!
IF YOU HAVE AN APPETITE ...
...
THANKS.
I'LL HAVE SOME.
SWIP
I'LL TAKE IT.
HUH?
HIS ARM'S WOUNDED. I'LL HAVE TO FEED HIM.
TH... THEN I COULD ...
TAKIKO!

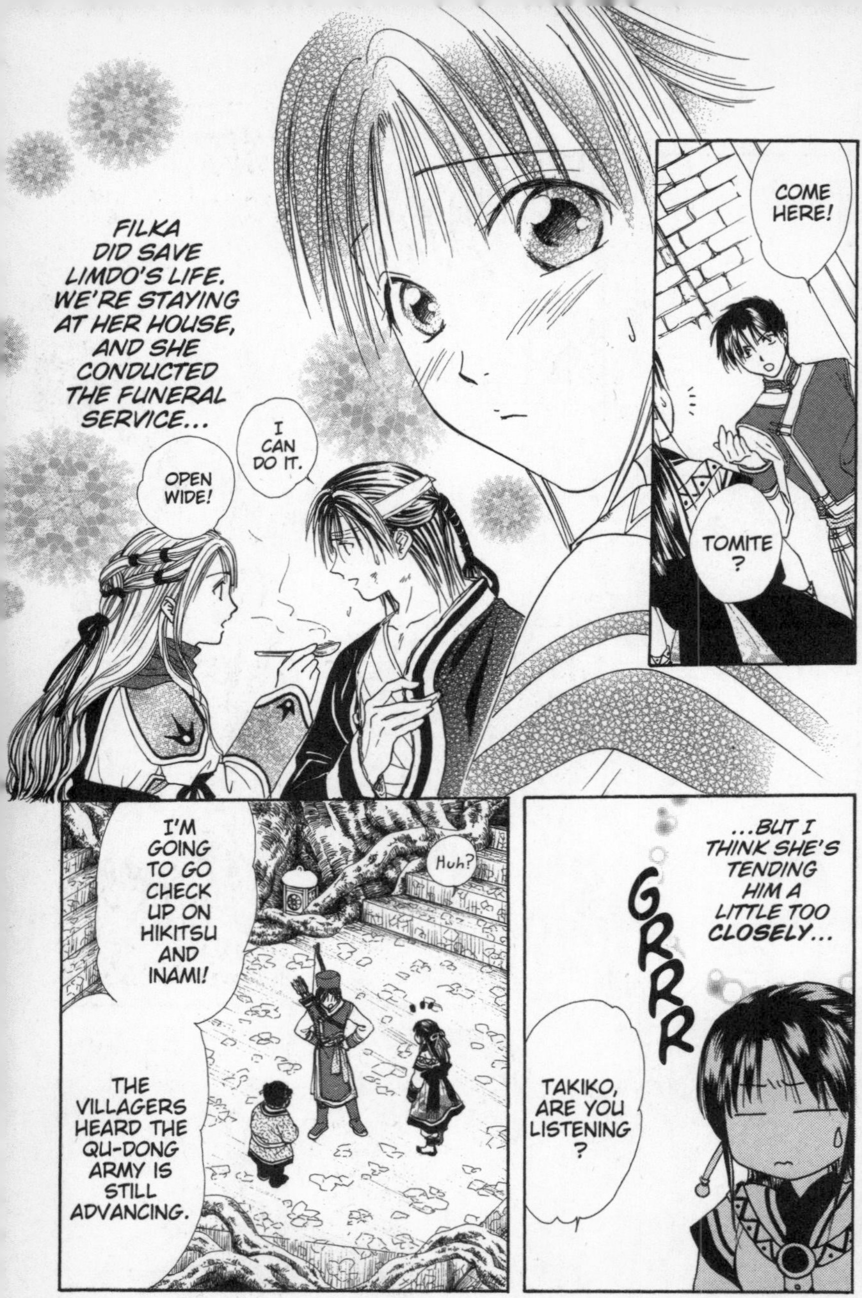
COME HERE!
TOMITE?
FILKA DID SAVE LIMDO'S LIFE. WE'RE STAYING AT HER HOUSE, AND SHE CONDUCTED THE FUNERAL SERVICE...
I CAN DO IT.
OPEN WIDE!
...BUT I THINK SHE'S TENDING HIM A LITTLE TOO CLOSELY...
GRRR
TAKIKO, ARE YOU LISTENING?
I'M GOING TO GO CHECK UP ON HIKITSU AND INAMI!
Huh?
THE VILLAGERS HEARD THE QU-DONG ARMY IS STILL ADVANCING.

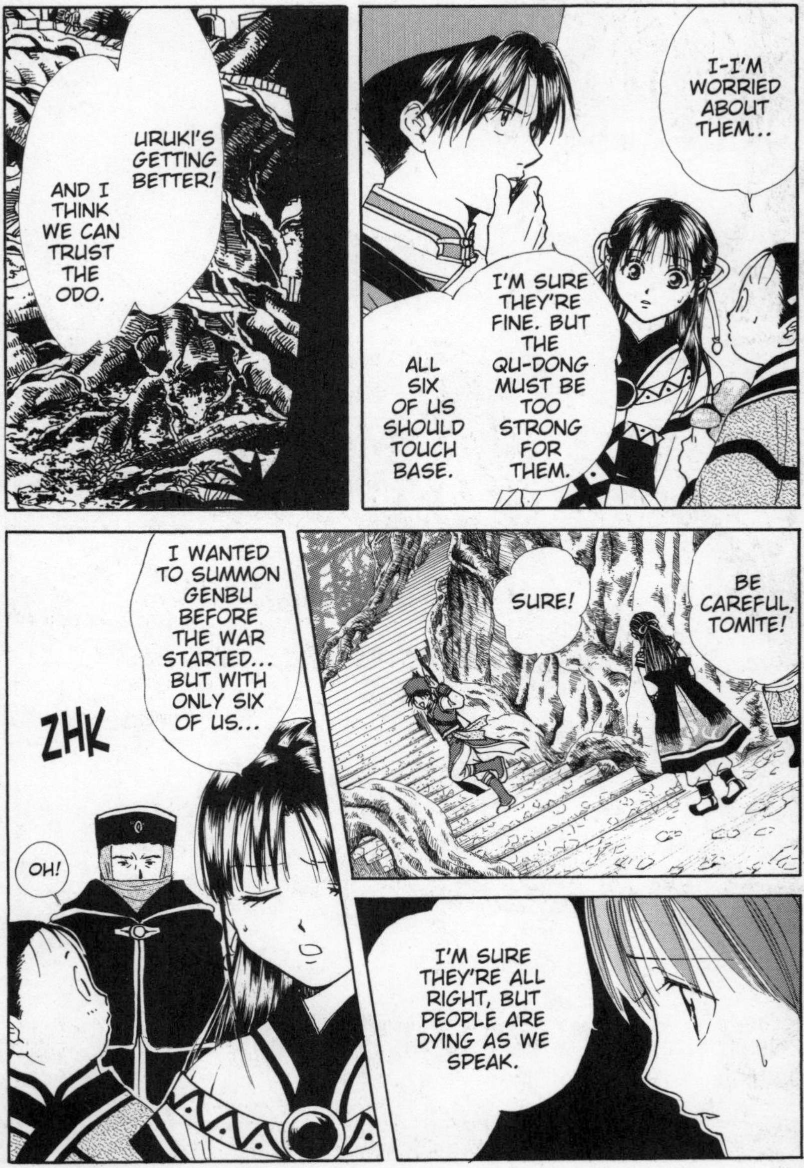
I-I'M WORRIED ABOUT THEM...
I'M SURE THEY'RE FINE. BUT THE QU-DONG MUST BE TOO STRONG FOR THEM.
ALL SIX OF US SHOULD TOUCH BASE.
URUKI'S GETTING BETTER!
AND I THINK WE CAN TRUST THE ODO.
BE CAREFUL, TOMITE!
SURE!
I'M SURE THEY'RE ALL RIGHT, BUT PEOPLE ARE DYING AS WE SPEAK.
I WANTED TO SUMMON GENBU BEFORE THE WAR STARTED... BUT WITH ONLY SIX OF US...
ZHK
OH!

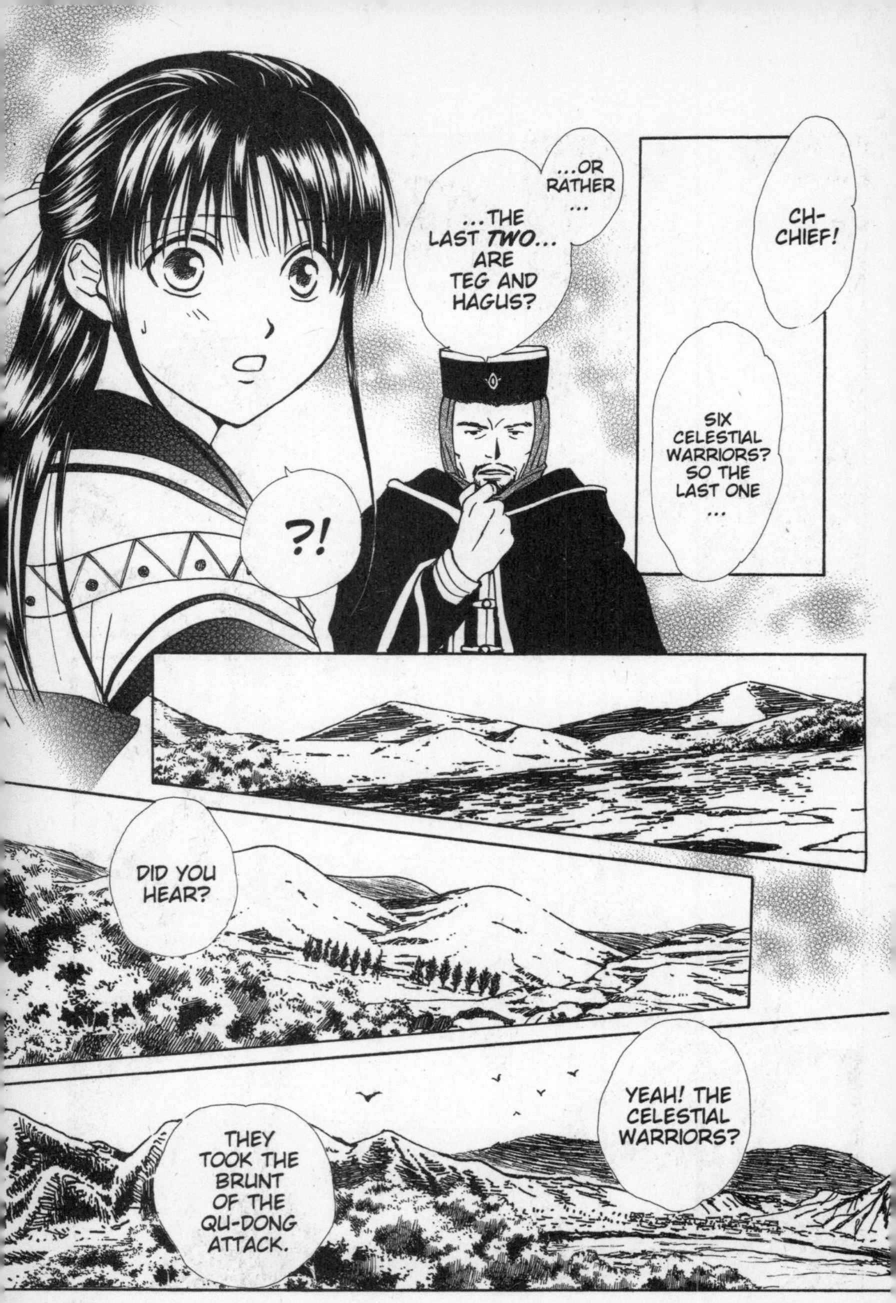
CH-CHIEF!
SIX CELESTIAL WARRIORS? SO THE LAST ONE ...
...OR RATHER ...
...THE LAST *TWO*... ARE TEG AND HAGUS?
?!
DID YOU HEAR?
YEAH! THE CELESTIAL WARRIORS?
THEY TOOK THE BRUNT OF THE QU-DONG ATTACK.

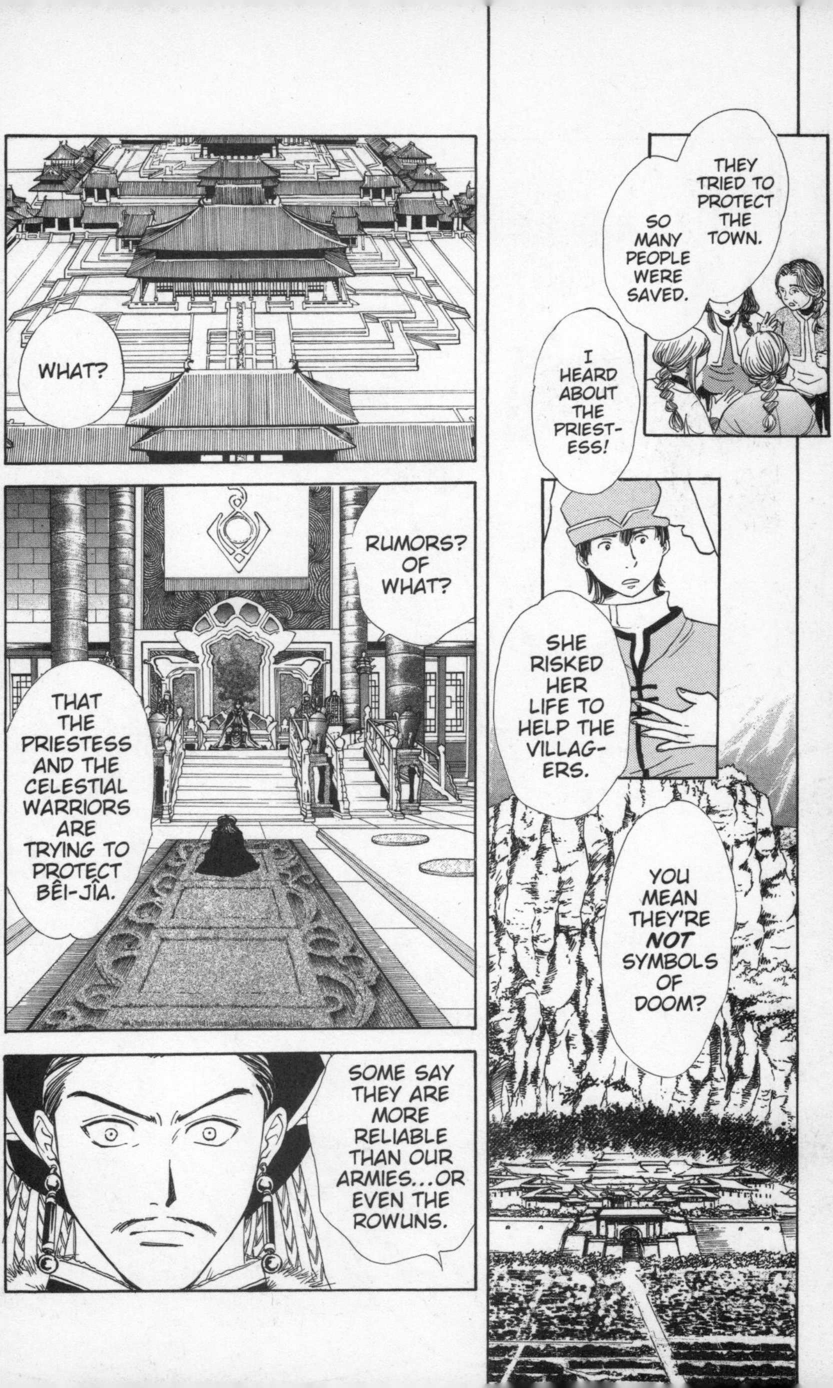
THEY TRIED TO PROTECT THE TOWN.
SO MANY PEOPLE WERE SAVED.
I HEARD ABOUT THE PRIEST-ESS!
SHE RISKED HER LIFE TO HELP THE VILLAG-ERS.
YOU MEAN THEY'RE ***NOT*** SYMBOLS OF DOOM?
WHAT?
RUMORS? OF WHAT?
THAT THE PRIESTESS AND THE CELESTIAL WARRIORS ARE TRYING TO PROTECT BÊI-JÎA.
SOME SAY THEY ARE MORE RELIABLE THAN OUR ARMIES...OR EVEN THE ROWUNS.

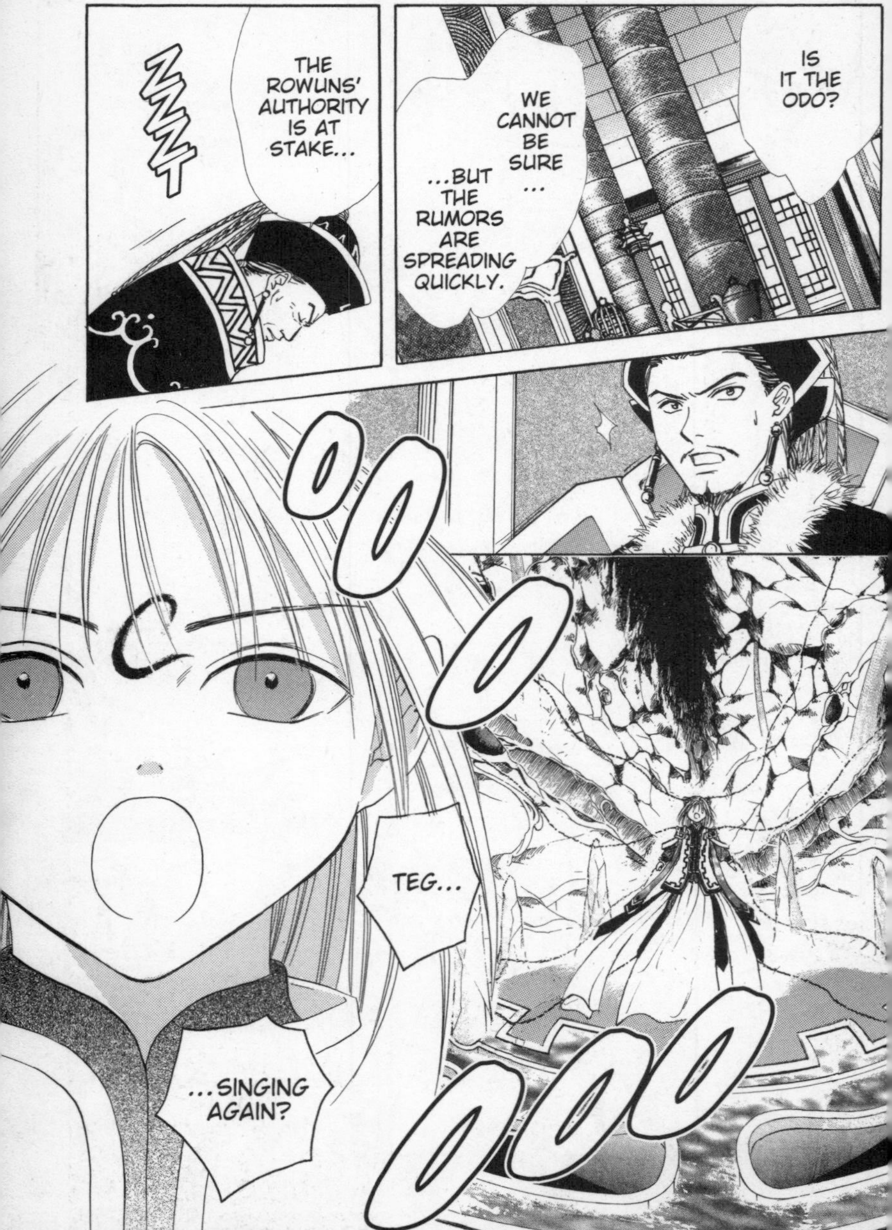
IS IT THE ODO?
WE CANNOT BE SURE...
...BUT THE RUMORS ARE SPREADING QUICKLY.
THE ROWLINS' AUTHORITY IS AT STAKE...
ZZZT
OOOO
TEG...
...SINGING AGAIN?
OOOO

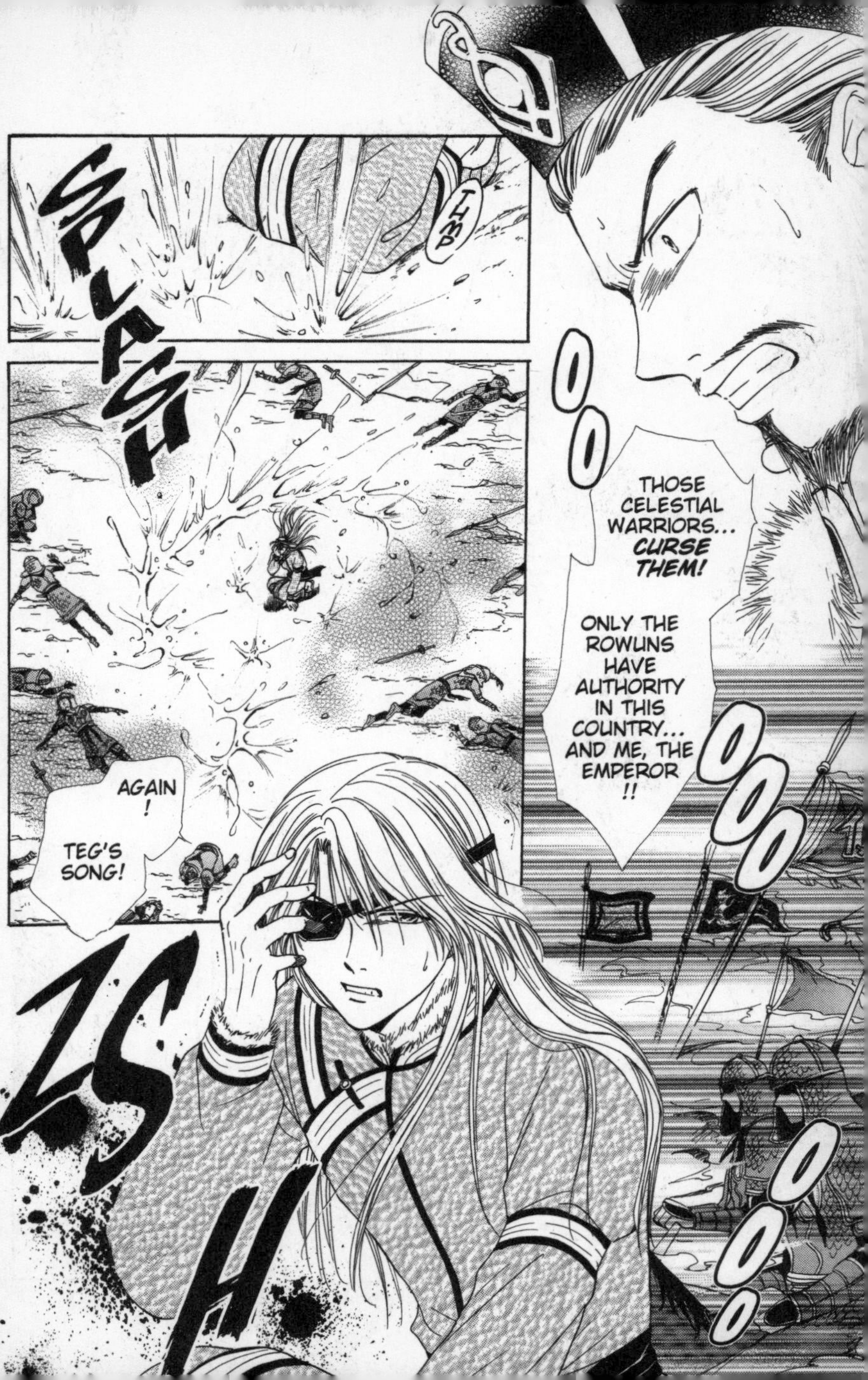
OO
THOSE CELESTIAL WARRIORS... CURSE THEM!
ONLY THE ROWUNS HAVE AUTHORITY IN THIS COUNTRY... AND ME, THE EMPEROR !!
OOO
OOOO
SPLASH
THUMP
AGAIN!
TEG'S SONG!
ZSH

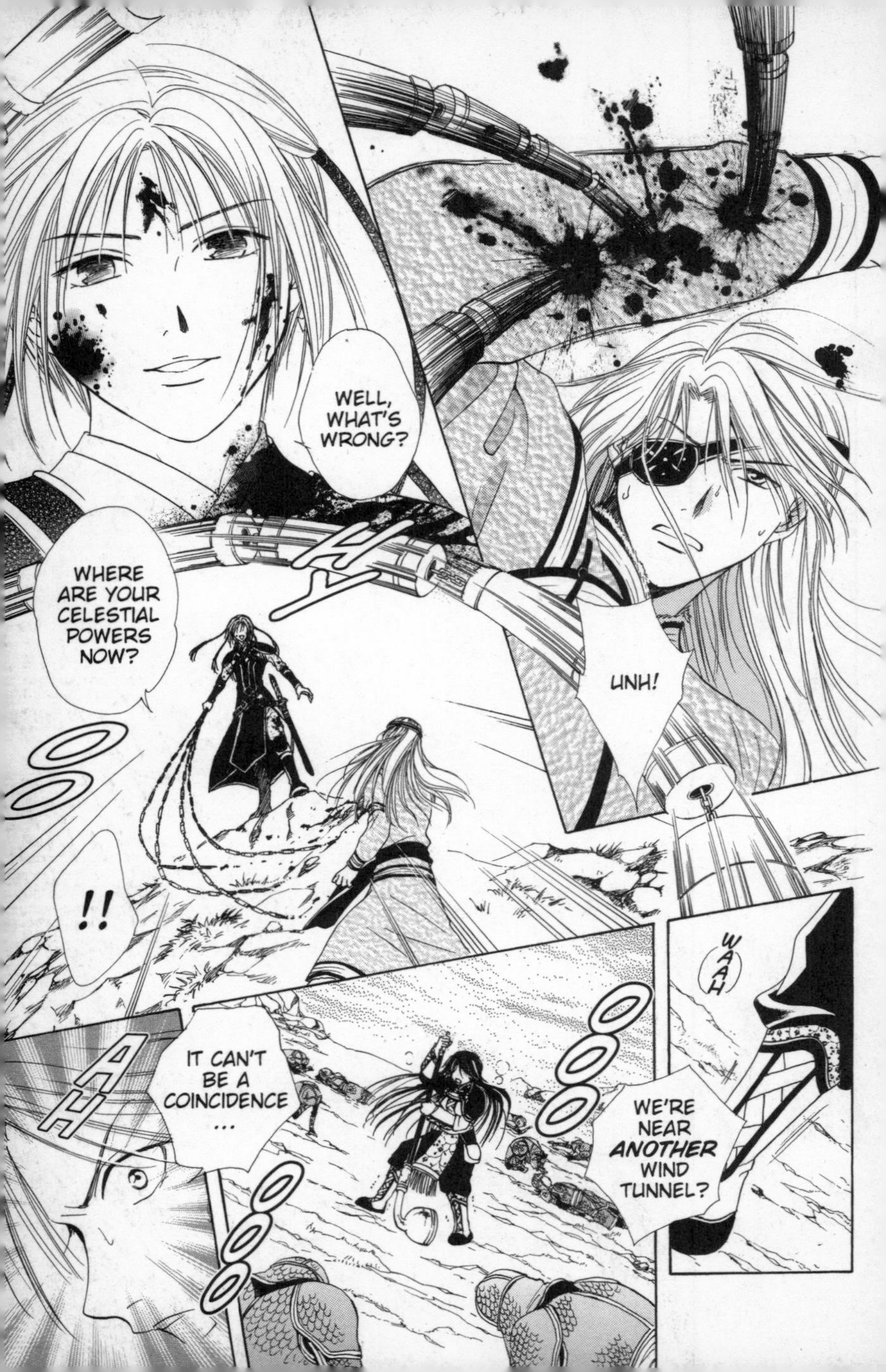
UNH!
HY
WELL, WHAT'S WRONG?
WHERE ARE YOUR CELESTIAL POWERS NOW?
OO
!!
WAAH
WE'RE NEAR *ANOTHER* WIND TUNNEL?
OOOOOOO
IT CAN'T BE A COINCIDENCE...
AH

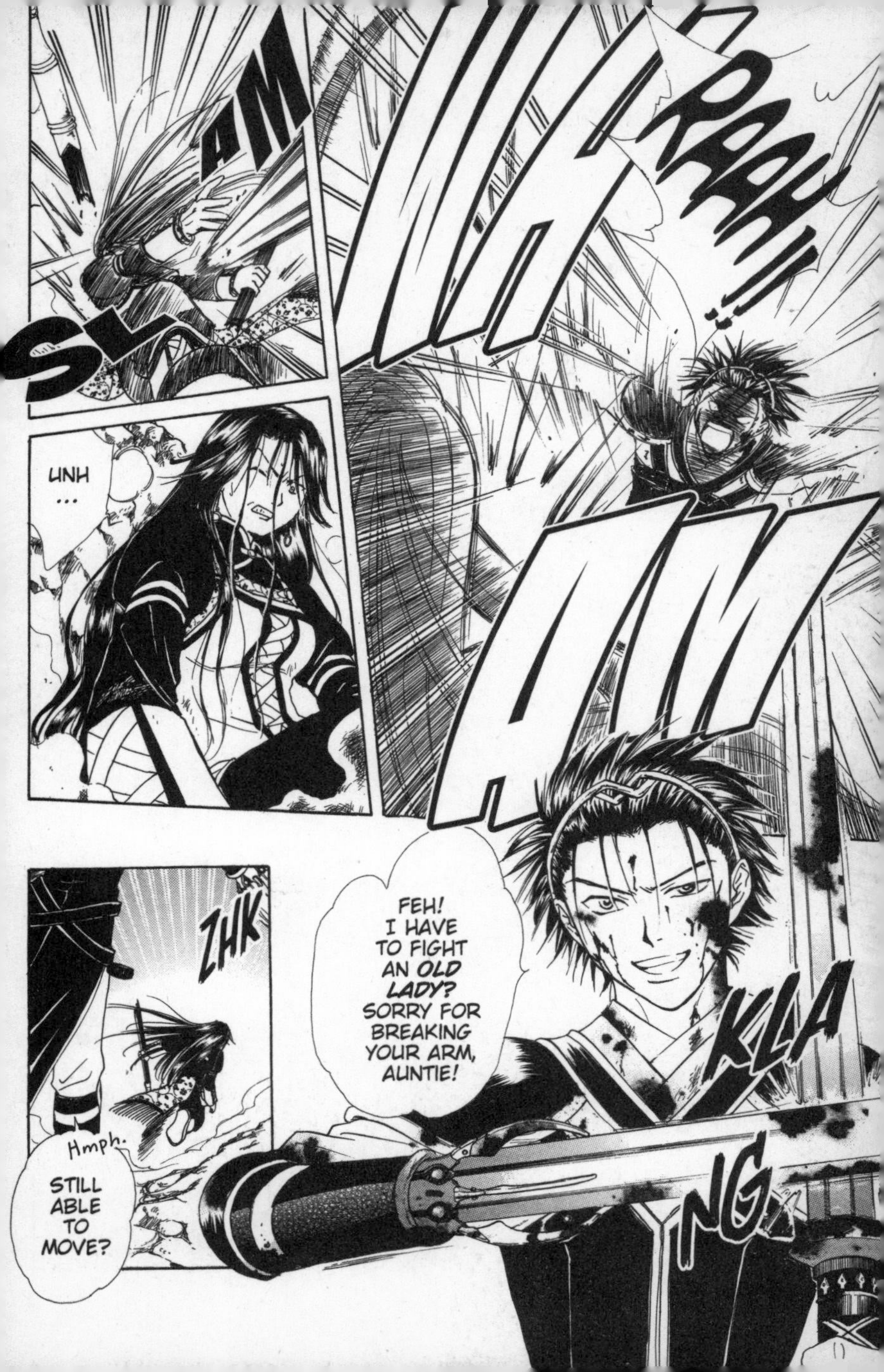
RAAH!!
FEH! I HAVE TO FIGHT AN *OLD LADY?* SORRY FOR BREAKING YOUR ARM, AUNTIE!
KLA
NG
SL
AM
UNH ...
ZHK
Hmph.
STILL ABLE TO MOVE?

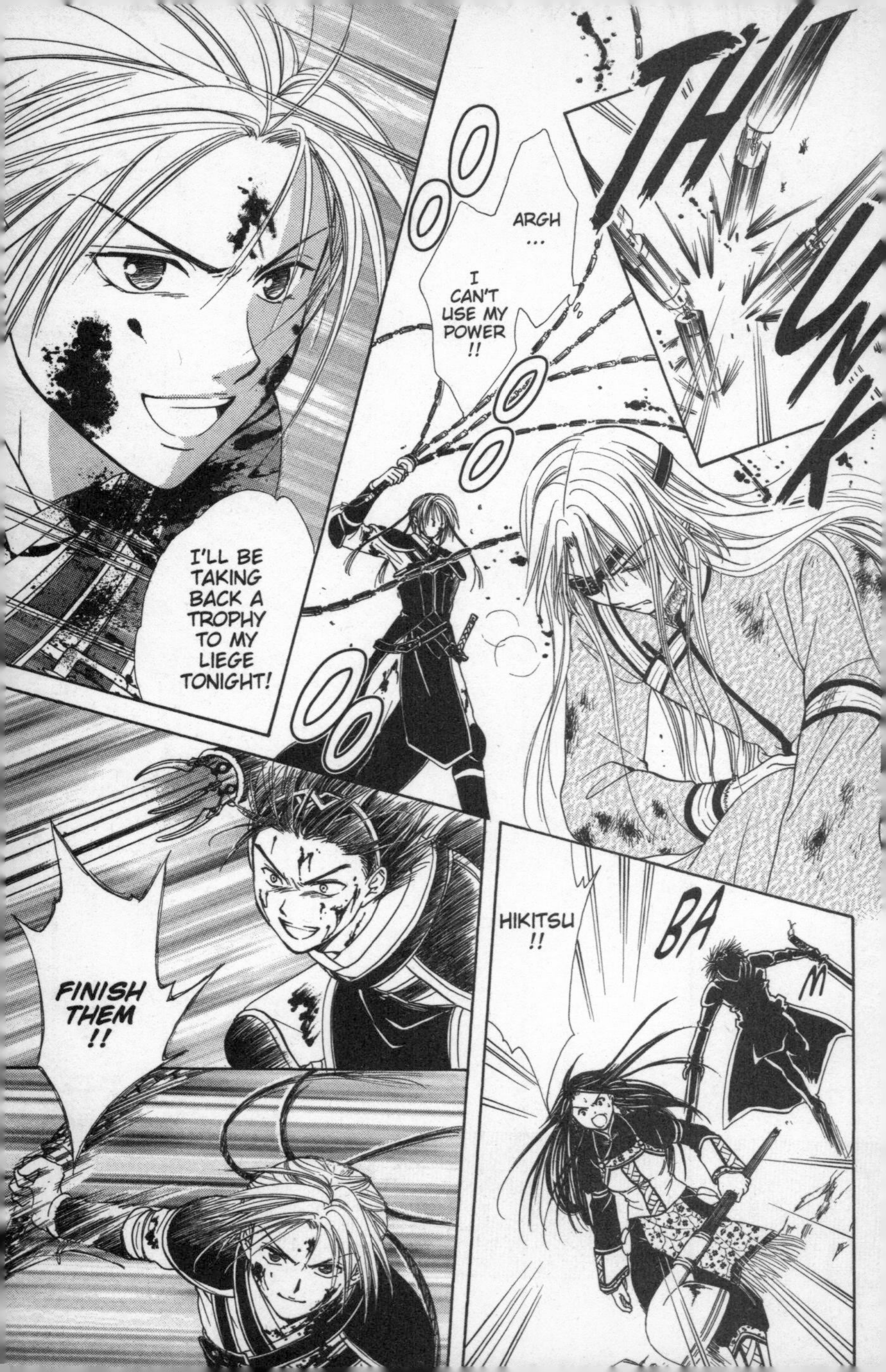
THUNK
ARGH ...
I CAN'T USE MY POWER !!
I'LL BE TAKING BACK A TROPHY TO MY LIEGE TONIGHT!
HIKITSU !!
BAM
FINISH THEM !!

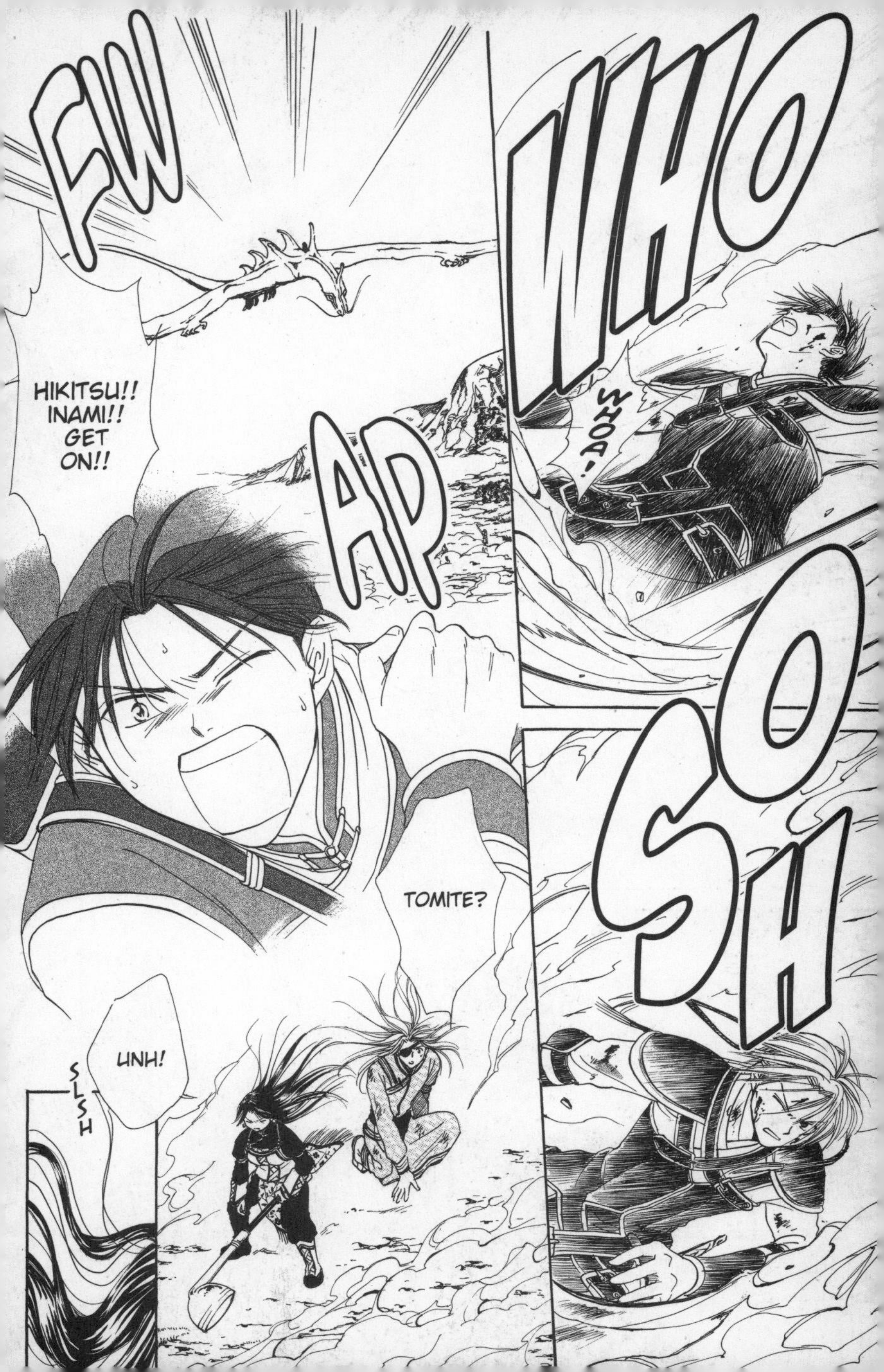
WHO
WHOA!
OSH
FW
HIKITSU!! INAMI!! GET ON!!
AP
TOMITE?
UNH!
SLSH

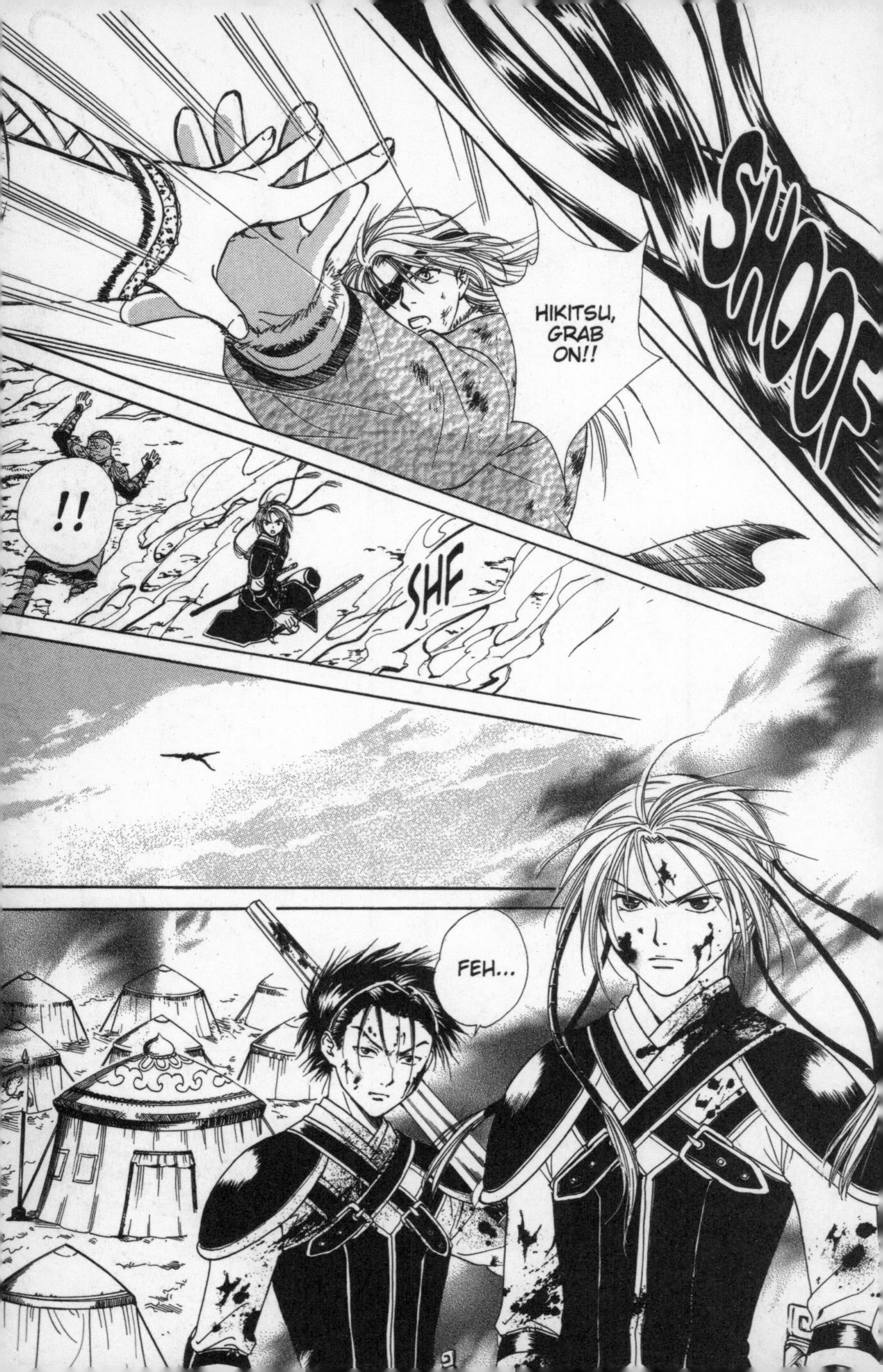
SHOOF
HIKITSU, GRAB ON!!
SHF
!!
FEH...

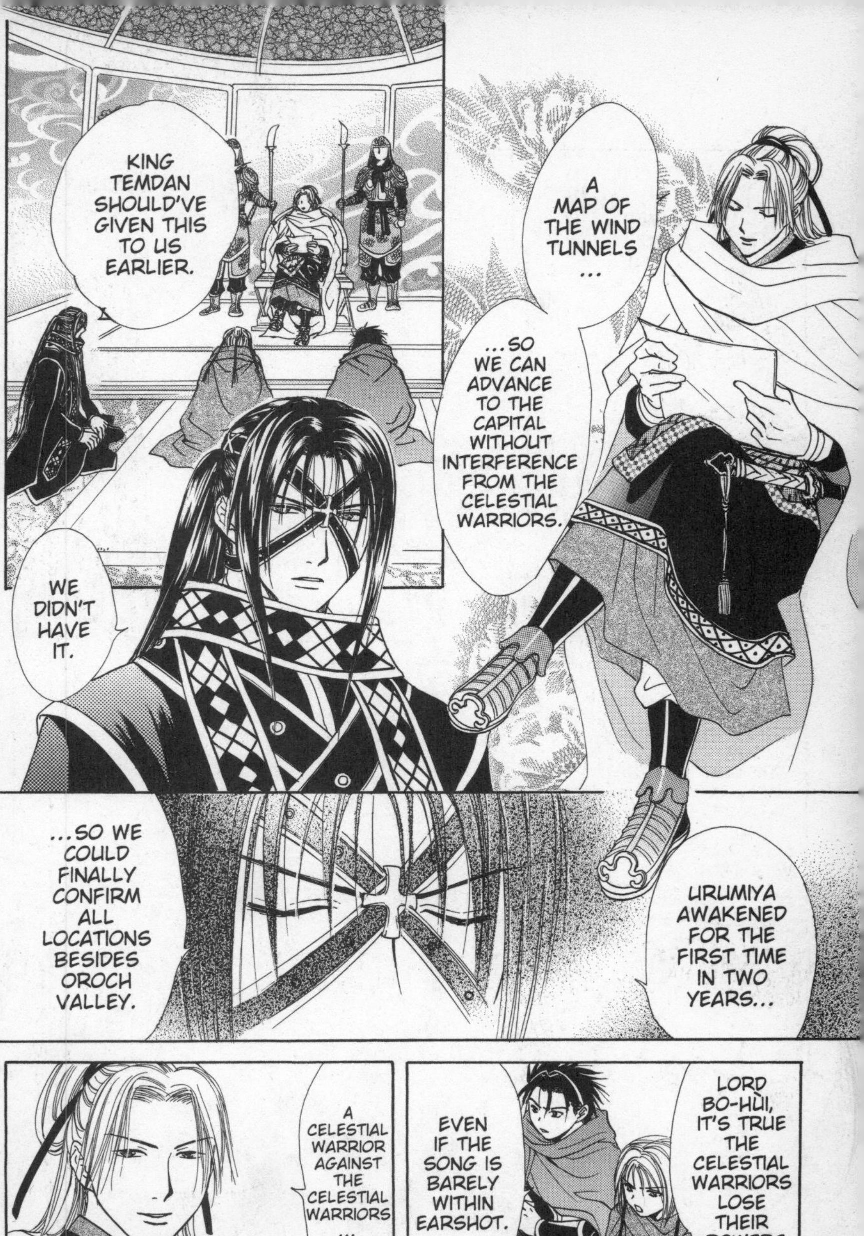
A MAP OF THE WIND TUNNELS...
...SO WE CAN ADVANCE TO THE CAPITAL WITHOUT INTERFERENCE FROM THE CELESTIAL WARRIORS.
KING TEMDAN SHOULD'VE GIVEN THIS TO US EARLIER.
WE DIDN'T HAVE IT.
URUMIYA AWAKENED FOR THE FIRST TIME IN TWO YEARS...
...SO WE COULD FINALLY CONFIRM ALL LOCATIONS BESIDES OROCH VALLEY.
LORD BO-HŬI, IT'S TRUE THE CELESTIAL WARRIORS LOSE THEIR POWERS.
EVEN IF THE SONG IS BARELY WITHIN EARSHOT.
A CELESTIAL WARRIOR AGAINST THE CELESTIAL WARRIORS...

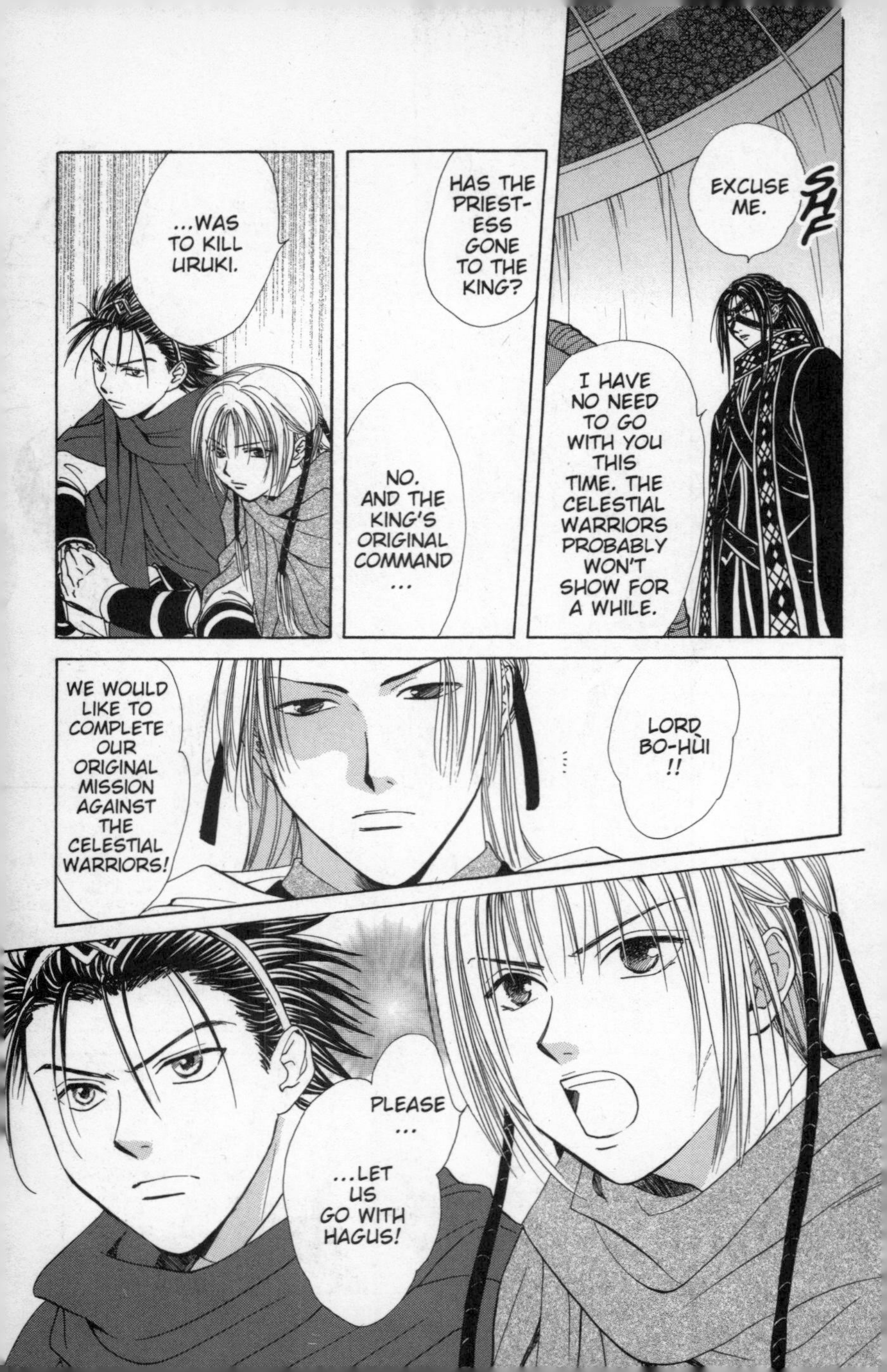
EXCUSE ME.
SHF
I HAVE NO NEED TO GO WITH YOU THIS TIME. THE CELESTIAL WARRIORS PROBABLY WON'T SHOW FOR A WHILE.
HAS THE PRIEST-ESS GONE TO THE KING?
NO. AND THE KING'S ORIGINAL COMMAND ...
...WAS TO KILL URUKI.
LORD BO-HÙI !!
WE WOULD LIKE TO COMPLETE OUR ORIGINAL MISSION AGAINST THE CELESTIAL WARRIORS!
PLEASE ...
...LET US GO WITH HAGUS!

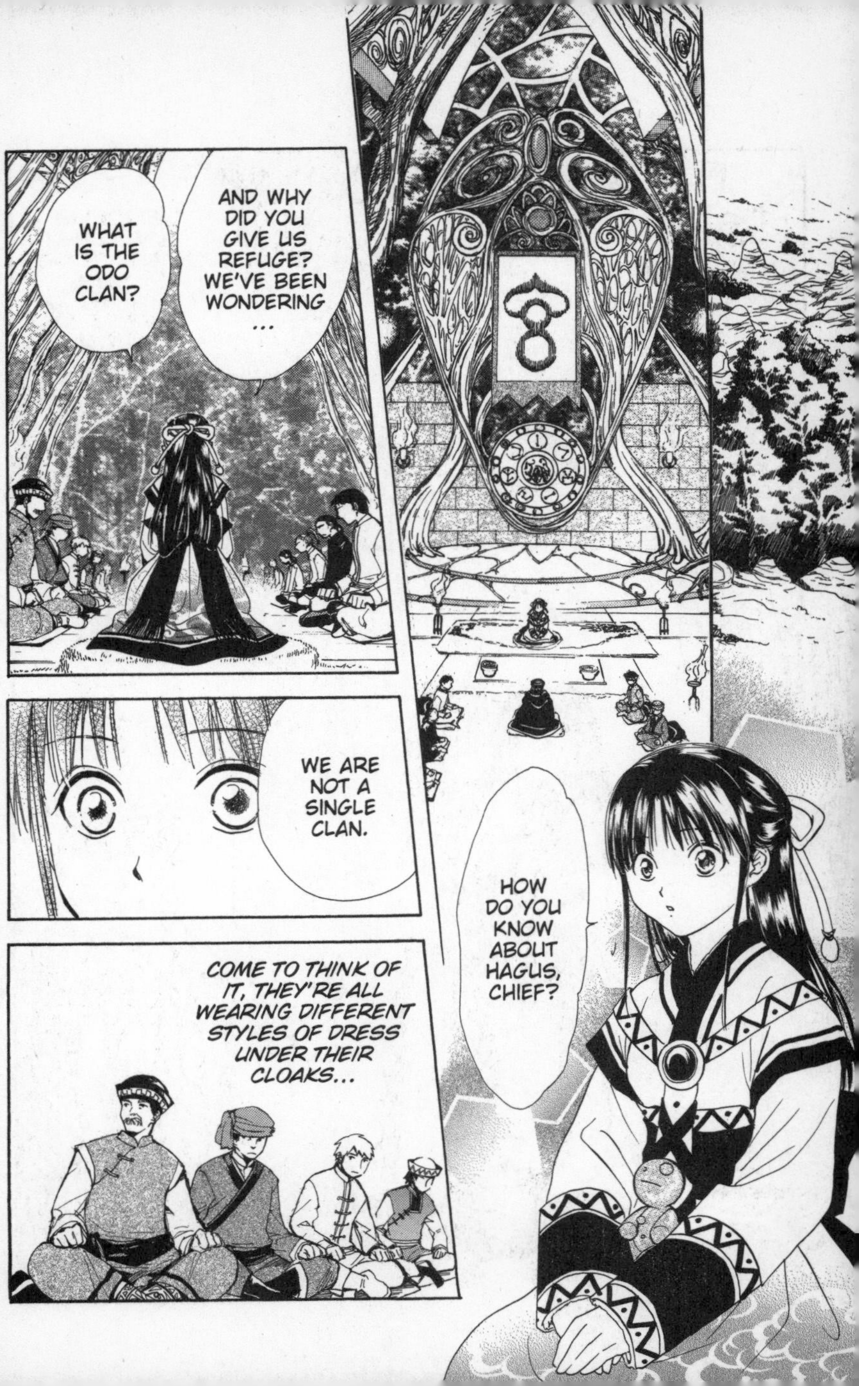
HOW DO YOU KNOW ABOUT HAGUS, CHIEF?
AND WHY DID YOU GIVE US REFUGE? WE'VE BEEN WONDERING ...
WHAT IS THE ODO CLAN?
WE ARE NOT A SINGLE CLAN.
COME TO THINK OF IT, THEY'RE ALL WEARING DIFFERENT STYLES OF DRESS UNDER THEIR CLOAKS...

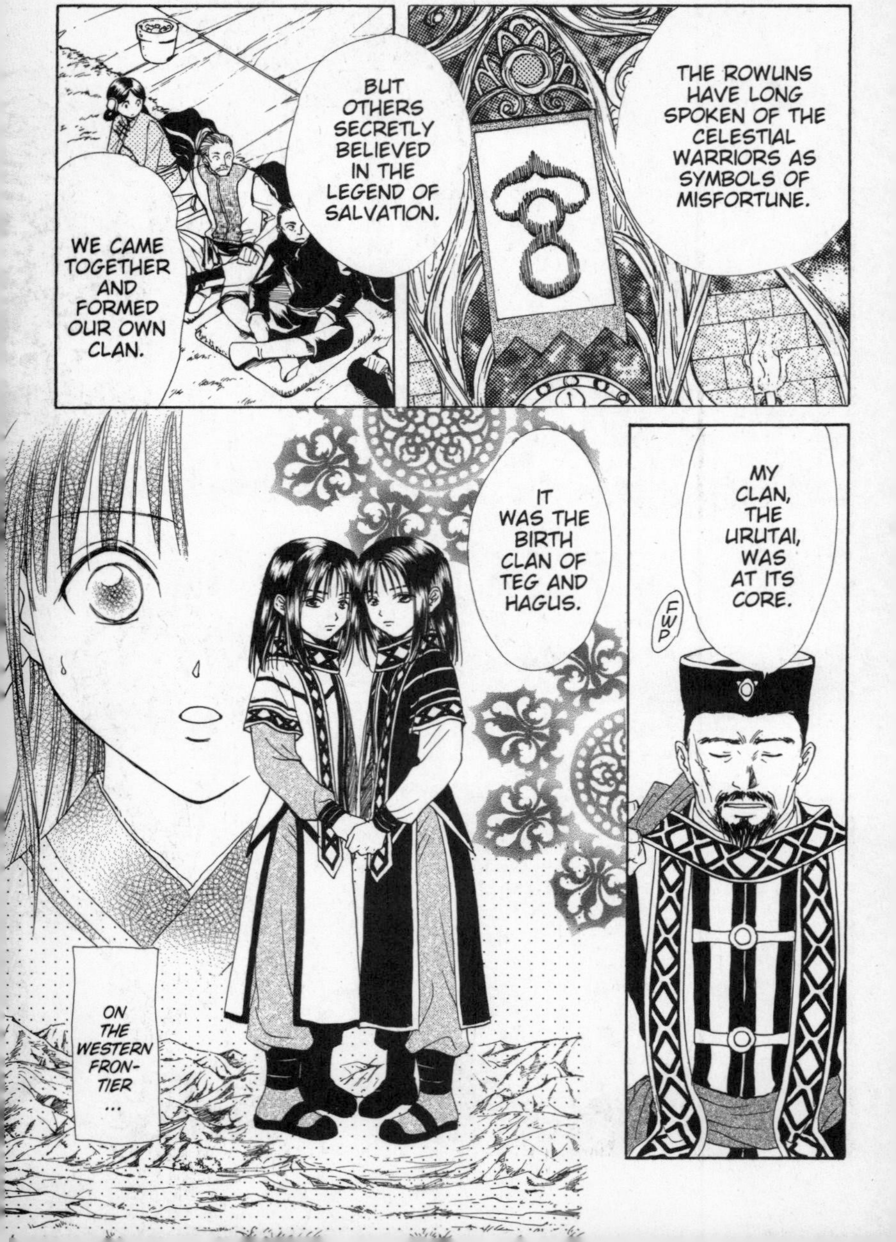
THE ROWUNS HAVE LONG SPOKEN OF THE CELESTIAL WARRIORS AS SYMBOLS OF MISFORTUNE.
BUT OTHERS SECRETLY BELIEVED IN THE LEGEND OF SALVATION.
WE CAME TOGETHER AND FORMED OUR OWN CLAN.
MY CLAN, THE URUTAI, WAS AT ITS CORE.
FWP
IT WAS THE BIRTH CLAN OF TEG AND HAGUS.
ON THE WESTERN FRONTIER...

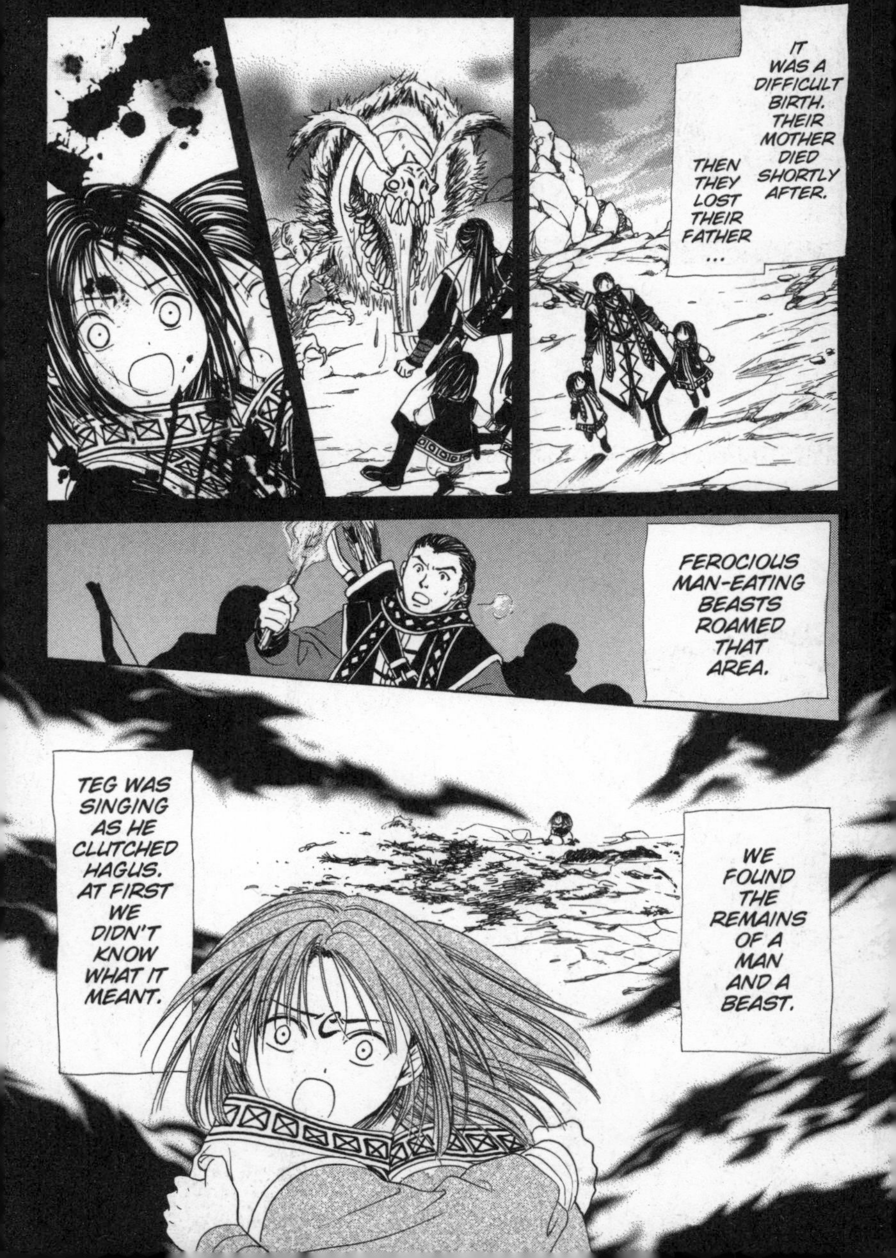
IT WAS A DIFFICULT BIRTH. THEIR MOTHER DIED SHORTLY AFTER.
THEN THEY LOST THEIR FATHER ...
FEROCIOUS MAN-EATING BEASTS ROAMED THAT AREA.
WE FOUND THE REMAINS OF A MAN AND A BEAST.
TEG WAS SINGING AS HE CLUTCHED HAGUS. AT FIRST WE DIDN'T KNOW WHAT IT MEANT.

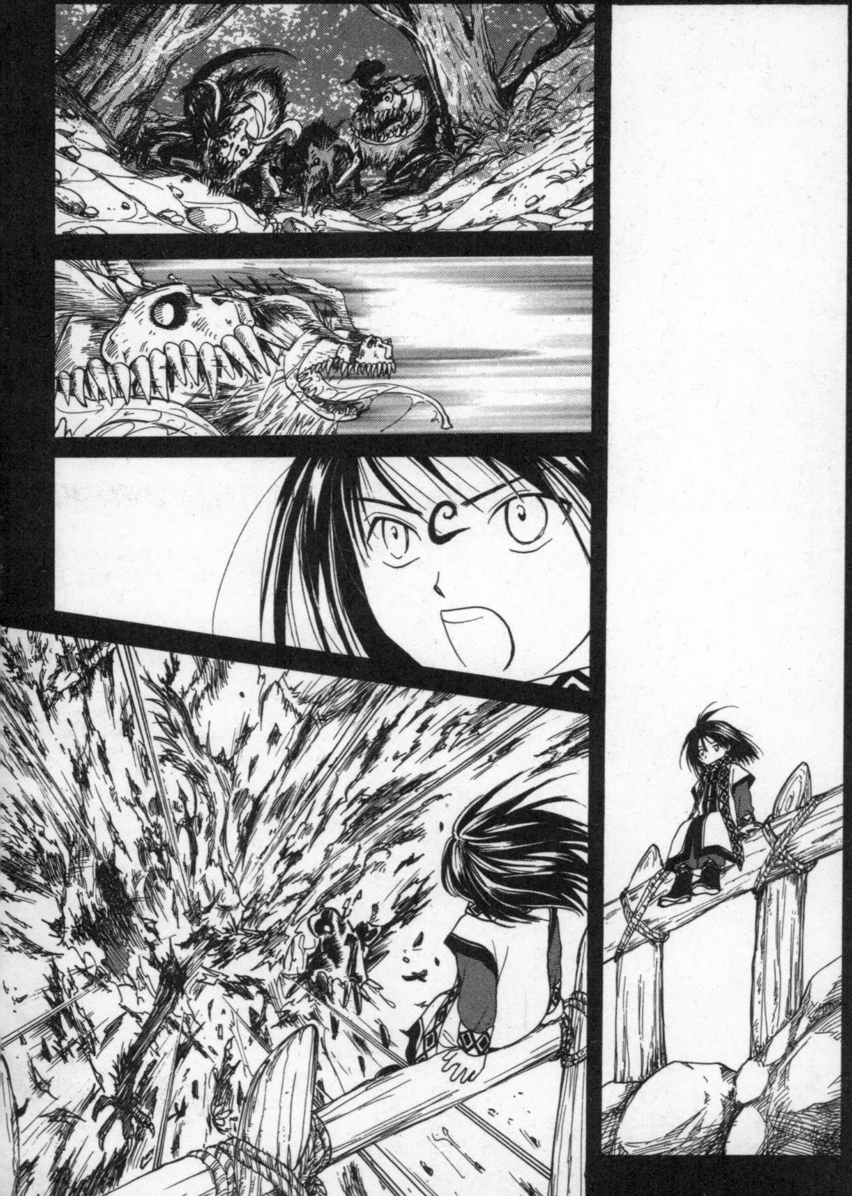

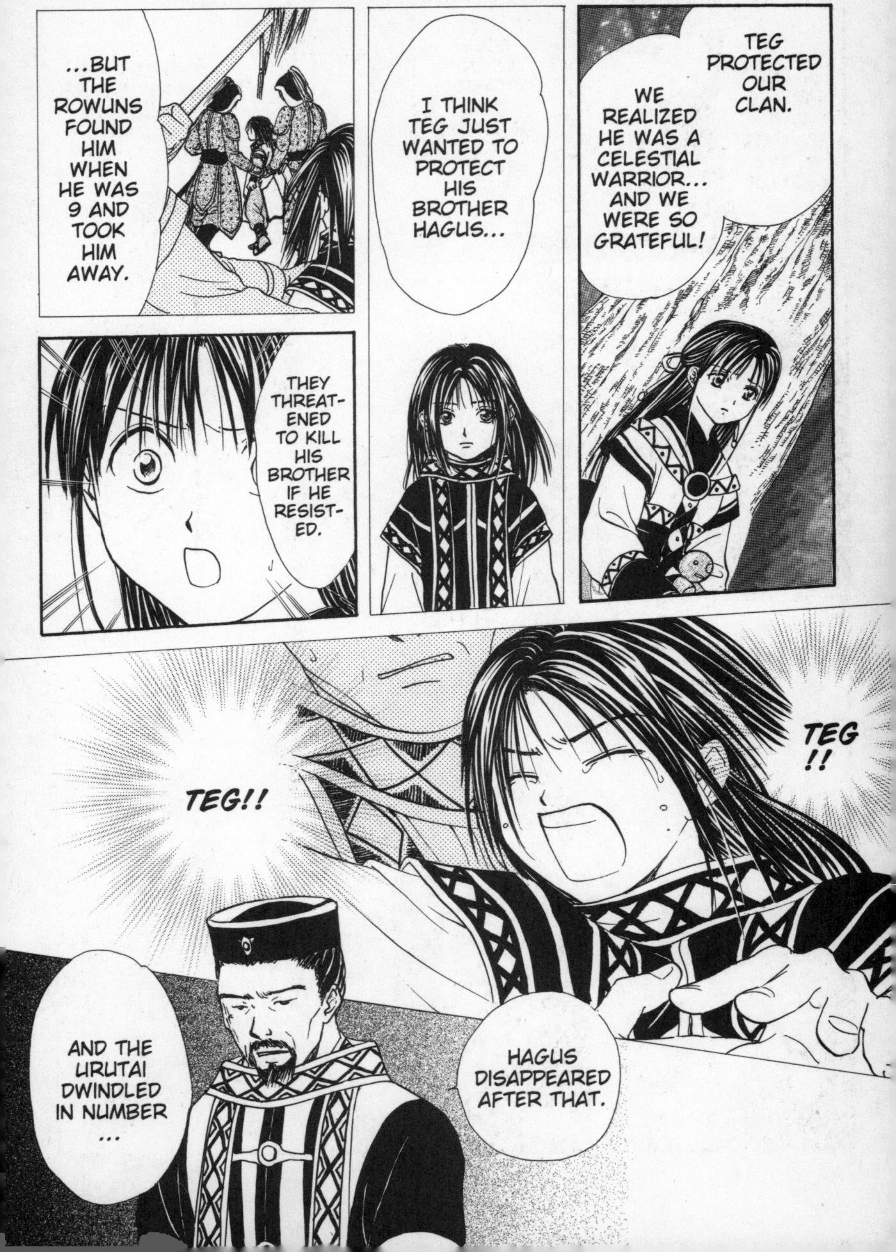
TEG PROTECTED OUR CLAN.
WE REALIZED HE WAS A CELESTIAL WARRIOR... AND WE WERE SO GRATEFUL!
I THINK TEG JUST WANTED TO PROTECT HIS BROTHER HAGUS...
...BUT THE ROWUNS FOUND HIM WHEN HE WAS 9 AND TOOK HIM AWAY.
THEY THREAT-ENED TO KILL HIS BROTHER IF HE RESIST-ED.
TEG !!
TEG!!
HAGUS DISAPPEARED AFTER THAT.
AND THE URUTAI DWINDLED IN NUMBER ...

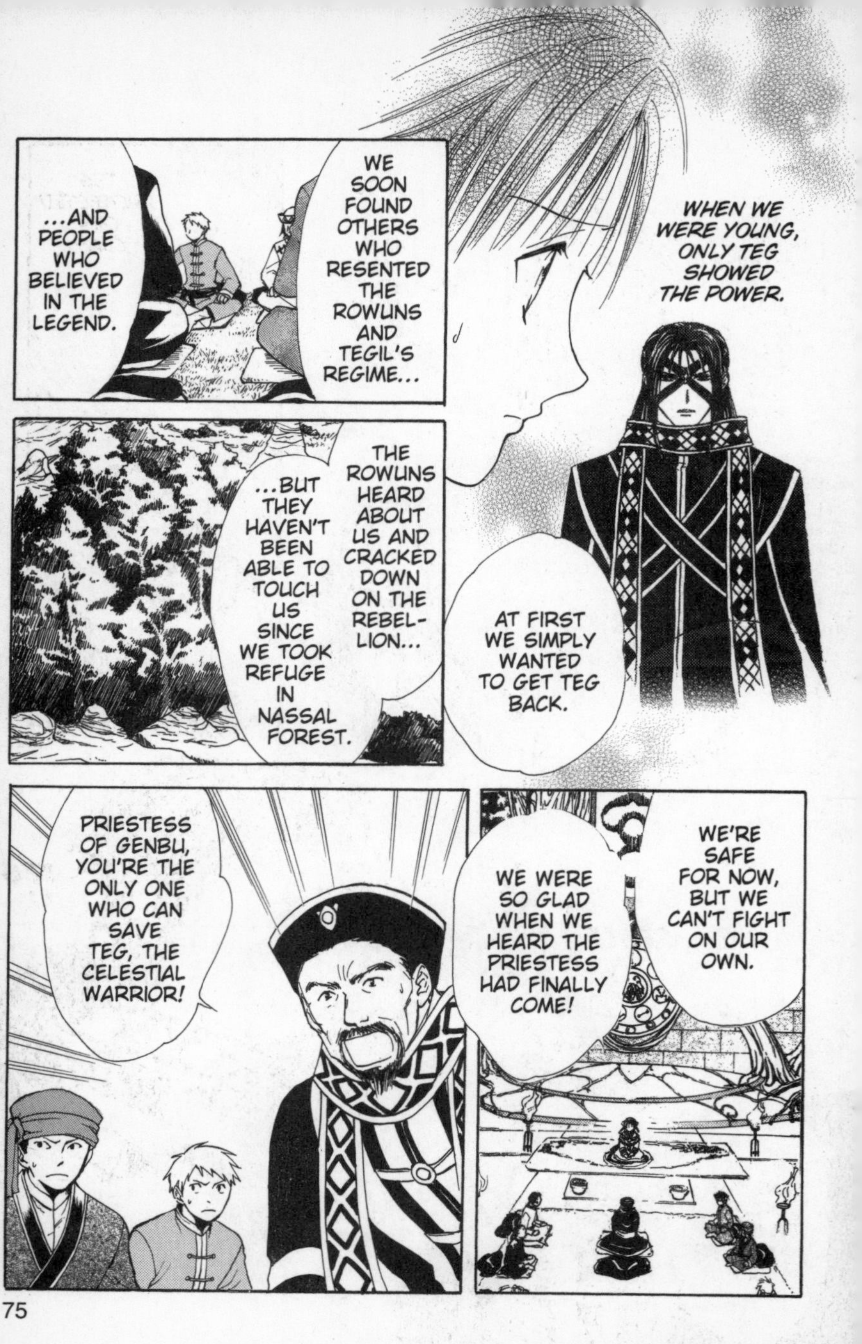
WHEN WE WERE YOUNG, ONLY TEG SHOWED THE POWER.
AT FIRST WE SIMPLY WANTED TO GET TEG BACK.
WE SOON FOUND OTHERS WHO RESENTED THE ROWUNS AND TEGIL'S REGIME...
...AND PEOPLE WHO BELIEVED IN THE LEGEND.
THE ROWUNS HEARD ABOUT US AND CRACKED DOWN ON THE REBEL-LION...
...BUT THEY HAVEN'T BEEN ABLE TO TOUCH US SINCE WE TOOK REFUGE IN NASSAL FOREST.
WE'RE SAFE FOR NOW, BUT WE CAN'T FIGHT ON OUR OWN.
WE WERE SO GLAD WHEN WE HEARD THE PRIESTESS HAD FINALLY COME!
PRIESTESS OF GENBU, YOU'RE THE ONLY ONE WHO CAN SAVE TEG, THE CELESTIAL WARRIOR!

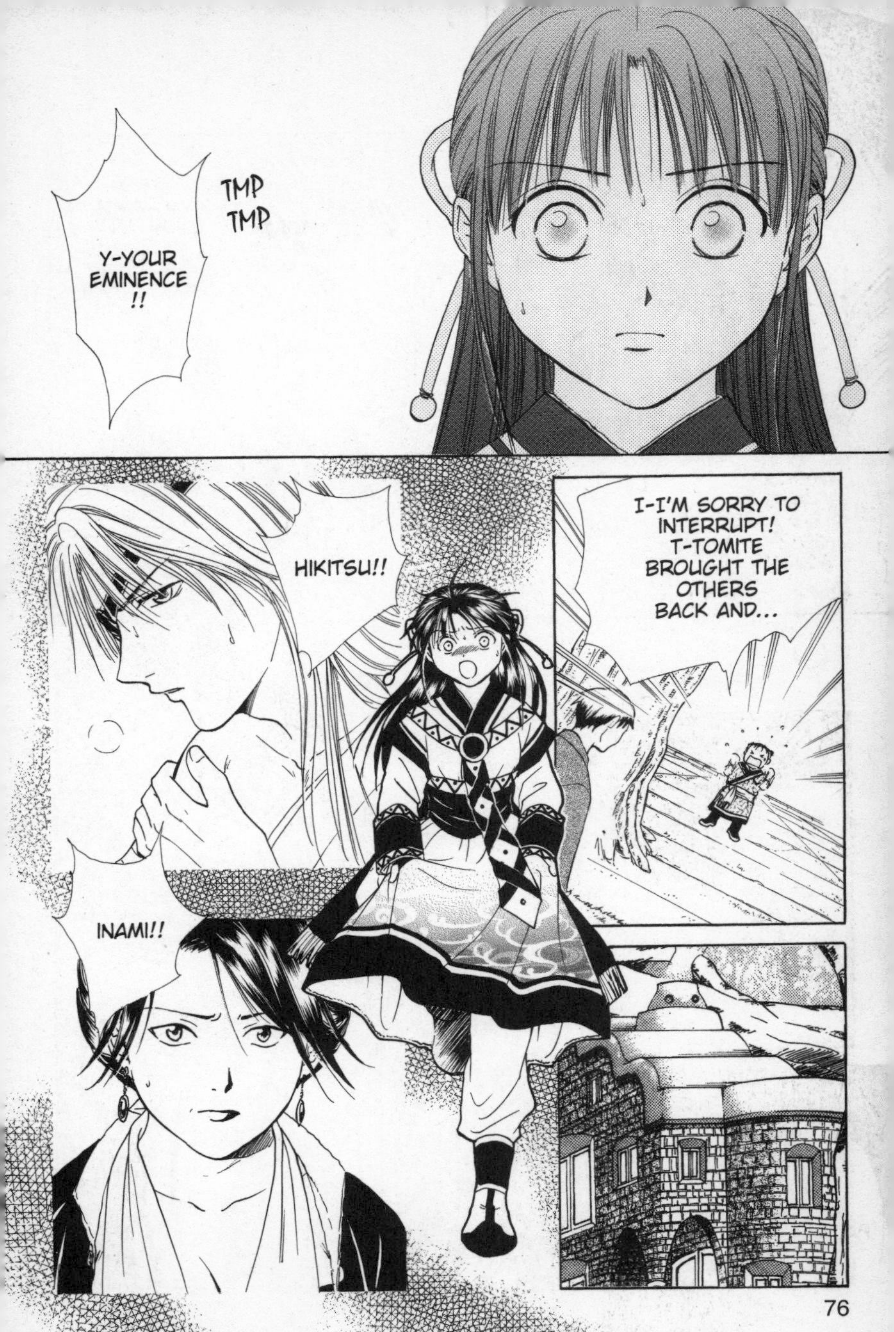
TMP
TMP
Y-YOUR EMINENCE!!
I-I'M SORRY TO INTERRUPT! T-TOMITE BROUGHT THE OTHERS BACK AND...
HIKITSU!!
INAMI!!

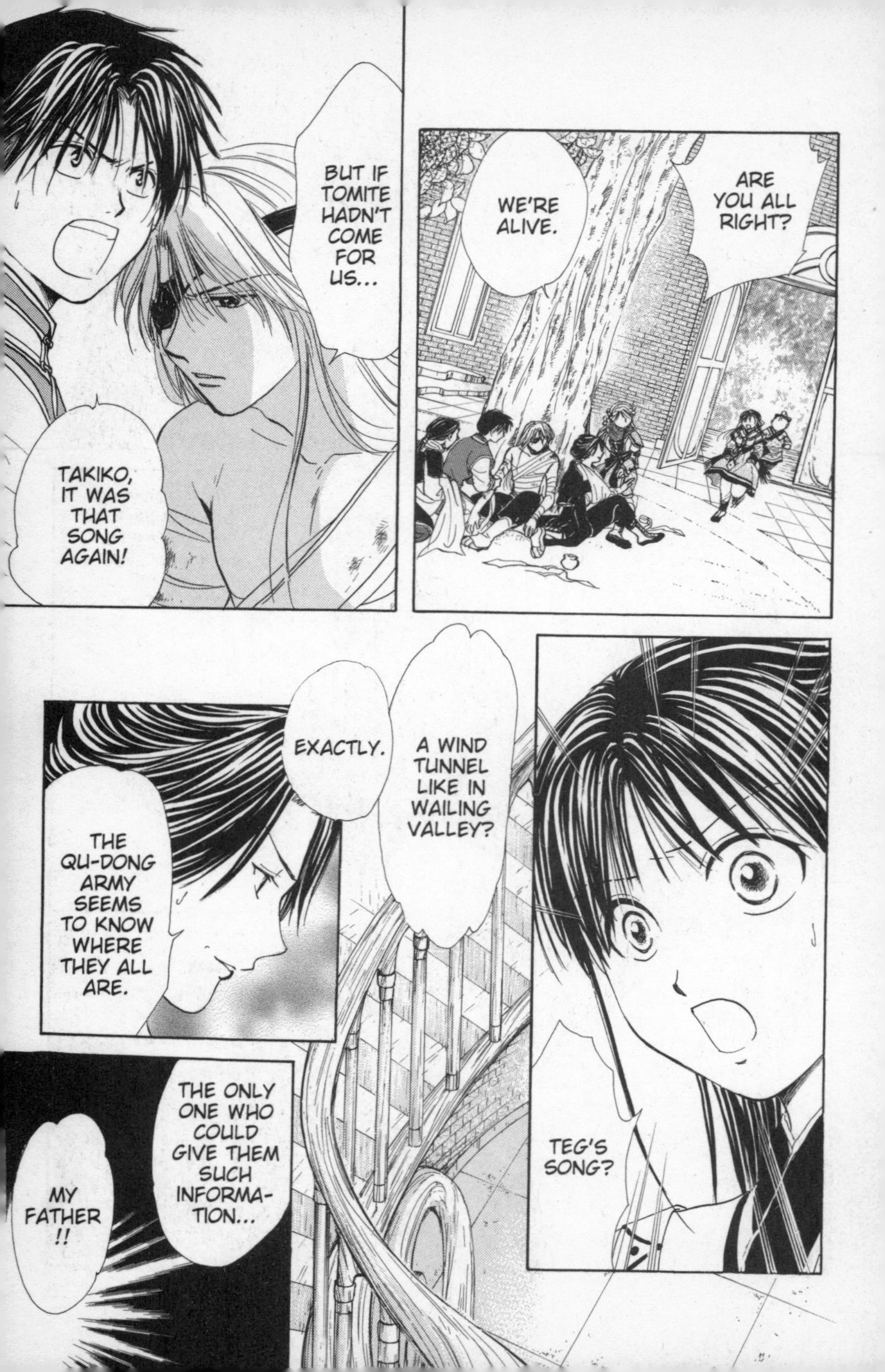
ARE YOU ALL RIGHT?
WE'RE ALIVE.
BUT IF TOMITE HADN'T COME FOR US...
TAKIKO, IT WAS THAT SONG AGAIN!
TEG'S SONG?
A WIND TUNNEL LIKE IN WAILING VALLEY?
EXACTLY.
THE QU-DONG ARMY SEEMS TO KNOW WHERE THEY ALL ARE.
THE ONLY ONE WHO COULD GIVE THEM SUCH INFORMA-TION...
MY FATHER!!

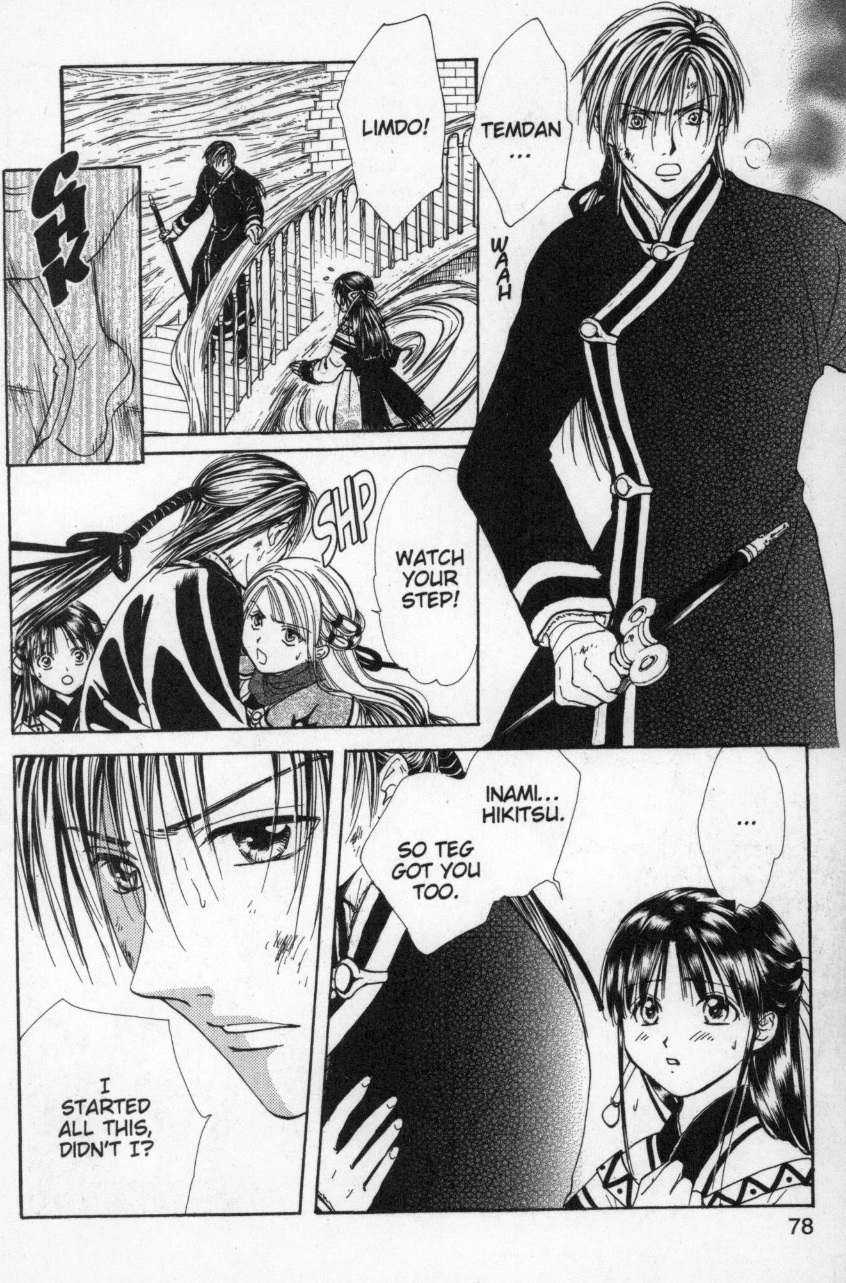
TEMDAN ...
LIMDO!
WAAH
CHK
SHP
WATCH YOUR STEP!
...
INAMI... HIKITSU.
SO TEG GOT YOU TOO.
I STARTED ALL THIS, DIDN'T I?

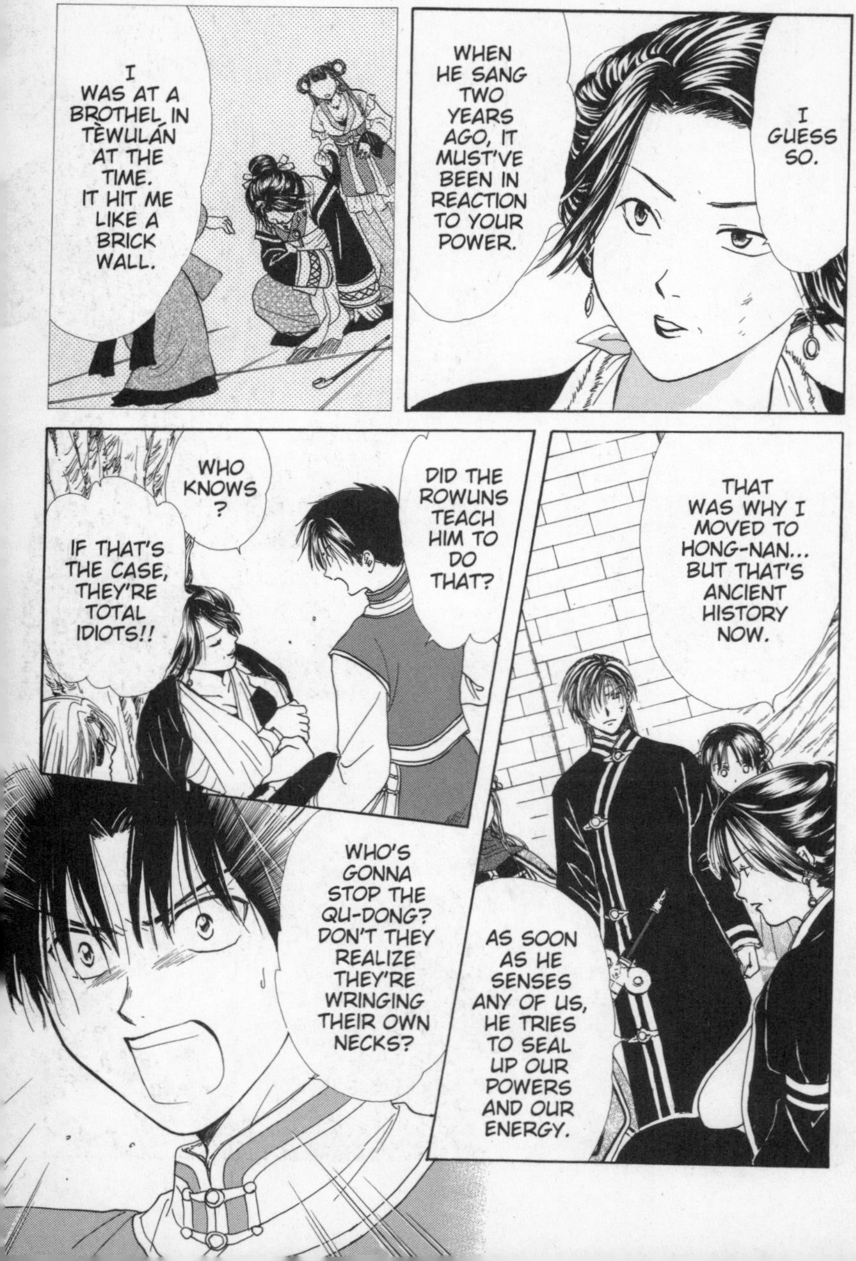
WHEN HE SANG TWO YEARS AGO, IT MUST'VE BEEN IN REACTION TO YOUR POWER.
I GUESS SO.
I WAS AT A BROTHEL IN TÈWULÁN AT THE TIME. IT HIT ME LIKE A BRICK WALL.
THAT WAS WHY I MOVED TO HONG-NAN... BUT THAT'S ANCIENT HISTORY NOW.
AS SOON AS HE SENSES ANY OF US, HE TRIES TO SEAL UP OUR POWERS AND OUR ENERGY.
DID THE ROWUNS TEACH HIM TO DO THAT?
WHO KNOWS?
IF THAT'S THE CASE, THEY'RE TOTAL IDIOTS!!
WHO'S GONNA STOP THE QU-DONG? DON'T THEY REALIZE THEY'RE WRINGING THEIR OWN NECKS?

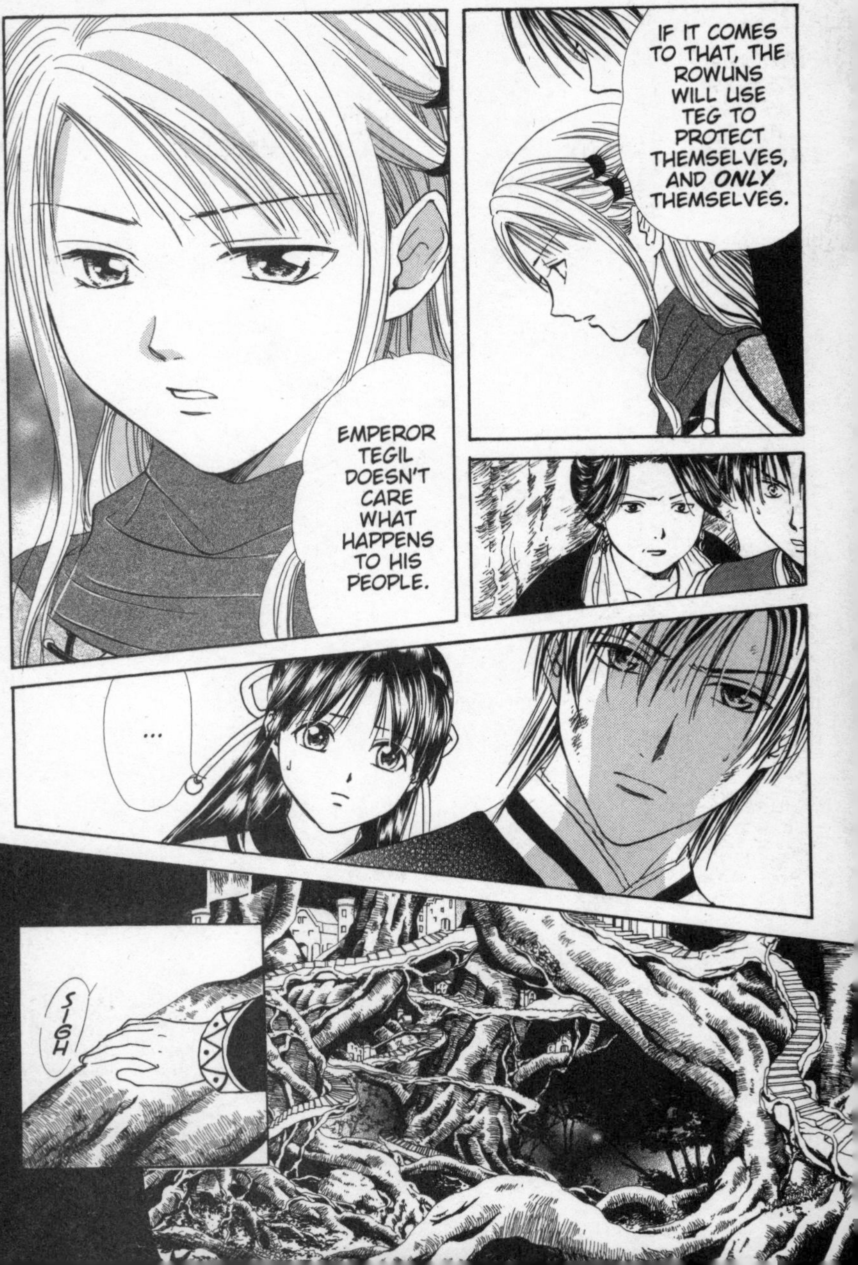
IF IT COMES TO THAT, THE ROWLINS WILL USE TEG TO PROTECT THEMSELVES, AND ONLY THEMSELVES.
EMPEROR TEGIL DOESN'T CARE WHAT HAPPENS TO HIS PEOPLE.
...
SIGH

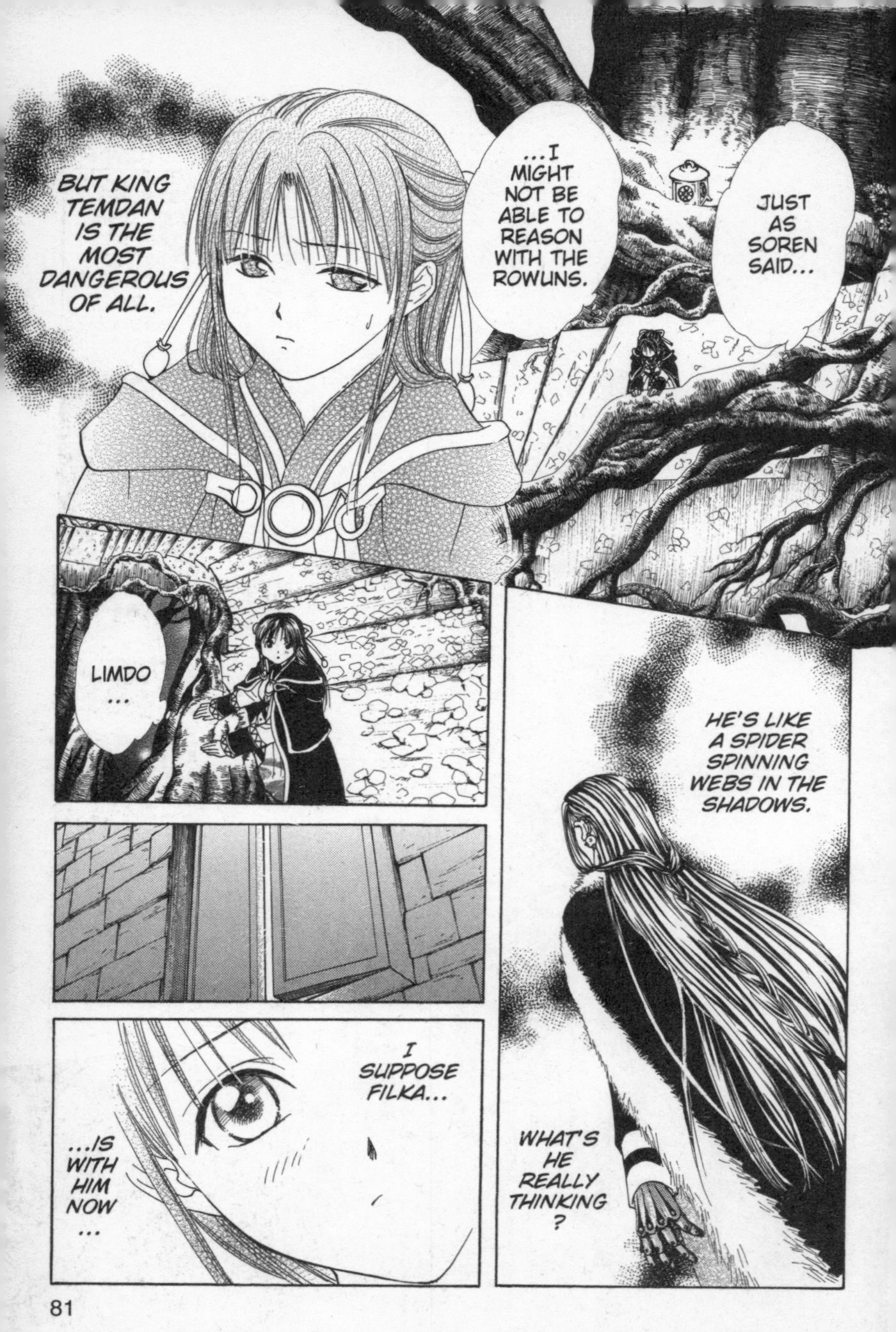
JUST AS SOREN SAID...
...I MIGHT NOT BE ABLE TO REASON WITH THE ROWUNS.
BUT KING TEMDAN IS THE MOST DANGEROUS OF ALL.
HE'S LIKE A SPIDER SPINNING WEBS IN THE SHADOWS.
WHAT'S HE REALLY THINKING?
LIMDO...
I SUPPOSE FILKA...
...IS WITH HIM NOW...

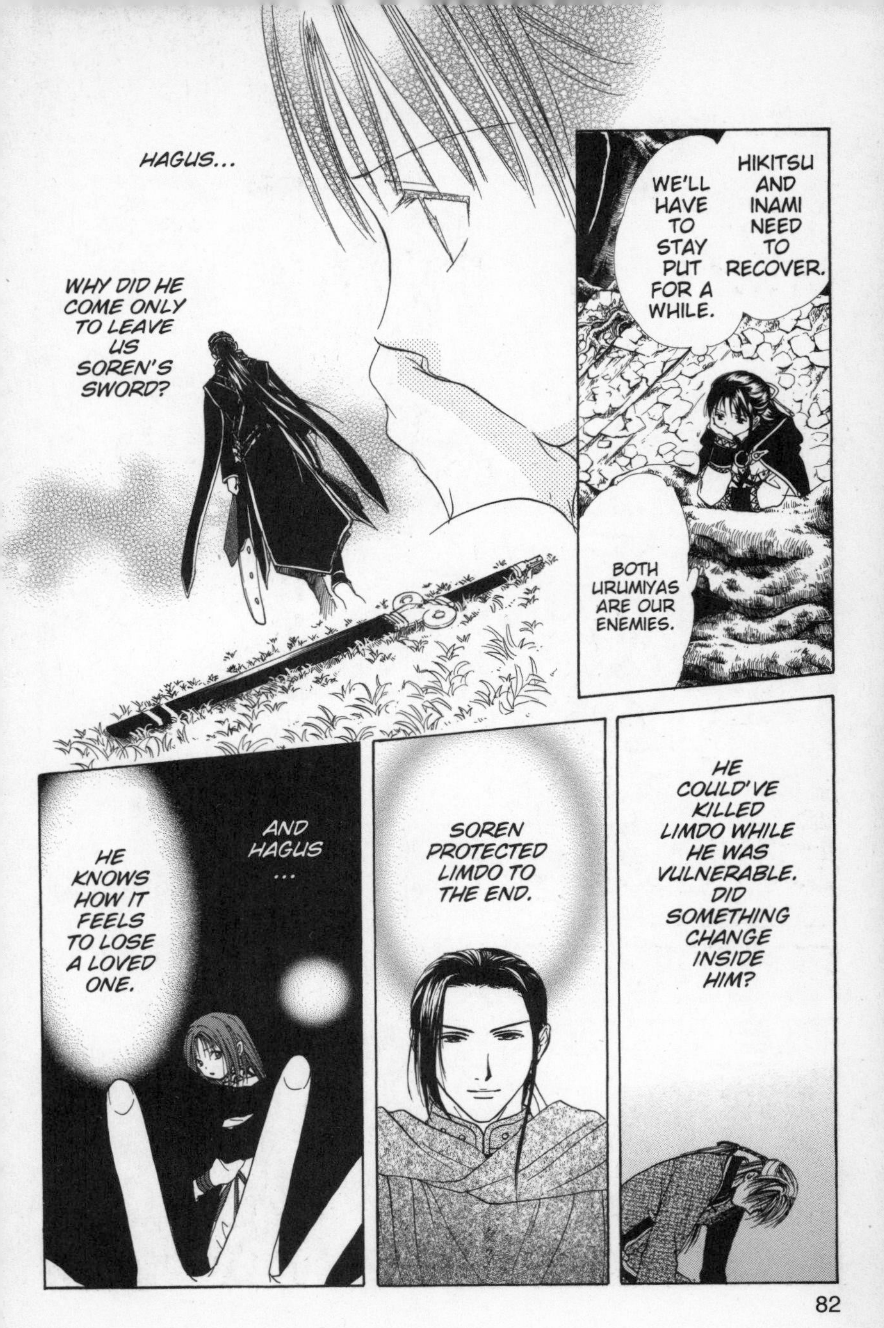
HAGUS...
WHY DID HE COME ONLY TO LEAVE US SOREN'S SWORD?
HIKITSU AND INAMI NEED TO RECOVER.
WE'LL HAVE TO STAY PUT FOR A WHILE.
BOTH URUMIYAS ARE OUR ENEMIES.
HE COULD'VE KILLED LIMDO WHILE HE WAS VULNERABLE. DID SOMETHING CHANGE INSIDE HIM?
SOREN PROTECTED LIMDO TO THE END.
AND HAGUS...
HE KNOWS HOW IT FEELS TO LOSE A LOVED ONE.

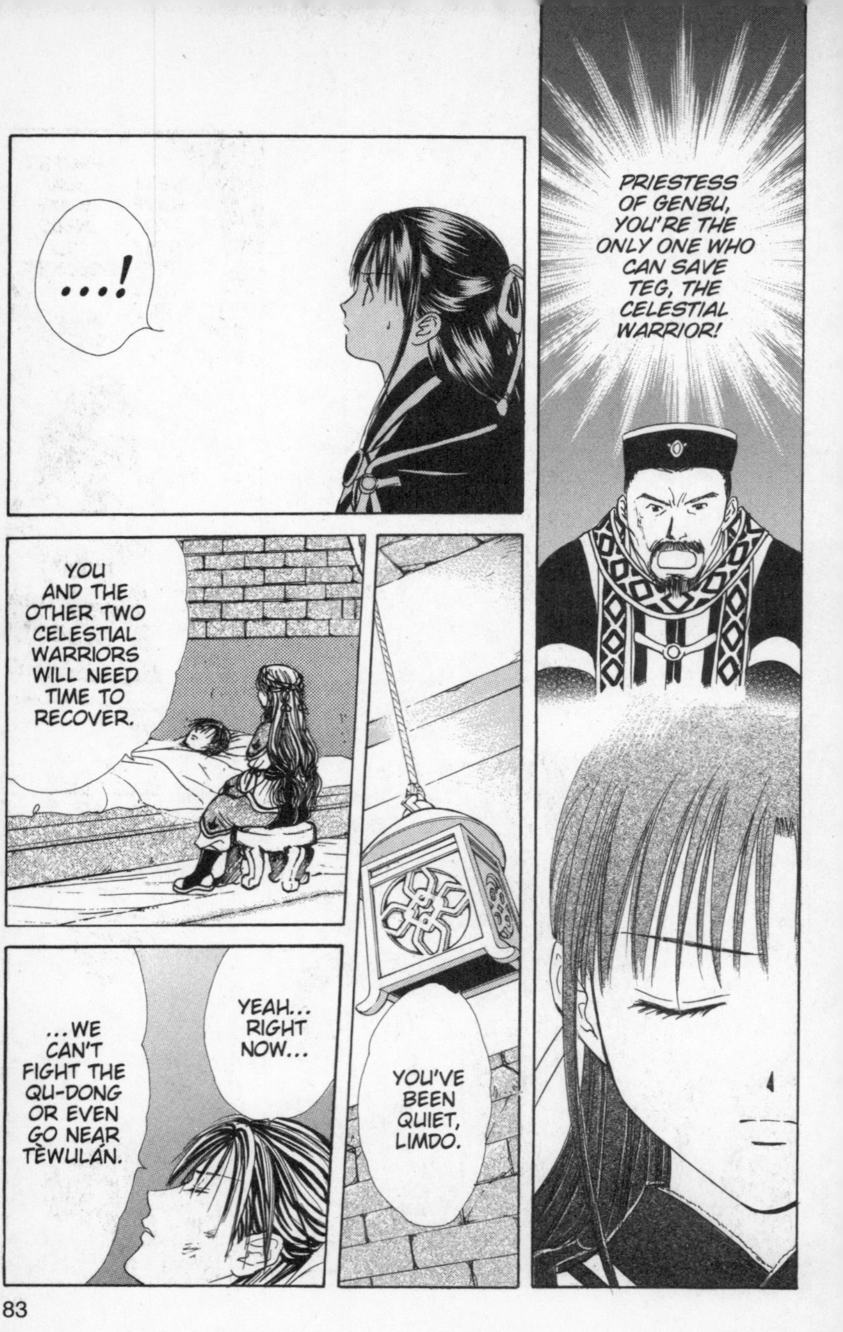
PRIESTESS OF GENBU, YOU'RE THE ONLY ONE WHO CAN SAVE TEG, THE CELESTIAL WARRIOR!
...!
YOU'VE BEEN QUIET, LIMDO.
YOU AND THE OTHER TWO CELESTIAL WARRIORS WILL NEED TIME TO RECOVER.
YEAH... RIGHT NOW...
...WE CAN'T FIGHT THE QU-DONG OR EVEN GO NEAR TÈWULÁN.

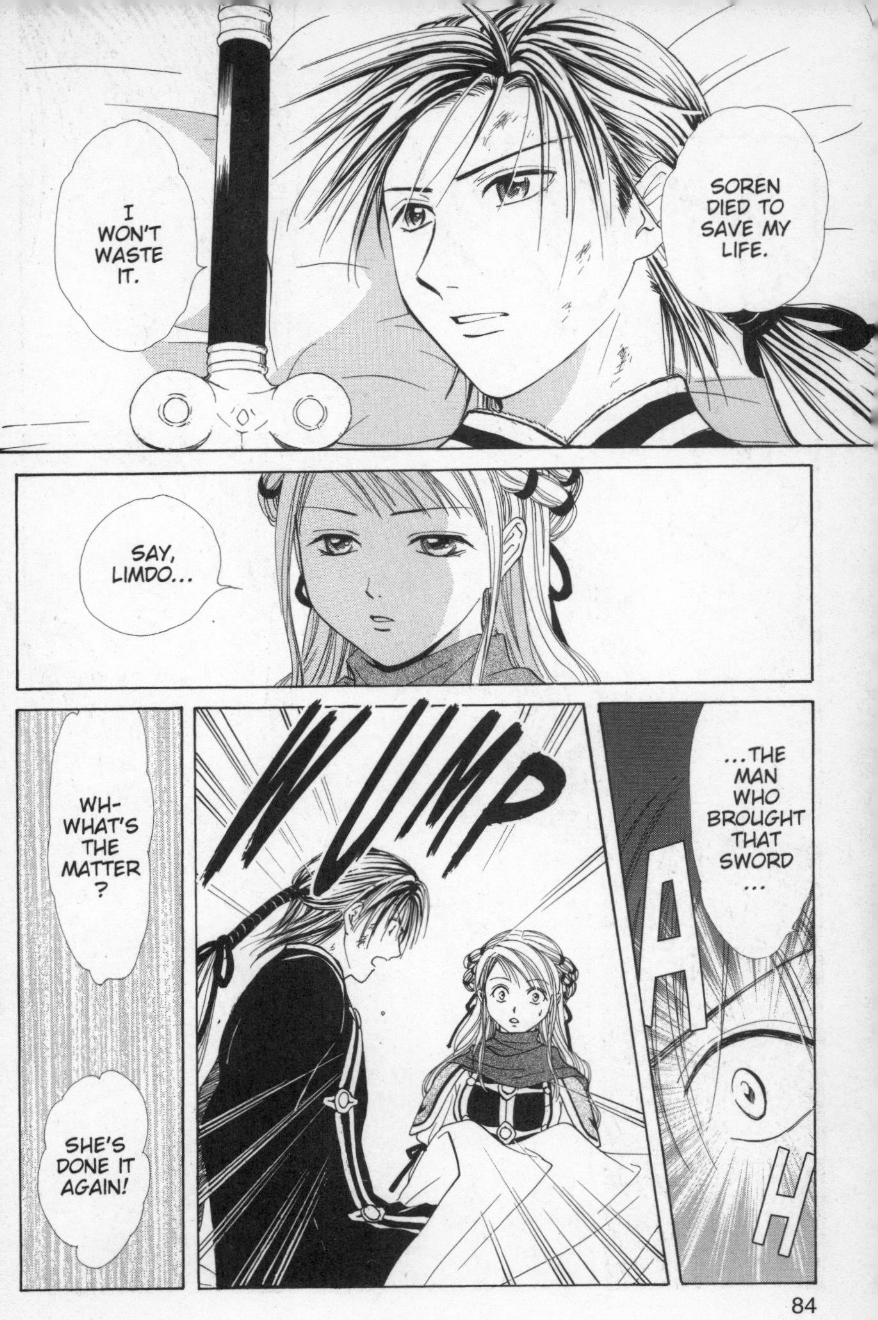
SOREN DIED TO SAVE MY LIFE.
I WON'T WASTE IT.
SAY, LIMDO...
...THE MAN WHO BROUGHT THAT SWORD...
AH
WUMP
WH-WHAT'S THE MATTER?
SHE'S DONE IT AGAIN!

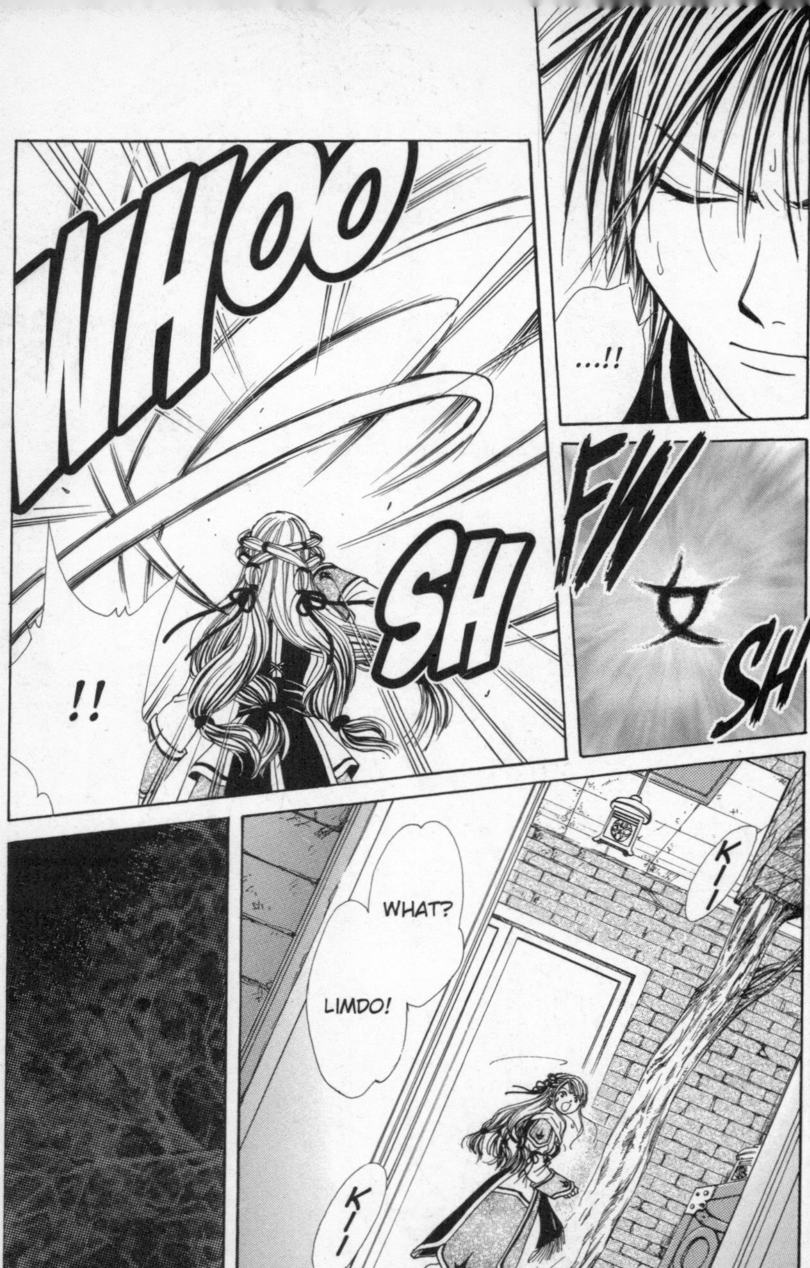
...!!
FW
SH
WHOO
SH
!!
KII
WHAT?
LIMDO!
KII

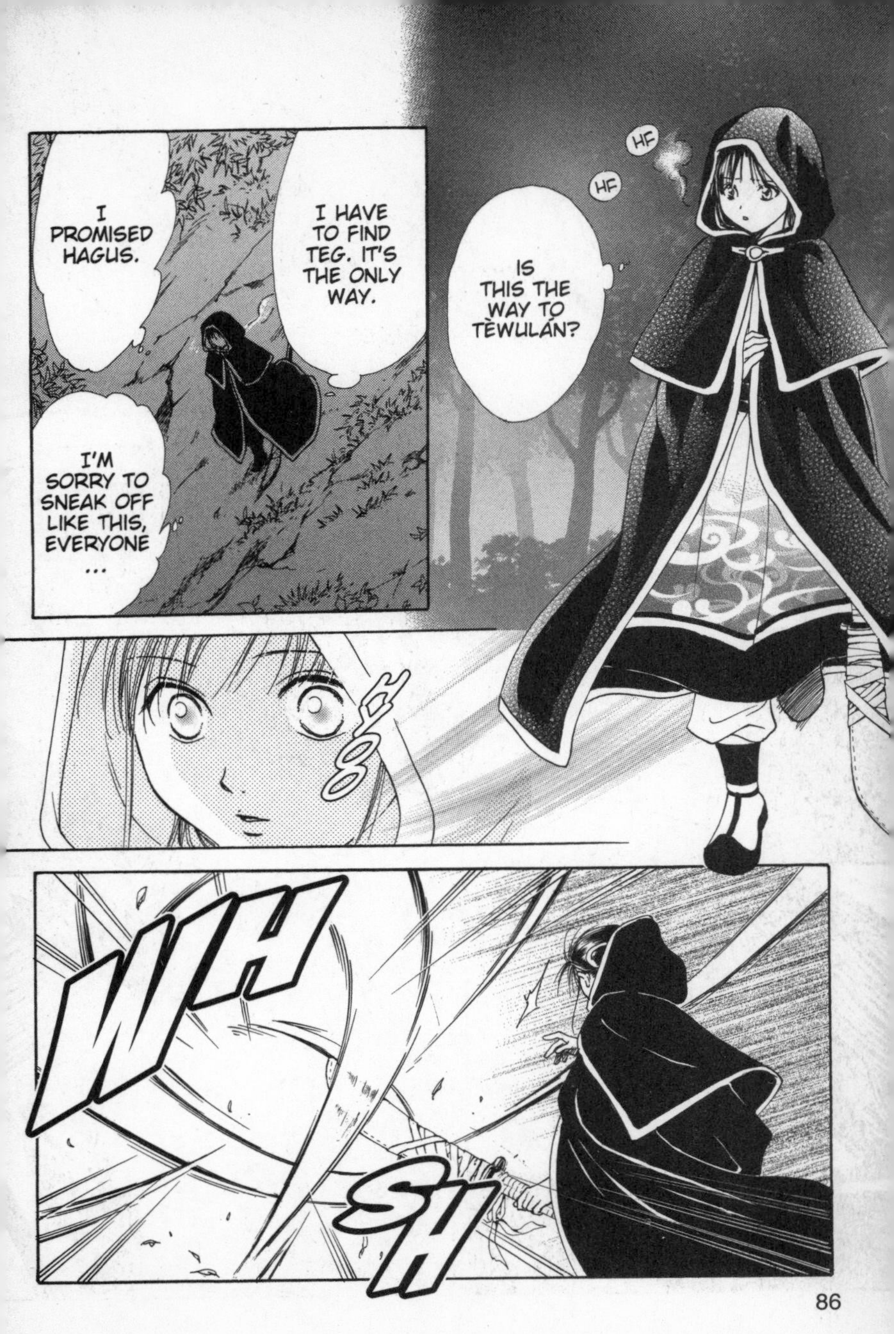
HF
HF
IS THIS THE WAY TO TÈWULÁN?
I HAVE TO FIND TEG. IT'S THE ONLY WAY.
I PROMISED HAGUS.
I'M SORRY TO SNEAK OFF LIKE THIS, EVERYONE ...
WH
SH

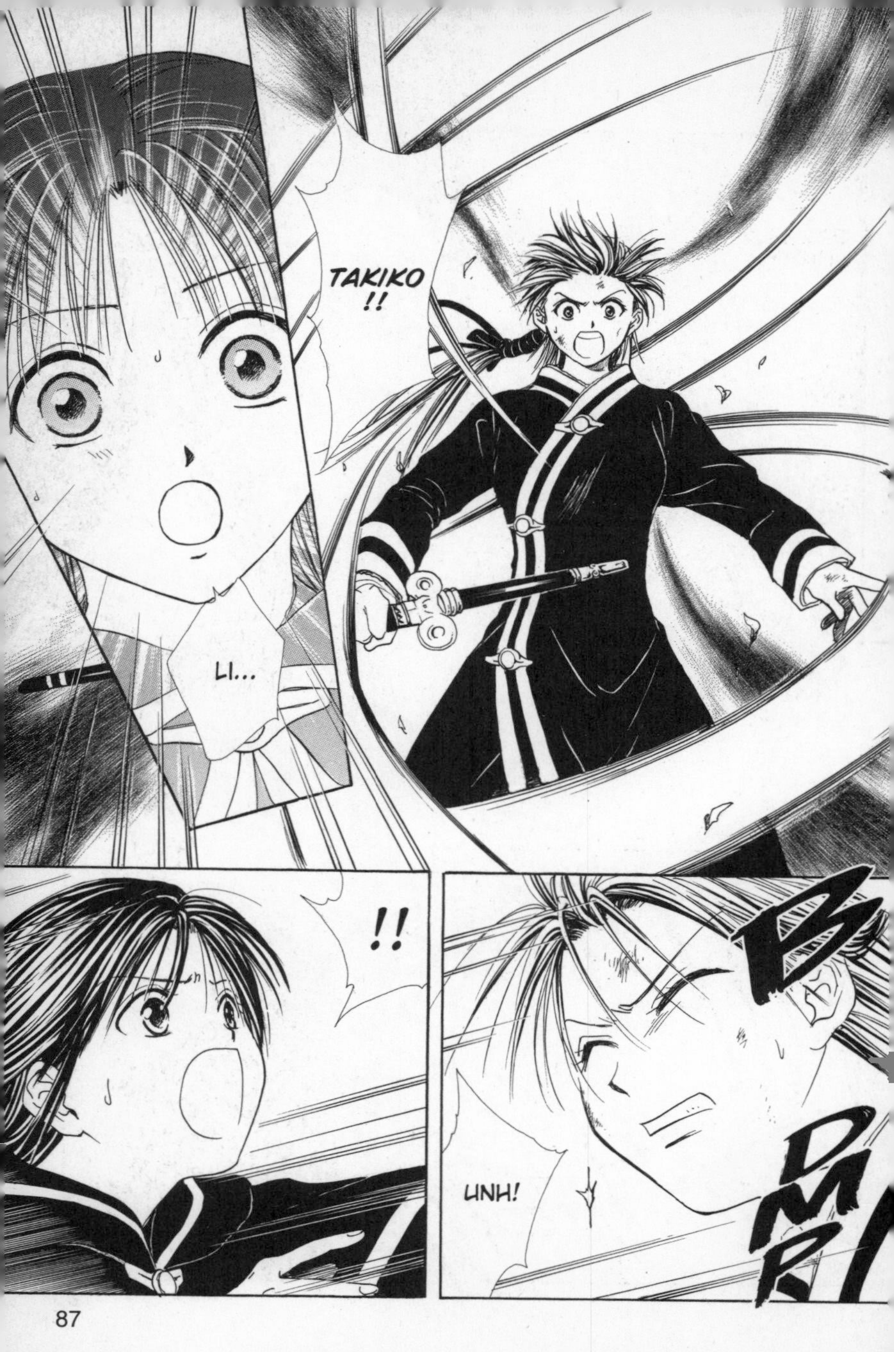
TAKIKO !!
LI...
UNH!
BDMP
!!

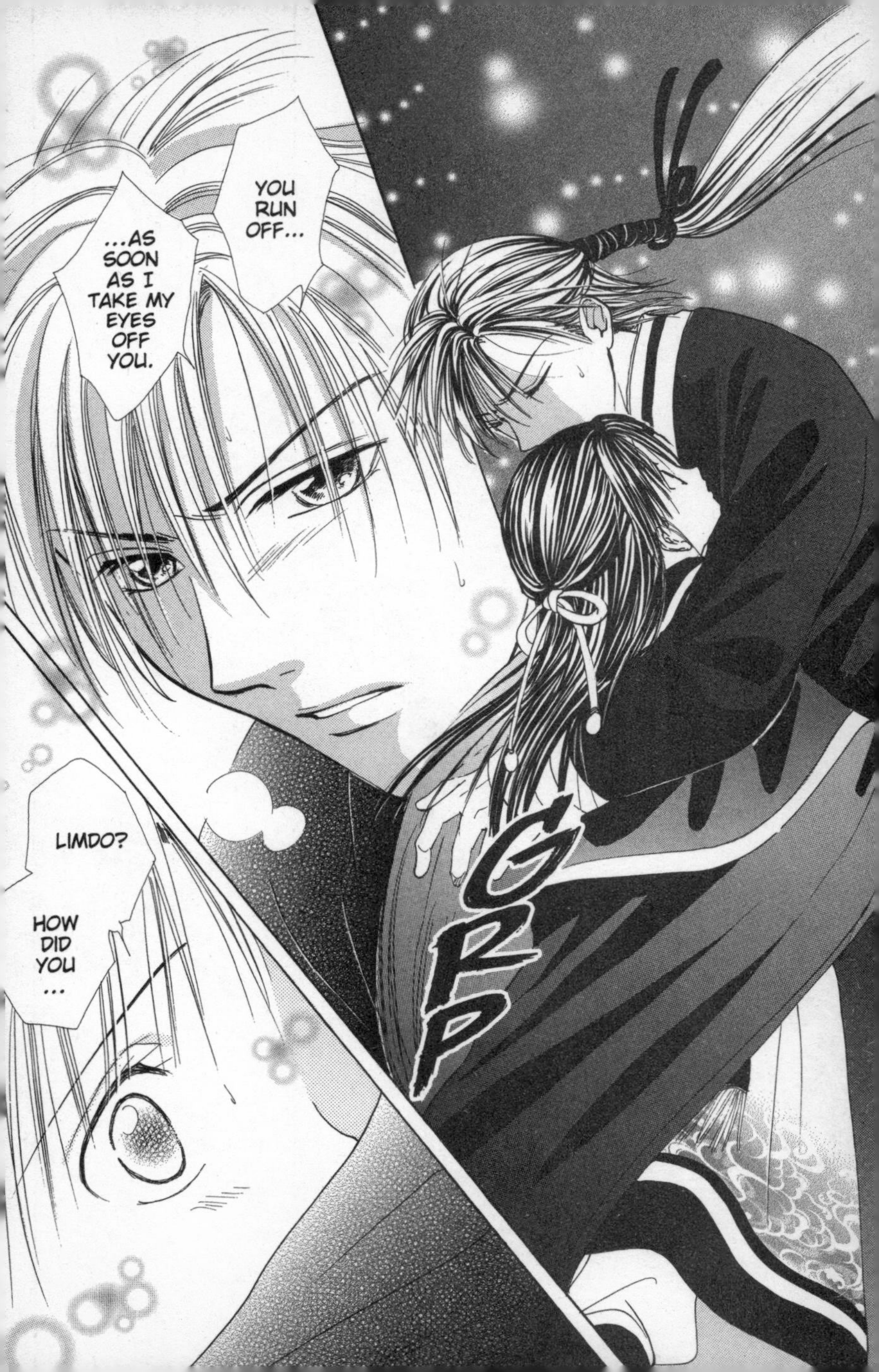
YOU RUN OFF...
...AS SOON AS I TAKE MY EYES OFF YOU.
GRP
LIMDO?
HOW DID YOU ...

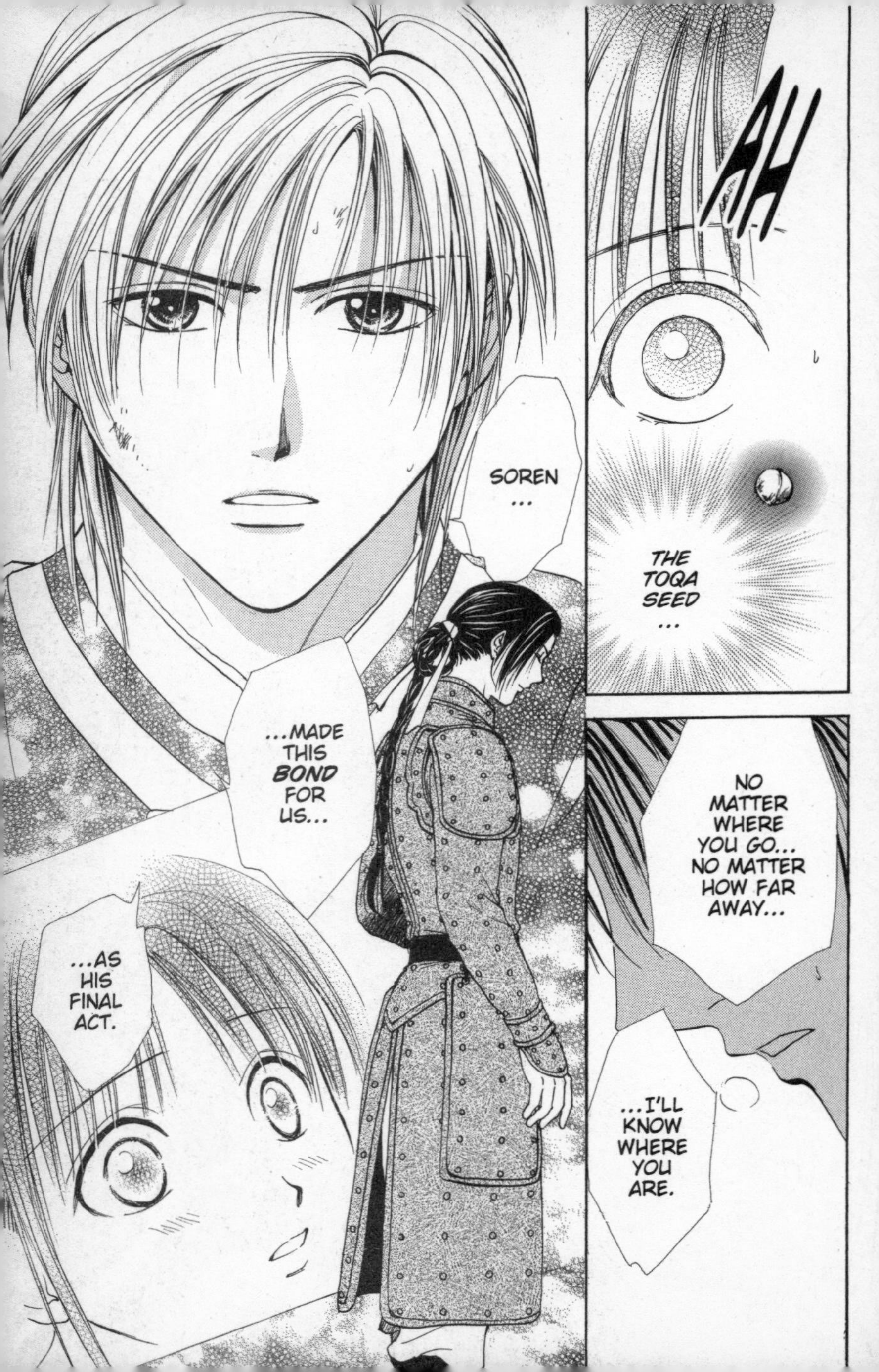
AH
THE TOQA SEED ...
NO MATTER WHERE YOU GO... NO MATTER HOW FAR AWAY...
...I'LL KNOW WHERE YOU ARE.
SOREN ...
...MADE THIS *BOND* FOR US...
...AS HIS FINAL ACT.

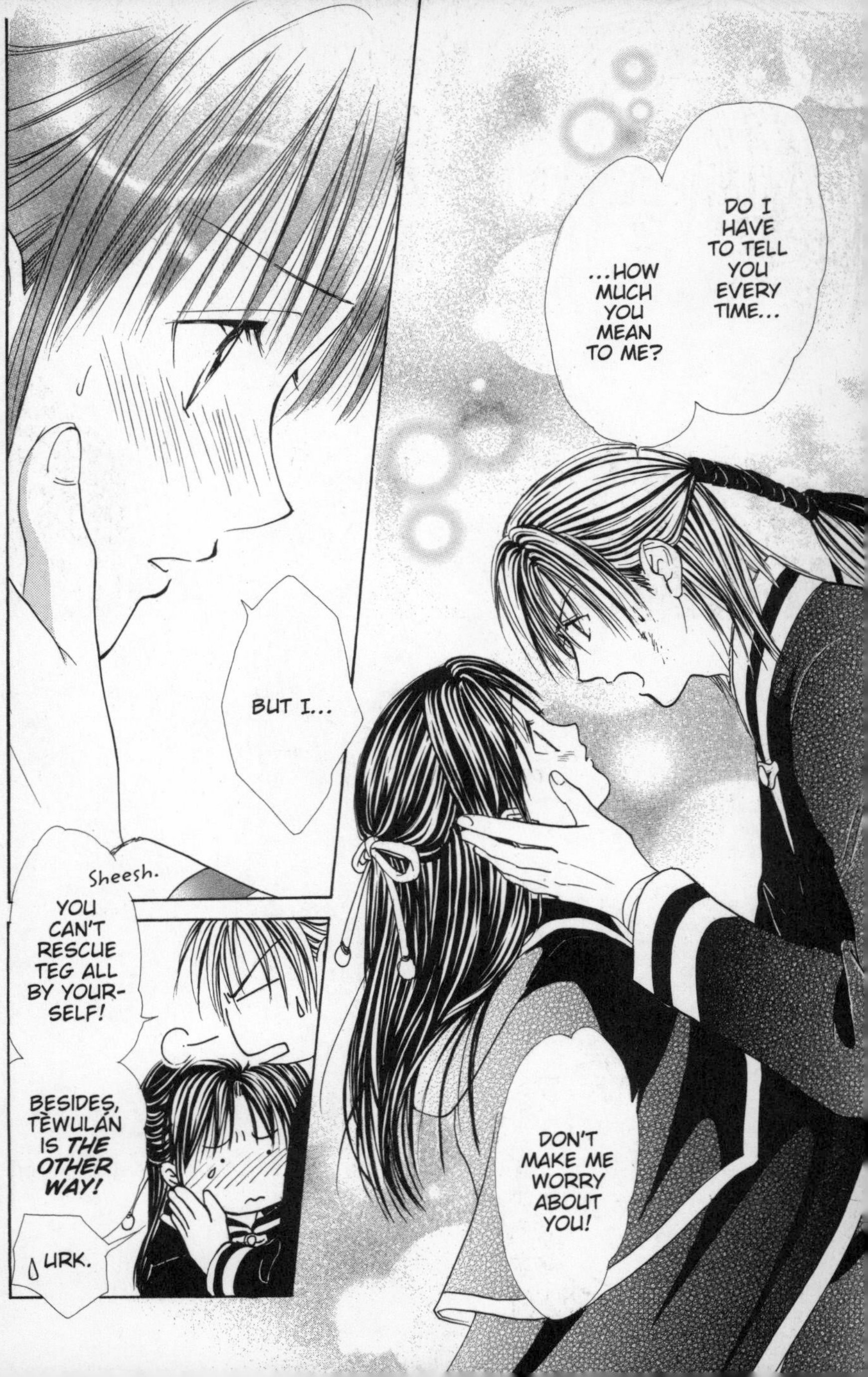
DO I HAVE TO TELL YOU EVERY TIME...
...HOW MUCH YOU MEAN TO ME?
DON'T MAKE ME WORRY ABOUT YOU!
BUT I...
Sheesh.
YOU CAN'T RESCUE TEG ALL BY YOUR-SELF!
BESIDES, TÈWULÁN IS ***THE OTHER WAY!***
URK.

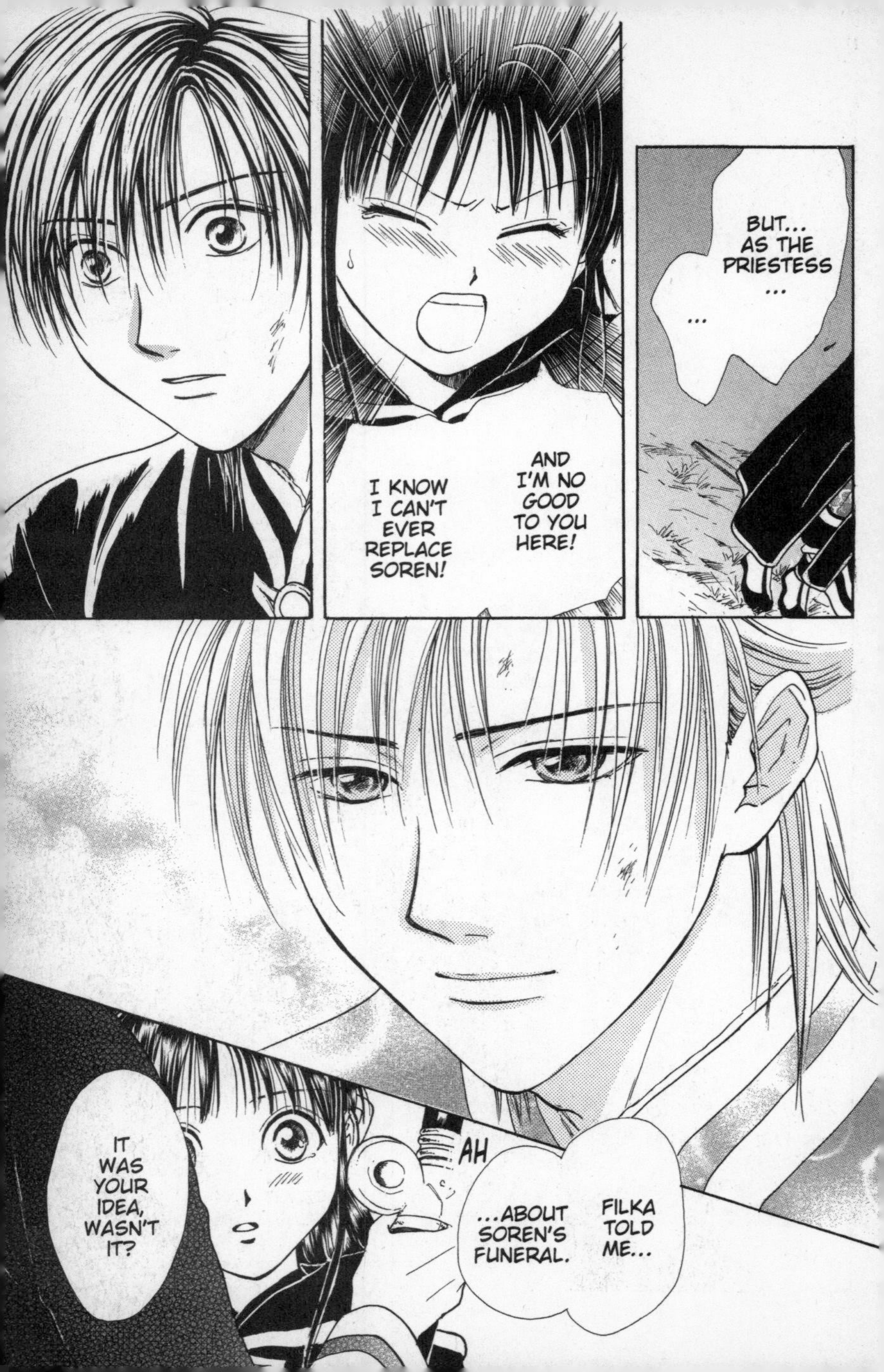
BUT... AS THE PRIESTESS ...
...
AND I'M NO GOOD TO YOU HERE!
I KNOW I CAN'T EVER REPLACE SOREN!
FILKA TOLD ME...
...ABOUT SOREN'S FUNERAL.
AH
IT WAS YOUR IDEA, WASN'T IT?

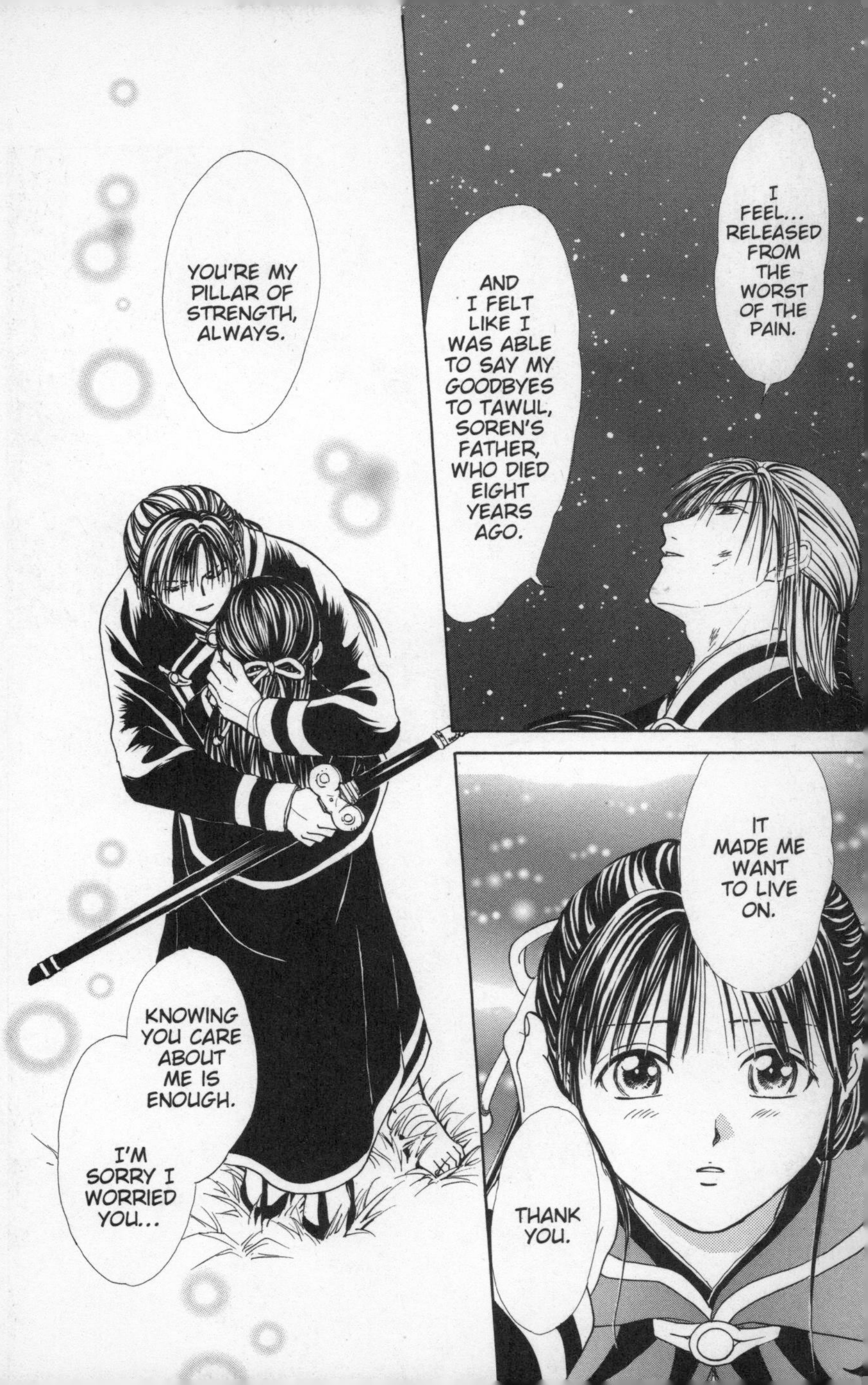
I FEEL... RELEASED FROM THE WORST OF THE PAIN.
AND I FELT LIKE I WAS ABLE TO SAY MY GOODBYES TO TAWUL, SOREN'S FATHER, WHO DIED EIGHT YEARS AGO.
IT MADE ME WANT TO LIVE ON.
THANK YOU.
YOU'RE MY PILLAR OF STRENGTH, ALWAYS.
KNOWING YOU CARE ABOUT ME IS ENOUGH.
I'M SORRY I WORRIED YOU...

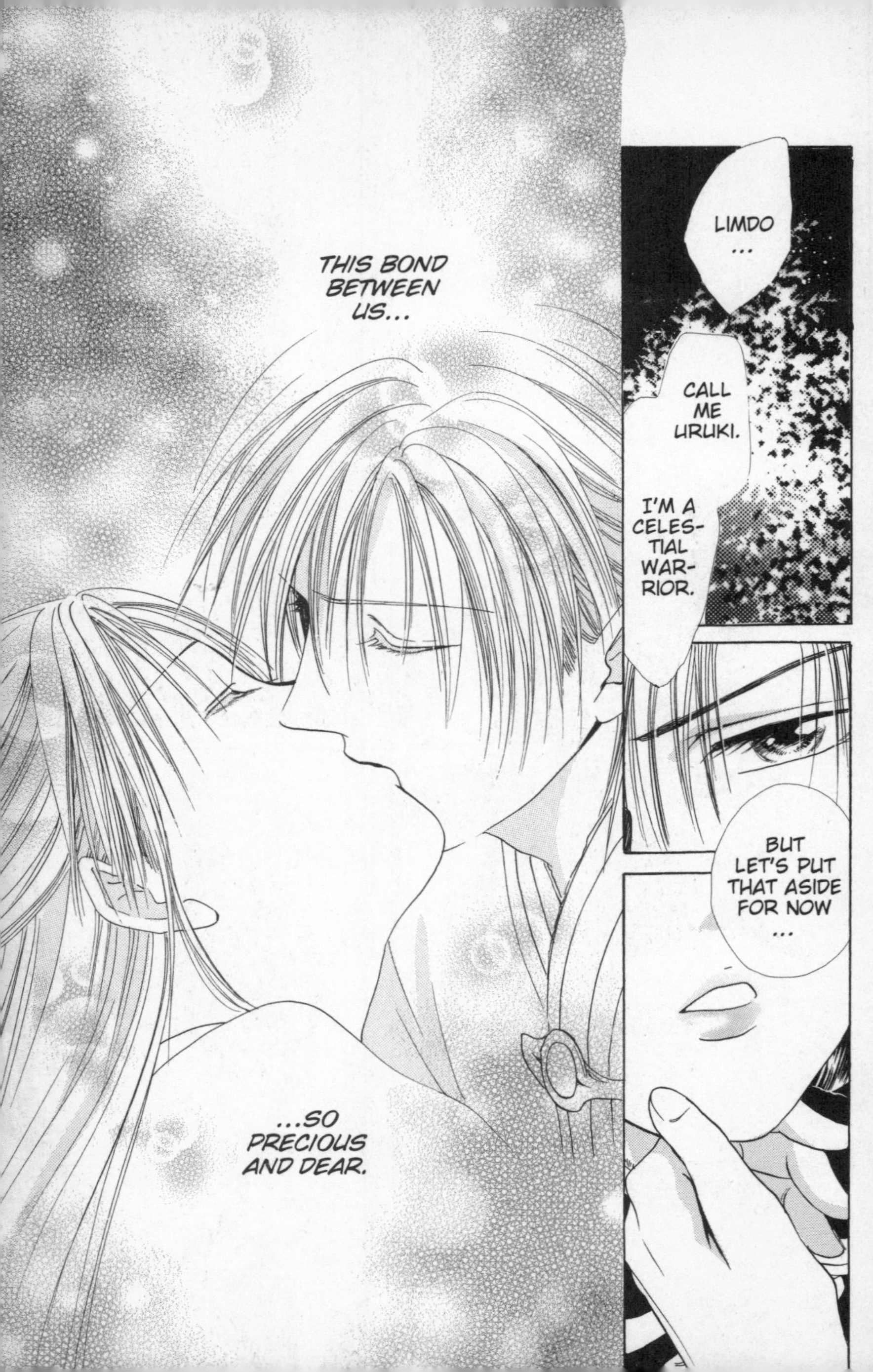
LIMDO...
CALL ME URUKI.
I'M A CELESTIAL WARRIOR.
BUT LET'S PUT THAT ASIDE FOR NOW...
THIS BOND BETWEEN US...
...SO PRECIOUS AND DEAR.

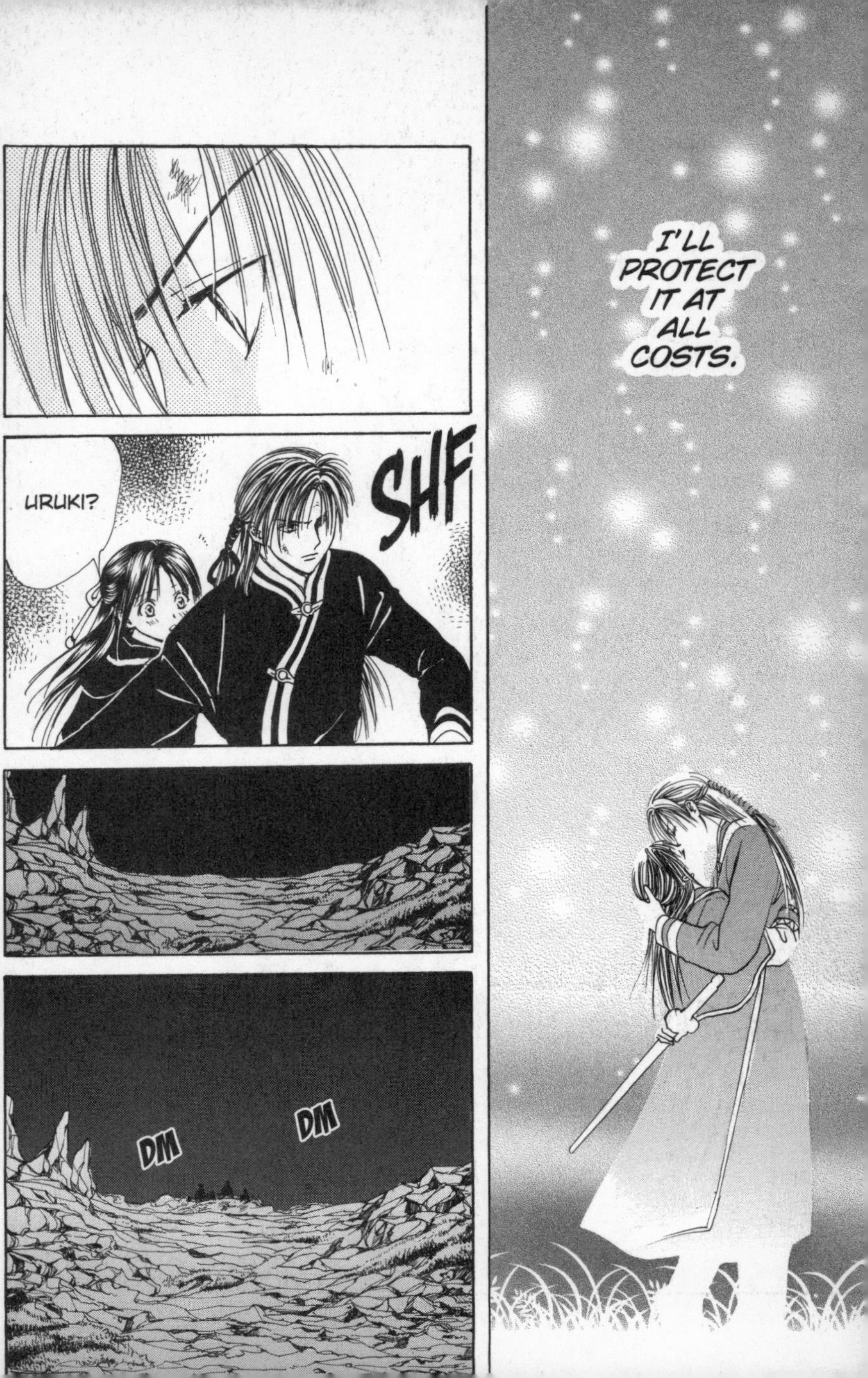
I'LL PROTECT IT AT ALL COSTS.
SHF
URUKI?
DM
DM

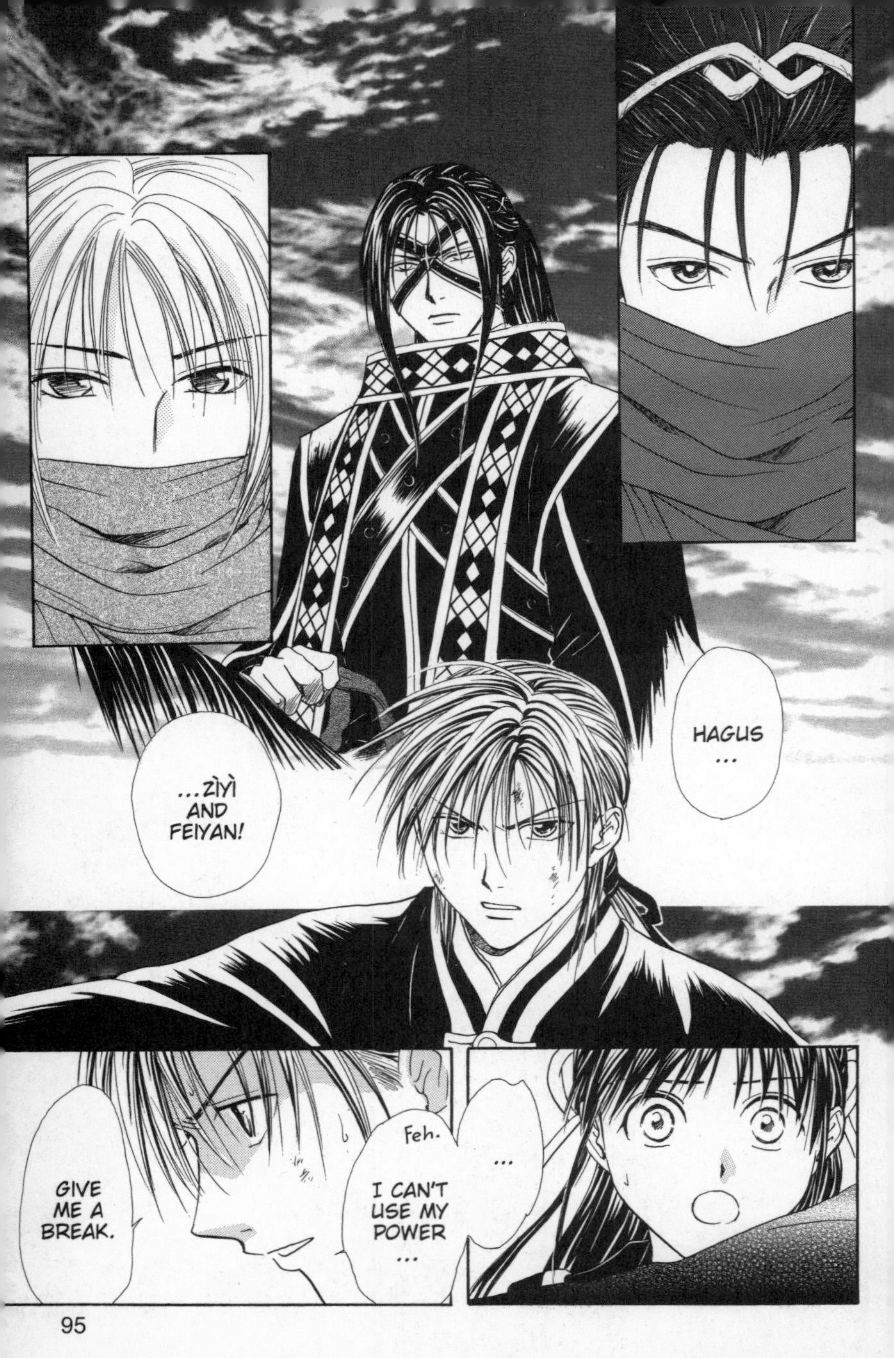
HAGUS ...
...ZÌYÌ AND FEIYAN!
...
Feh.
I CAN'T USE MY POWER ...
GIVE ME A BREAK.

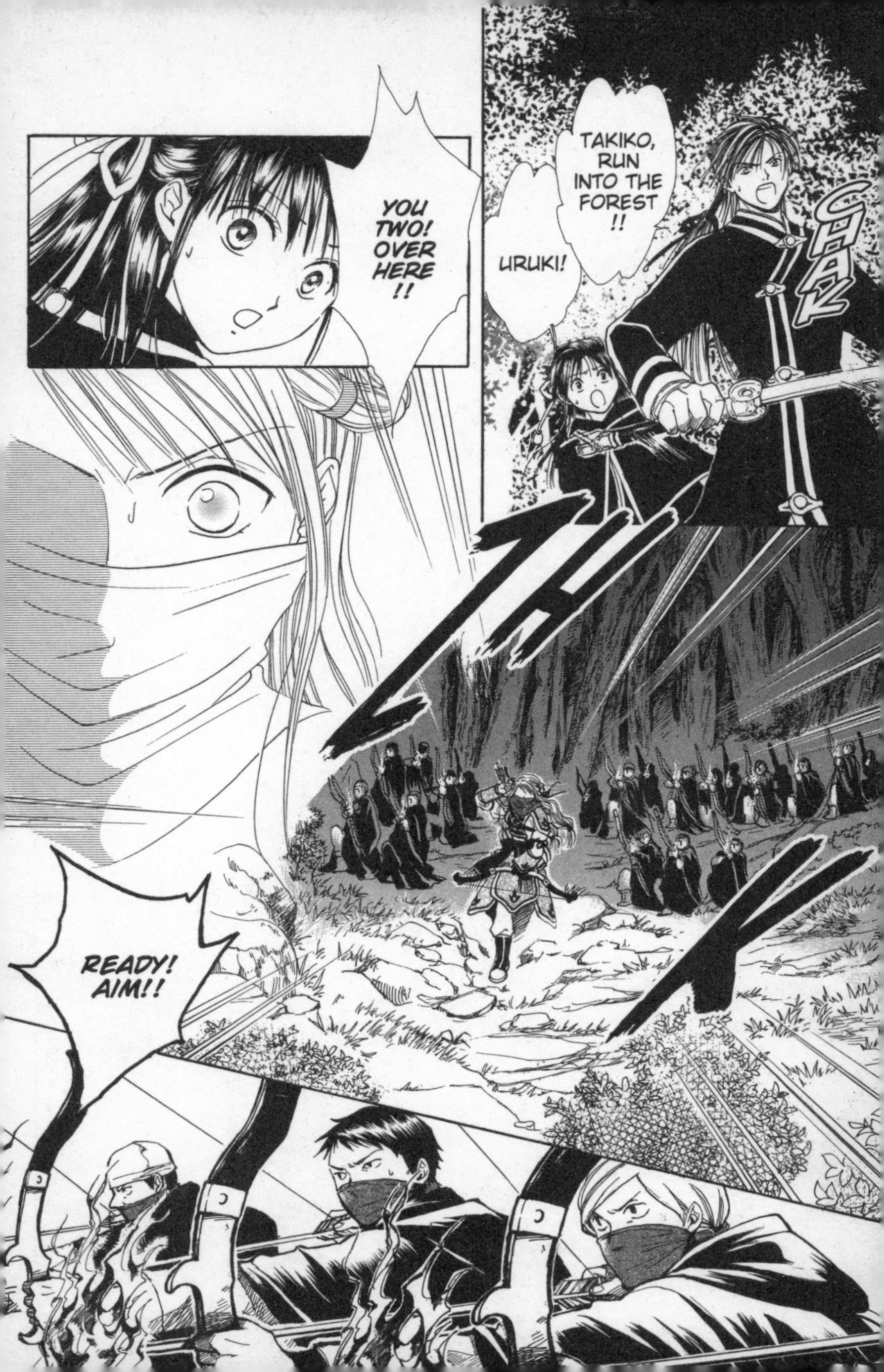
TAKIKO, RUN INTO THE FOREST !!
URUKI!
CHAK
YOU TWO! OVER HERE !!
READY! AIM!!

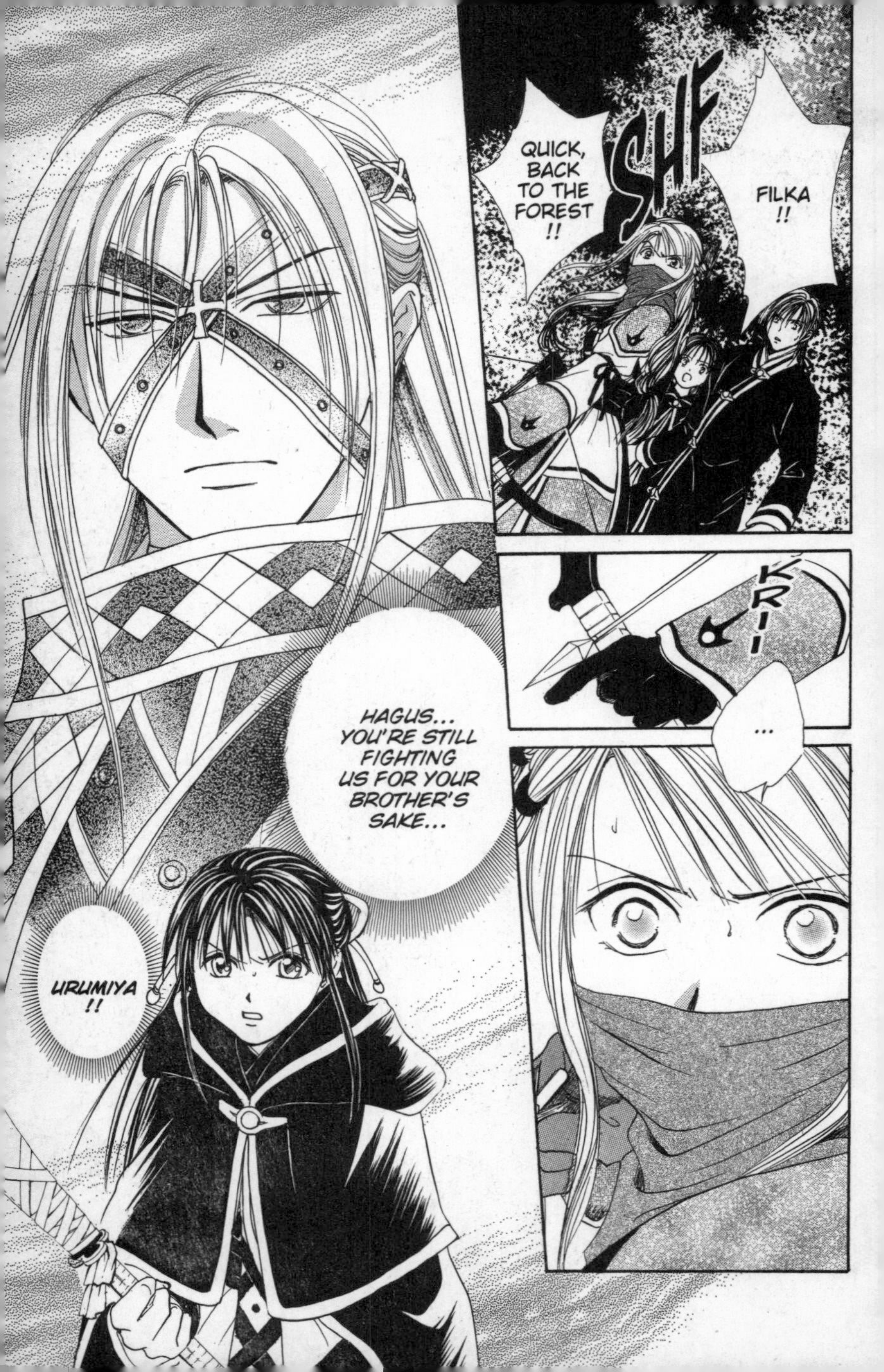
FILKA !!
SHF
QUICK, BACK TO THE FOREST !!
KRII
...
HAGUS... YOU'RE STILL FIGHTING US FOR YOUR BROTHER'S SAKE...
URUMIYA !!

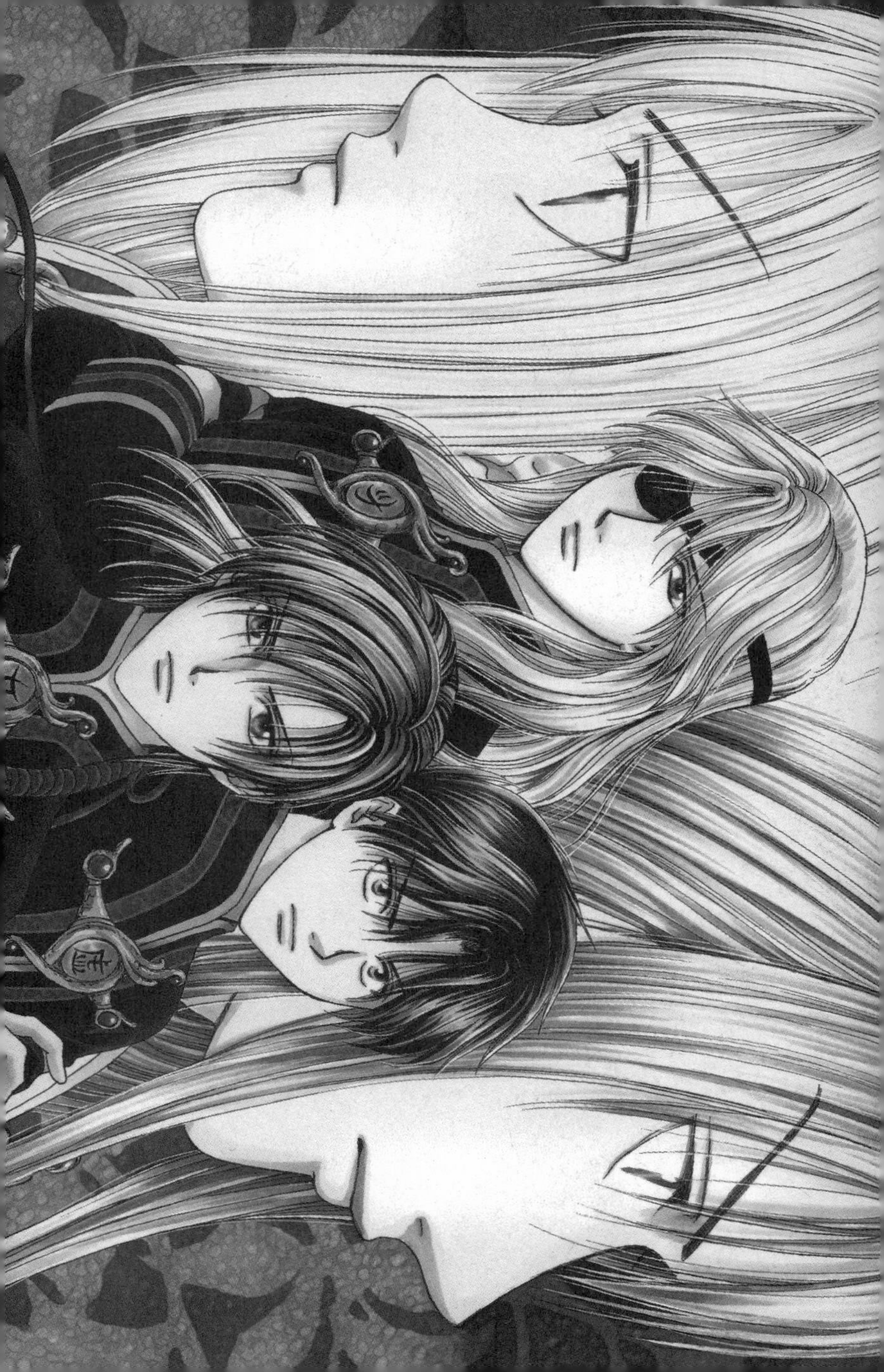

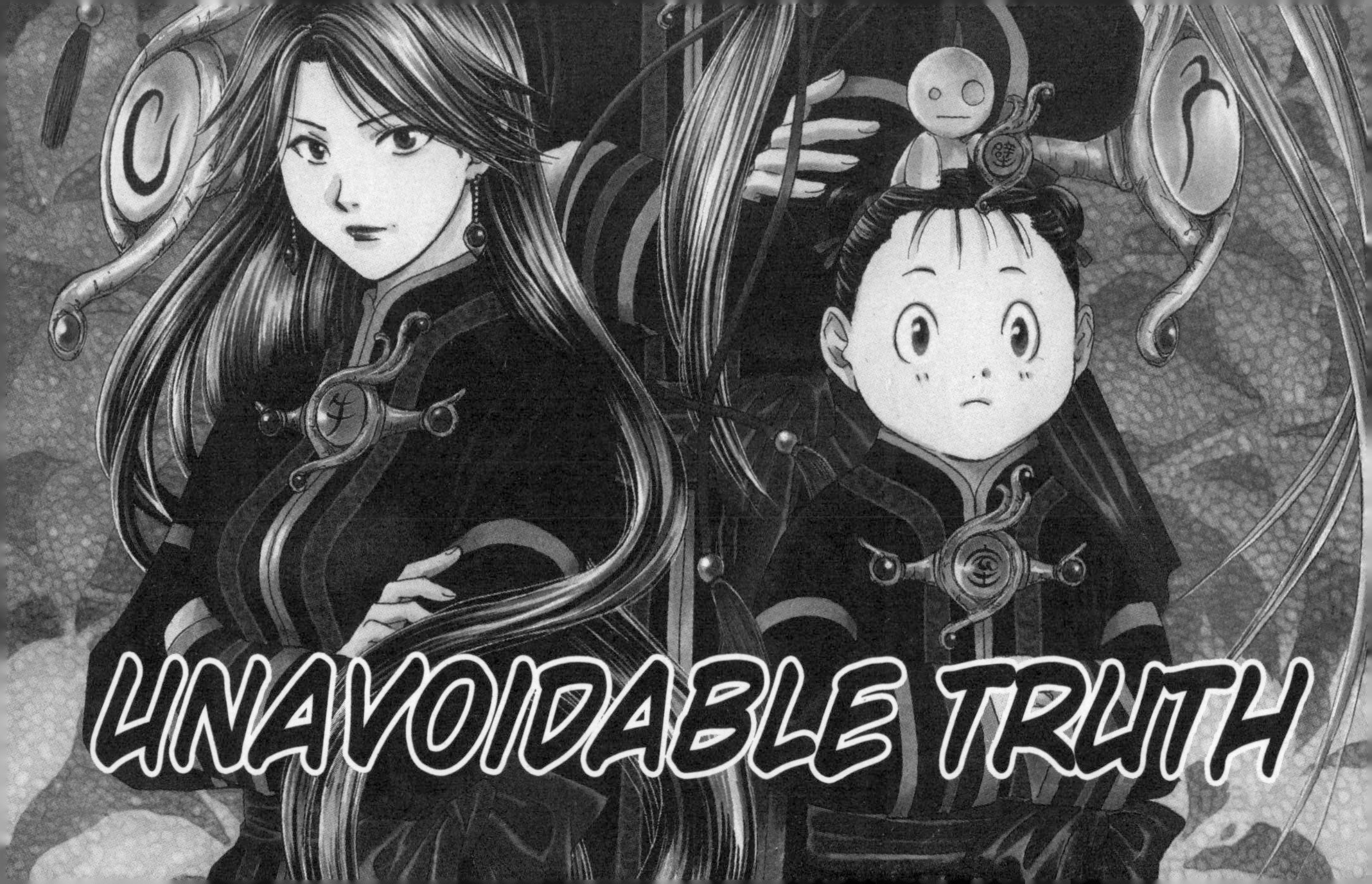
UNAVOIDABLE TRUTH

1

It's me, Watase! Please enjoy ***Genbu*** Volume 8. Goodbye.

Just kidding. I'm sleep deprived again.

So...things went badly for Soren in the last volume. Apparently when some fans learned that this story would have a "loyal attendant," they guessed his storyline would end in betrayal or death. I included a "betrayal" in a different sense. A matter of the heart. I really like the scene at the cliff because it shows Soren's human side.

I got some good feedback on Limdo's reaction, even from my editors. He and Soren cared about each other so much. I love master-servant relationships, not because one waits on the other, but because of the deep bonds of trust. I've said this before, but it feels so unconditional. By the way, a light novel about Limdo and Soren, ***Ties that Bind,*** is coming out in Japan in June! There will be two editions: the standard edition and one that comes with the drama CD (but the contents are the same).

There's a funeral in this volume. I wanted the stages of Limdo's grief to be very realistic. I myself suffered several losses of loved ones recently, both human and canine. First you're numb with shock and disbelief, then comes anger at nothing and everything. Once the reality starts to sink in, you're overwhelmed with sadness, and then you finally come to terms and accept the loss. Anyone who has experienced it once can understand. Since 2006 I've become acutely sensitive to the magnitude of life...

2

Okay! Let's change the subject to the new character, Filka. Some people are concerned about what's going to happen between her and Limdo/Uruki. :) In terms of love, that is! We'll see... It's fun drawing female characters. This series has had a lot of younger girls like Anlu and Ayla, so it's nice to have an older girl (around 16) gracing the page along with Takiko. What's that? Uruki? Sure, his female half, when it appears, is gorgeous. But he hasn't transformed lately! He hasn't been able to use his powers much...

Oh yeah! The PS2 game ***Fushigi Yugi: Suzaku Ibun*** is hitting the shelves in May! The story is based on the original series, with the Suzaku/Seiryu arc, but the player gets to be the game-original Priestess of Suzaku. It's basically a dating sim for girls where you work toward a relationship with the Celestial Warrior of your choice. But there are 13 volumes' worth of story, so it's quite an adventure too. You can choose to play with any name you want! There's also a friendship-only option, so guys can enjoy playing it too, just following the story. People have always said ***Fushigi Yugi*** would make a great dating sim. There were plans when the anime was produced, but they fell through... So this makes me happy. And they've lowered the price of the previous game, ***Priestess in the Mirror,*** so if you're interested, it might be less stress on your wallet.

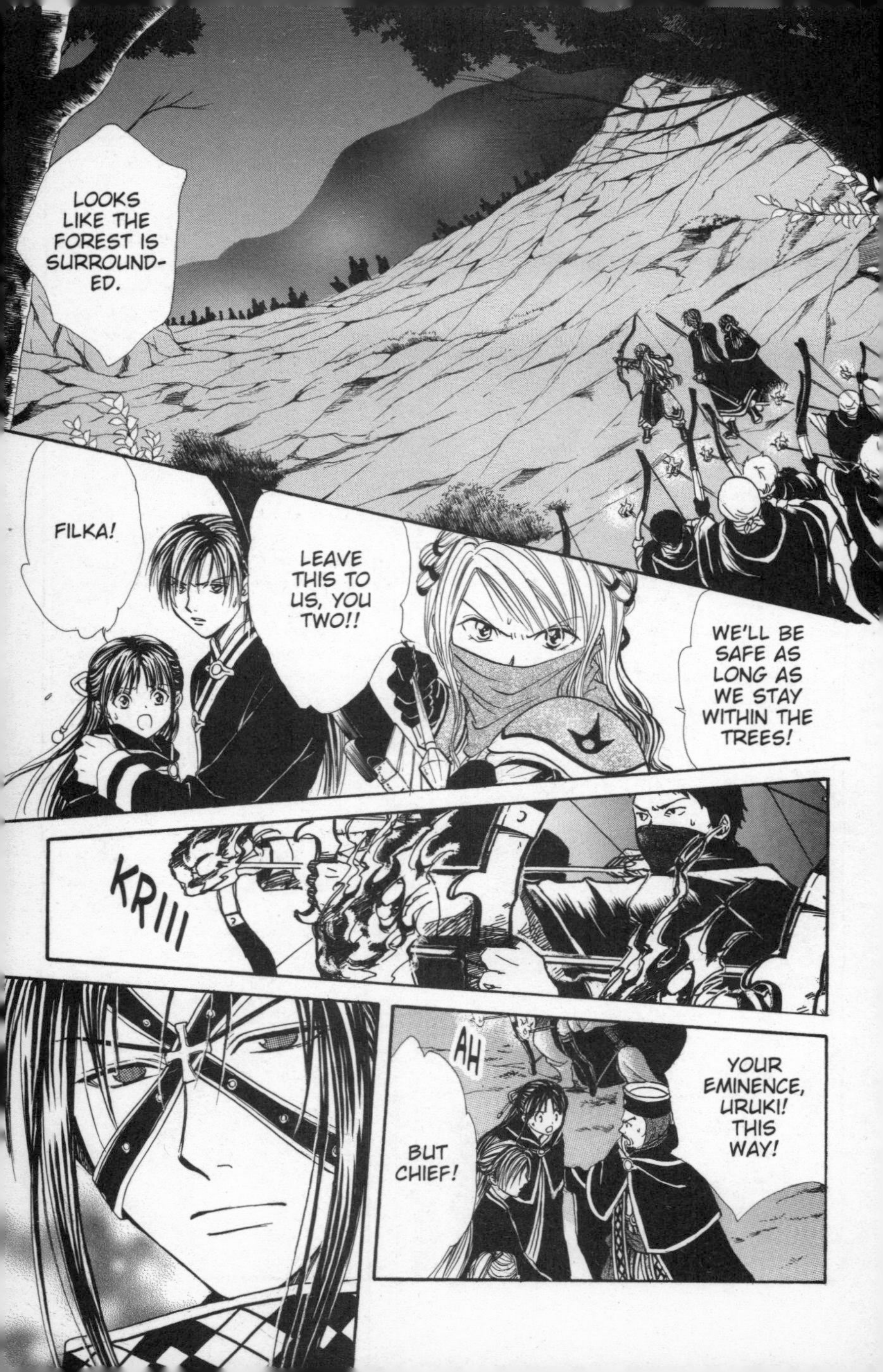
LOOKS LIKE THE FOREST IS SURROUND-ED.
WE'LL BE SAFE AS LONG AS WE STAY WITHIN THE TREES!
LEAVE THIS TO US, YOU TWO!!
FILKA!
KRIII
YOUR EMINENCE, URUKI! THIS WAY!
AH
BUT CHIEF!

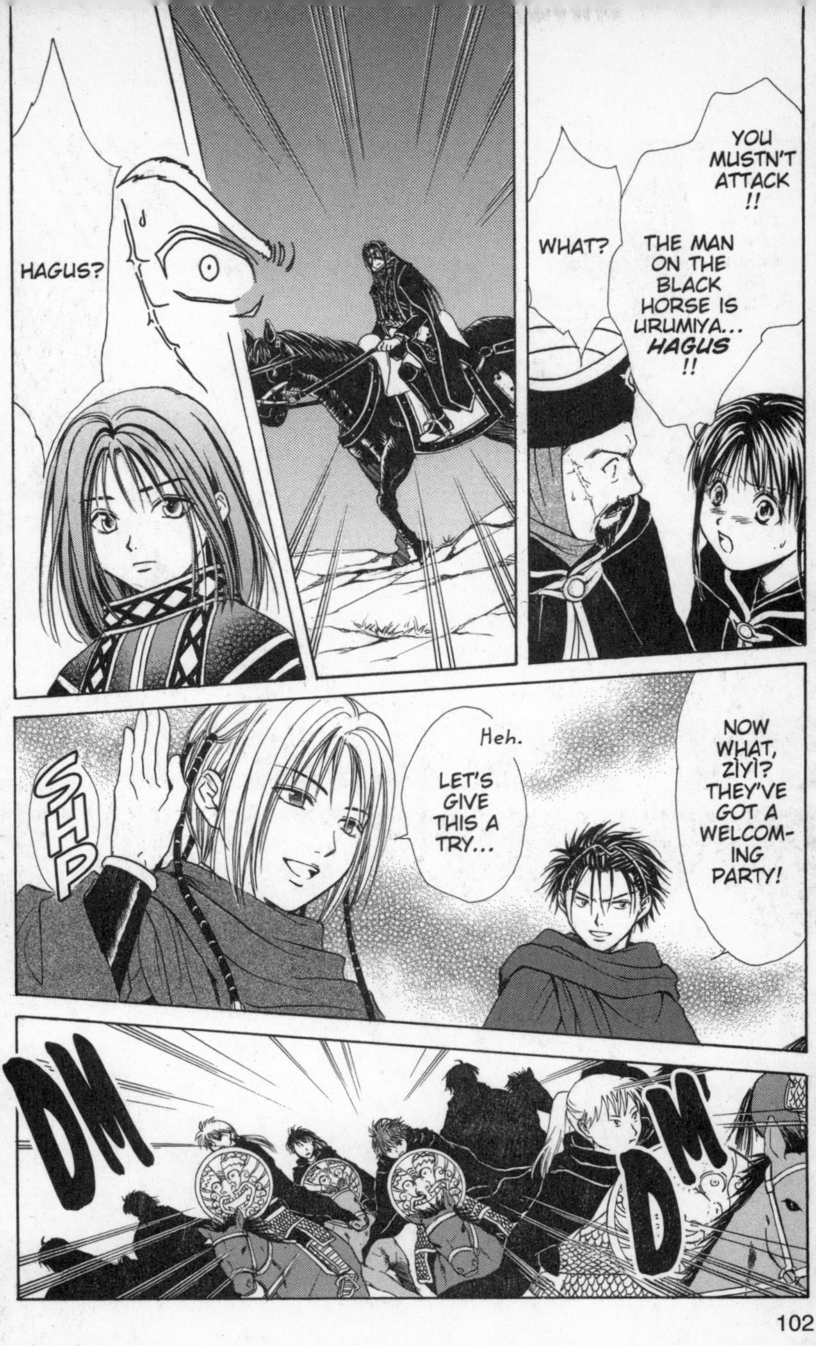
YOU MUSTN'T ATTACK !!
THE MAN ON THE BLACK HORSE IS URUMIYA... HAGUS !!
WHAT?
HAGUS?
NOW WHAT, ZIYI? THEY'VE GOT A WELCOMING PARTY!
Heh.
LET'S GIVE THIS A TRY...
SHP
DM
DM

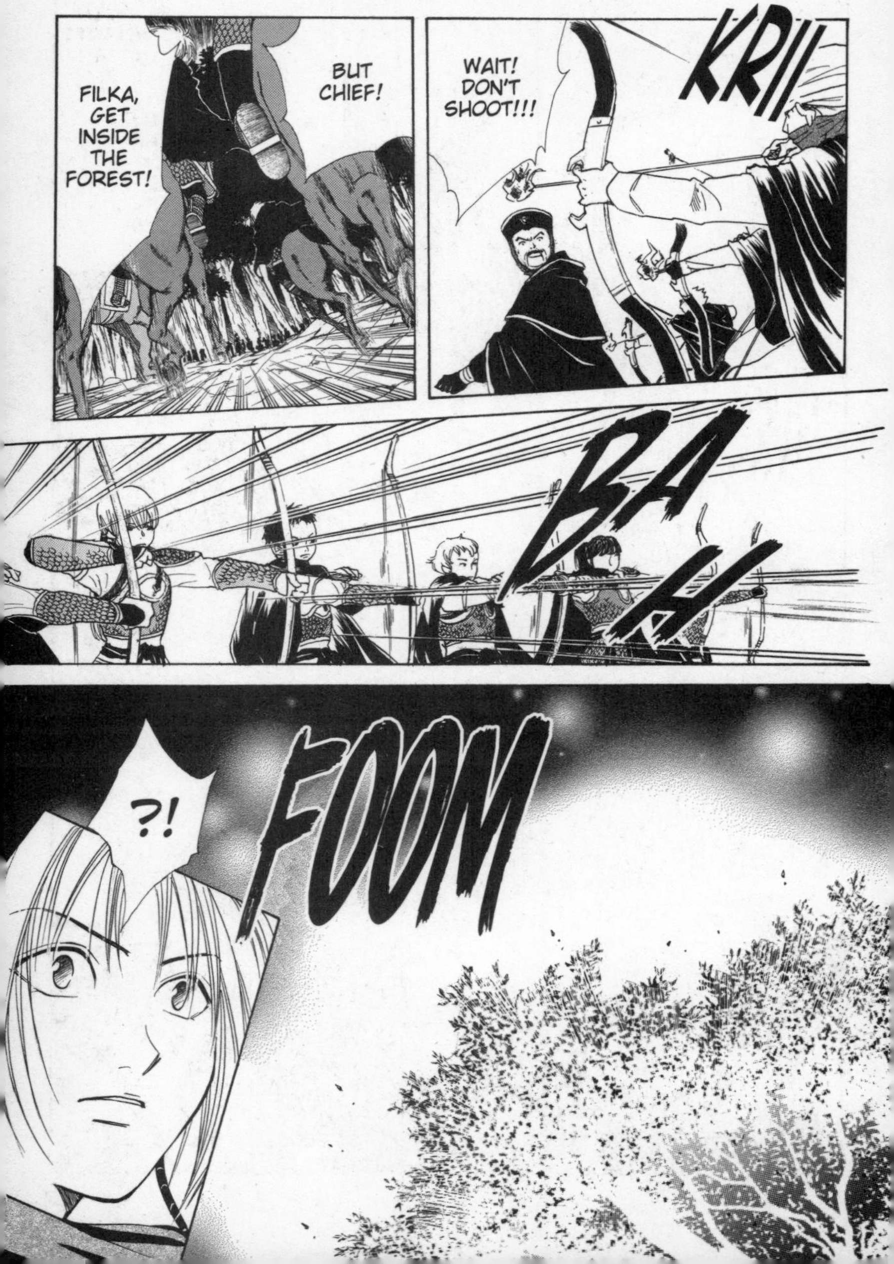
KRIII
WAIT! DON'T SHOOT!!!
BUT CHIEF!
FILKA, GET INSIDE THE FOREST!
BAH
FOOM
?!

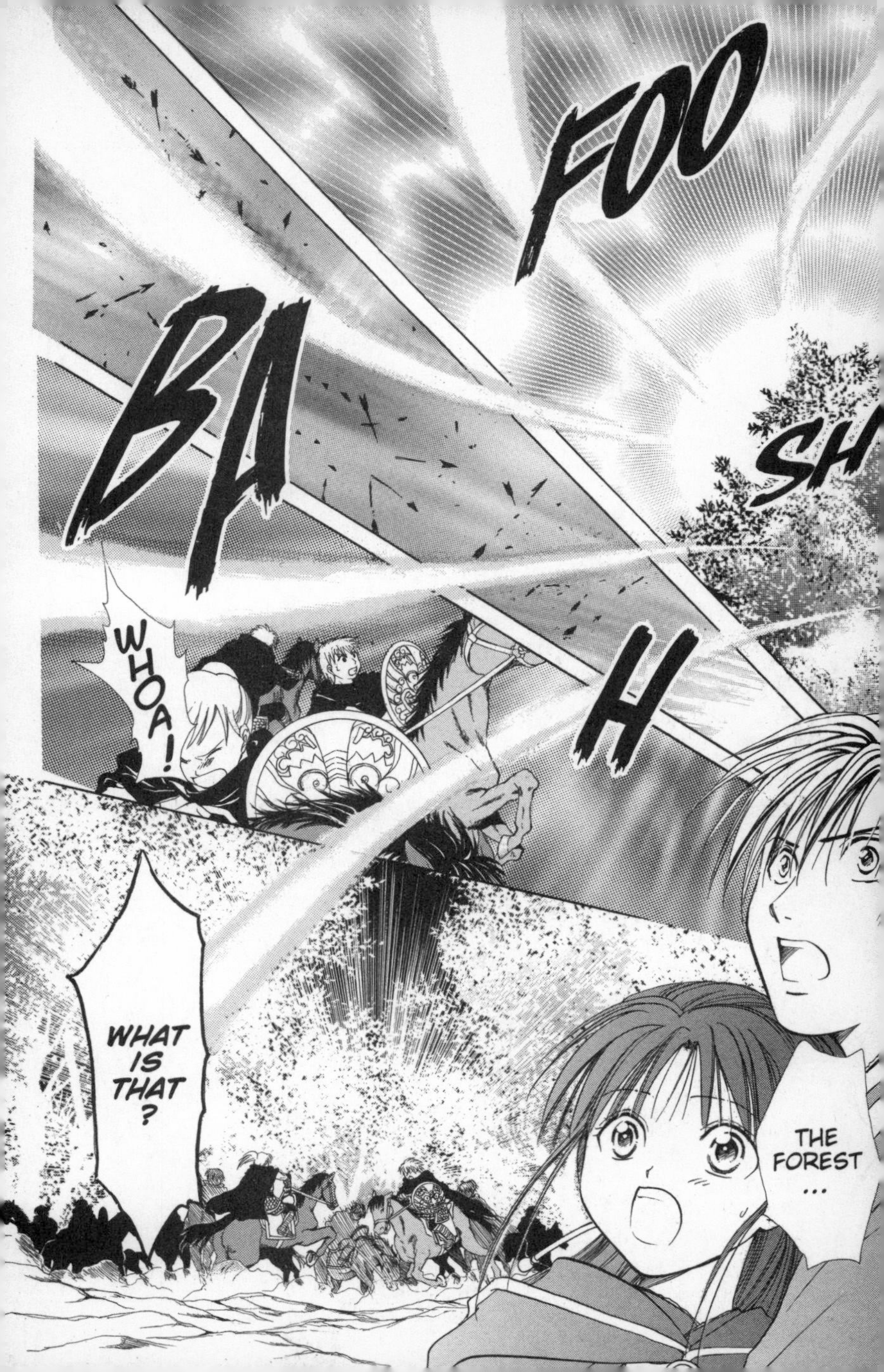
FOO
SH
H
BA
WHOA!
THE FOREST ...
WHAT IS THAT?

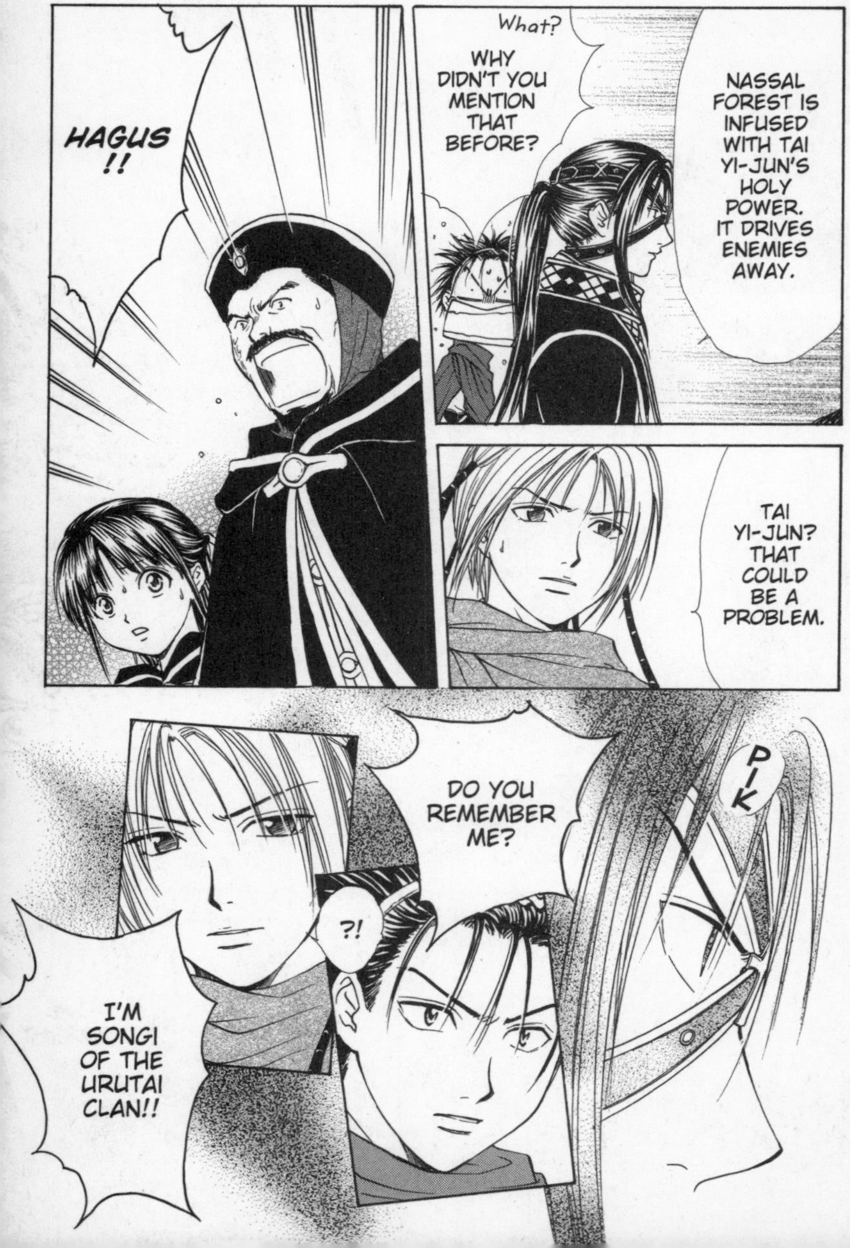
NASSAL FOREST IS INFUSED WITH TAI YI-JUN'S HOLY POWER. IT DRIVES ENEMIES AWAY.
What?
WHY DIDN'T YOU MENTION THAT BEFORE?
TAI YI-JUN? THAT COULD BE A PROBLEM.
HAGUS!!
PIK
DO YOU REMEMBER ME?
?!
I'M SONGI OF THE URUTAI CLAN!!

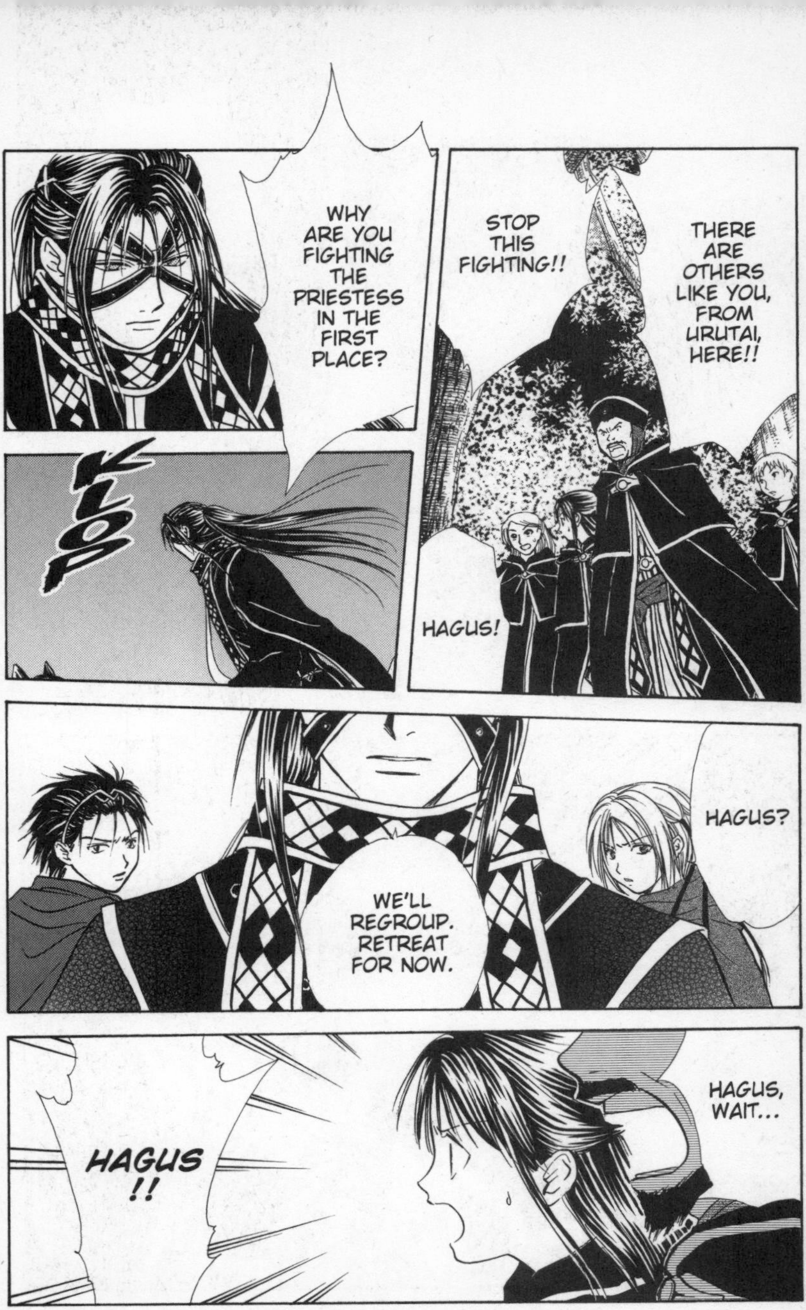
THERE ARE OTHERS LIKE YOU, FROM URUTAI, HERE!!
STOP THIS FIGHTING!!
HAGUS!
WHY ARE YOU FIGHTING THE PRIESTESS IN THE FIRST PLACE?
FLOP
HAGUS?
WE'LL REGROUP. RETREAT FOR NOW.
HAGUS, WAIT...
HAGUS !!

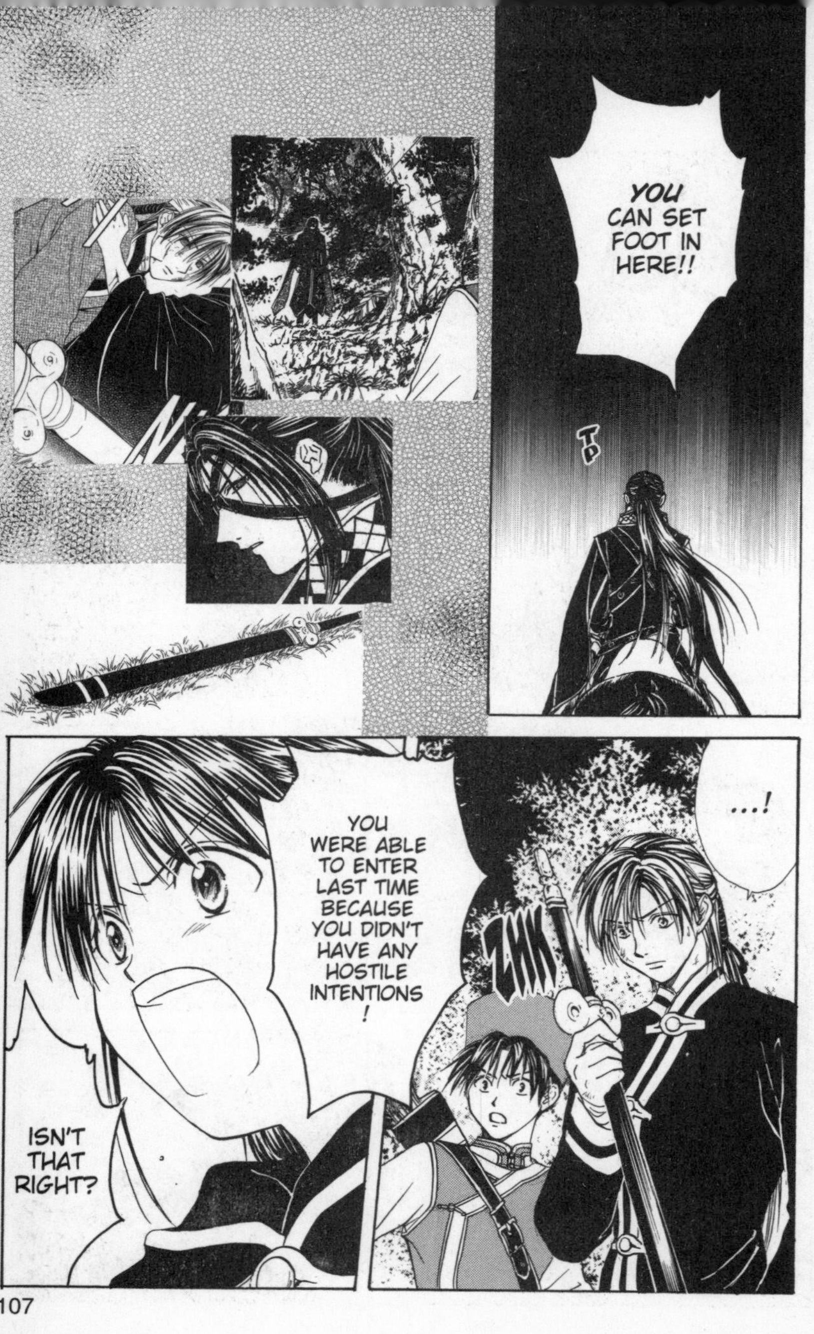
YOU CAN SET FOOT IN HERE!!
TP
...!
ZHK
YOU WERE ABLE TO ENTER LAST TIME BECAUSE YOU DIDN'T HAVE ANY HOSTILE INTENTIONS!
ISN'T THAT RIGHT?

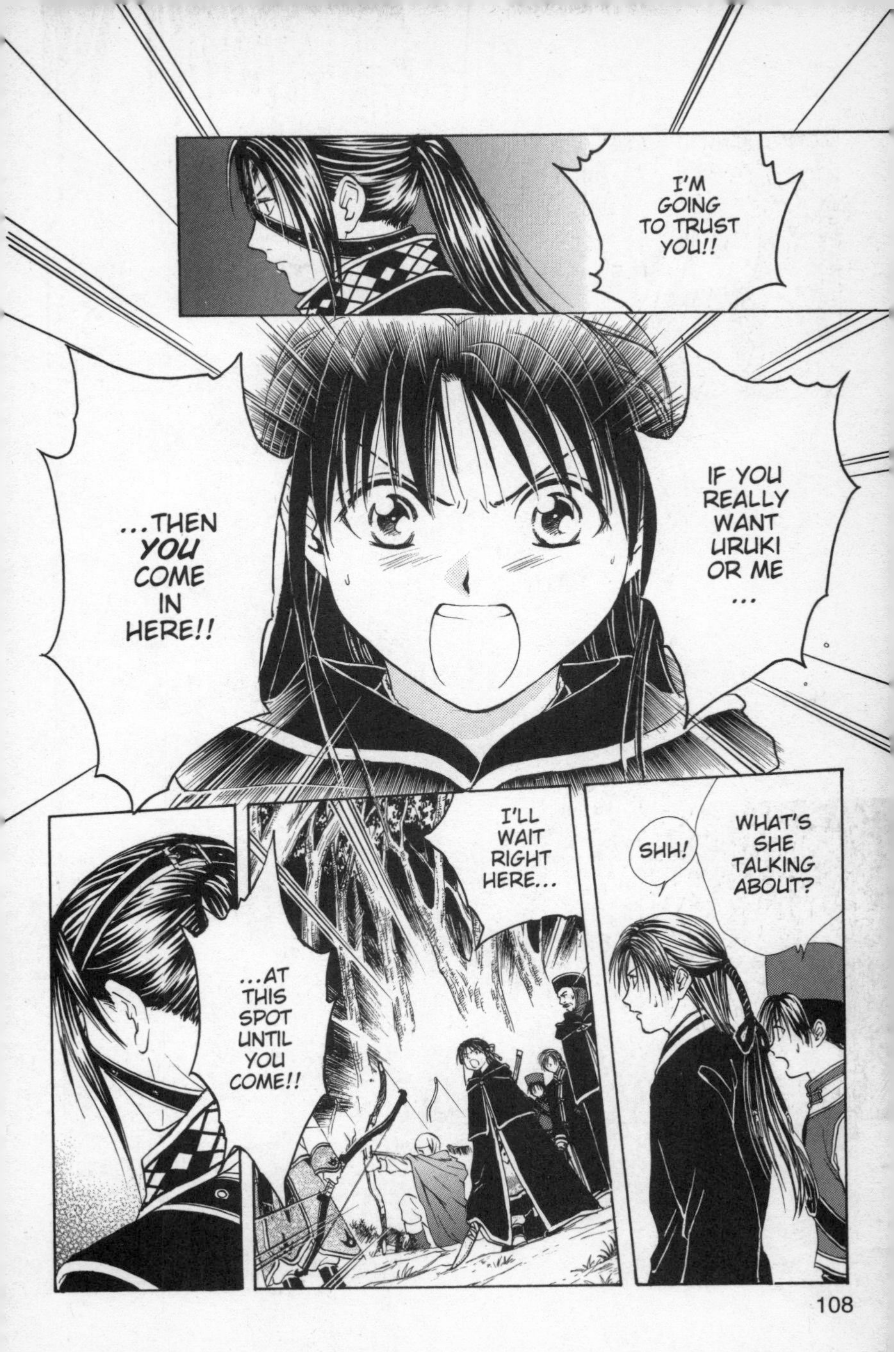
I'M GOING TO TRUST YOU!!
IF YOU REALLY WANT URUKI OR ME ...
...THEN *YOU* COME IN HERE!!
WHAT'S SHE TALKING ABOUT?
SHH!
I'LL WAIT RIGHT HERE...
...AT THIS SPOT UNTIL YOU COME!!

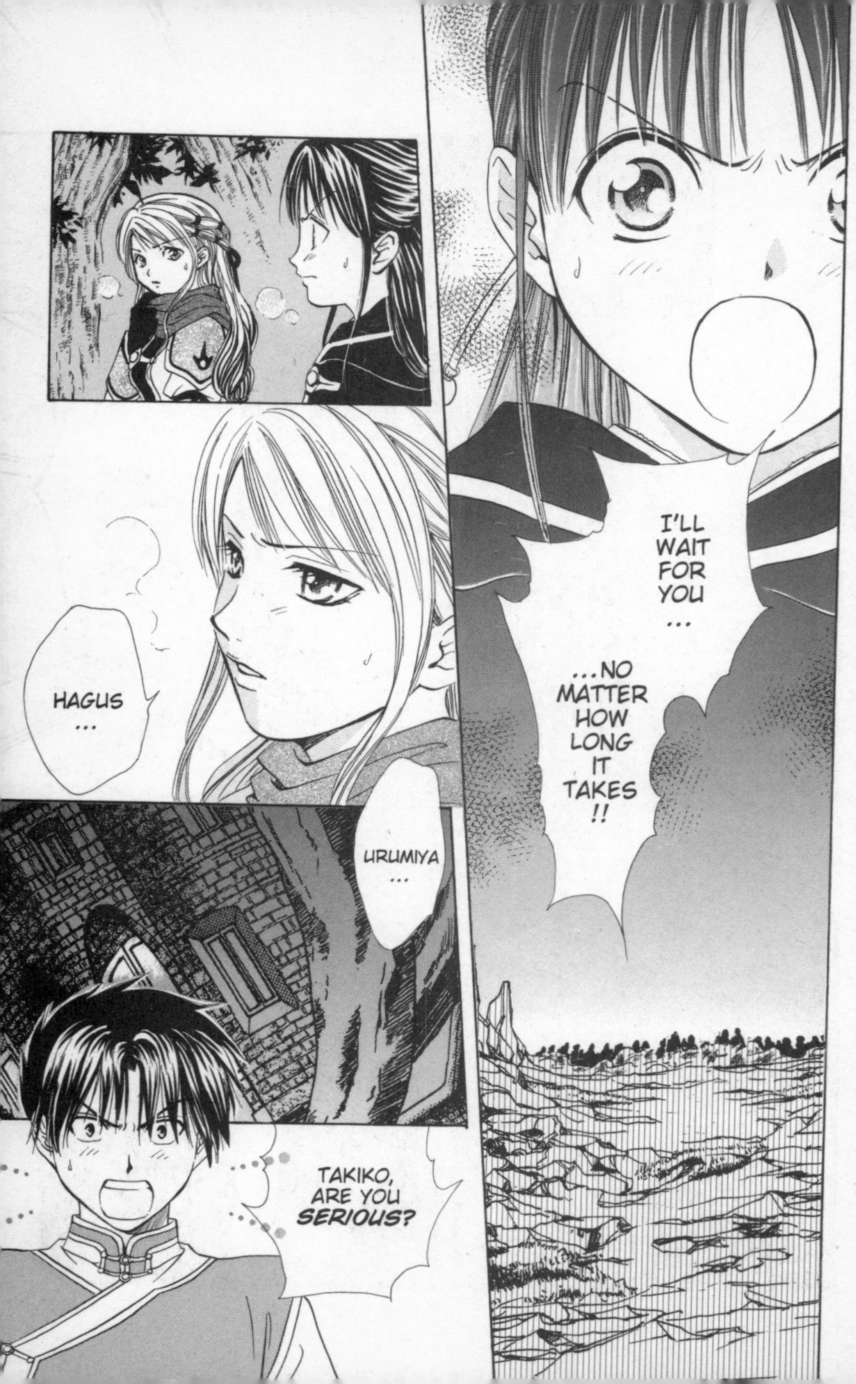
I'LL WAIT FOR YOU ...
...NO MATTER HOW LONG IT TAKES !!
HAGUS ...
URUMIYA ...
TAKIKO, ARE YOU SERIOUS?

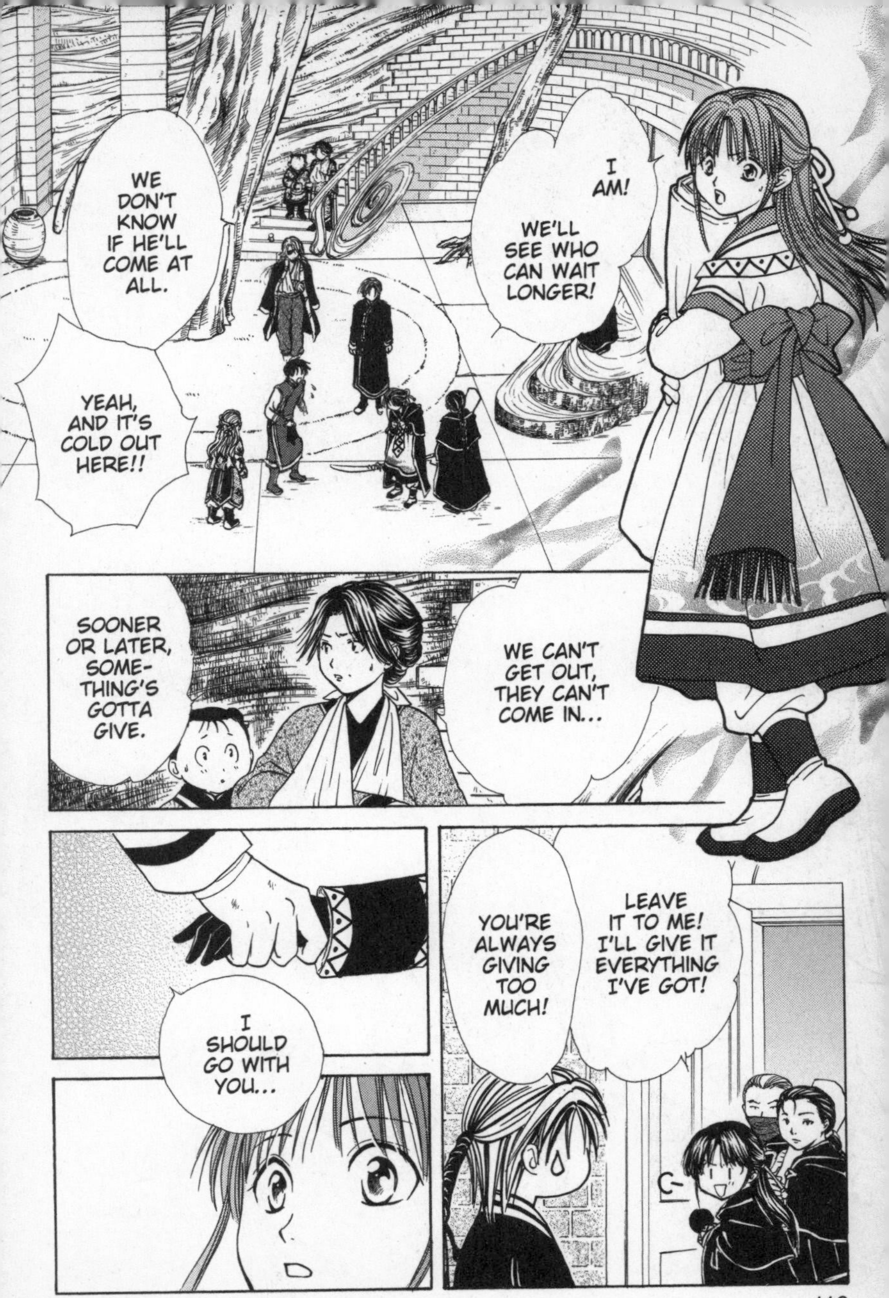
I AM!
WE'LL SEE WHO CAN WAIT LONGER!
WE DON'T KNOW IF HE'LL COME AT ALL.
YEAH, AND IT'S COLD OUT HERE!!
WE CAN'T GET OUT, THEY CAN'T COME IN...
SOONER OR LATER, SOME-THING'S GOTTA GIVE.
LEAVE IT TO ME! I'LL GIVE IT EVERYTHING I'VE GOT!
YOU'RE ALWAYS GIVING TOO MUCH!
I SHOULD GO WITH YOU...

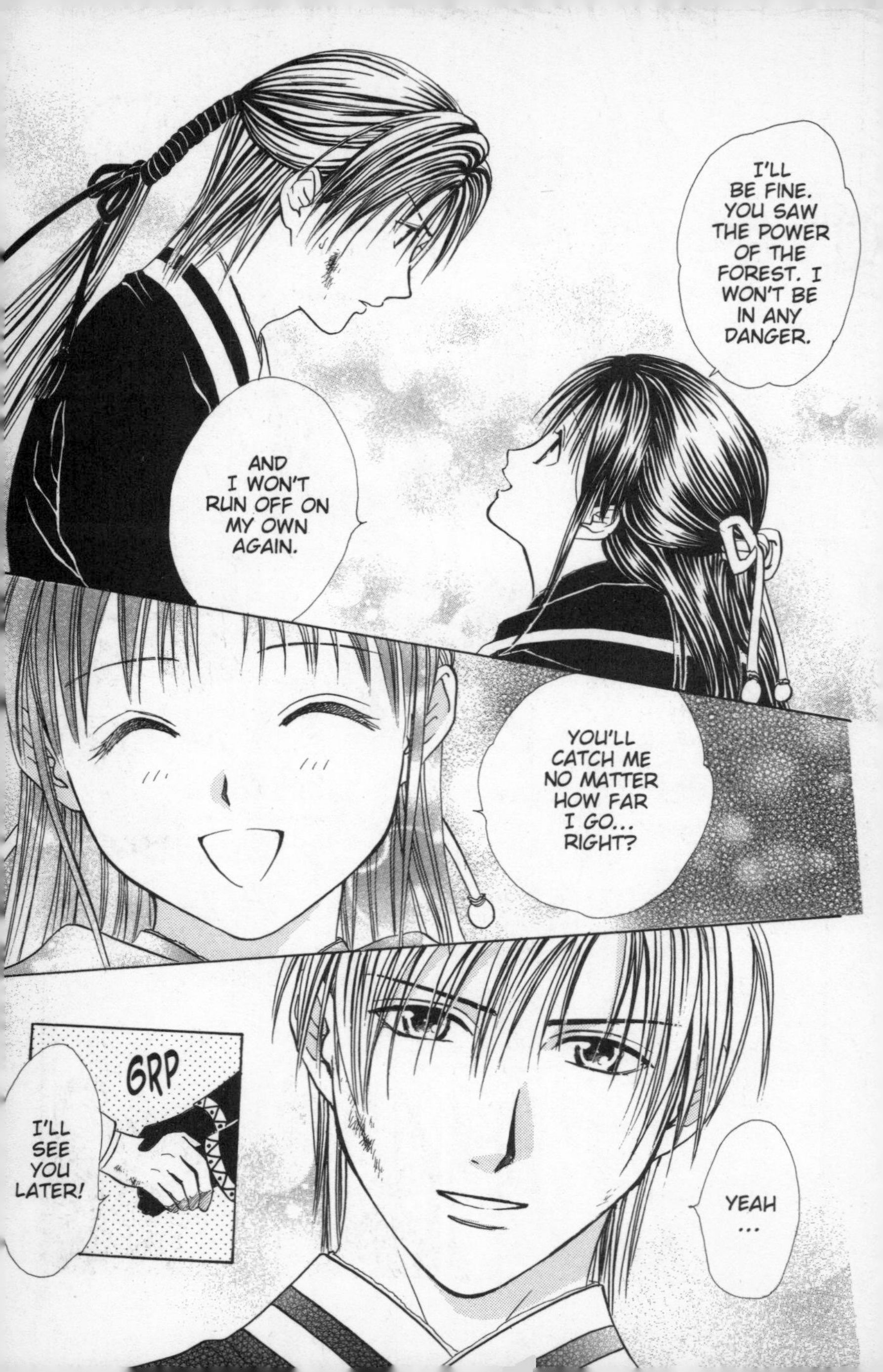
I'LL BE FINE. YOU SAW THE POWER OF THE FOREST. I WON'T BE IN ANY DANGER.
AND I WON'T RUN OFF ON MY OWN AGAIN.
YOU'LL CATCH ME NO MATTER HOW FAR I GO... RIGHT?
GRP
I'LL SEE YOU LATER!
YEAH ...

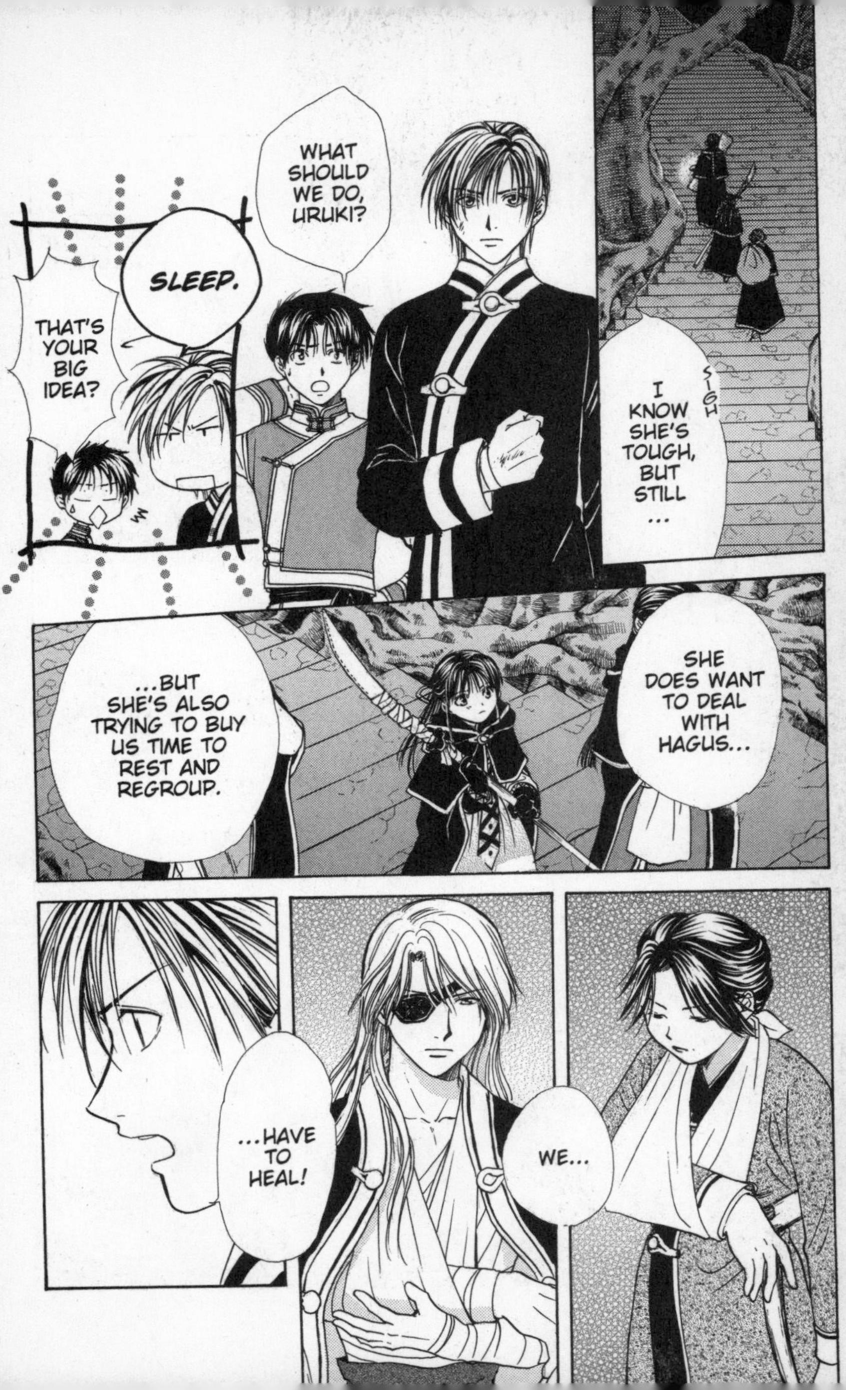
SIGH
I KNOW SHE'S TOUGH, BUT STILL...
WHAT SHOULD WE DO, URUKI?
SLEEP.
THAT'S YOUR BIG IDEA?
SHE DOES WANT TO DEAL WITH HAGUS...
...BUT SHE'S ALSO TRYING TO BUY US TIME TO REST AND REGROUP.
WE...
...HAVE TO HEAL!

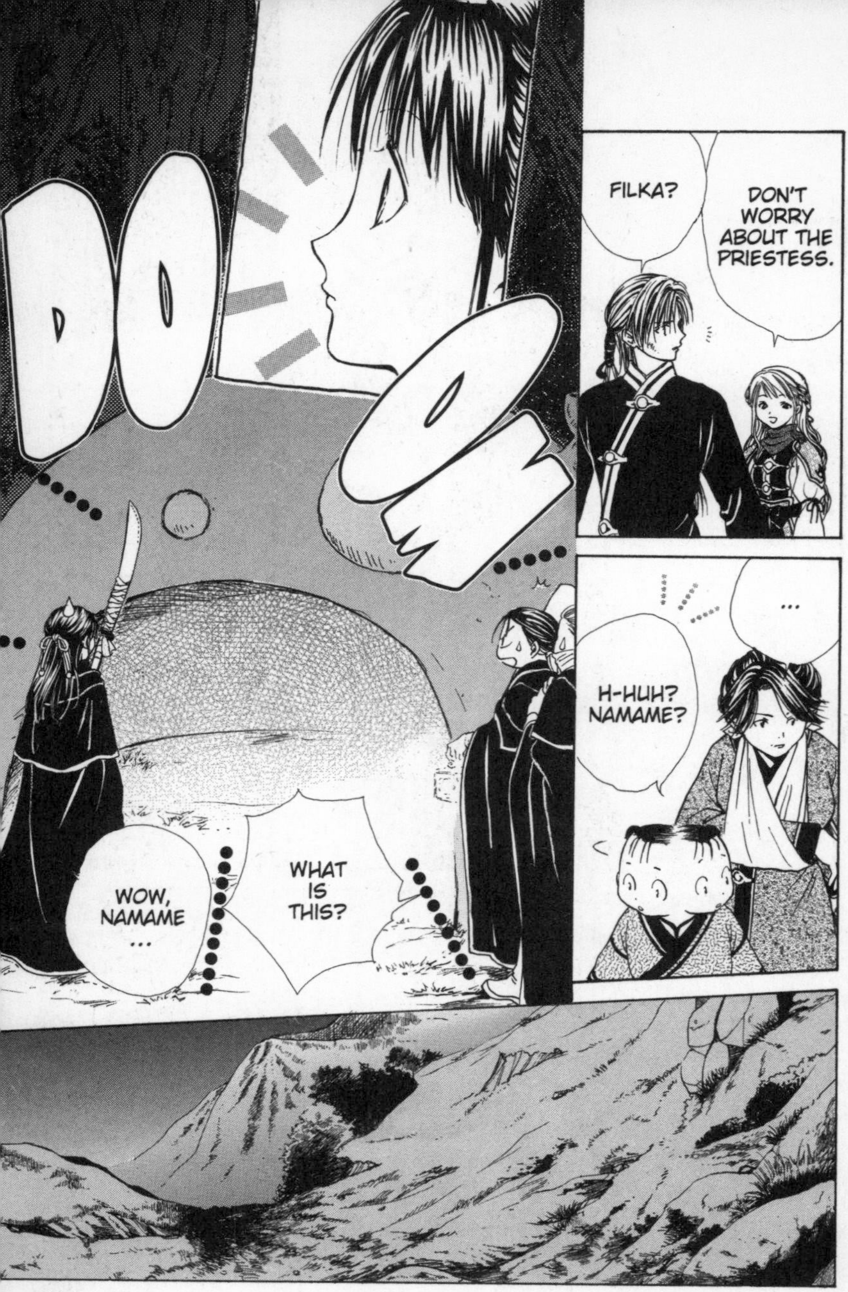

FILKA?
DON'T WORRY ABOUT THE PRIESTESS.
...
H-HUH? NAMAME?
DOOOM
WHAT IS THIS?
WOW, NAMAME ...

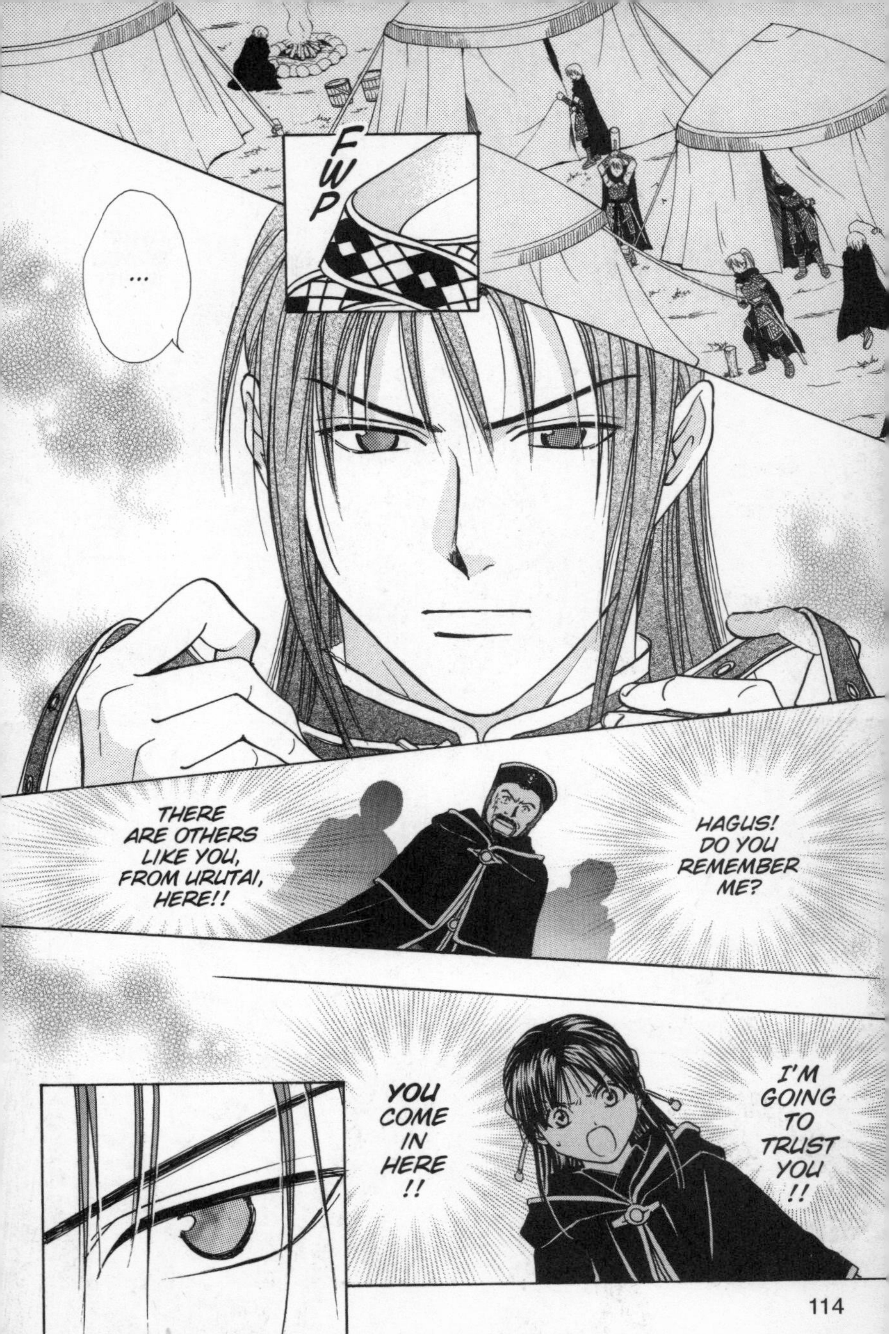
FWP
...
HAGUS! DO YOU REMEMBER ME?
THERE ARE OTHERS LIKE YOU, FROM URUTAI, HERE!!
I'M GOING TO TRUST YOU !!
YOU COME IN HERE !!

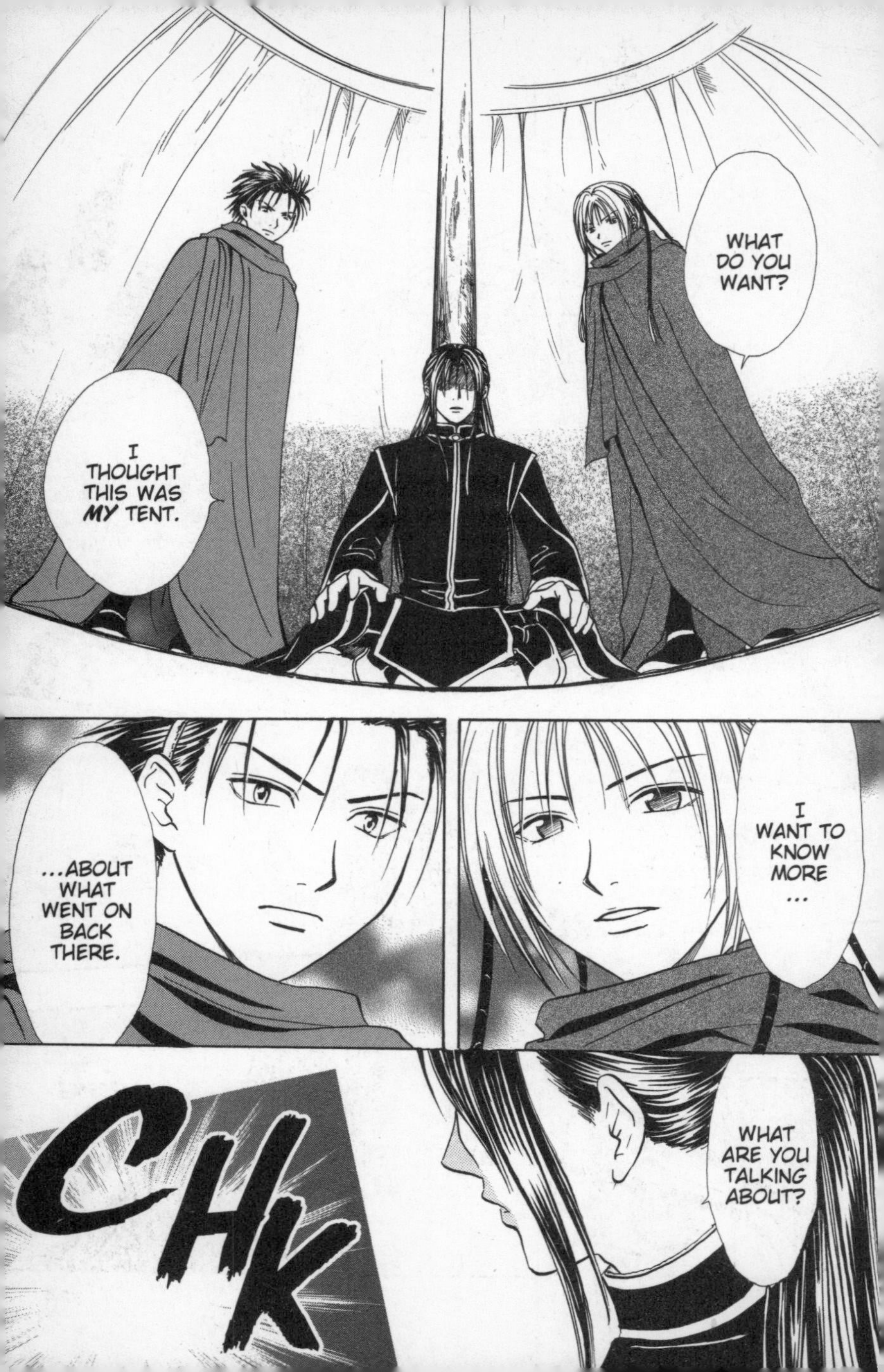
WHAT DO YOU WANT?
I THOUGHT THIS WAS *MY* TENT.
I WANT TO KNOW MORE ...
...ABOUT WHAT WENT ON BACK THERE.
WHAT ARE YOU TALKING ABOUT?
CHK

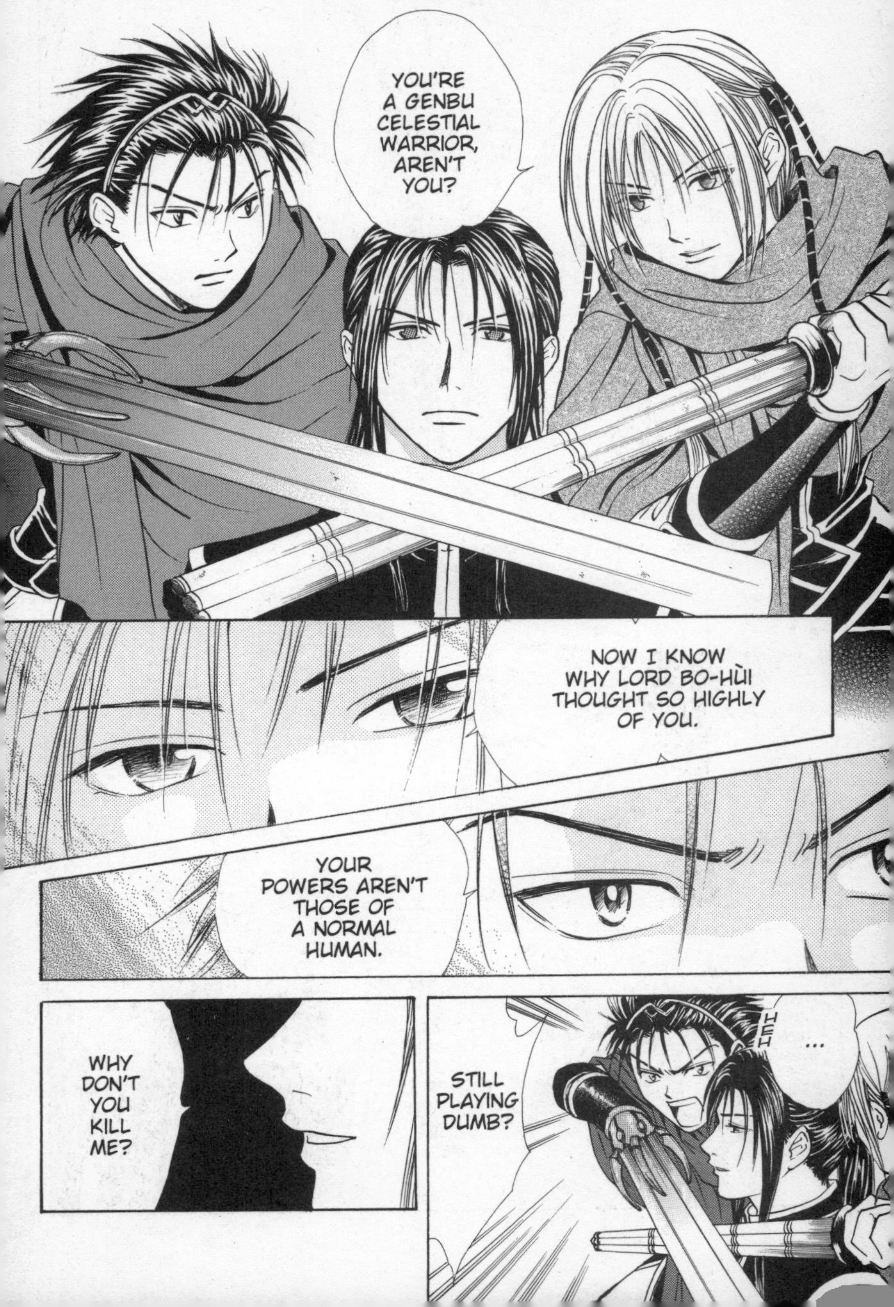
YOU'RE A GENBU CELESTIAL WARRIOR, AREN'T YOU?
NOW I KNOW WHY LORD BO-HÙI THOUGHT SO HIGHLY OF YOU.
YOUR POWERS AREN'T THOSE OF A NORMAL HUMAN.
...
HEH
STILL PLAYING DUMB?
WHY DON'T YOU KILL ME?

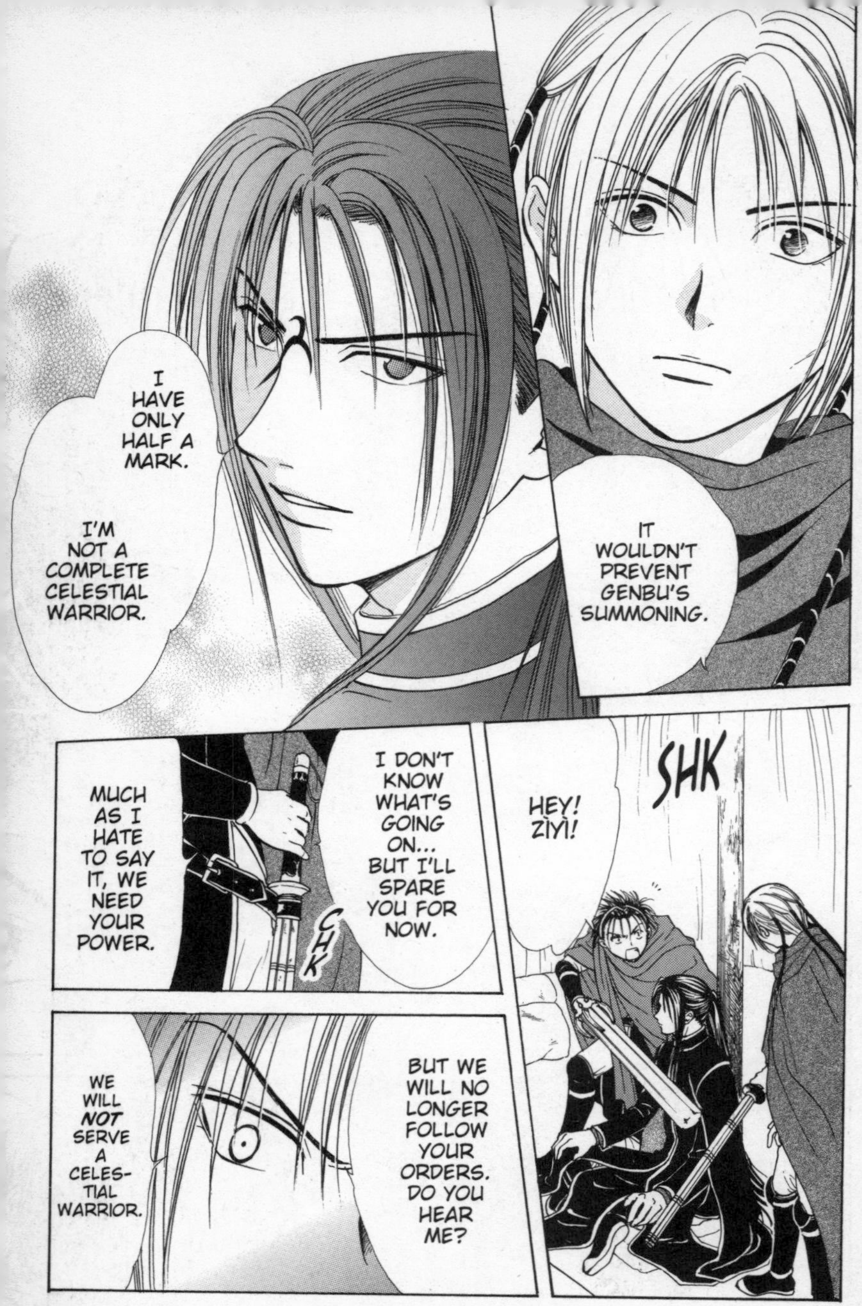
IT WOULDN'T PREVENT GENBU'S SUMMONING.
I HAVE ONLY HALF A MARK.
I'M NOT A COMPLETE CELESTIAL WARRIOR.
SHK
HEY! ZIYI!
I DON'T KNOW WHAT'S GOING ON... BUT I'LL SPARE YOU FOR NOW.
CHK
MUCH AS I HATE TO SAY IT, WE NEED YOUR POWER.
BUT WE WILL NO LONGER FOLLOW YOUR ORDERS. DO YOU HEAR ME?
WE WILL *NOT* SERVE A CELES-TIAL WARRIOR.

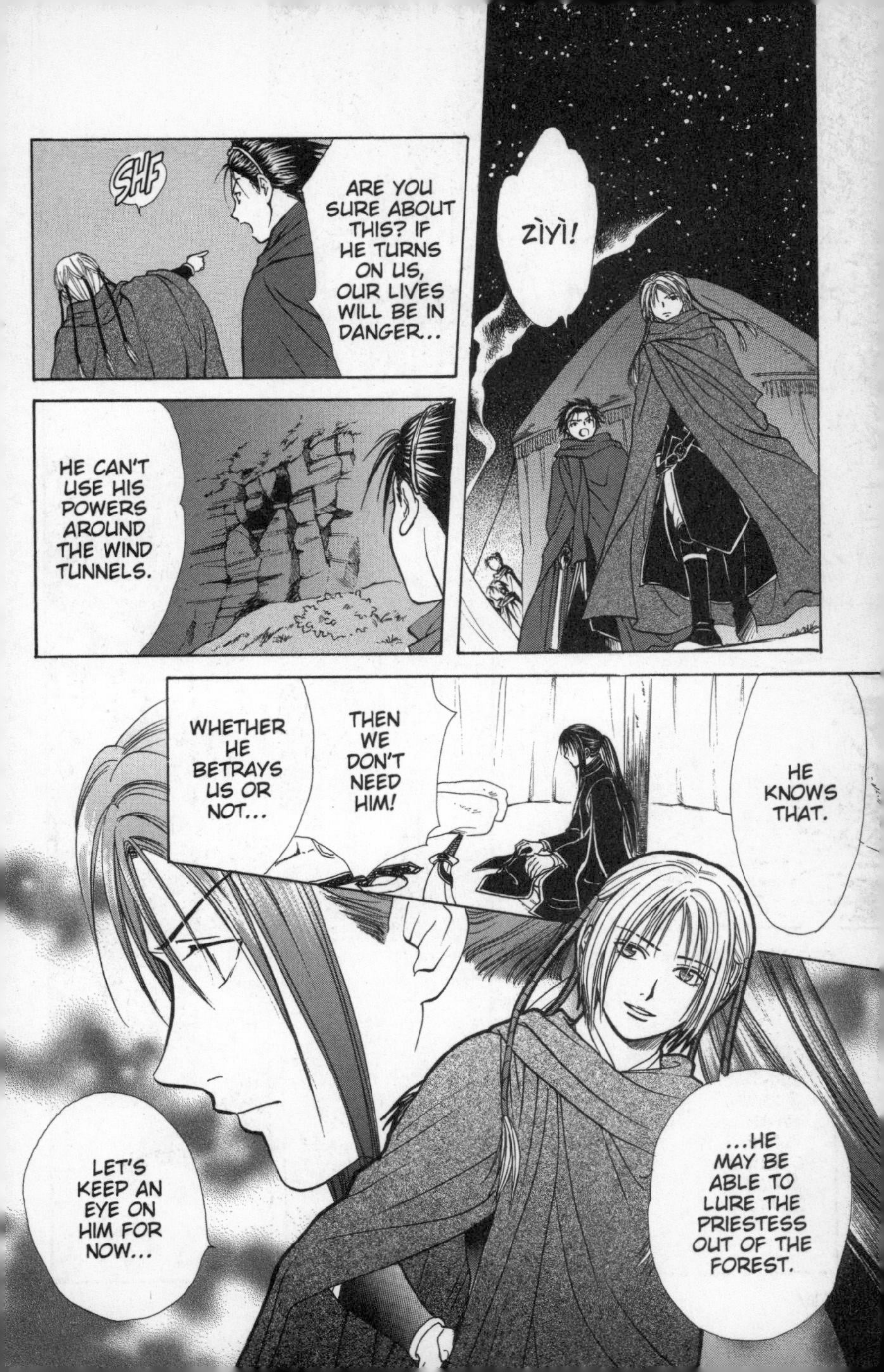
ZÌYÌ!
ARE YOU SURE ABOUT THIS? IF HE TURNS ON US, OUR LIVES WILL BE IN DANGER...
SHF
HE CAN'T USE HIS POWERS AROUND THE WIND TUNNELS.
HE KNOWS THAT.
THEN WE DON'T NEED HIM!
WHETHER HE BETRAYS US OR NOT...
...HE MAY BE ABLE TO LURE THE PRIESTESS OUT OF THE FOREST.
LET'S KEEP AN EYE ON HIM FOR NOW...

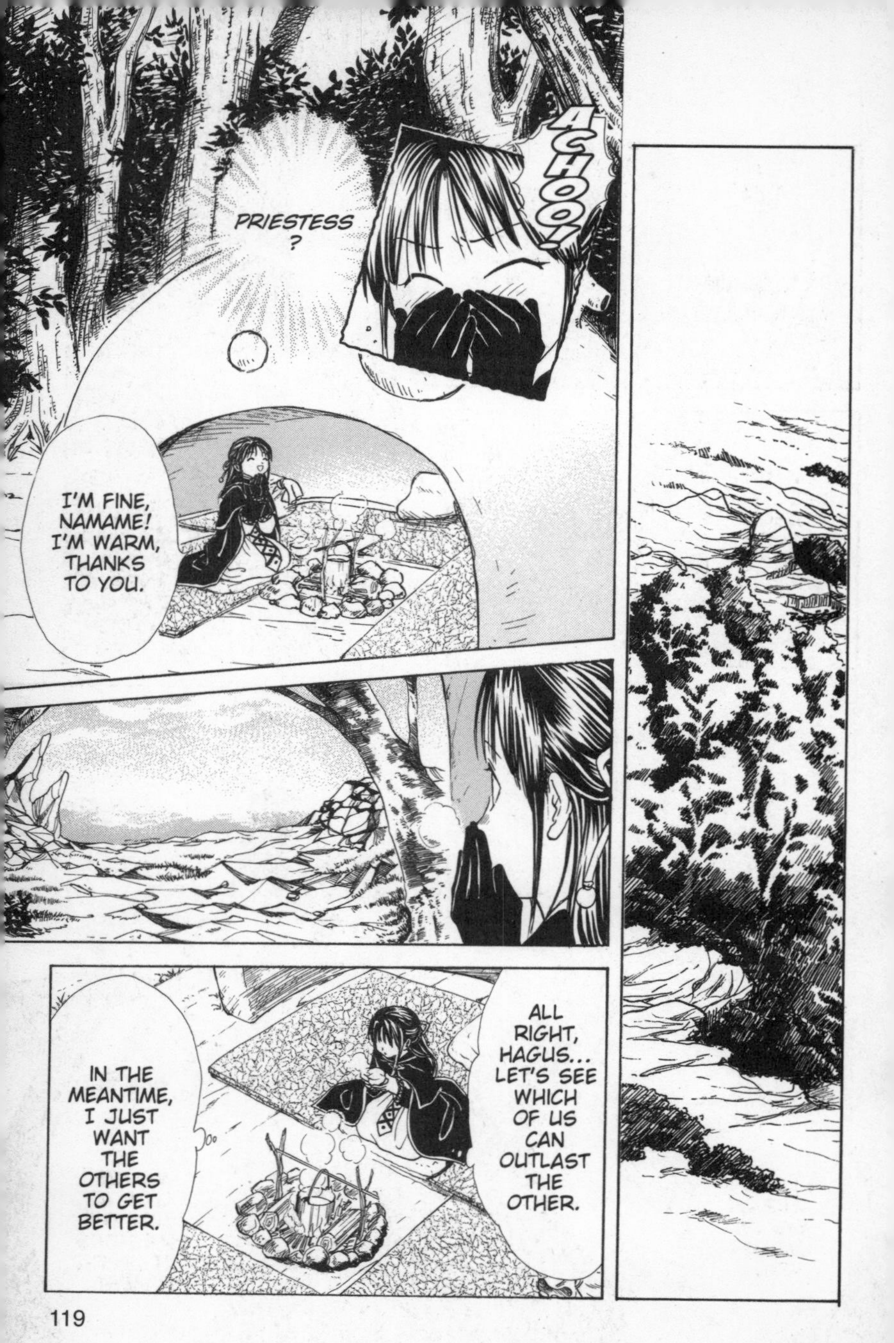
ACHOO!
PRIESTESS ?
I'M FINE, NAMAME! I'M WARM, THANKS TO YOU.
ALL RIGHT, HAGUS... LET'S SEE WHICH OF US CAN OUTLAST THE OTHER.
IN THE MEANTIME, I JUST WANT THE OTHERS TO GET BETTER.

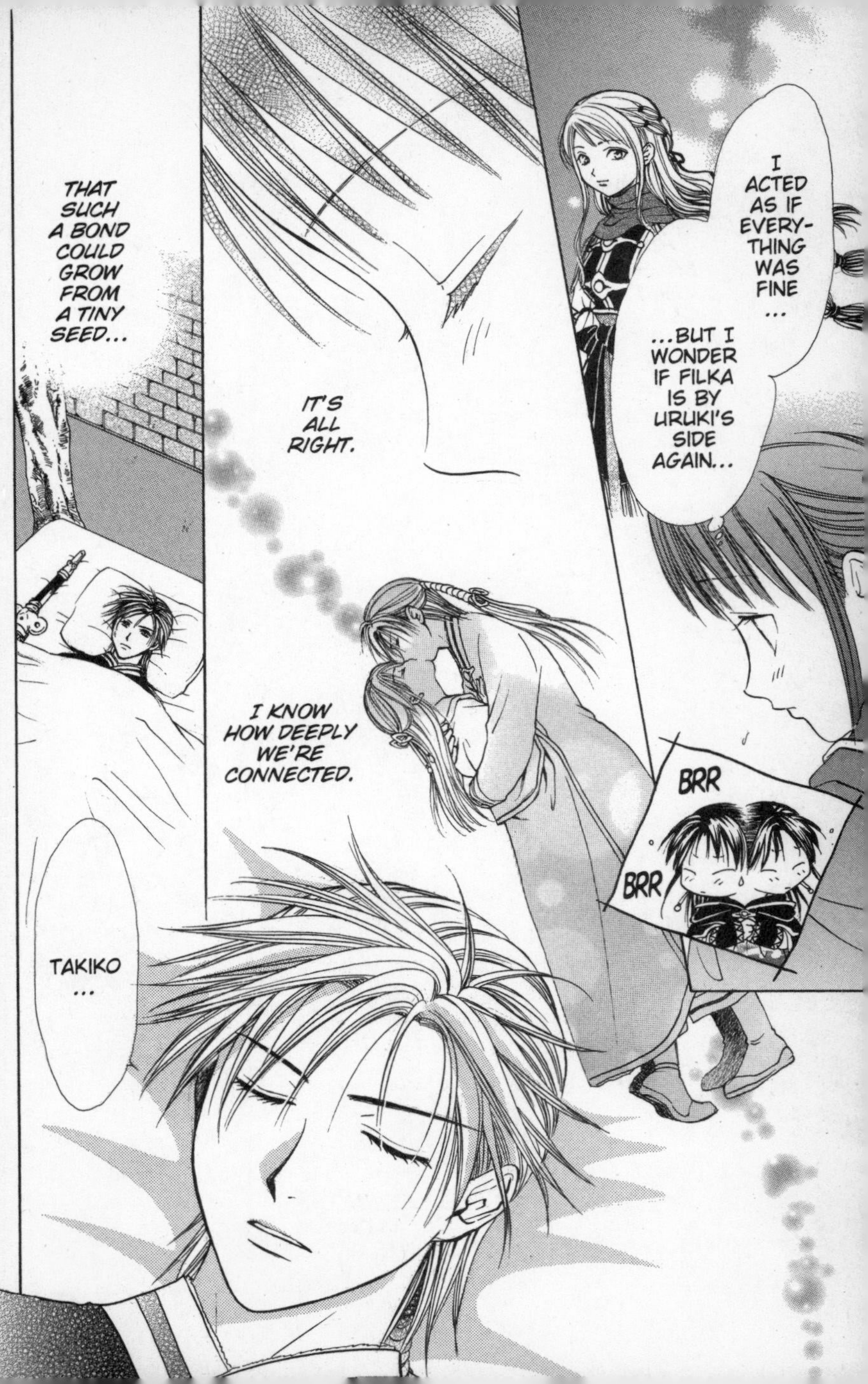
I ACTED AS IF EVERYTHING WAS FINE...
...BUT I WONDER IF FILKA IS BY URUKI'S SIDE AGAIN...
BRR
BRR
IT'S ALL RIGHT.
I KNOW HOW DEEPLY WE'RE CONNECTED.
THAT SUCH A BOND COULD GROW FROM A TINY SEED...
TAKIKO...

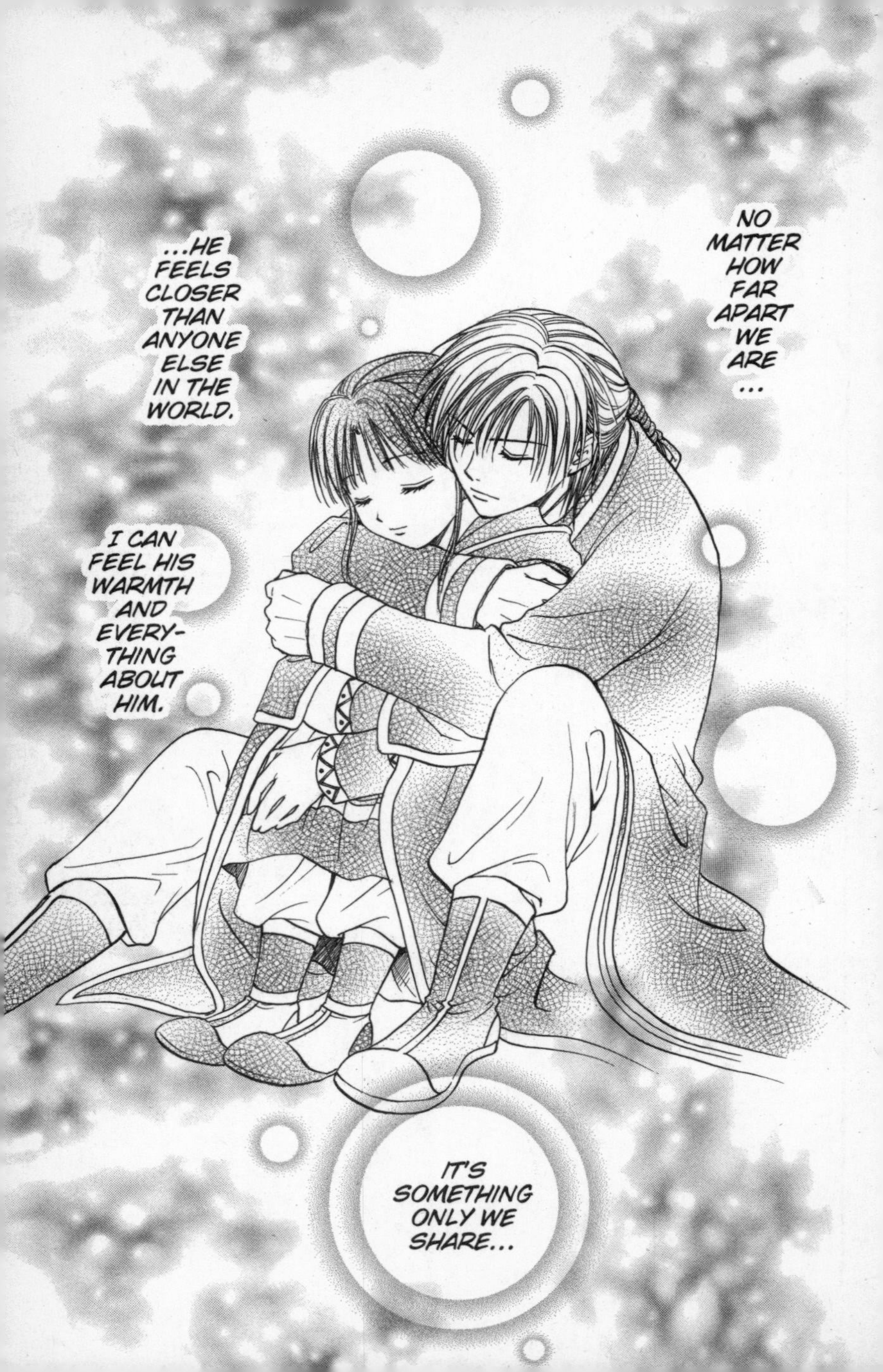
NO MATTER HOW FAR APART WE ARE...
...HE FEELS CLOSER THAN ANYONE ELSE IN THE WORLD.
I CAN FEEL HIS WARMTH AND EVERY-THING ABOUT HIM.
IT'S SOMETHING ONLY WE SHARE...

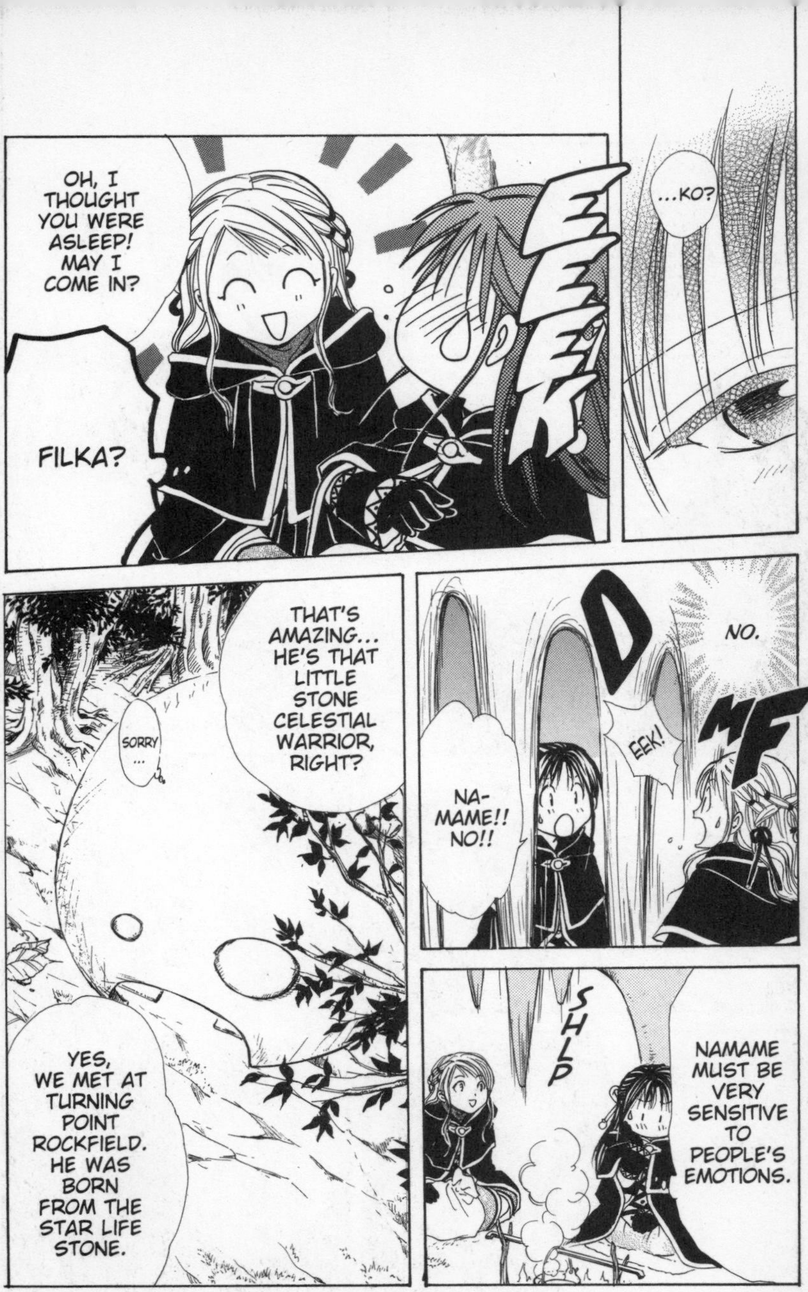
...KO?
EEEEK
FILKA?
OH, I THOUGHT YOU WERE ASLEEP! MAY I COME IN?
NO.
D
MF
EEK!
NA-MAME!! NO!!
SHLP
NAMAME MUST BE VERY SENSITIVE TO PEOPLE'S EMOTIONS.
THAT'S AMAZING... HE'S THAT LITTLE STONE CELESTIAL WARRIOR, RIGHT?
SORRY ...
YES, WE MET AT TURNING POINT ROCKFIELD. HE WAS BORN FROM THE STAR LIFE STONE.

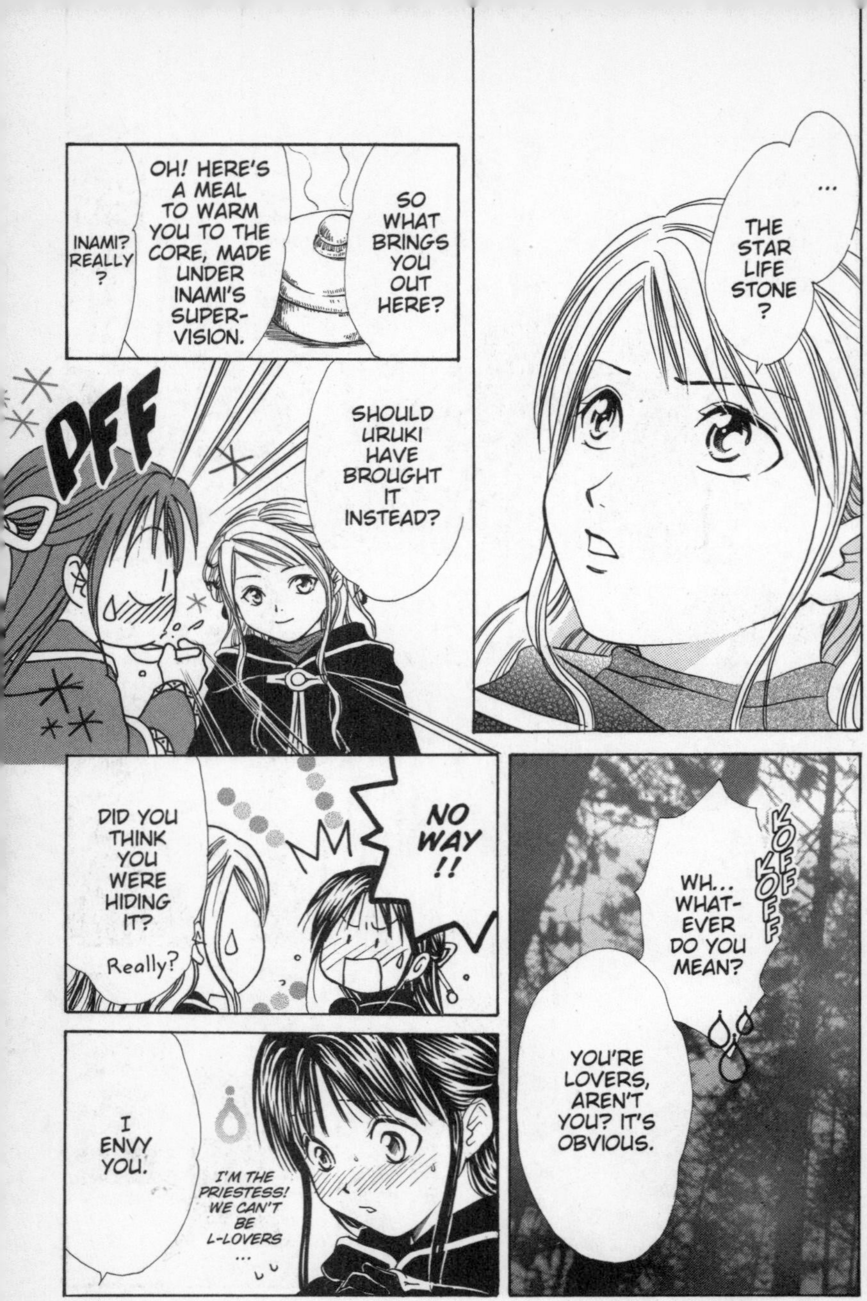
...
THE STAR LIFE STONE?
SO WHAT BRINGS YOU OUT HERE?
OH! HERE'S A MEAL TO WARM YOU TO THE CORE, MADE UNDER INAMI'S SUPER-VISION.
INAMI? REALLY?
SHOULD URUKI HAVE BROUGHT IT INSTEAD?
PFF
KOFF KOFF
WH... WHAT-EVER DO YOU MEAN?
YOU'RE LOVERS, AREN'T YOU? IT'S OBVIOUS.
NO WAY!!
DID YOU THINK YOU WERE HIDING IT?
Really?
I'M THE PRIESTESS! WE CAN'T BE L-LOVERS...
I ENVY YOU.

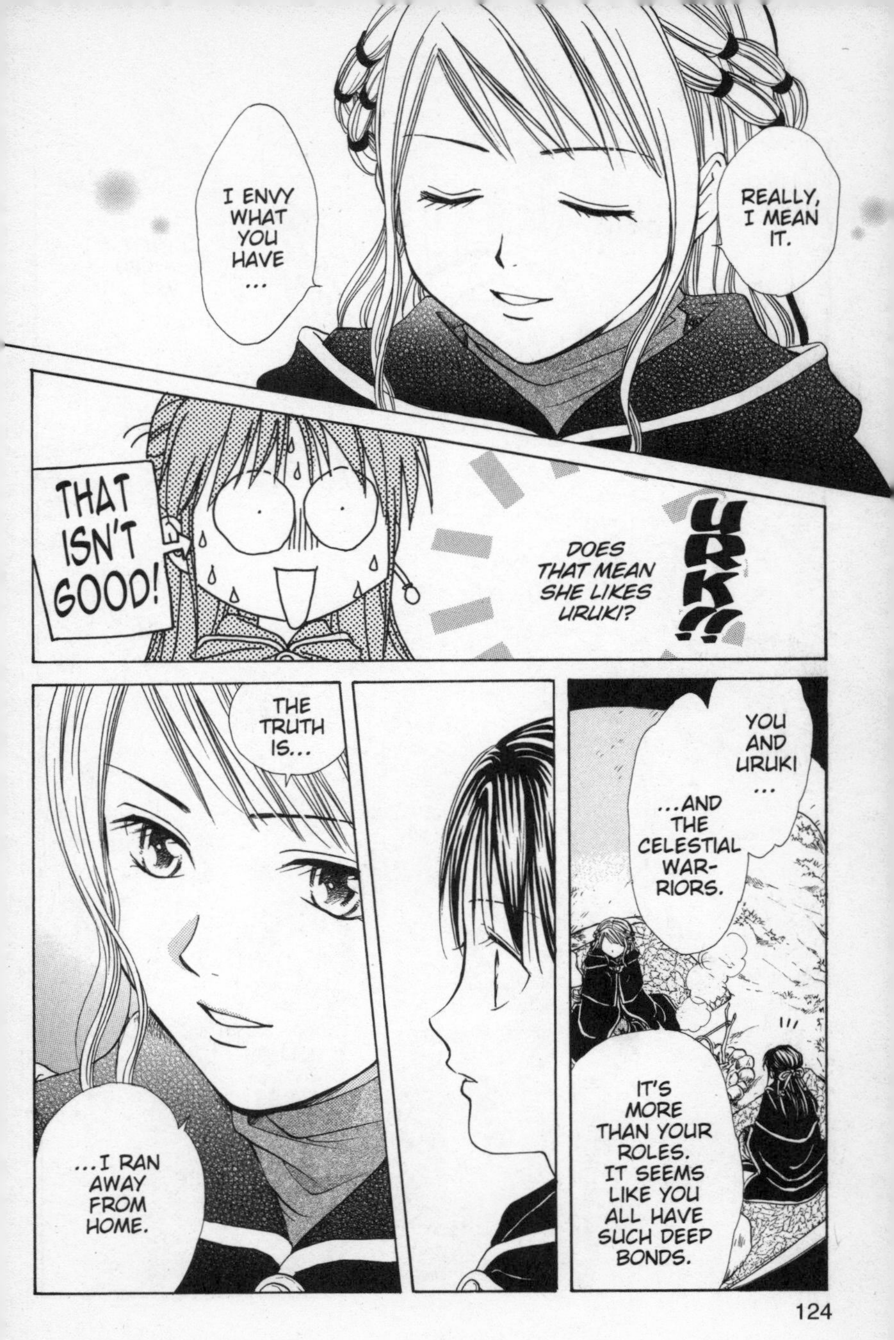
REALLY, I MEAN IT.
I ENVY WHAT YOU HAVE ...
URK!!
DOES THAT MEAN SHE LIKES URUKI?
THAT ISN'T GOOD!
YOU AND URUKI ...
...AND THE CELESTIAL WAR-RIORS.
IT'S MORE THAN YOUR ROLES. IT SEEMS LIKE YOU ALL HAVE SUCH DEEP BONDS.
THE TRUTH IS...
...I RAN AWAY FROM HOME.

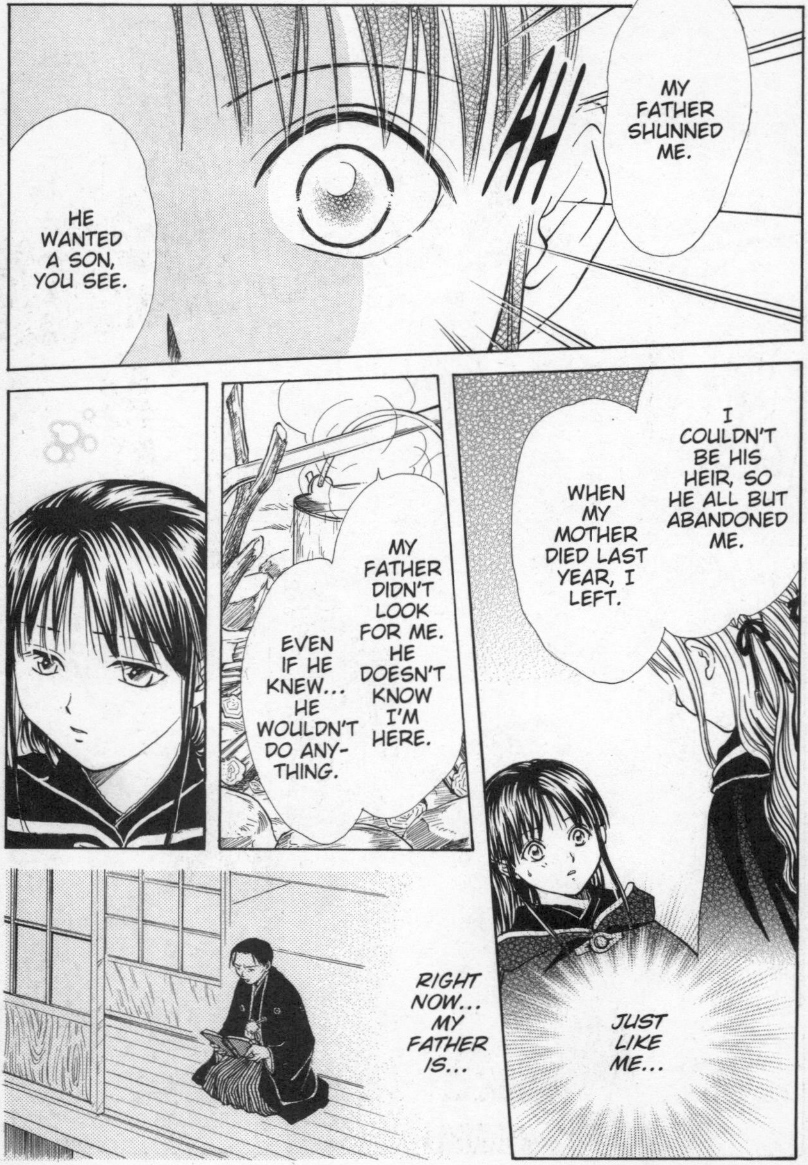
MY FATHER SHUNNED ME.
AH
HE WANTED A SON, YOU SEE.
I COULDN'T BE HIS HEIR, SO HE ALL BUT ABANDONED ME.
WHEN MY MOTHER DIED LAST YEAR, I LEFT.
JUST LIKE ME...
MY FATHER DIDN'T LOOK FOR ME. HE DOESN'T KNOW I'M HERE.
EVEN IF HE KNEW... HE WOULDN'T DO ANY-THING.
RIGHT NOW... MY FATHER IS...

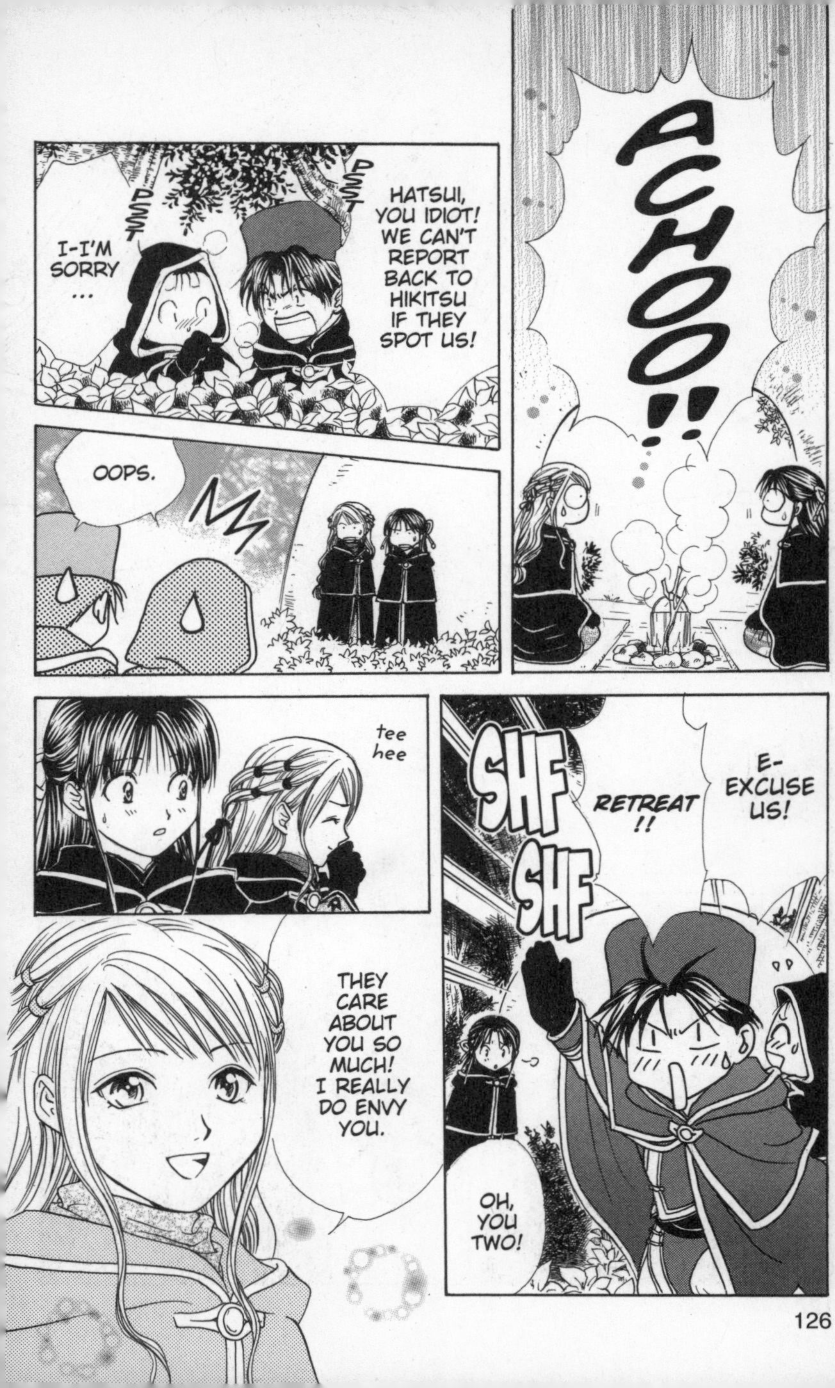
ACHOO!!
PSST PSST
HATSUI, YOU IDIOT! WE CAN'T REPORT BACK TO HIKITSU IF THEY SPOT US!
I-I'M SORRY ...
OOPS.
E-EXCUSE US!
RETREAT !!
SHF SHF
OH, YOU TWO!
tee hee
THEY CARE ABOUT YOU SO MUCH! I REALLY DO ENVY YOU.

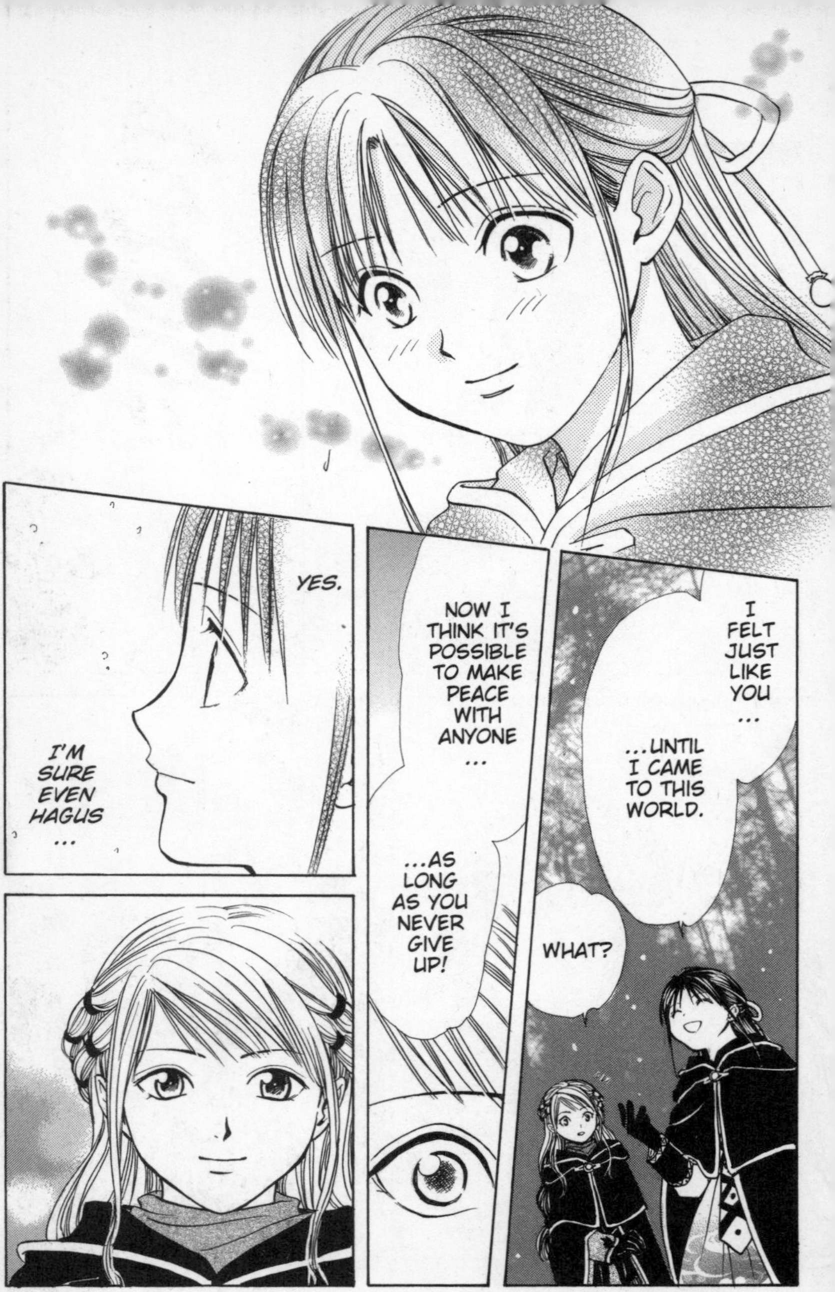
I FELT JUST LIKE YOU ...
...UNTIL I CAME TO THIS WORLD.
WHAT?
NOW I THINK IT'S POSSIBLE TO MAKE PEACE WITH ANYONE ...
...AS LONG AS YOU NEVER GIVE UP!
YES.
I'M SURE EVEN HAGUS ...

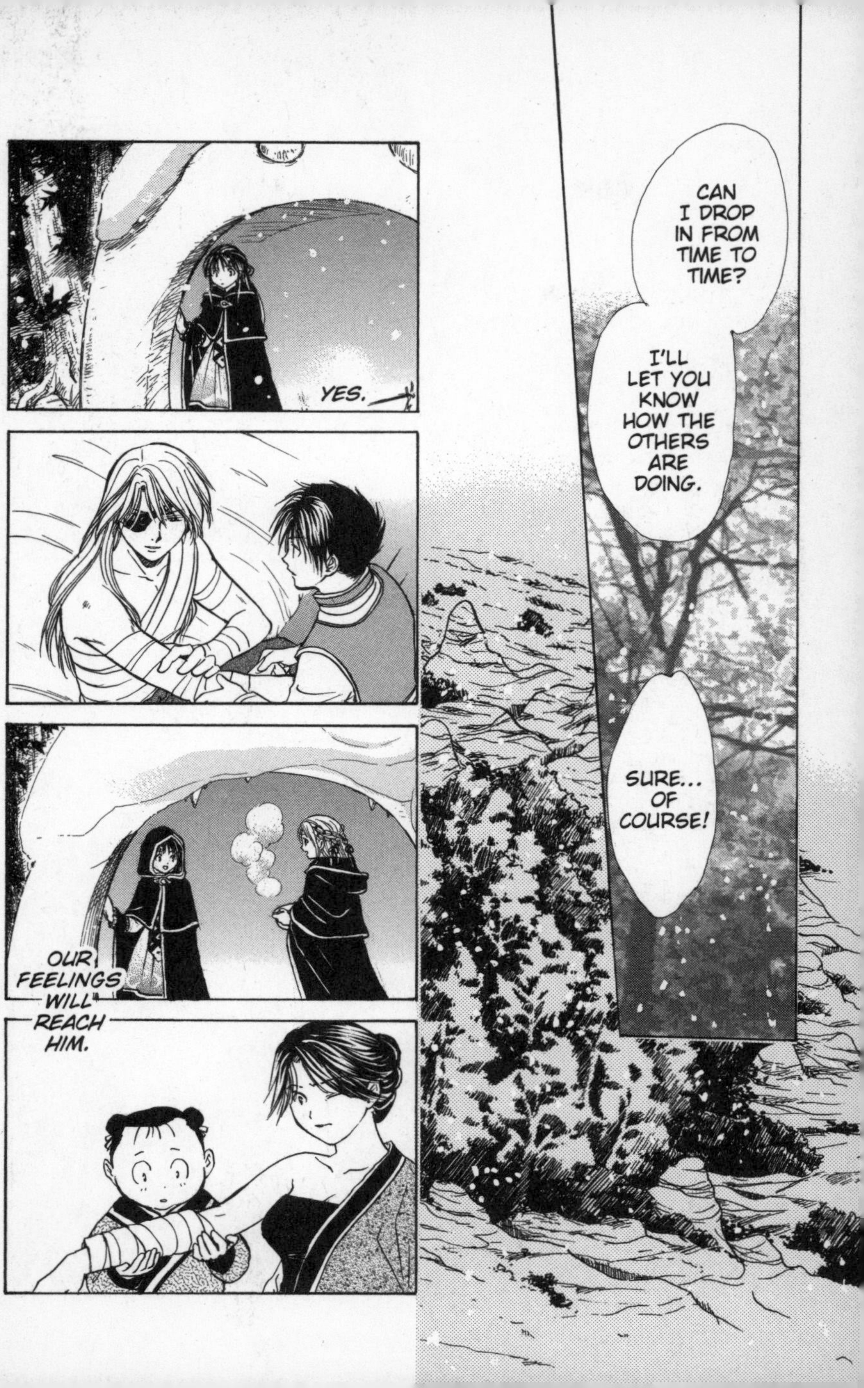
CAN I DROP IN FROM TIME TO TIME?
I'LL LET YOU KNOW HOW THE OTHERS ARE DOING.
SURE... OF COURSE!
YES.
OUR FEELINGS WILL REACH HIM.

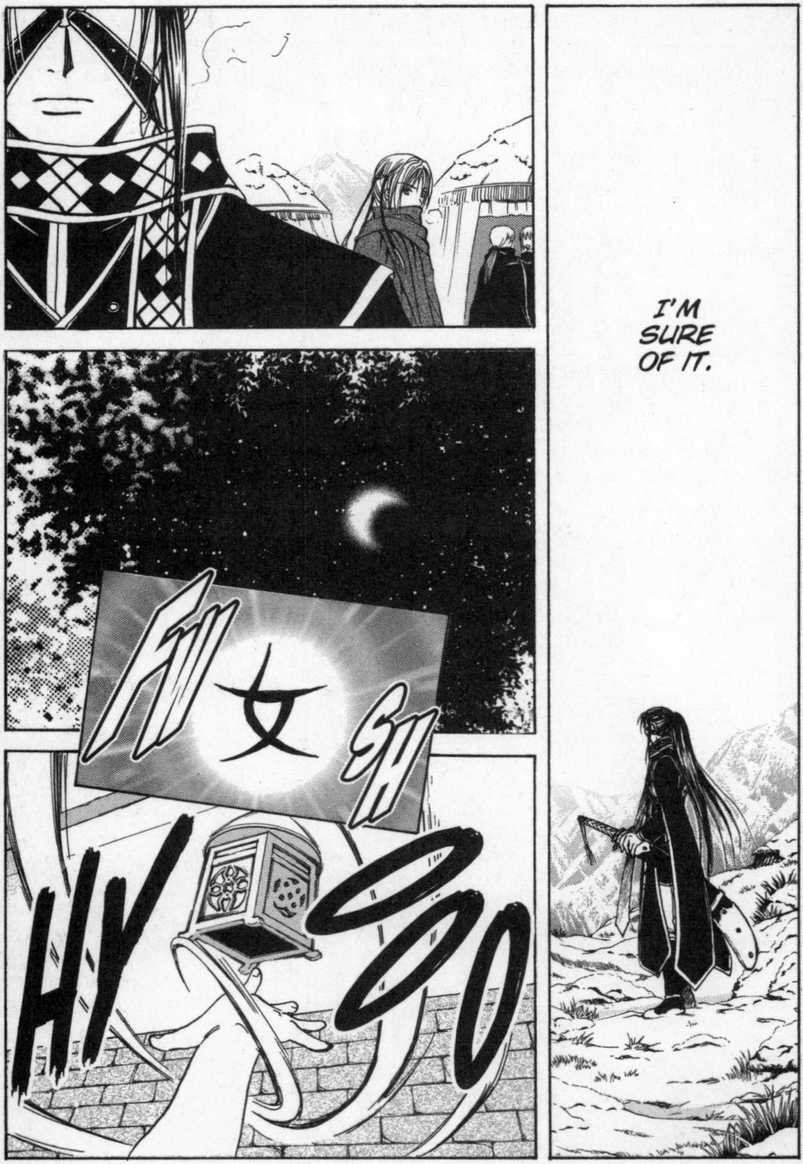
I'M SURE OF IT.
FL
SH
HY
OO

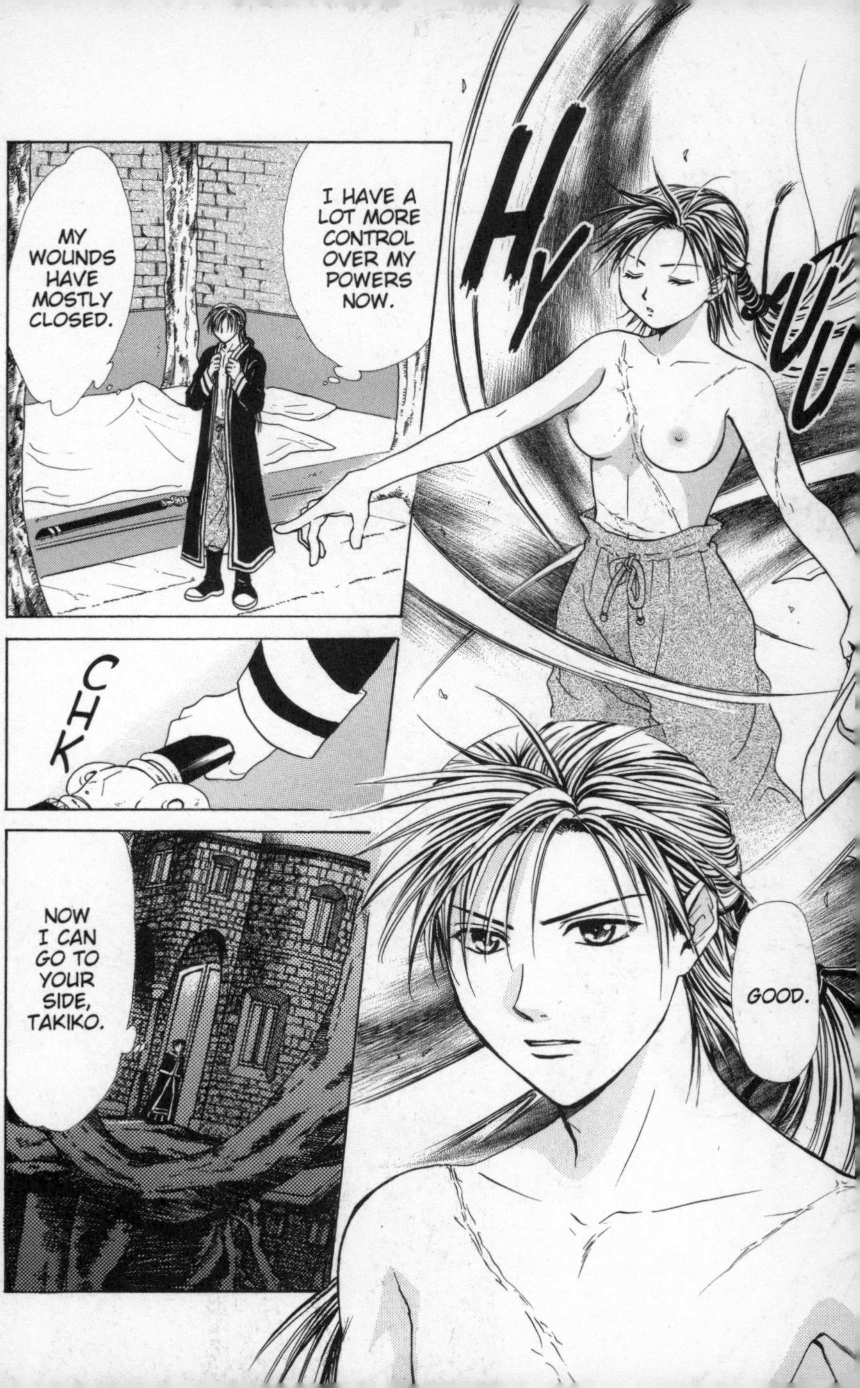
HYUUU
GOOD.
I HAVE A LOT MORE CONTROL OVER MY POWERS NOW.
MY WOUNDS HAVE MOSTLY CLOSED.
CHK
NOW I CAN GO TO YOUR SIDE, TAKIKO.

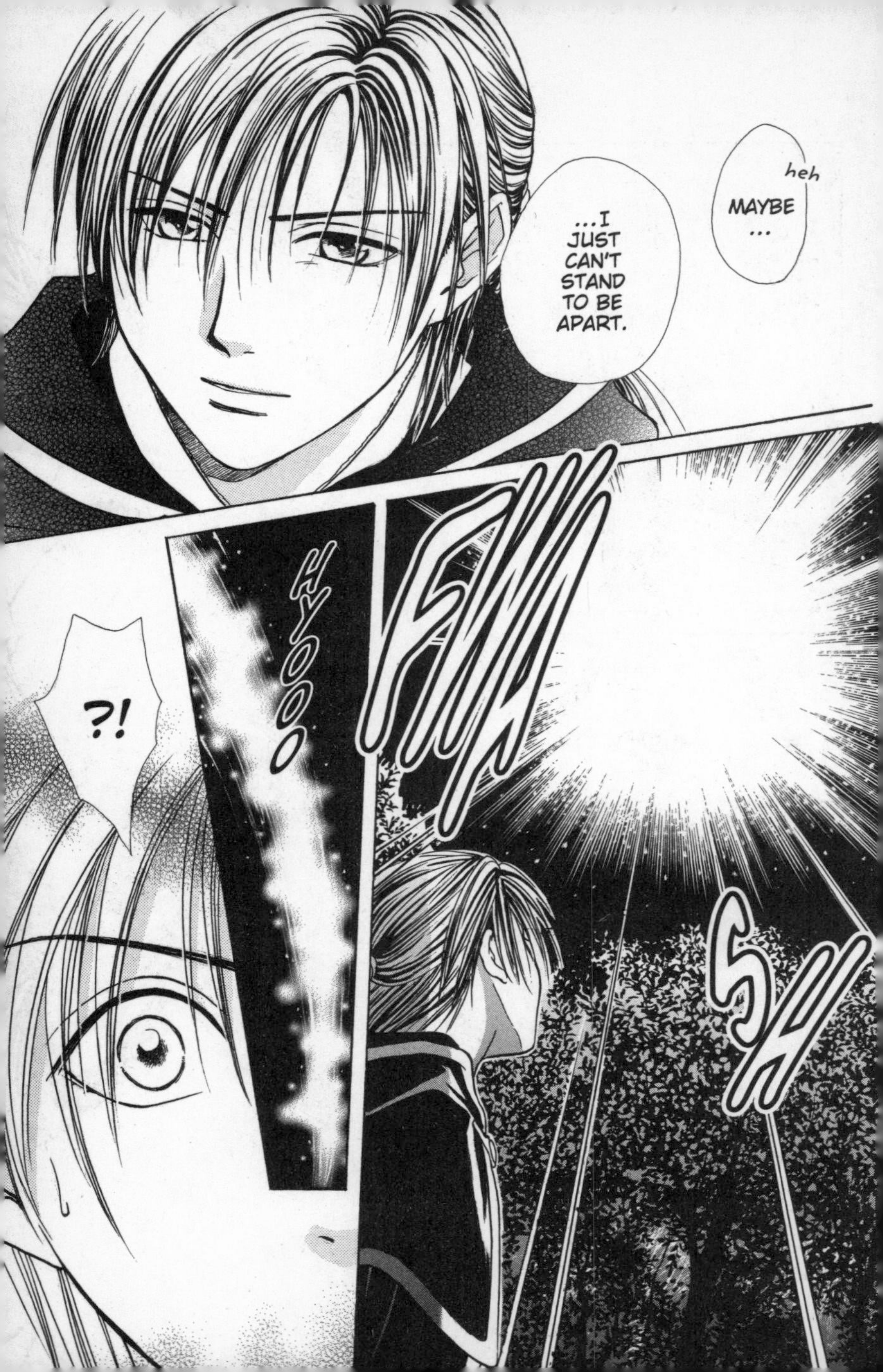
heh
MAYBE ...
...I JUST CAN'T STAND TO BE APART.
HYOOO
?!

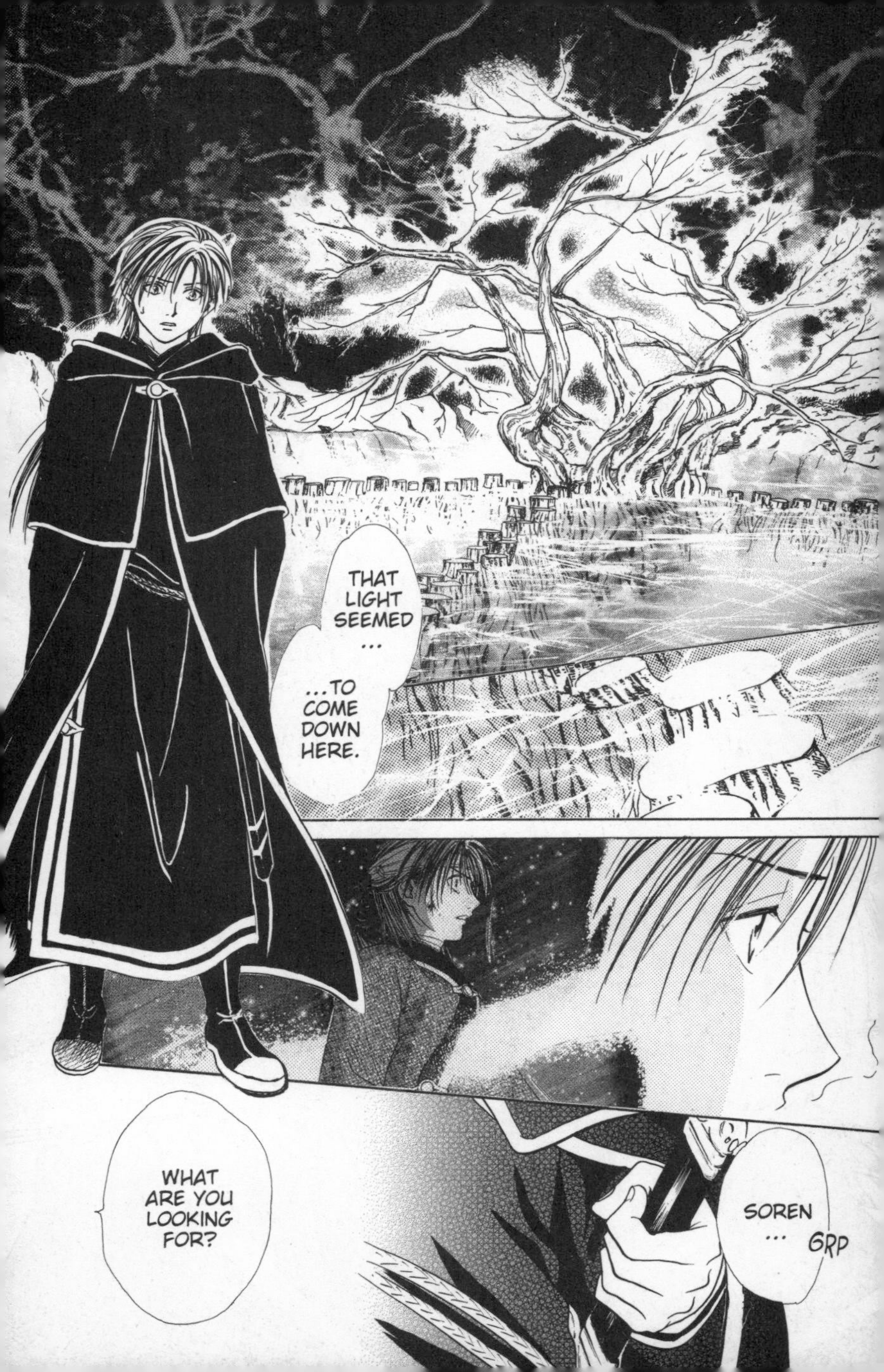
THAT LIGHT SEEMED ...
...TO COME DOWN HERE.
SOREN ...
GRP
WHAT ARE YOU LOOKING FOR?

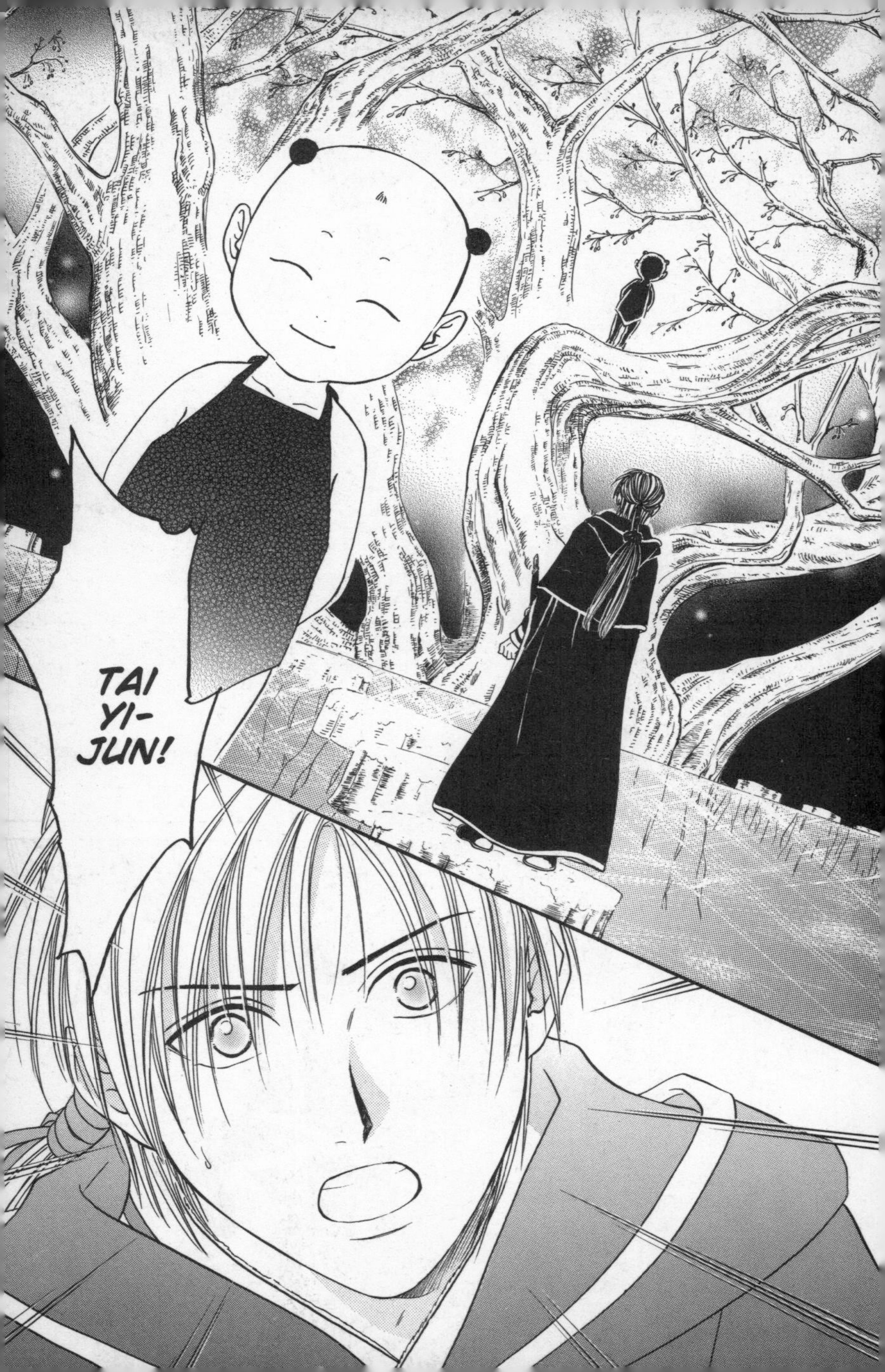
TAI YI-JUN!

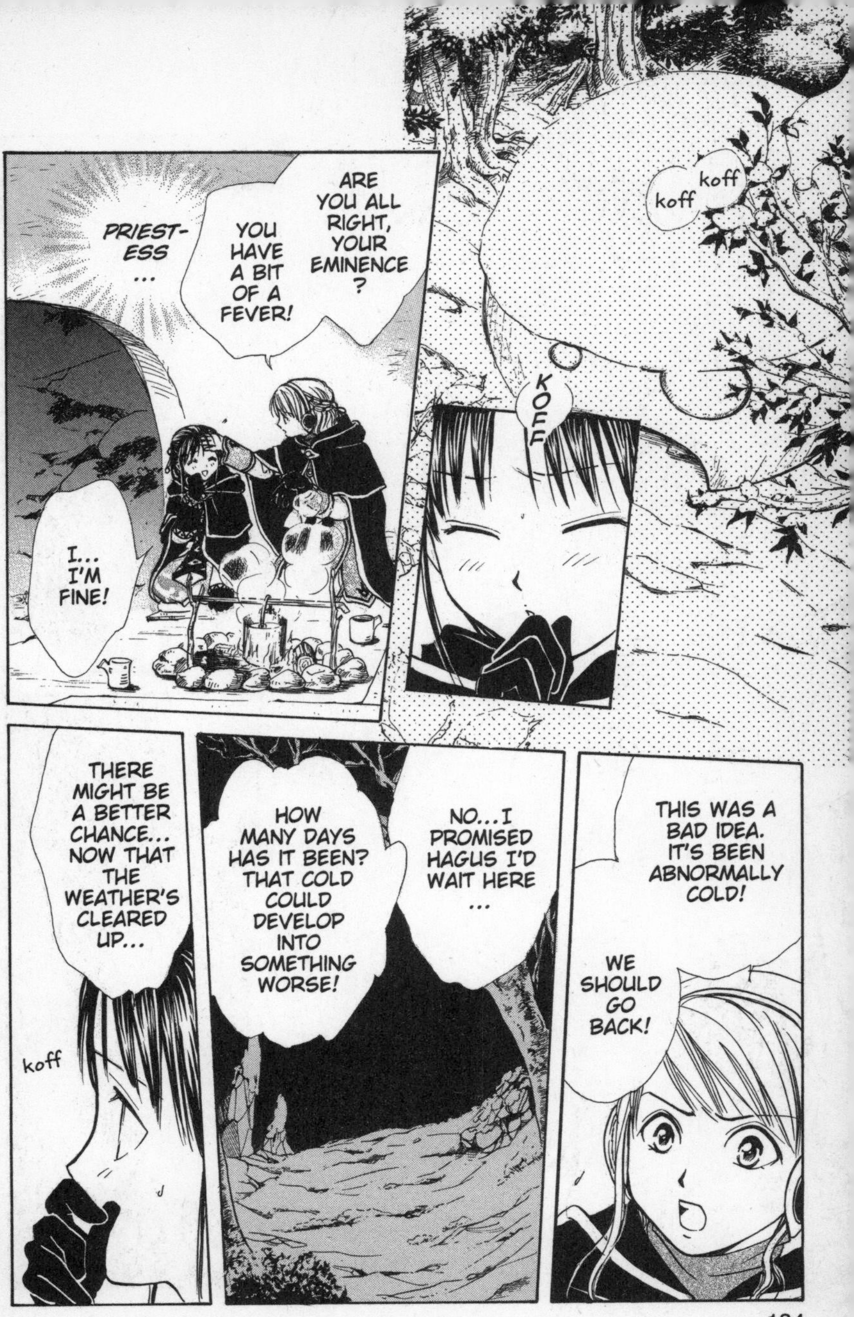

koff koff
KOFF
ARE YOU ALL RIGHT, YOUR EMINENCE?
YOU HAVE A BIT OF A FEVER!
PRIEST-ESS...
I... I'M FINE!
THIS WAS A BAD IDEA. IT'S BEEN ABNORMALLY COLD!
WE SHOULD GO BACK!
NO...I PROMISED HAGUS I'D WAIT HERE...
HOW MANY DAYS HAS IT BEEN? THAT COLD COULD DEVELOP INTO SOMETHING WORSE!
THERE MIGHT BE A BETTER CHANCE... NOW THAT THE WEATHER'S CLEARED UP...
koff

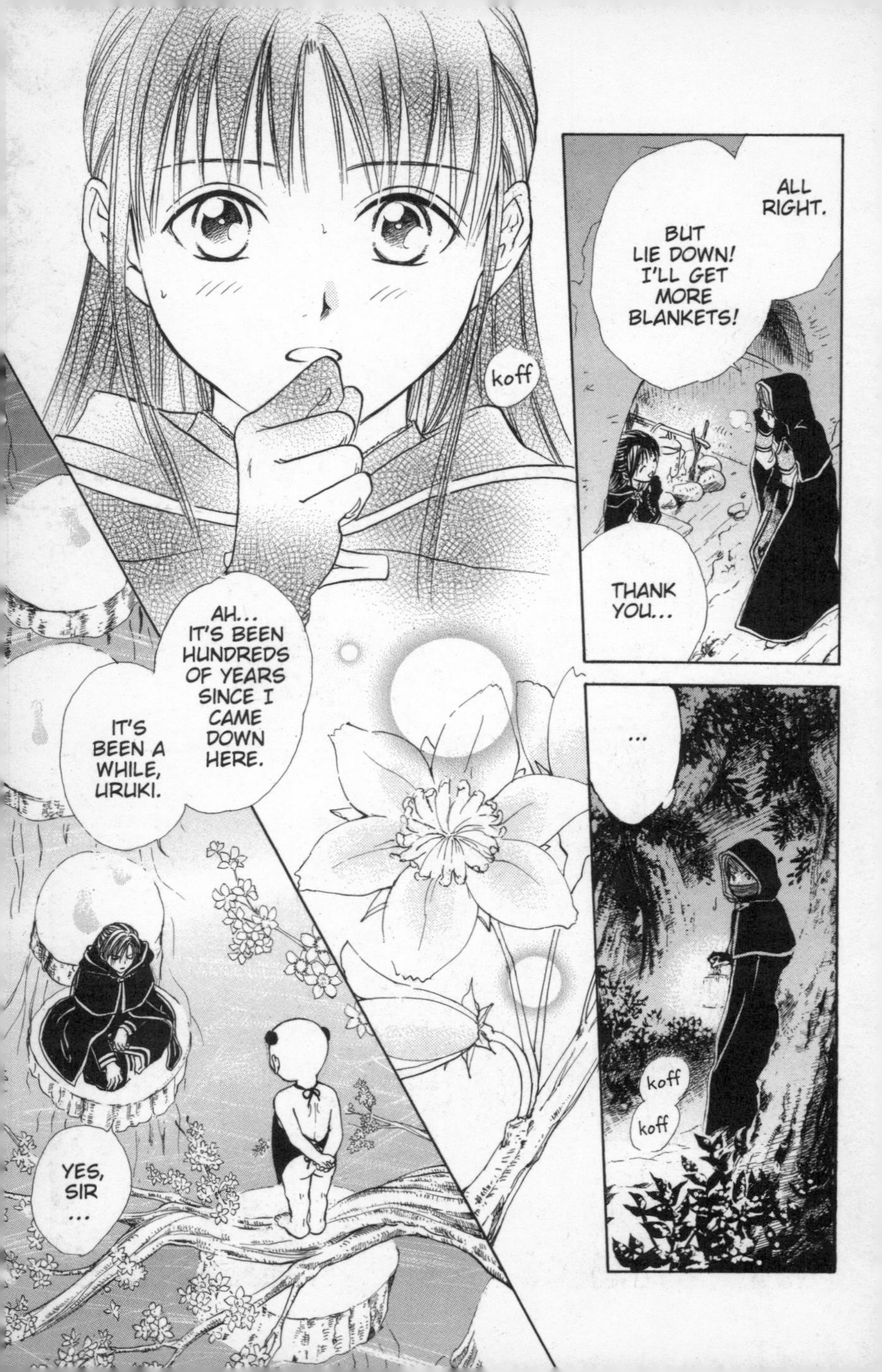
ALL RIGHT.
BUT LIE DOWN! I'LL GET MORE BLANKETS!
THANK YOU...
...
koff
koff
koff
AH... IT'S BEEN HUNDREDS OF YEARS SINCE I CAME DOWN HERE.
IT'S BEEN A WHILE, URUKI.
YES, SIR ...

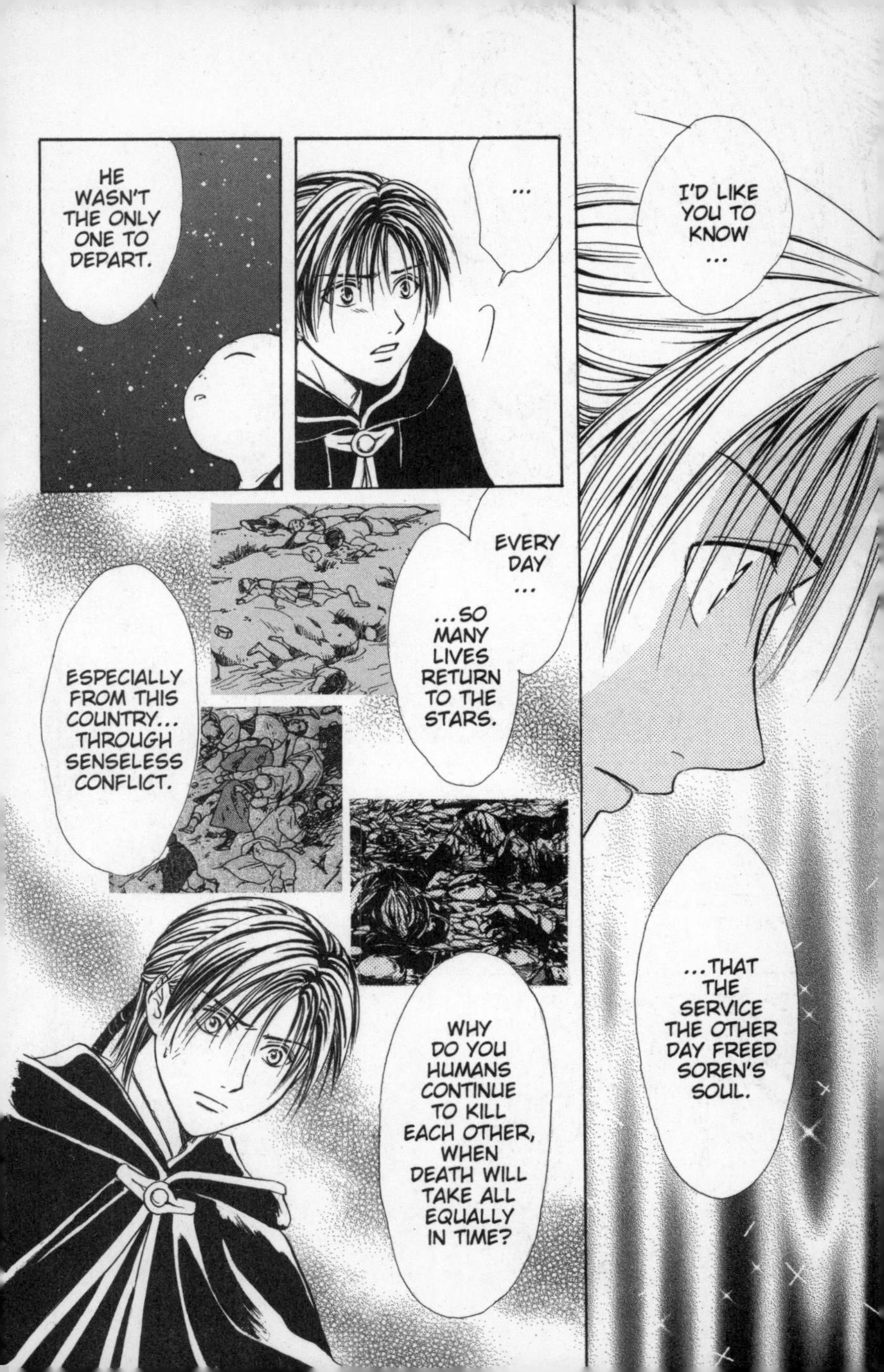
I'D LIKE YOU TO KNOW ...
...THAT THE SERVICE THE OTHER DAY FREED SOREN'S SOUL.
...
HE WASN'T THE ONLY ONE TO DEPART.
EVERY DAY ...
...SO MANY LIVES RETURN TO THE STARS.
ESPECIALLY FROM THIS COUNTRY... THROUGH SENSELESS CONFLICT.
WHY DO YOU HUMANS CONTINUE TO KILL EACH OTHER, WHEN DEATH WILL TAKE ALL EQUALLY IN TIME?

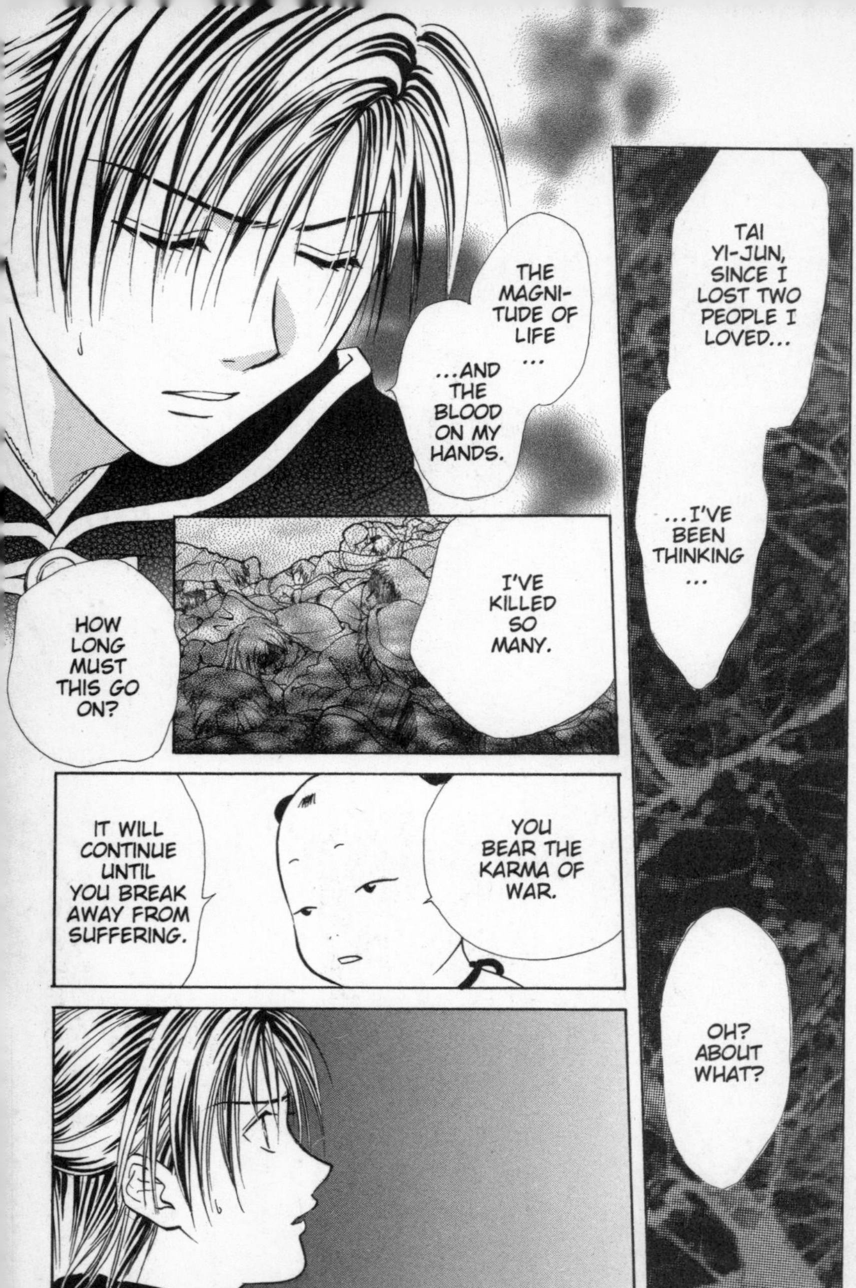
TAI YI-JUN, SINCE I LOST TWO PEOPLE I LOVED...
...I'VE BEEN THINKING...
OH? ABOUT WHAT?
THE MAGNITUDE OF LIFE...
...AND THE BLOOD ON MY HANDS.
I'VE KILLED SO MANY.
HOW LONG MUST THIS GO ON?
YOU BEAR THE KARMA OF WAR.
IT WILL CONTINUE UNTIL YOU BREAK AWAY FROM SUFFERING.

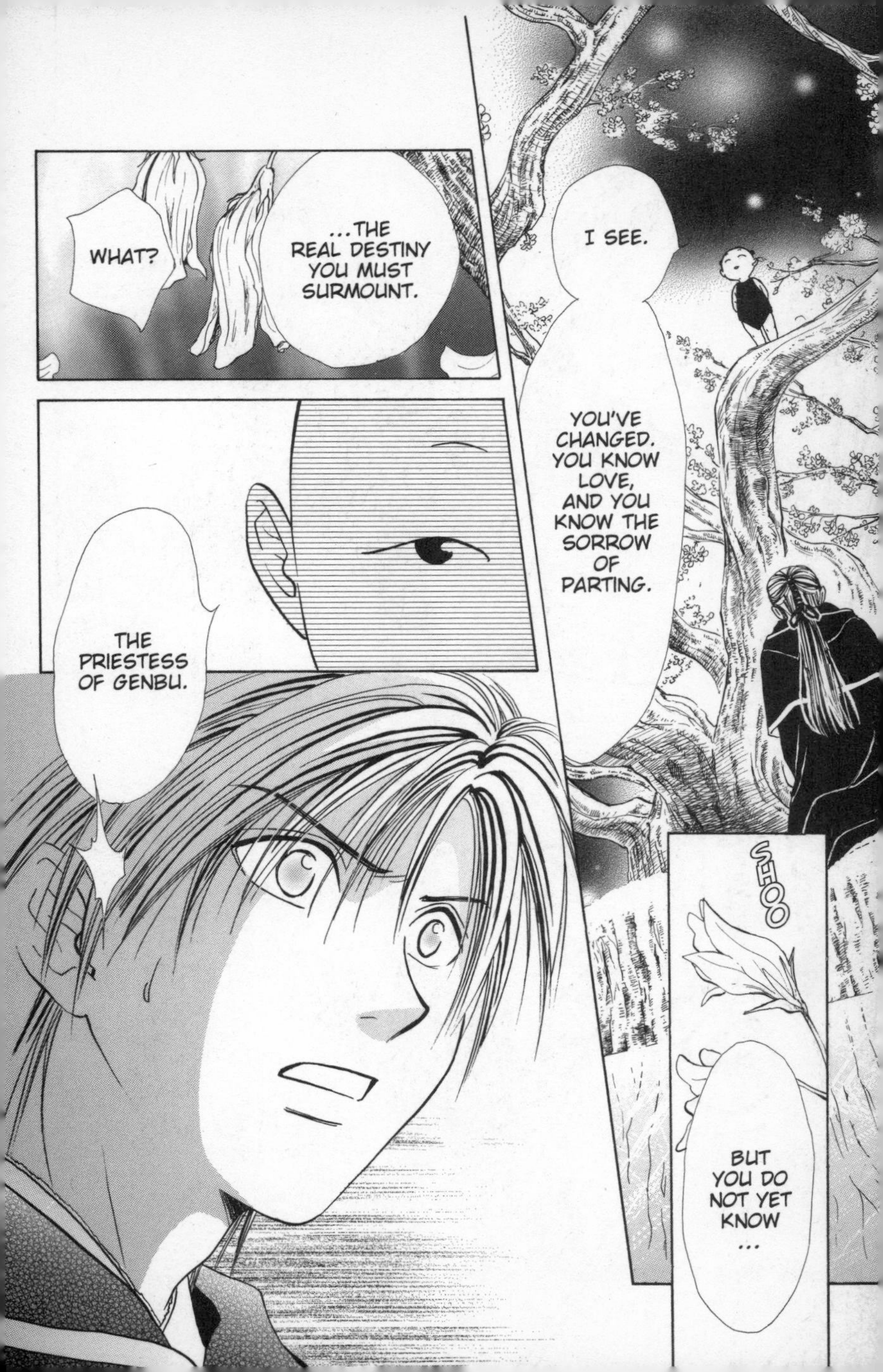
I SEE.
YOU'VE CHANGED. YOU KNOW LOVE, AND YOU KNOW THE SORROW OF PARTING.
SHOO
BUT YOU DO NOT YET KNOW ...
...THE REAL DESTINY YOU MUST SURMOUNT.
WHAT?
THE PRIESTESS OF GENBU.

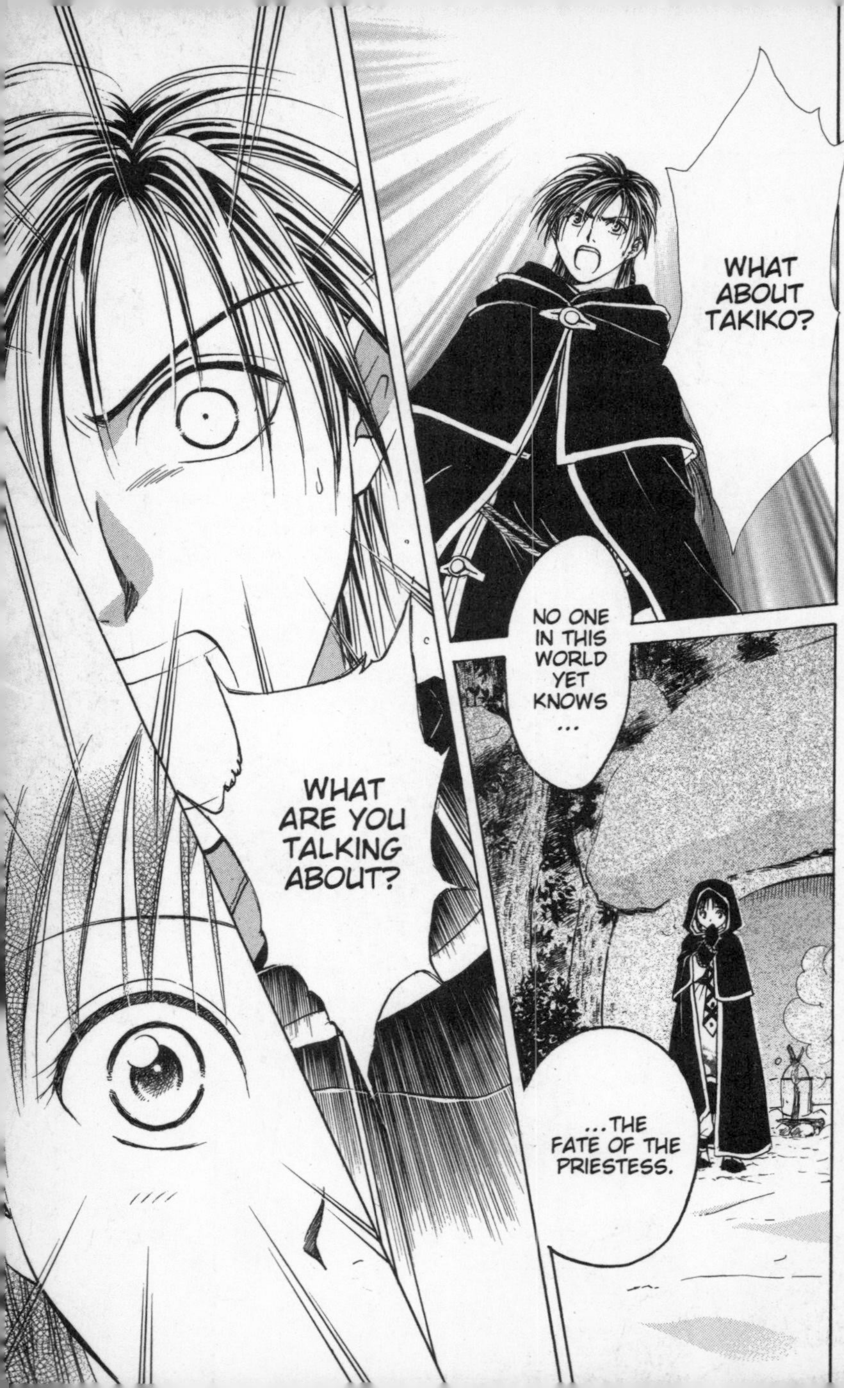
WHAT ABOUT TAKIKO?
NO ONE IN THIS WORLD YET KNOWS...
...THE FATE OF THE PRIESTESS.
WHAT ARE YOU TALKING ABOUT?

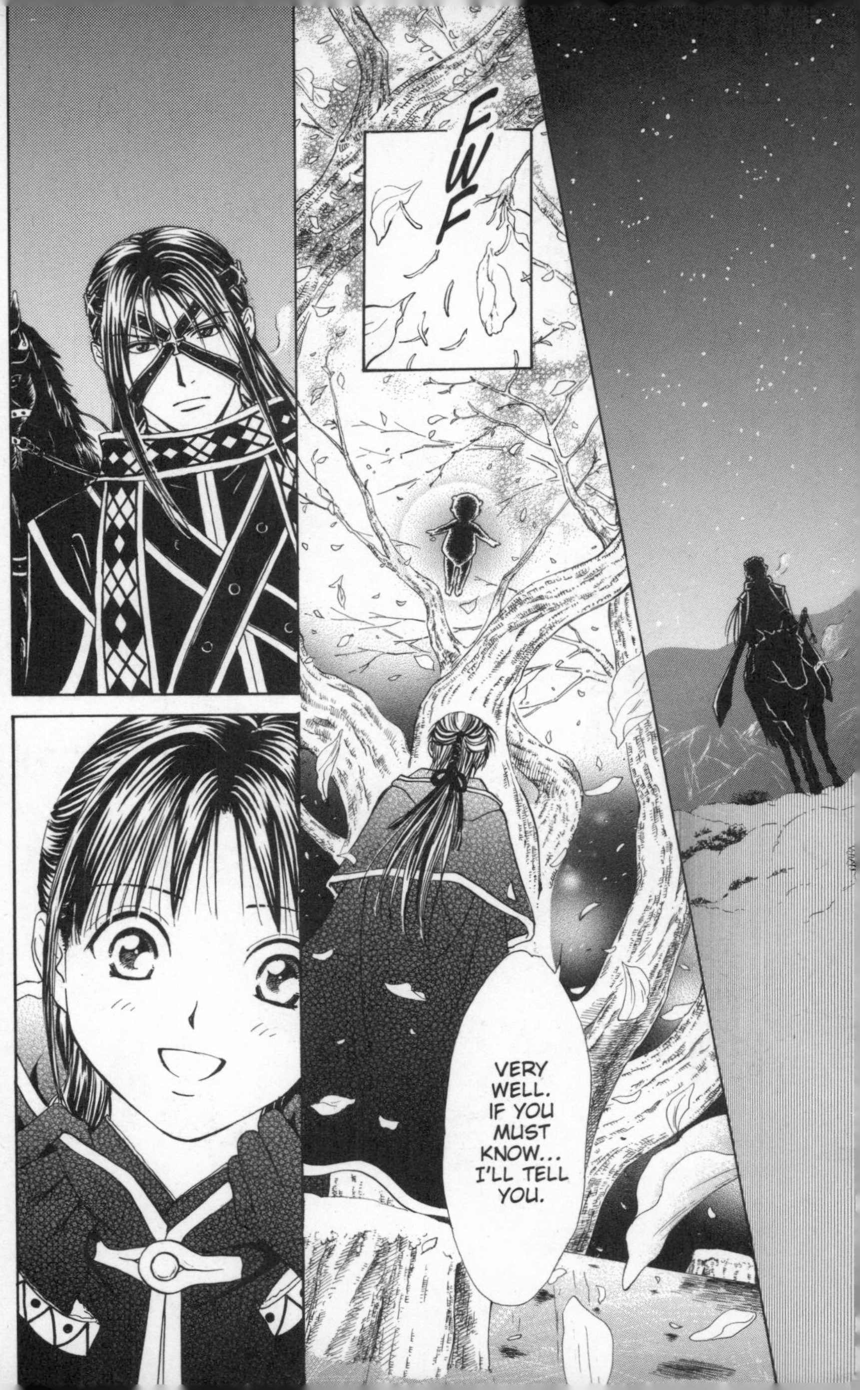
FWF
VERY WELL. IF YOU MUST KNOW... I'LL TELL YOU.

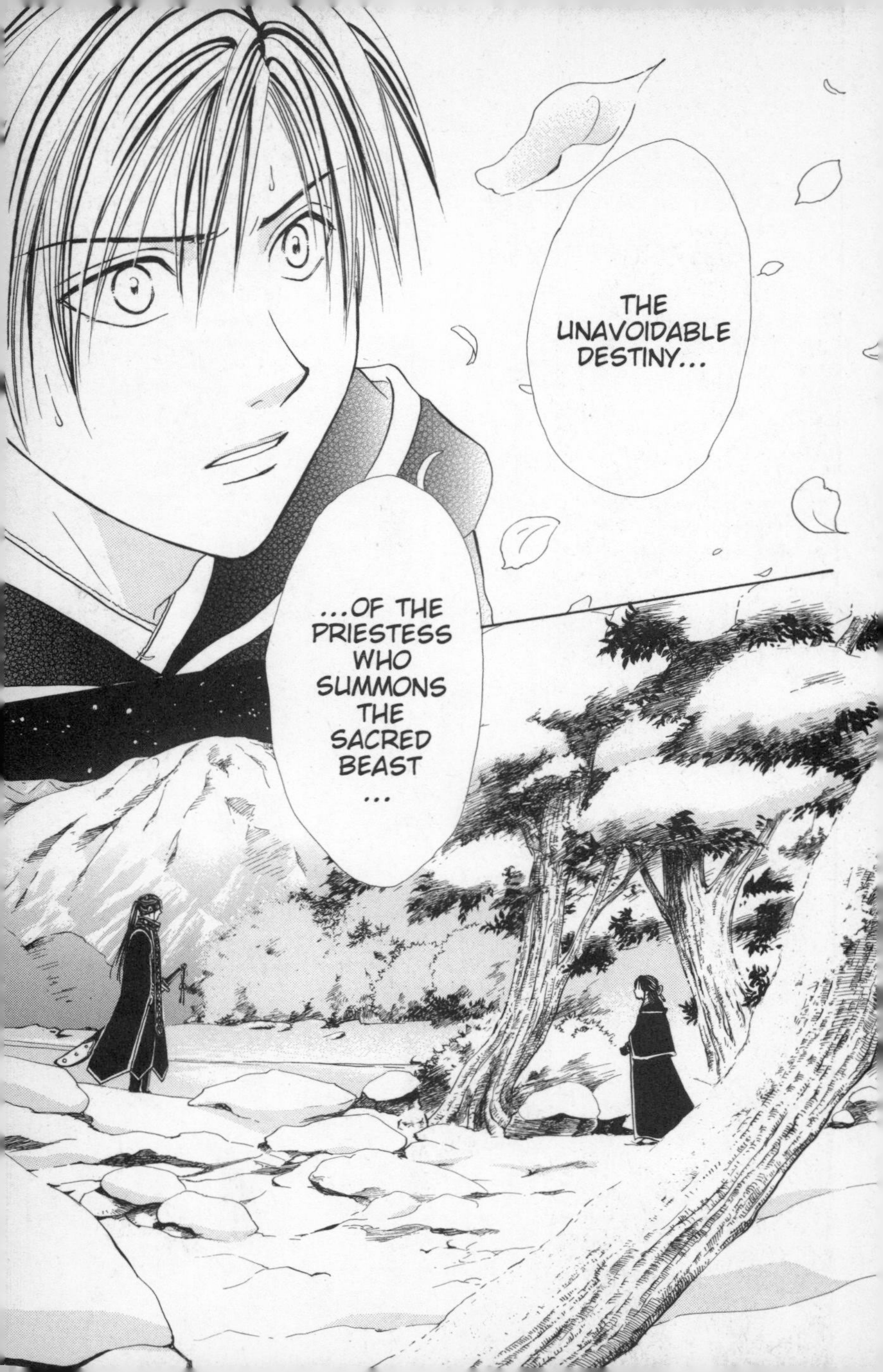
THE UNAVOIDABLE DESTINY...
...OF THE PRIESTESS WHO SUMMONS THE SACRED BEAST ...

3

I'm kind of going backward in terms of announcements, but in April, **Absolute Boyfriend** is going to be a drama series on TV! Wow! This is the first time one of my series has been adapted into live action. The characters will be older than they are the manga, and there are other changes, but the basic story will be the same (I know drama series often change the story a lot). I just hope it'll be entertaining even if it ends up completely different.

I feel the same way about anime adaptations. I like it when the adaptations build on the original manga to become good in their own way. They could even be better! I'd feel jealous... but also happy. I'd learn from it and do better next time! I hope you'll check out the drama series, games and novels and send me your comments. These days, readers seem to be satisfied just writing their opinions on blogs, and fewer people write directly to the creator.

It's a sign of the times...

I'm not as eager to write if I don't get any feedback. Hm, speaking of feedback...I've received some letters insisting that "Urumiya" should be spelled "Uruyami"... I got some mail like that during the first FY too. As I explained at the time, there are several possible readings of the Celestial names, so the spelling may be different depending on which reference book you read. I used whichever spelling I thought looked coolest. They're not wrong.

4

Another reading for "Tamahome" is "Tamaono." I have to admit, now I think "Hoto-ori" might have been better than "Hotohori." Too late...It's a very unusual name (can't change it now).

Oh, one more thing...the first volume of my new manga **Sakura Gari** will be out in mid-April. I wrote in Volume 6 that I don't recommend it for kids under 15... and a 15-year-old girl wrote to ask me, "Why?" Don't make me spell it out for you! I-it's because the story is very "mature"!! I guess in this day and age, younger people are reading more risqué stories, so maybe it doesn't matter. (Make up your mind, Watase!) It's not geared for young readers, so it might not be as fun to read. It's a very dark, serious story about the unpleasant side of humanity, so you need to be a certain age to fully appreciate what's going on. It's pretty expensive too. Though there are only going to be three volumes total. Sorry...

I had a one-shot story published in **Shonen Sunday** at the beginning of the year. I plan to do more work like that. I'll work hard on **Genbu** too, of course, as long as I have fans who want to read it. There are a lot of series I want to do. My official website is going through a redesign. Please check it out if you can. I don't know yet how it's going to look... Anyway, my manga are like my children, so I'll put my heart and soul into them. I don't have time to stay in bed with a hernia!!

See you in the next (tumultuous) volume!

MOST DISTANT PARTING

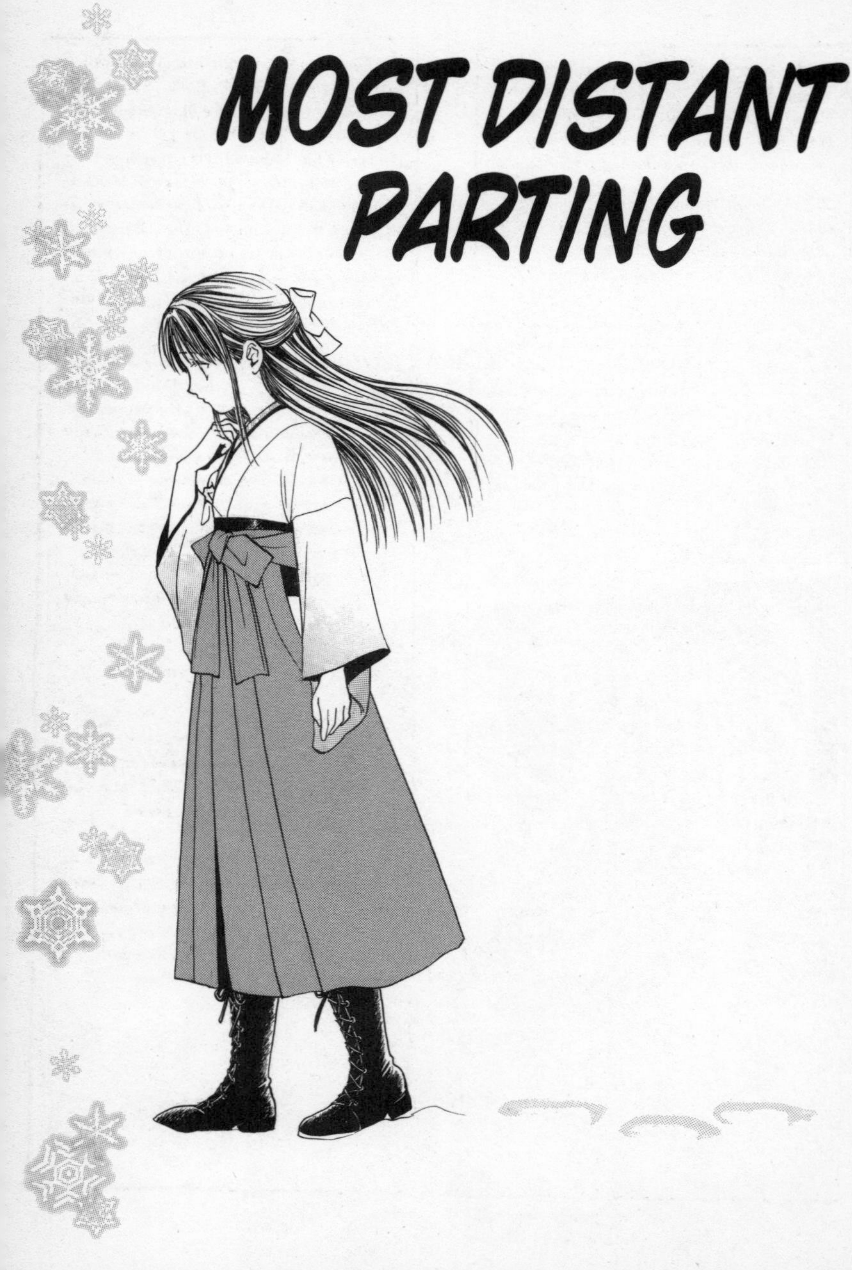

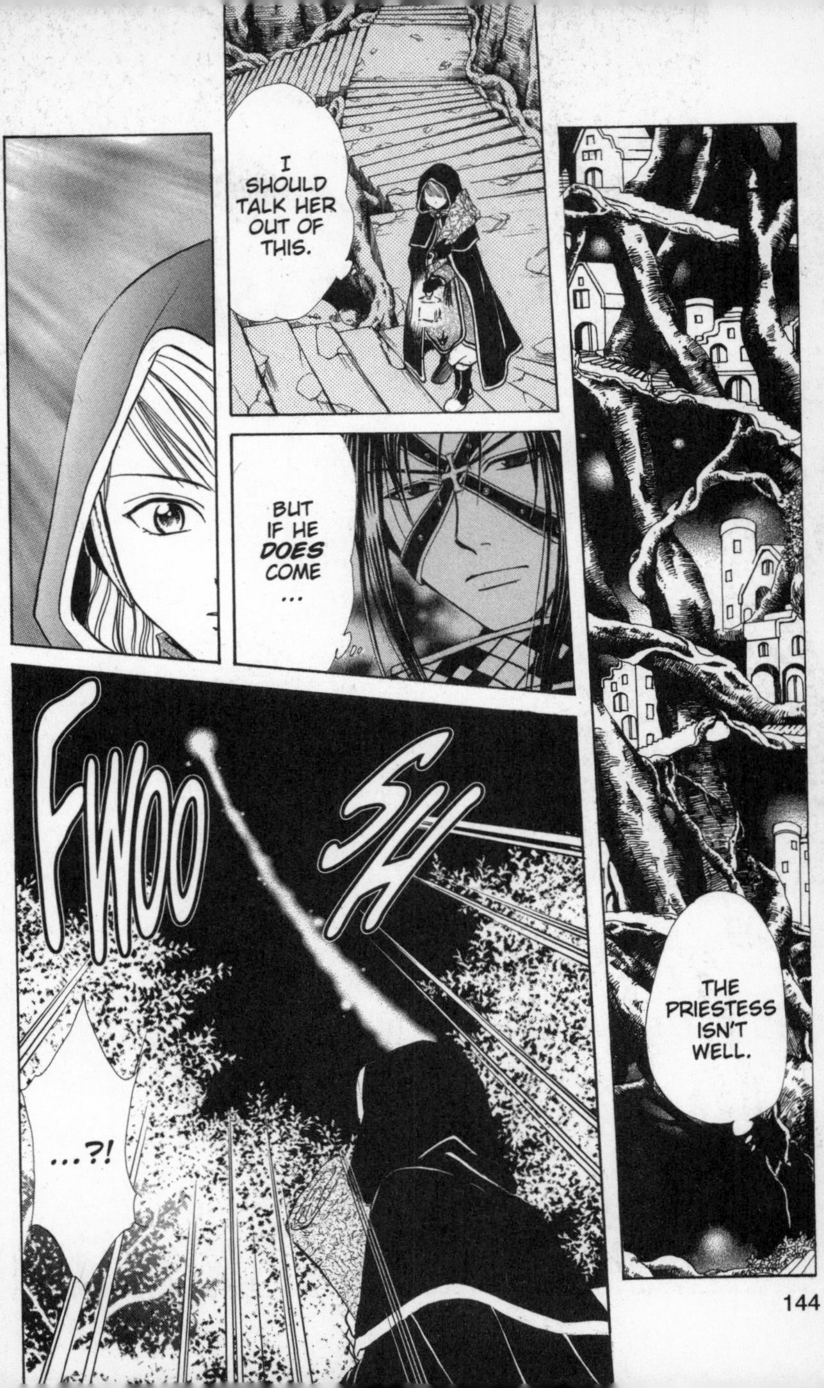
THE PRIESTESS ISN'T WELL.
I SHOULD TALK HER OUT OF THIS.
BUT IF HE *DOES* COME ...
FWOOSH
...?!

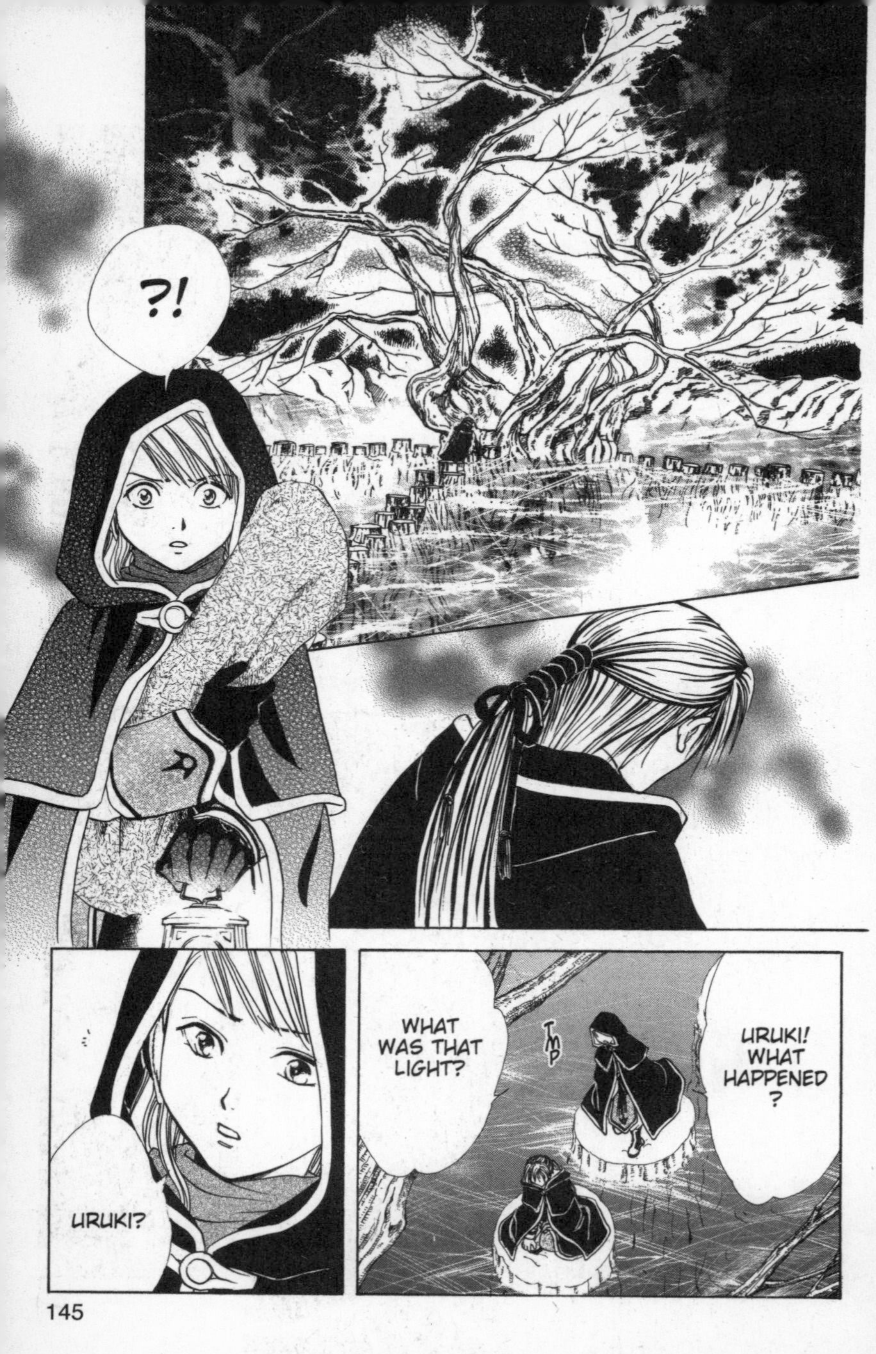
?!
URUKI! WHAT HAPPENED?
WHAT WAS THAT LIGHT?
TMP
URUKI?

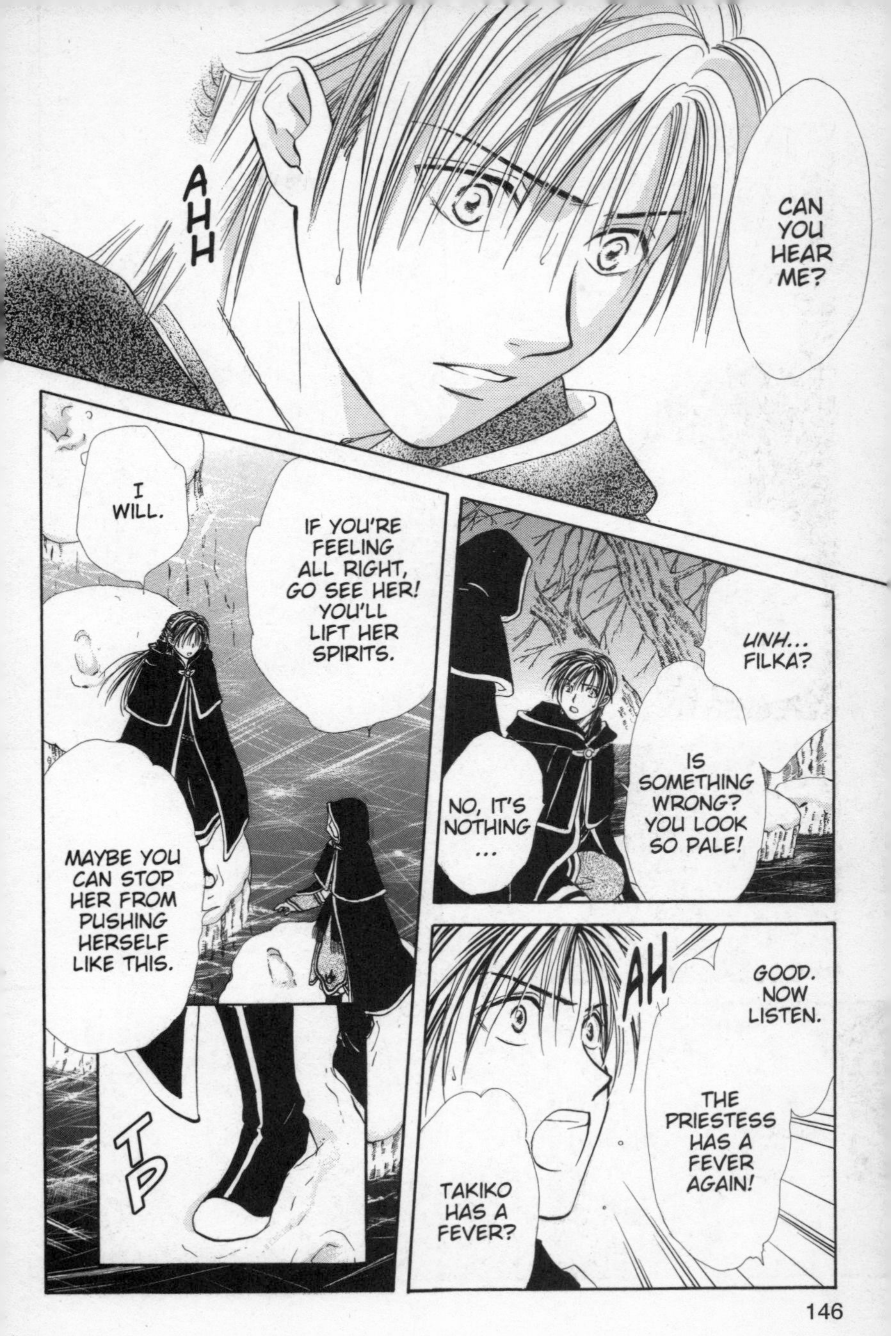
CAN YOU HEAR ME?
AHH
UNH... FILKA?
IS SOMETHING WRONG? YOU LOOK SO PALE!
NO, IT'S NOTHING ...
AH
GOOD. NOW LISTEN.
THE PRIESTESS HAS A FEVER AGAIN!
TAKIKO HAS A FEVER?
IF YOU'RE FEELING ALL RIGHT, GO SEE HER! YOU'LL LIFT HER SPIRITS.
I WILL.
MAYBE YOU CAN STOP HER FROM PUSHING HERSELF LIKE THIS.
TP

WHY ARE YOU ACTING SO STRANGE?

URUKI?

I'M SORRY.

YOU TAKE CARE OF TAKIKO...

...

HAGUS... YOU CAME!

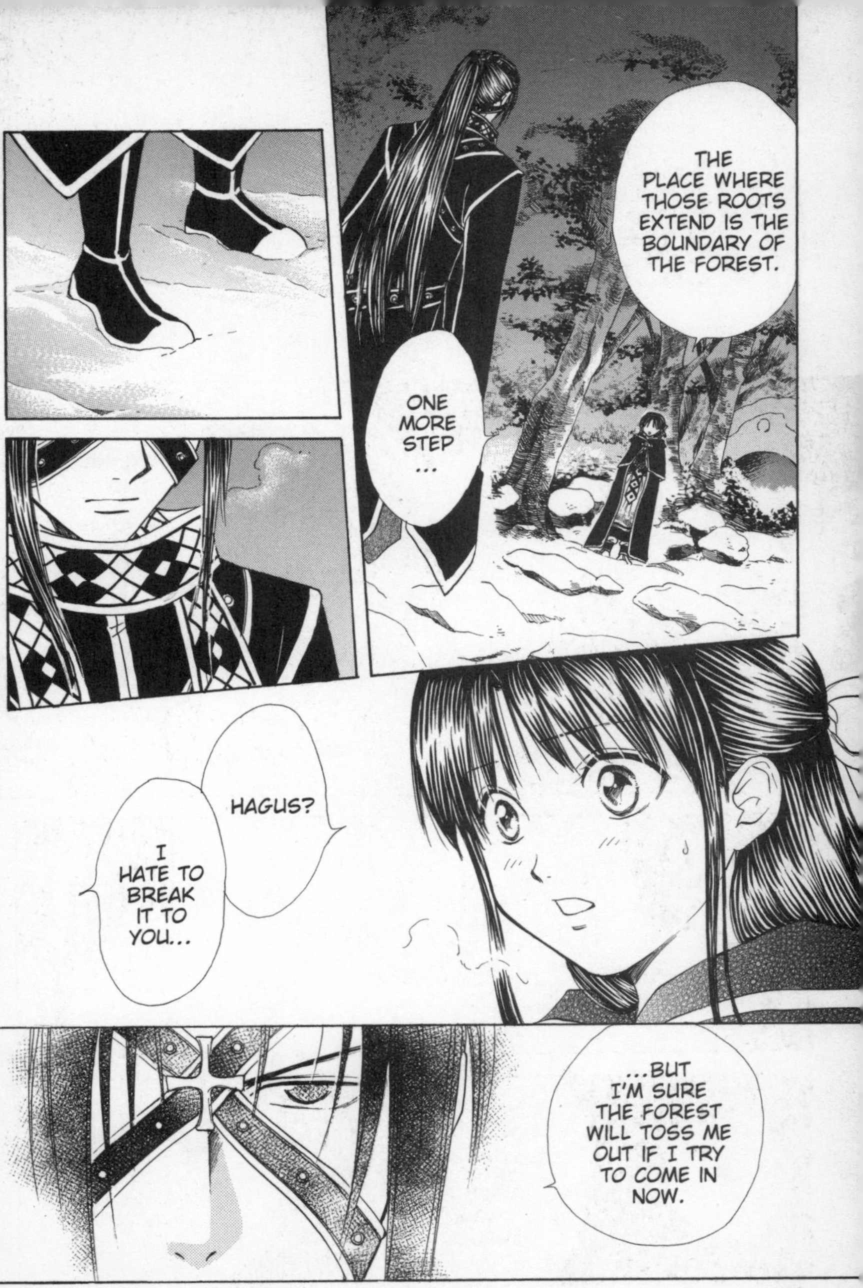
THE PLACE WHERE THOSE ROOTS EXTEND IS THE BOUNDARY OF THE FOREST.
ONE MORE STEP...
HAGUS?
I HATE TO BREAK IT TO YOU...
...BUT I'M SURE THE FOREST WILL TOSS ME OUT IF I TRY TO COME IN NOW.

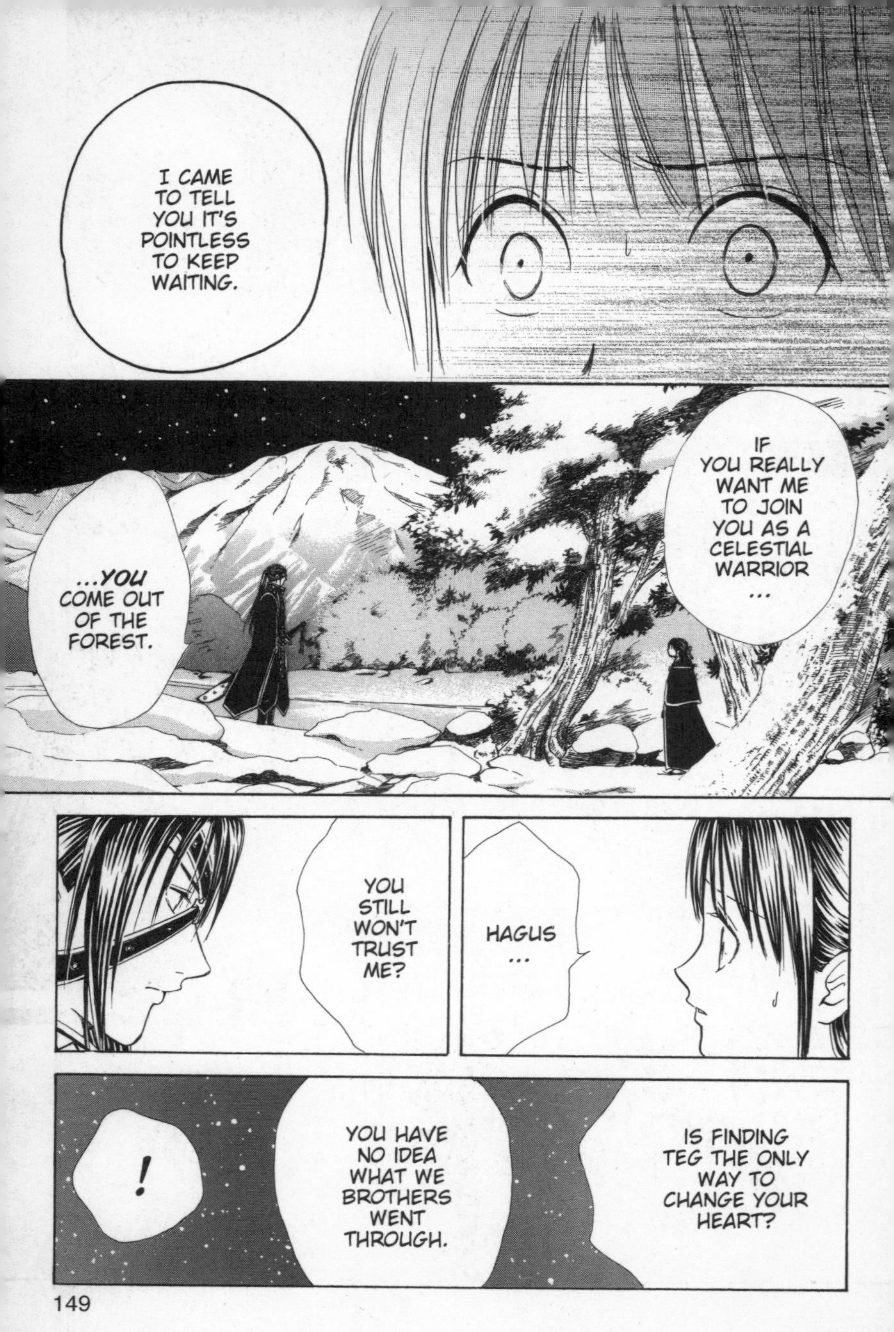
I CAME TO TELL YOU IT'S POINTLESS TO KEEP WAITING.
IF YOU REALLY WANT ME TO JOIN YOU AS A CELESTIAL WARRIOR ...
...*YOU* COME OUT OF THE FOREST.
HAGUS ...
YOU STILL WON'T TRUST ME?
IS FINDING TEG THE ONLY WAY TO CHANGE YOUR HEART?
YOU HAVE NO IDEA WHAT WE BROTHERS WENT THROUGH.
!

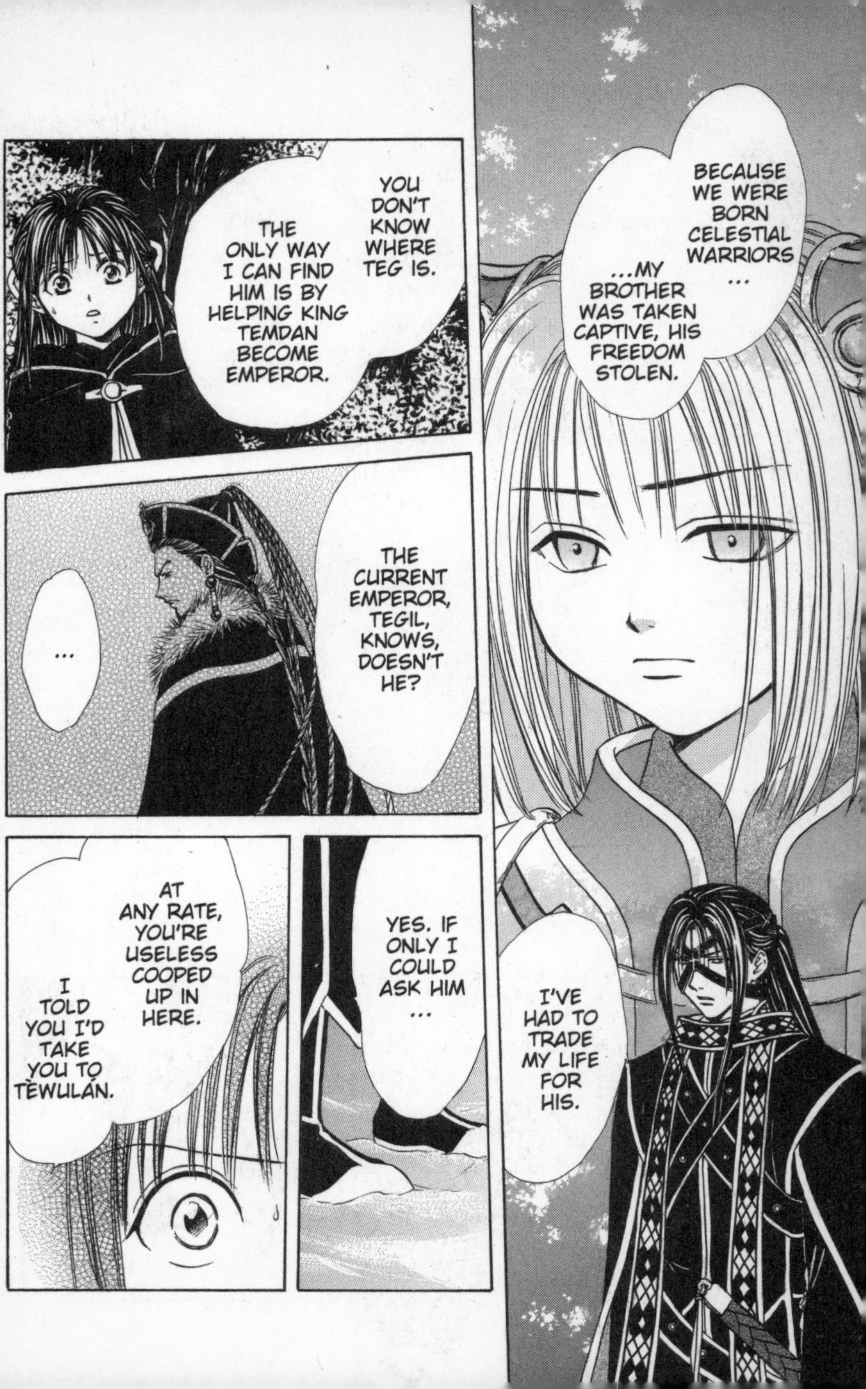
BECAUSE WE WERE BORN CELESTIAL WARRIORS...
...MY BROTHER WAS TAKEN CAPTIVE, HIS FREEDOM STOLEN.
I'VE HAD TO TRADE MY LIFE FOR HIS.
YOU DON'T KNOW WHERE TEG IS.
THE ONLY WAY I CAN FIND HIM IS BY HELPING KING TEMDAN BECOME EMPEROR.
THE CURRENT EMPEROR, TEGIL, KNOWS, DOESN'T HE?
...
YES. IF ONLY I COULD ASK HIM...
AT ANY RATE, YOU'RE USELESS COOPED UP IN HERE.
I TOLD YOU I'D TAKE YOU TO TÈWULÁN.

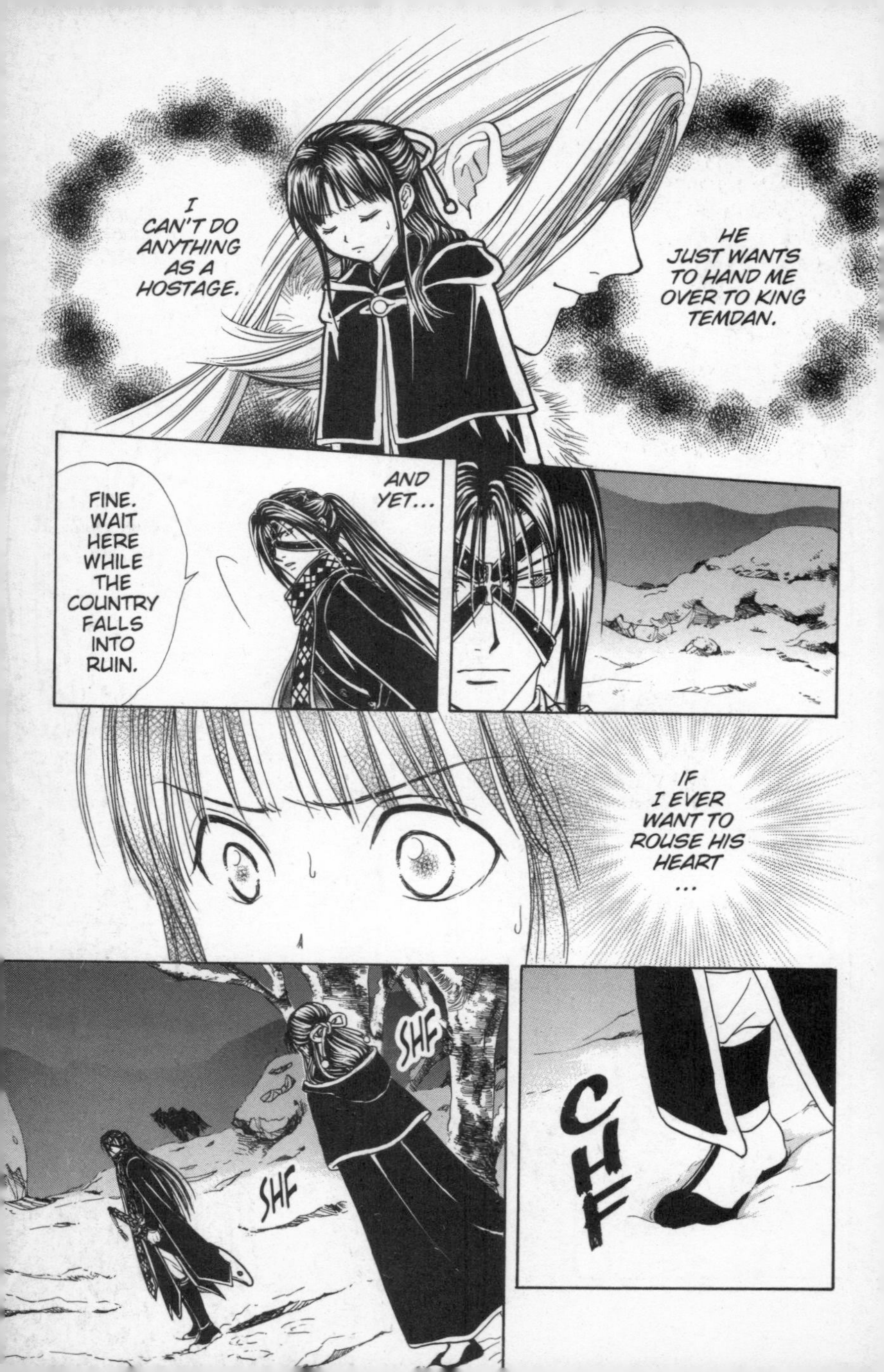
HE JUST WANTS TO HAND ME OVER TO KING TEMDAN.
I CAN'T DO ANYTHING AS A HOSTAGE.
AND YET...
FINE. WAIT HERE WHILE THE COUNTRY FALLS INTO RUIN.
IF I EVER WANT TO ROUSE HIS HEART ...
CHF
SHF
SHF

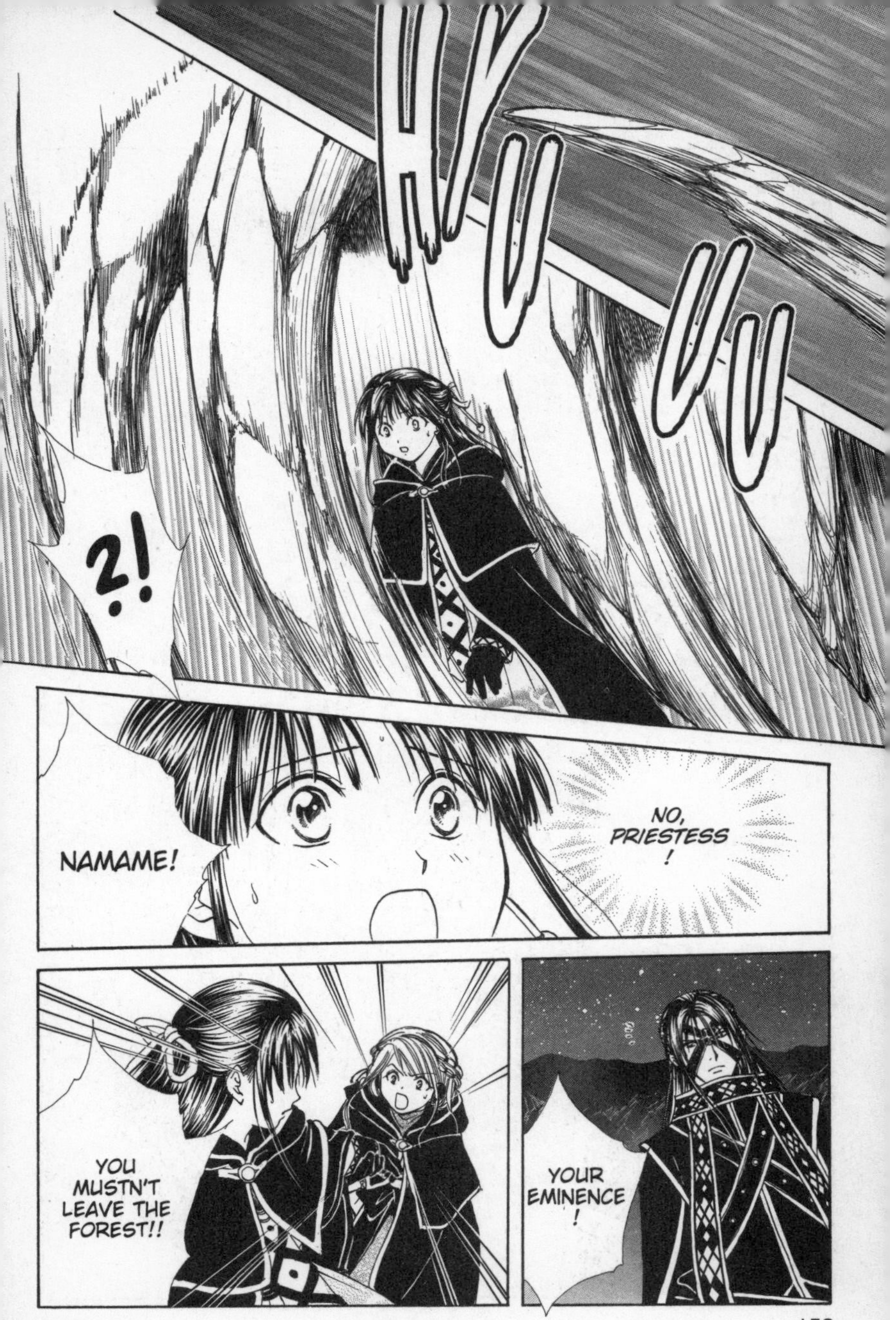
HYUUU
?!
NO, PRIESTESS!
NAMAME!
YOUR EMINENCE!
YOU MUSTN'T LEAVE THE FOREST!!

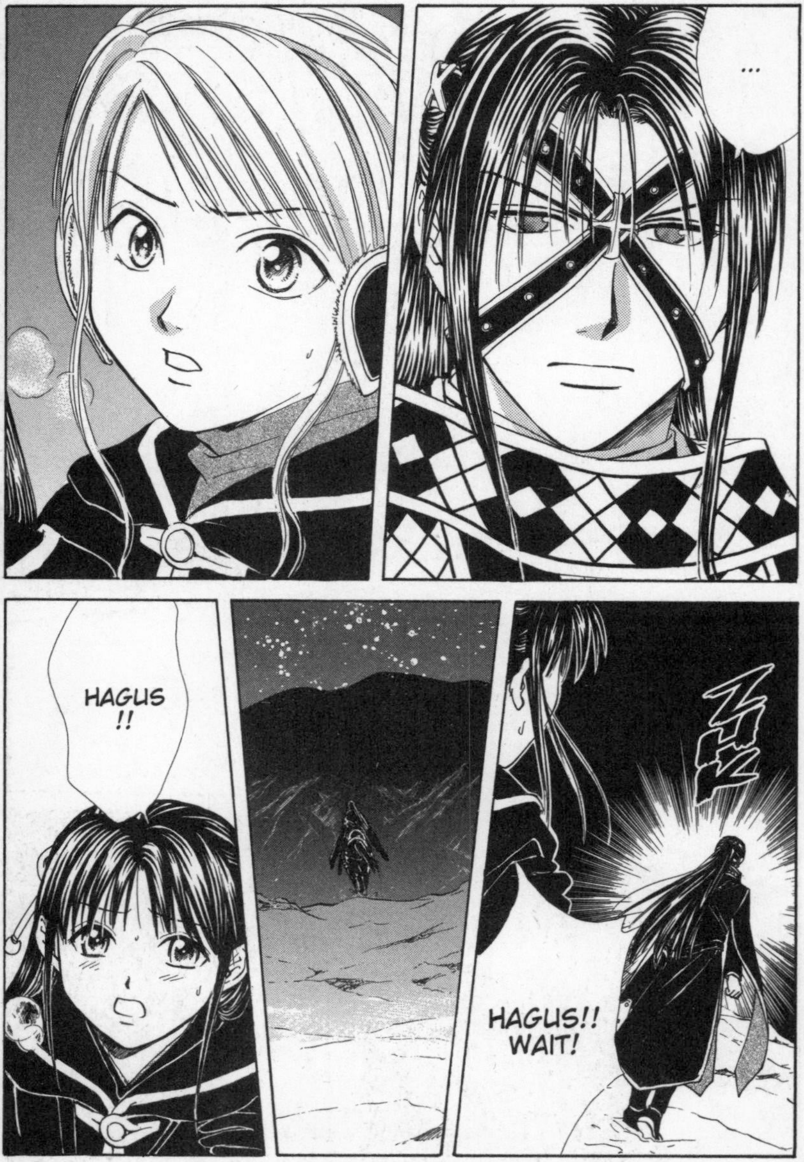
...
HAGUS!! WAIT!
HAGUS !!

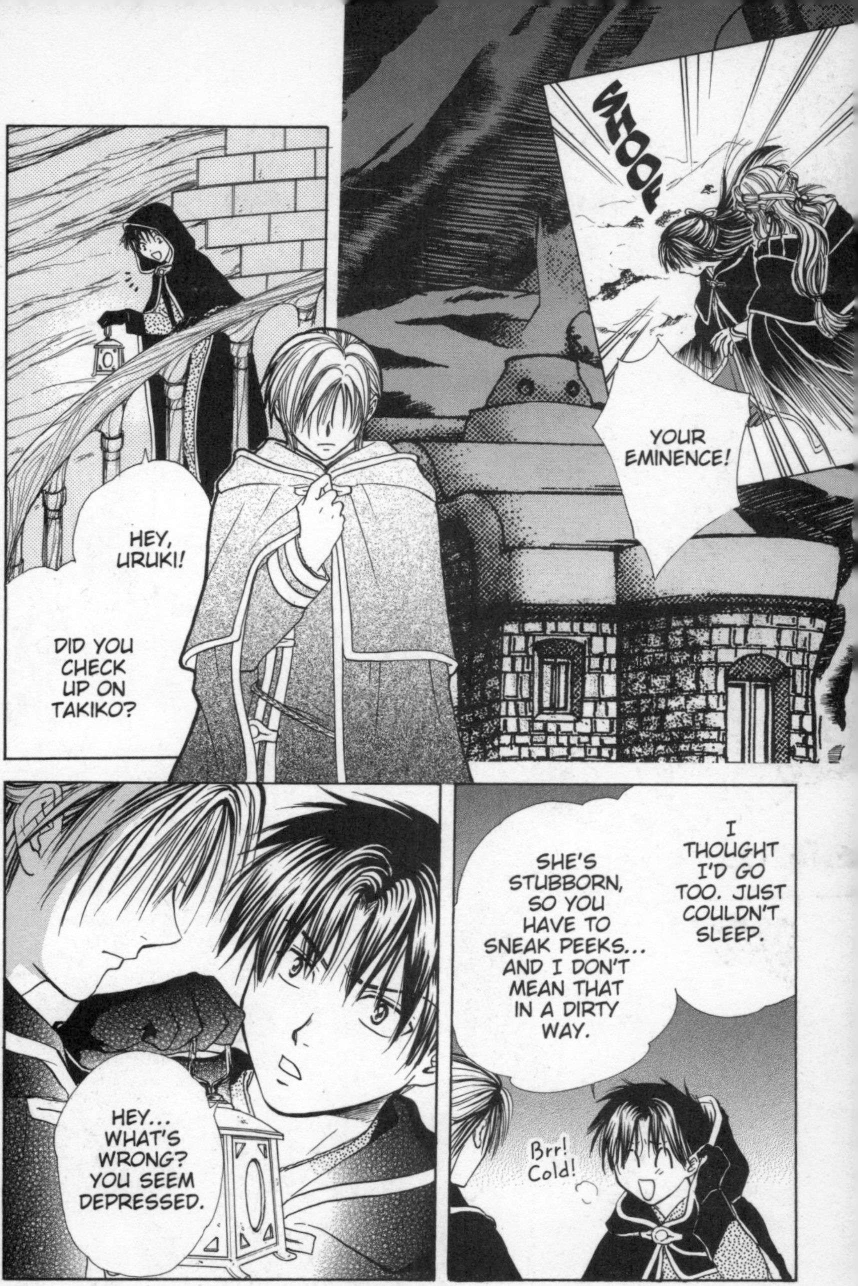
SHOOF
YOUR EMINENCE!
HEY, URUKI!
DID YOU CHECK UP ON TAKIKO?
I THOUGHT I'D GO TOO. JUST COULDN'T SLEEP.
SHE'S STUBBORN, SO YOU HAVE TO SNEAK PEEKS... AND I DON'T MEAN THAT IN A DIRTY WAY.
Brr! Cold!
HEY... WHAT'S WRONG? YOU SEEM DEPRESSED.

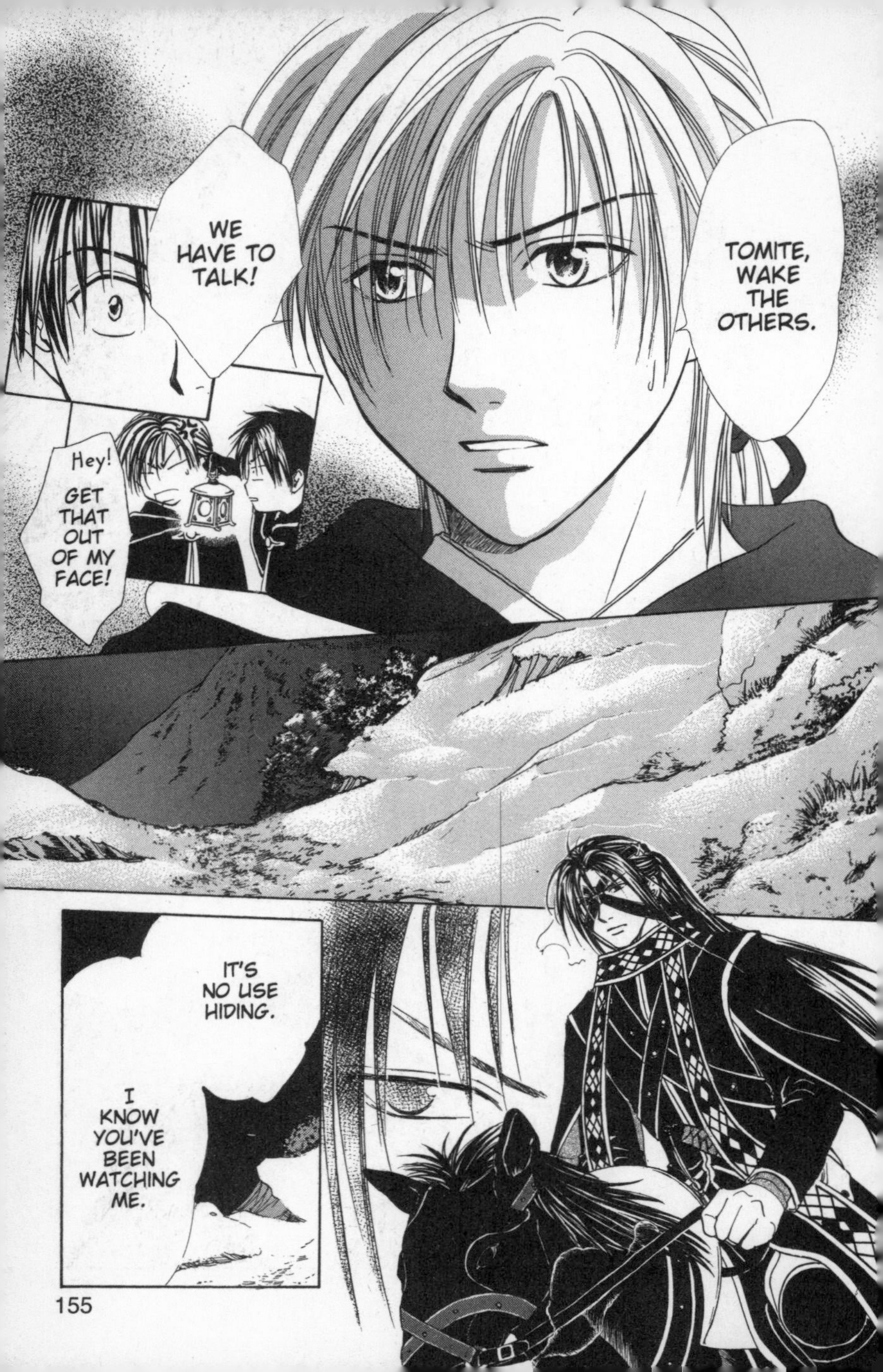
TOMITE, WAKE THE OTHERS.
WE HAVE TO TALK!
Hey! GET THAT OUT OF MY FACE!
IT'S NO USE HIDING.
I KNOW YOU'VE BEEN WATCHING ME.

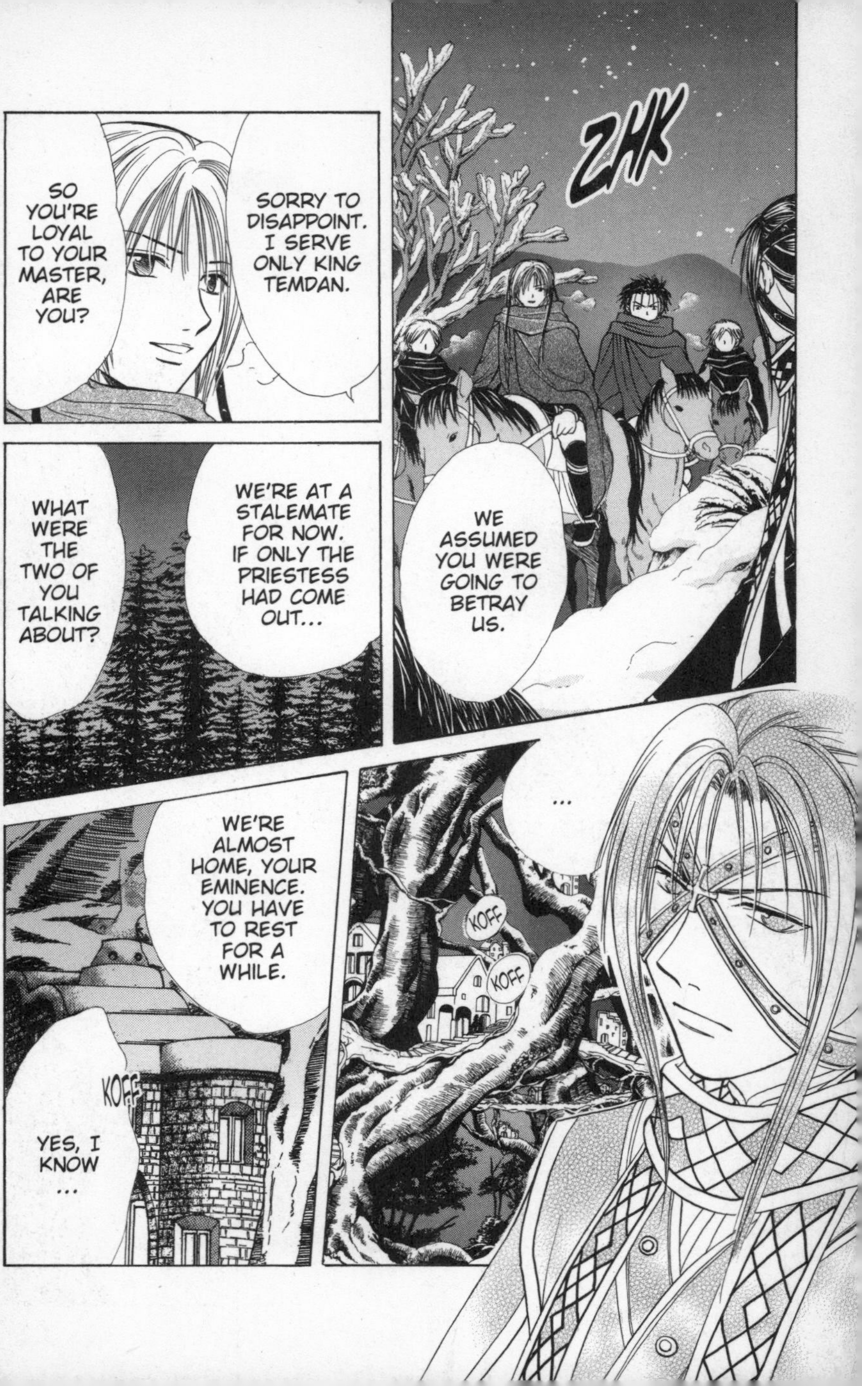
ZHK
WE ASSUMED YOU WERE GOING TO BETRAY US.
SORRY TO DISAPPOINT. I SERVE ONLY KING TEMDAN.
SO YOU'RE LOYAL TO YOUR MASTER, ARE YOU?
WE'RE AT A STALEMATE FOR NOW. IF ONLY THE PRIESTESS HAD COME OUT...
WHAT WERE THE TWO OF YOU TALKING ABOUT?
...
KOFF
KOFF
WE'RE ALMOST HOME, YOUR EMINENCE. YOU HAVE TO REST FOR A WHILE.
KOFF
YES, I KNOW ...

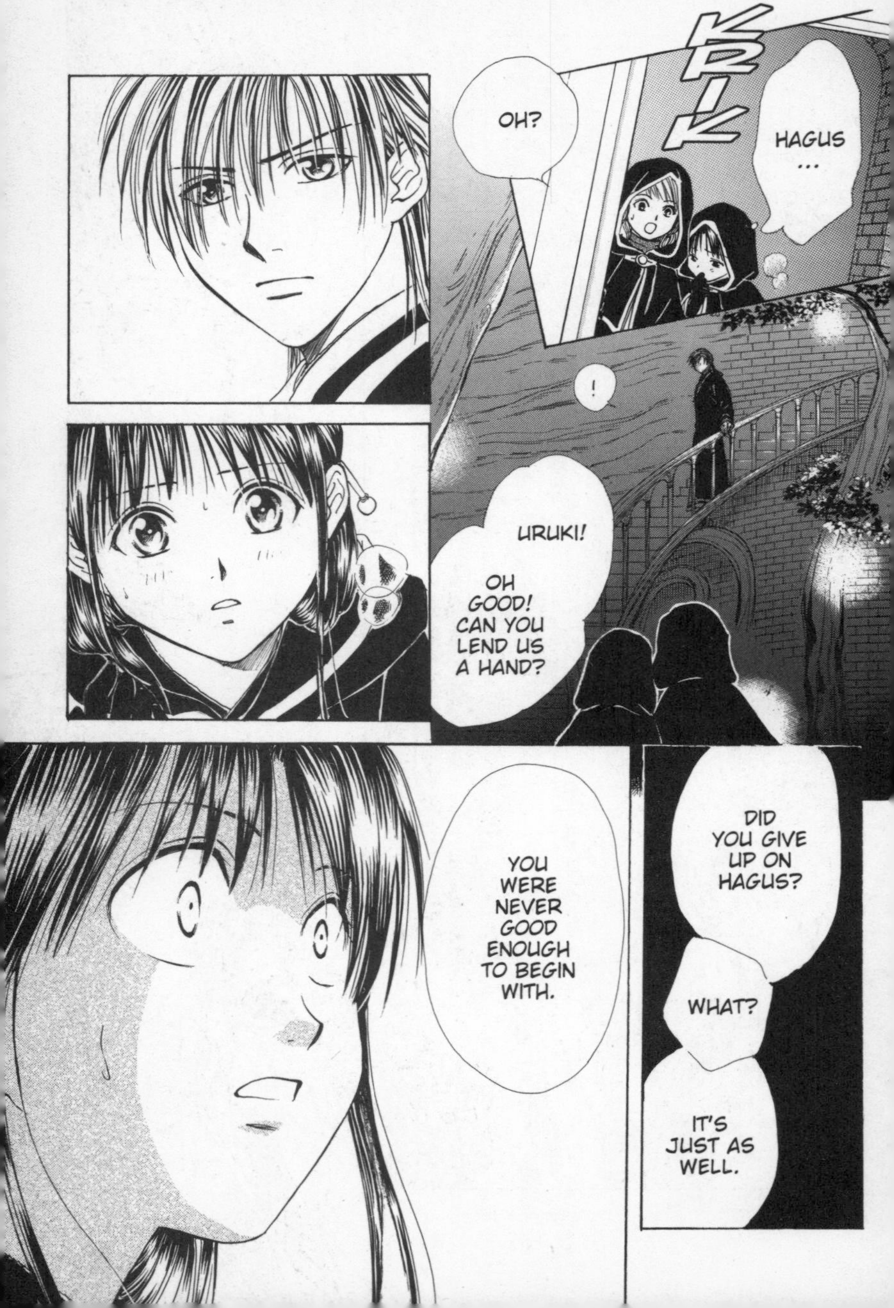
KRIK
HAGUS ...
OH?
!
URUKI!
OH GOOD! CAN YOU LEND US A HAND?
DID YOU GIVE UP ON HAGUS?
WHAT?
IT'S JUST AS WELL.
YOU WERE NEVER GOOD ENOUGH TO BEGIN WITH.

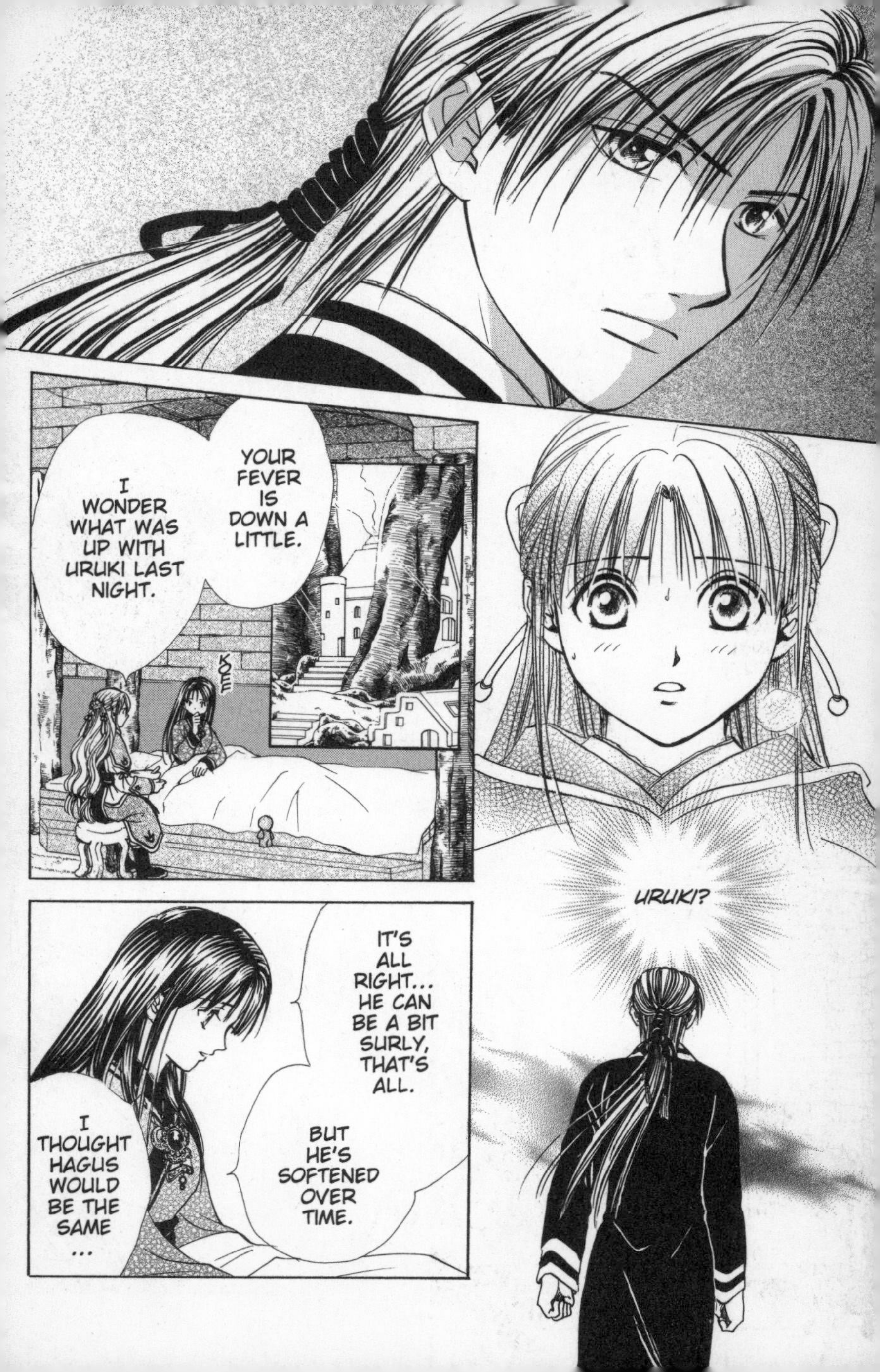
URUKI?
YOUR FEVER IS DOWN A LITTLE.
I WONDER WHAT WAS UP WITH URUKI LAST NIGHT.
KOFF
IT'S ALL RIGHT... HE CAN BE A BIT SURLY, THAT'S ALL.
BUT HE'S SOFTENED OVER TIME.
I THOUGHT HAGUS WOULD BE THE SAME ...

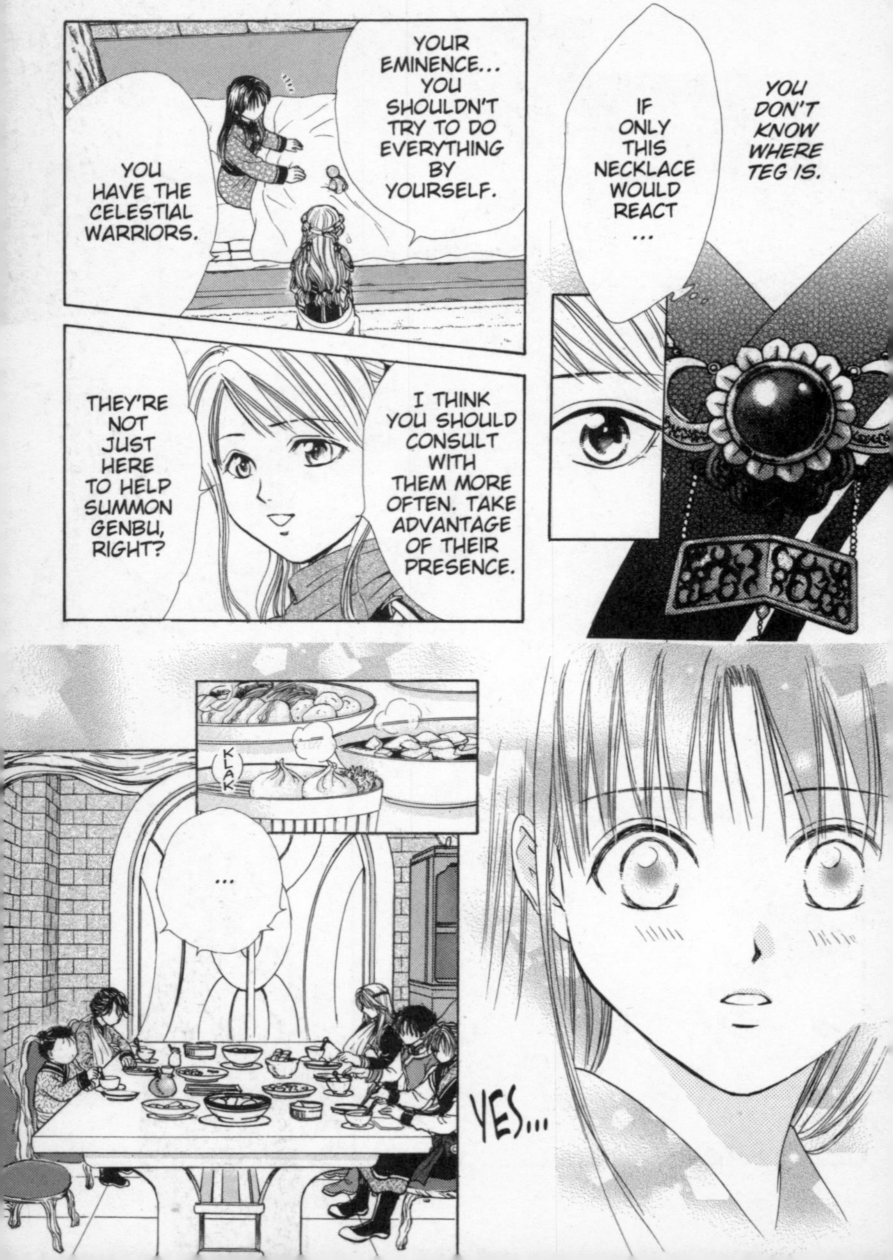
YOU DON'T KNOW WHERE TEG IS.
IF ONLY THIS NECKLACE WOULD REACT...
YOUR EMINENCE... YOU SHOULDN'T TRY TO DO EVERYTHING BY YOURSELF.
YOU HAVE THE CELESTIAL WARRIORS.
I THINK YOU SHOULD CONSULT WITH THEM MORE OFTEN. TAKE ADVANTAGE OF THEIR PRESENCE.
THEY'RE NOT JUST HERE TO HELP SUMMON GENBU, RIGHT?
YES...
KLAK
...

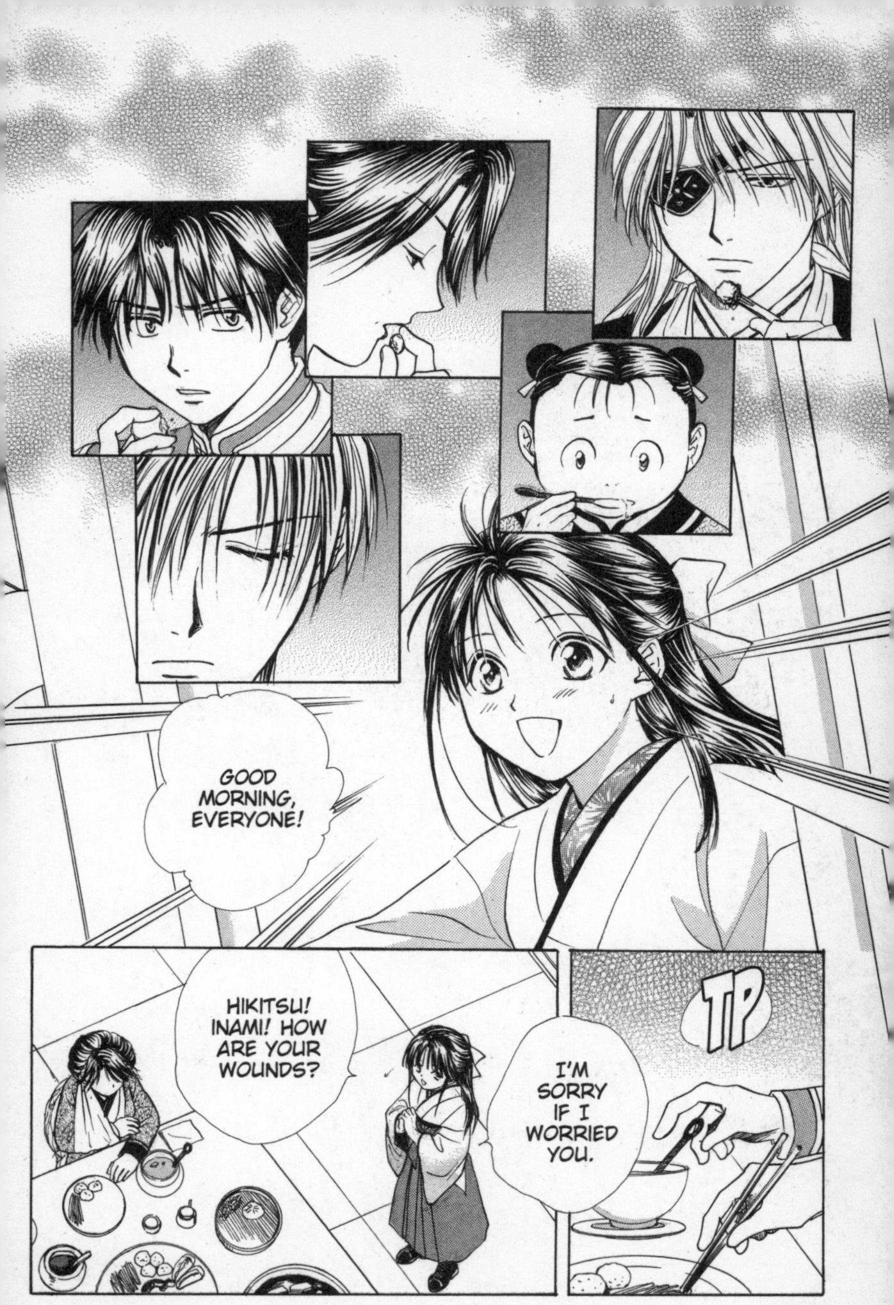
GOOD MORNING, EVERYONE!
TP
HIKITSU! INAMI! HOW ARE YOUR WOUNDS?
I'M SORRY IF I WORRIED YOU.

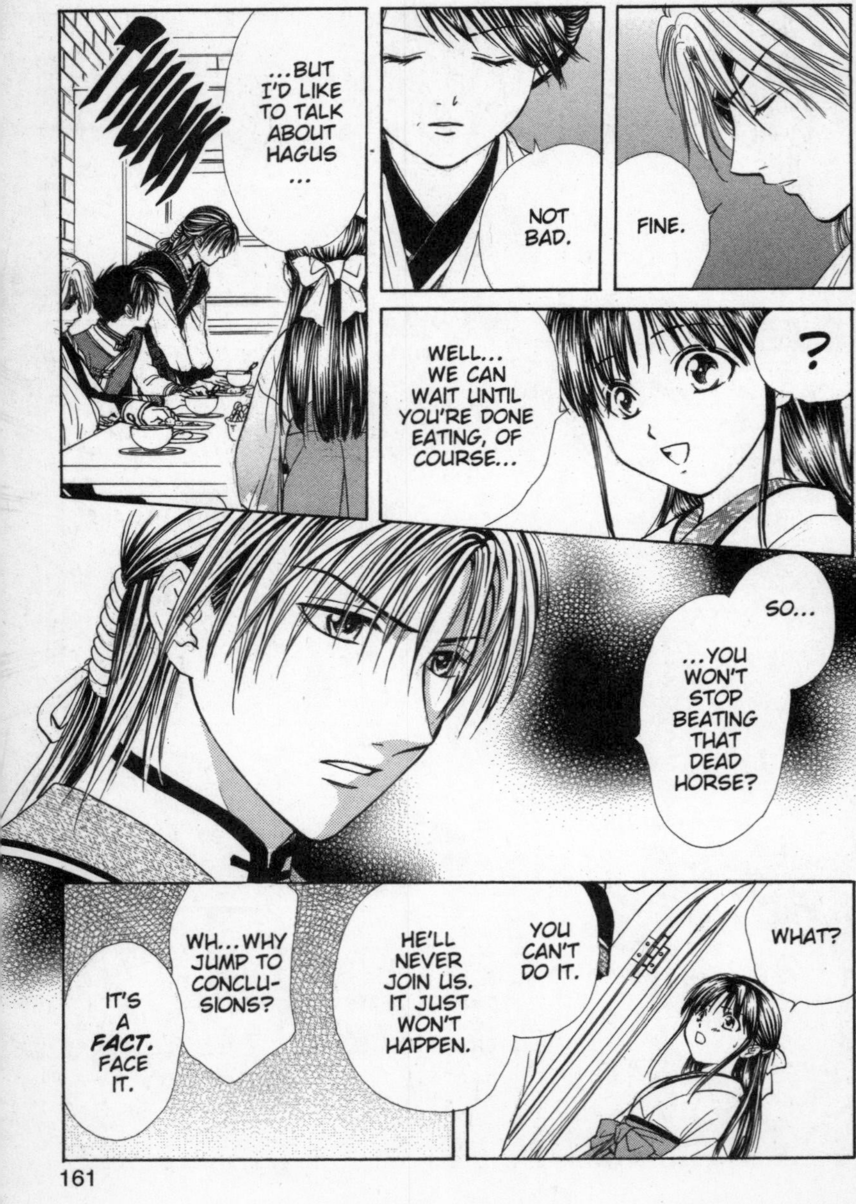
FINE.
NOT BAD.
WELL... WE CAN WAIT UNTIL YOU'RE DONE EATING, OF COURSE...
?
THUNK
...BUT I'D LIKE TO TALK ABOUT HAGUS...
SO...
...YOU WON'T STOP BEATING THAT DEAD HORSE?
WHAT?
YOU CAN'T DO IT.
HE'LL NEVER JOIN US. IT JUST WON'T HAPPEN.
WH...WHY JUMP TO CONCLUSIONS?
IT'S A FACT. FACE IT.

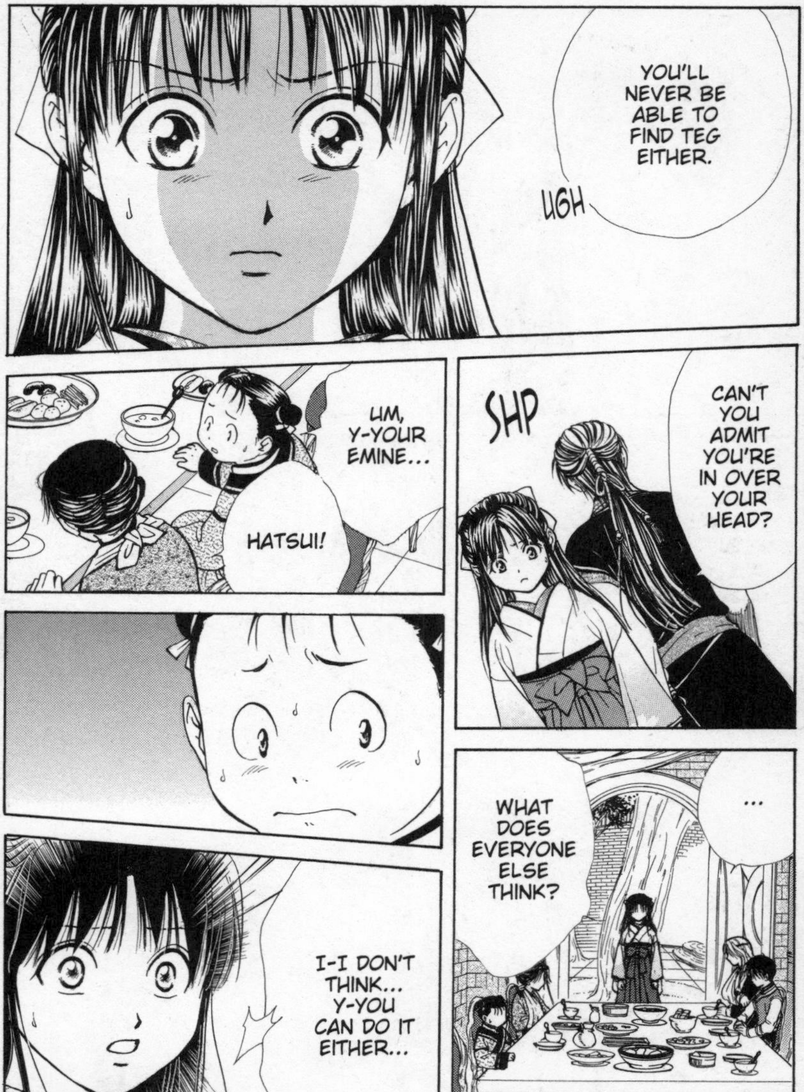
YOU'LL NEVER BE ABLE TO FIND TEG EITHER.
UGH
SHP
CAN'T YOU ADMIT YOU'RE IN OVER YOUR HEAD?
UM, Y-YOUR EMINE...
HATSUI!
...
WHAT DOES EVERYONE ELSE THINK?
I-I DON'T THINK... Y-YOU CAN DO IT EITHER...

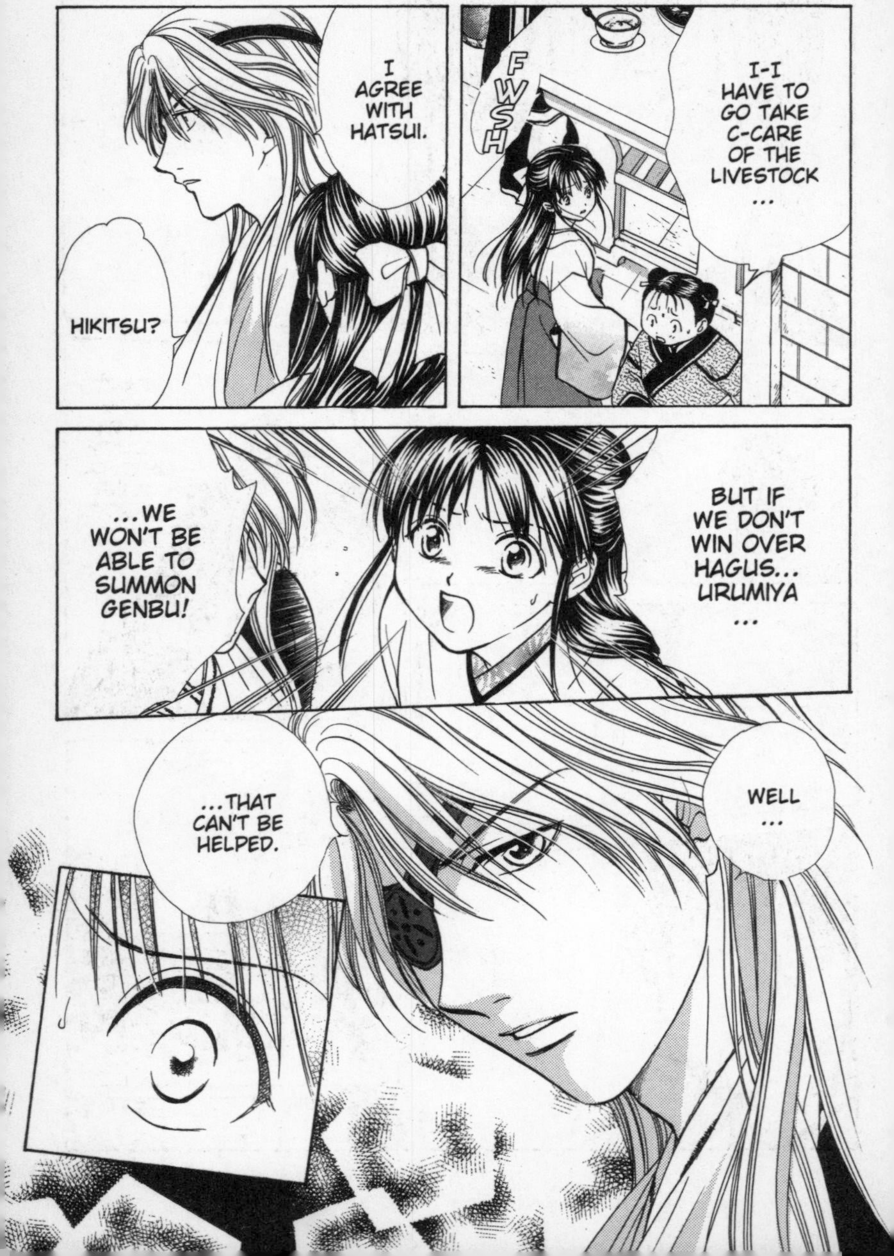
FWSH
I-I HAVE TO GO TAKE C-CARE OF THE LIVESTOCK ...
I AGREE WITH HATSUI.
HIKITSU?
BUT IF WE DON'T WIN OVER HAGUS... URUMIYA ...
...WE WON'T BE ABLE TO SUMMON GENBU!
WELL ...
...THAT CAN'T BE HELPED.

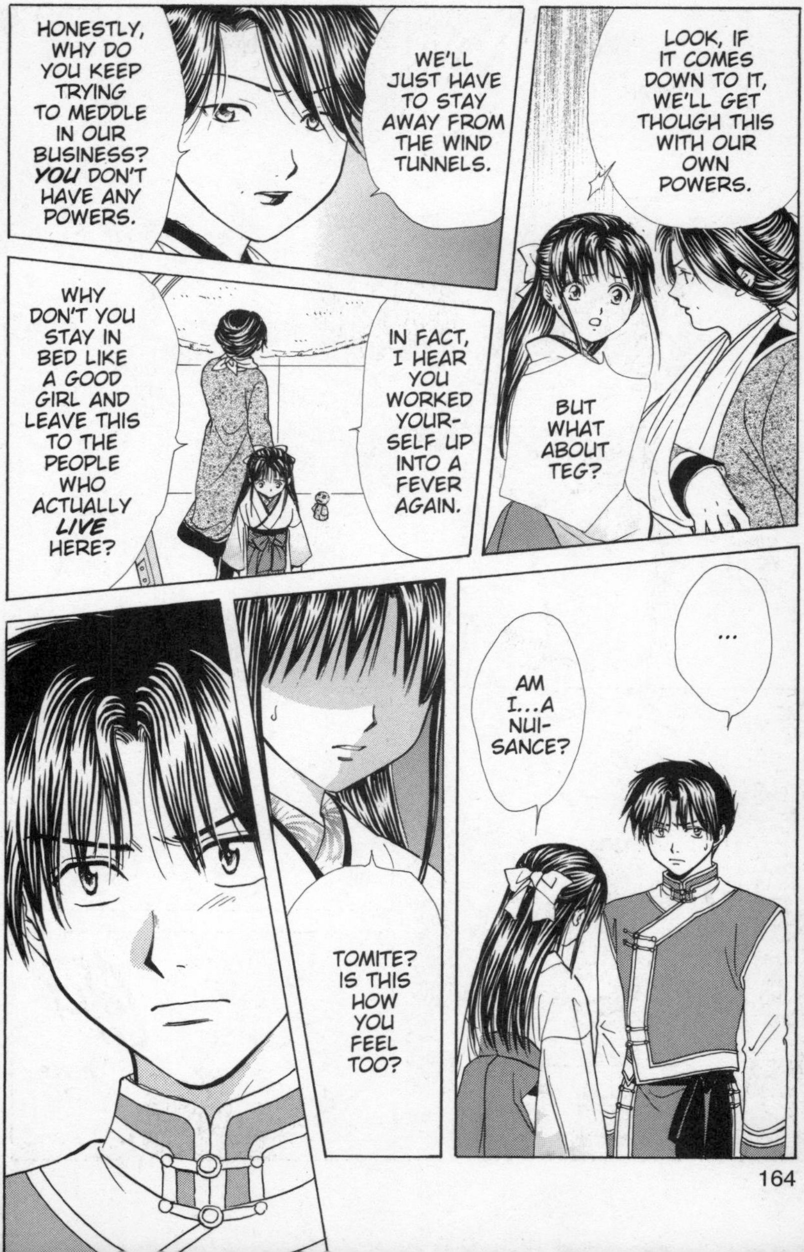
LOOK, IF IT COMES DOWN TO IT, WE'LL GET THOUGH THIS WITH OUR OWN POWERS.
BUT WHAT ABOUT TEG?
WE'LL JUST HAVE TO STAY AWAY FROM THE WIND TUNNELS.
HONESTLY, WHY DO YOU KEEP TRYING TO MEDDLE IN OUR BUSINESS? *YOU* DON'T HAVE ANY POWERS.
IN FACT, I HEAR YOU WORKED YOUR-SELF UP INTO A FEVER AGAIN.
WHY DON'T YOU STAY IN BED LIKE A GOOD GIRL AND LEAVE THIS TO THE PEOPLE WHO ACTUALLY *LIVE* HERE?
...
AM I...A NUI-SANCE?
TOMITE? IS THIS HOW YOU FEEL TOO?

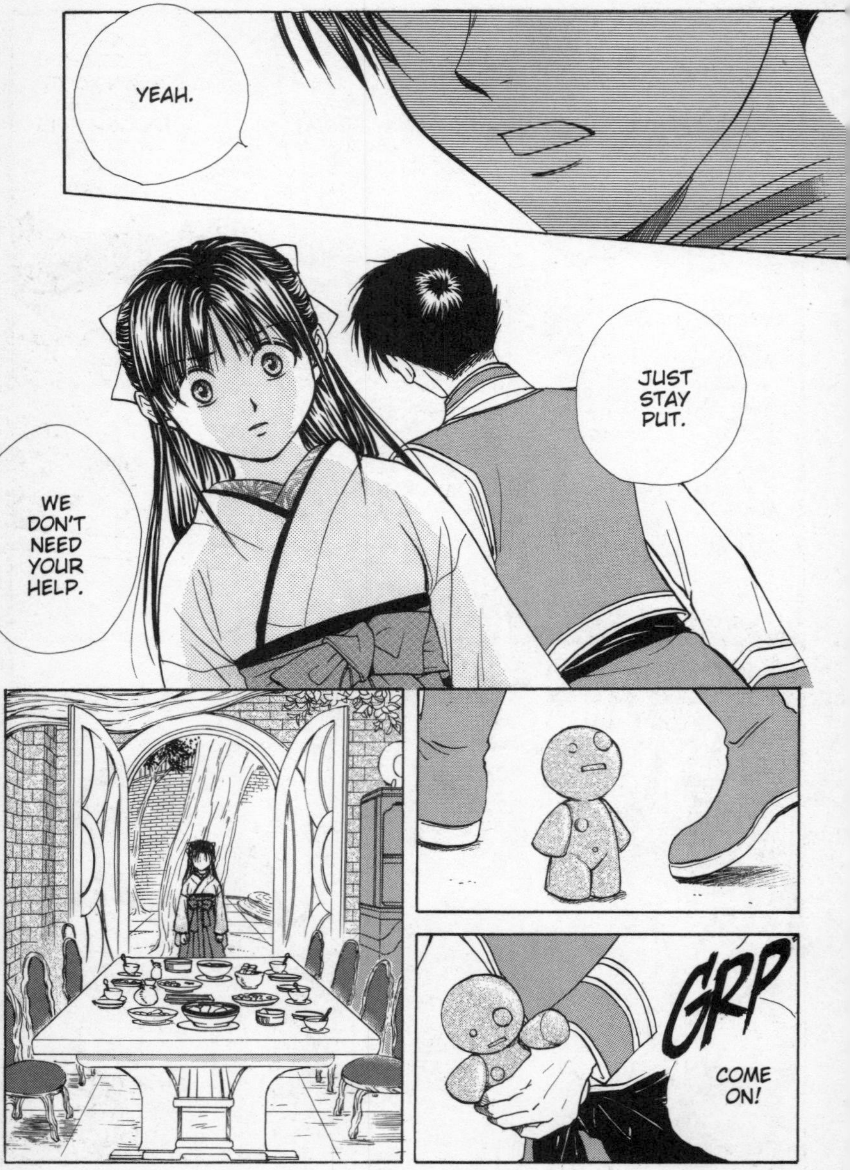
YEAH.
JUST STAY PUT.
WE DON'T NEED YOUR HELP.
GRP
COME ON!

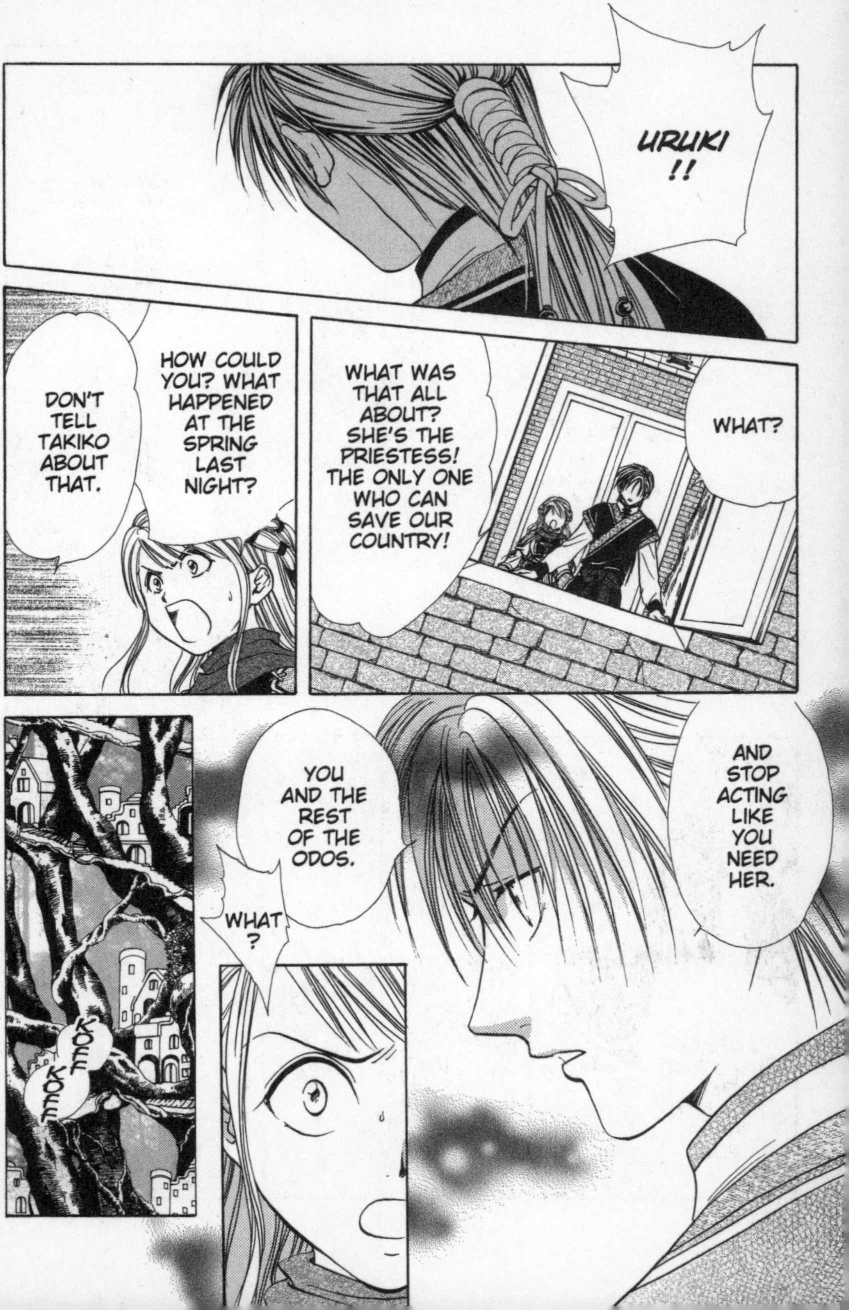
URUKI !!
WHAT?
WHAT WAS THAT ALL ABOUT? SHE'S THE PRIESTESS! THE ONLY ONE WHO CAN SAVE OUR COUNTRY!
HOW COULD YOU? WHAT HAPPENED AT THE SPRING LAST NIGHT?
DON'T TELL TAKIKO ABOUT THAT.
AND STOP ACTING LIKE YOU NEED HER.
YOU AND THE REST OF THE ODOS.
WHAT ?
KOFF KOFF

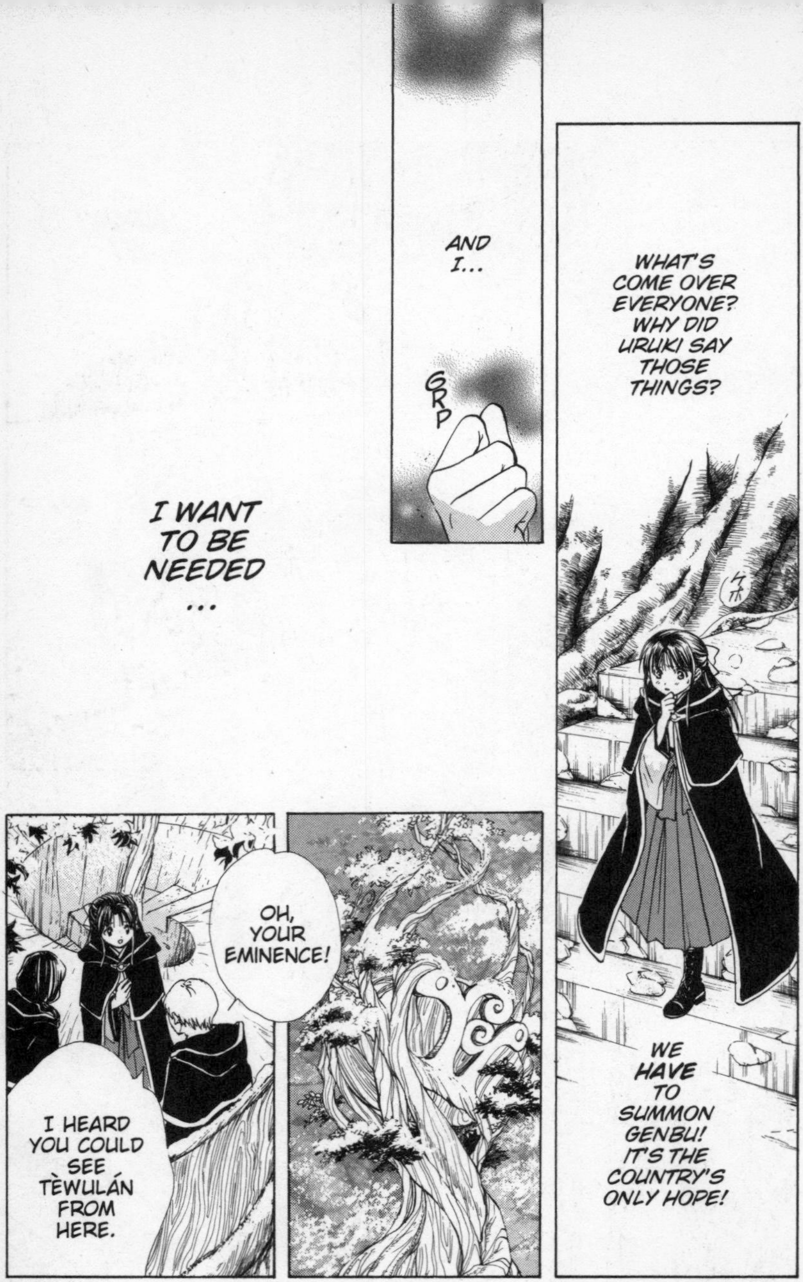
WHAT'S COME OVER EVERYONE? WHY DID URUKI SAY THOSE THINGS?
WE HAVE TO SUMMON GENBU! IT'S THE COUNTRY'S ONLY HOPE!
AND I...
GRP
I WANT TO BE NEEDED...
OH, YOUR EMINENCE!
I HEARD YOU COULD SEE TÈWULÁN FROM HERE.

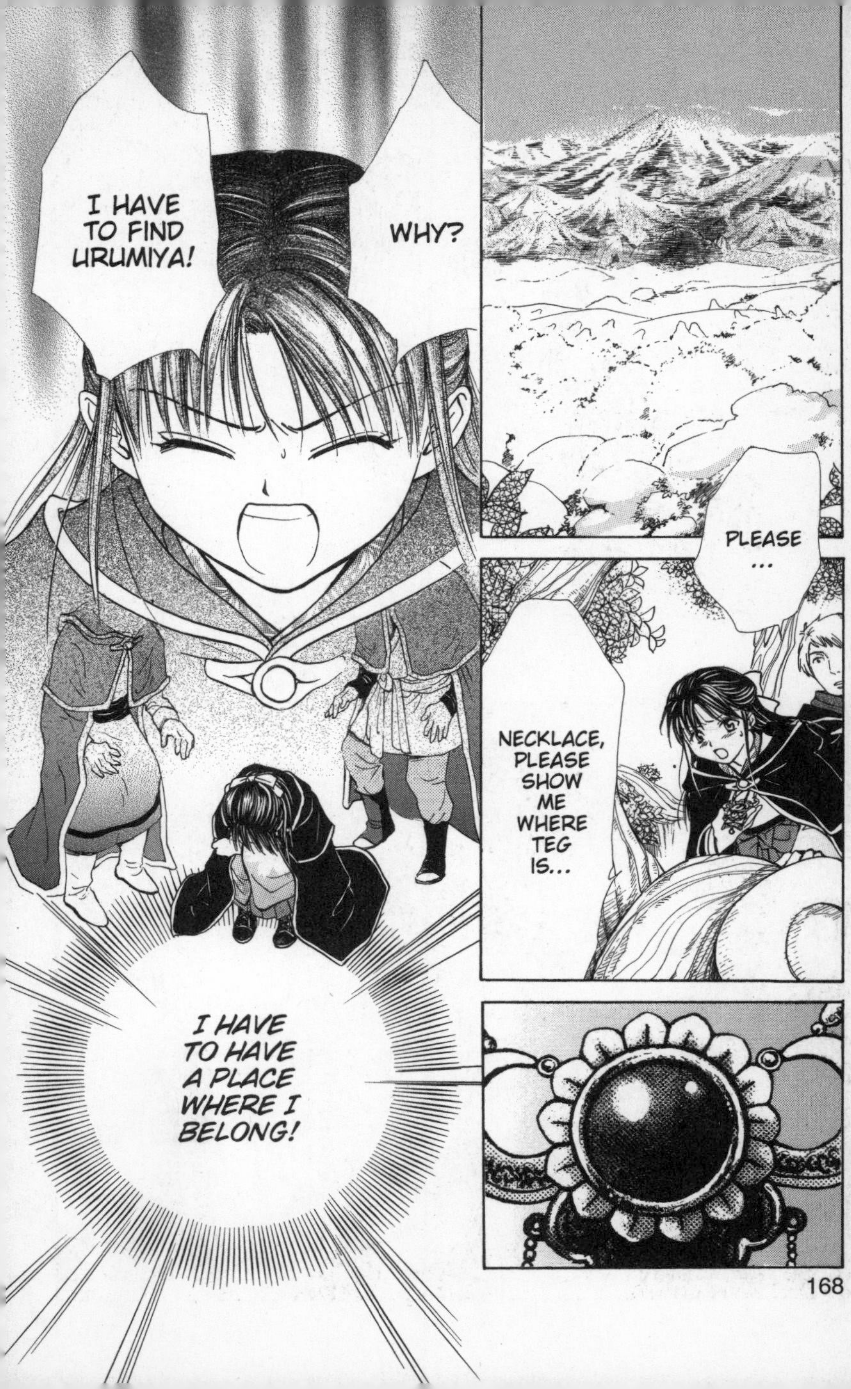
PLEASE ...
NECKLACE, PLEASE SHOW ME WHERE TEG IS...
WHY?
I HAVE TO FIND URUMIYA!
I HAVE TO HAVE A PLACE WHERE I BELONG!

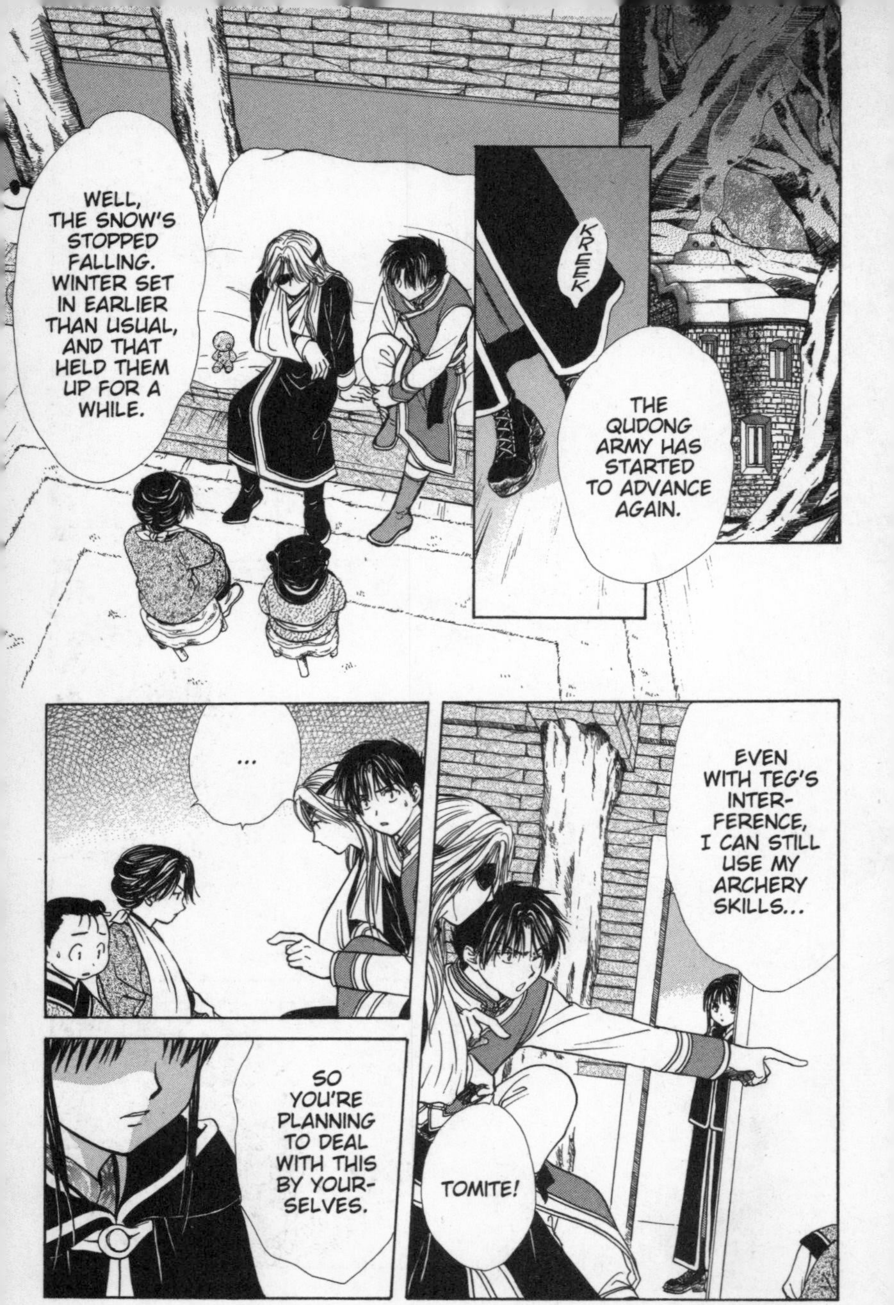
KREEK
THE QUDONG ARMY HAS STARTED TO ADVANCE AGAIN.
WELL, THE SNOW'S STOPPED FALLING. WINTER SET IN EARLIER THAN USUAL, AND THAT HELD THEM UP FOR A WHILE.
EVEN WITH TEG'S INTER-FERENCE, I CAN STILL USE MY ARCHERY SKILLS...
TOMITE!
...
SO YOU'RE PLANNING TO DEAL WITH THIS BY YOUR-SELVES.

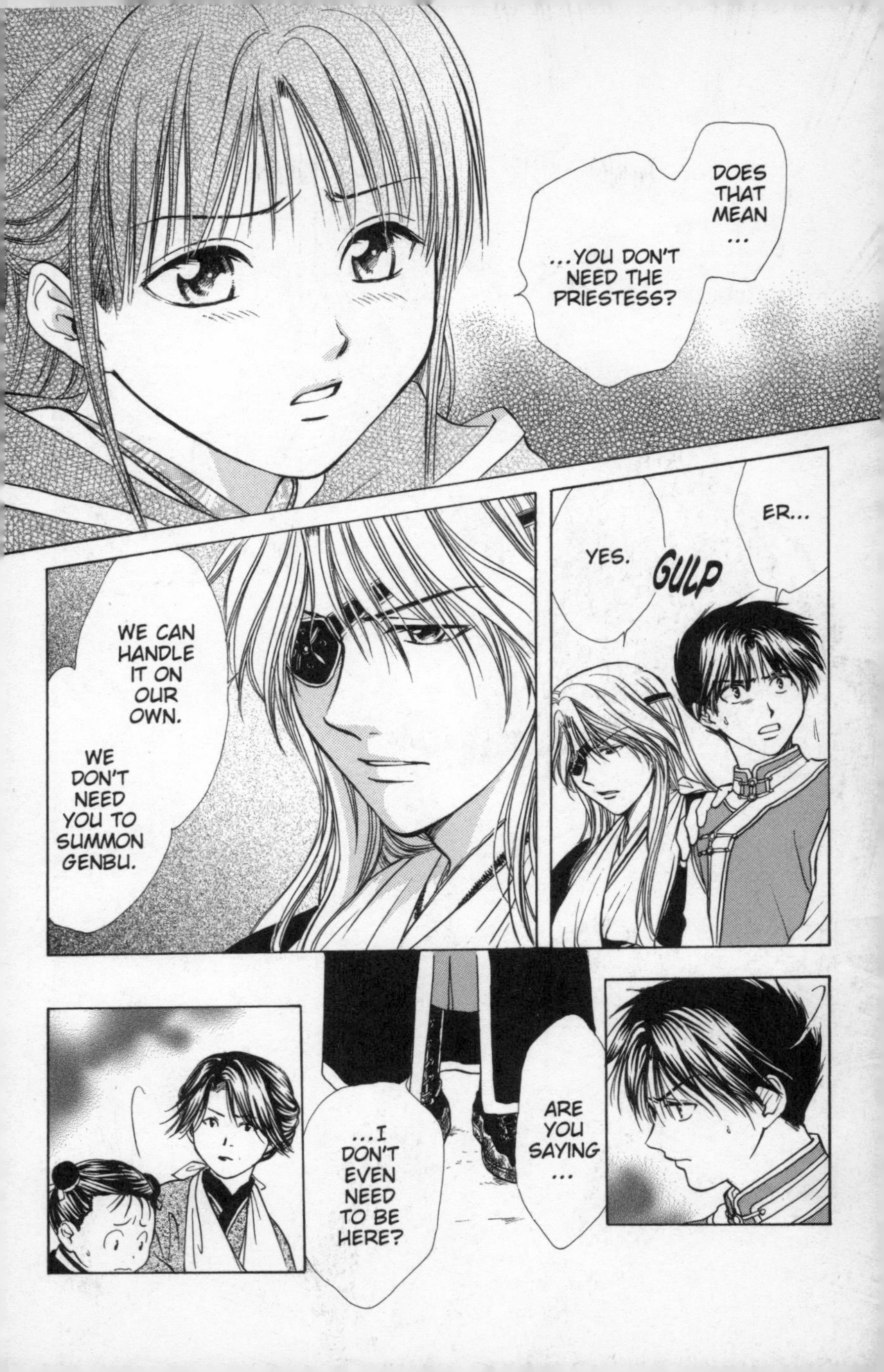
DOES THAT MEAN ...
...YOU DON'T NEED THE PRIESTESS?
ER...
YES.
GULP
WE CAN HANDLE IT ON OUR OWN.
WE DON'T NEED YOU TO SUMMON GENBU.
ARE YOU SAYING ...
...I DON'T EVEN NEED TO BE HERE?

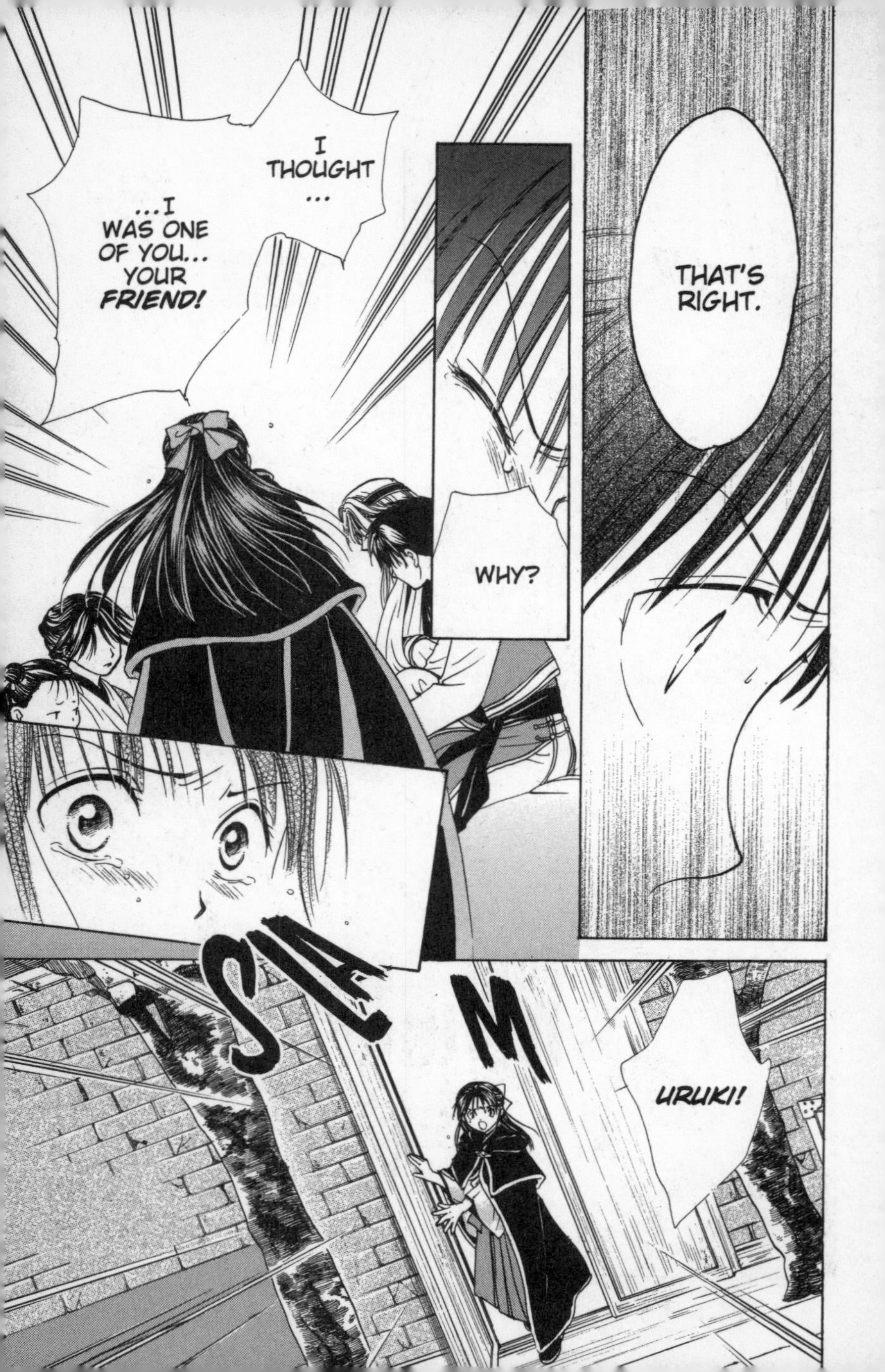
THAT'S RIGHT.
WHY?
I THOUGHT...
...I WAS ONE OF YOU... YOUR FRIEND!
URUKI!
SLAM

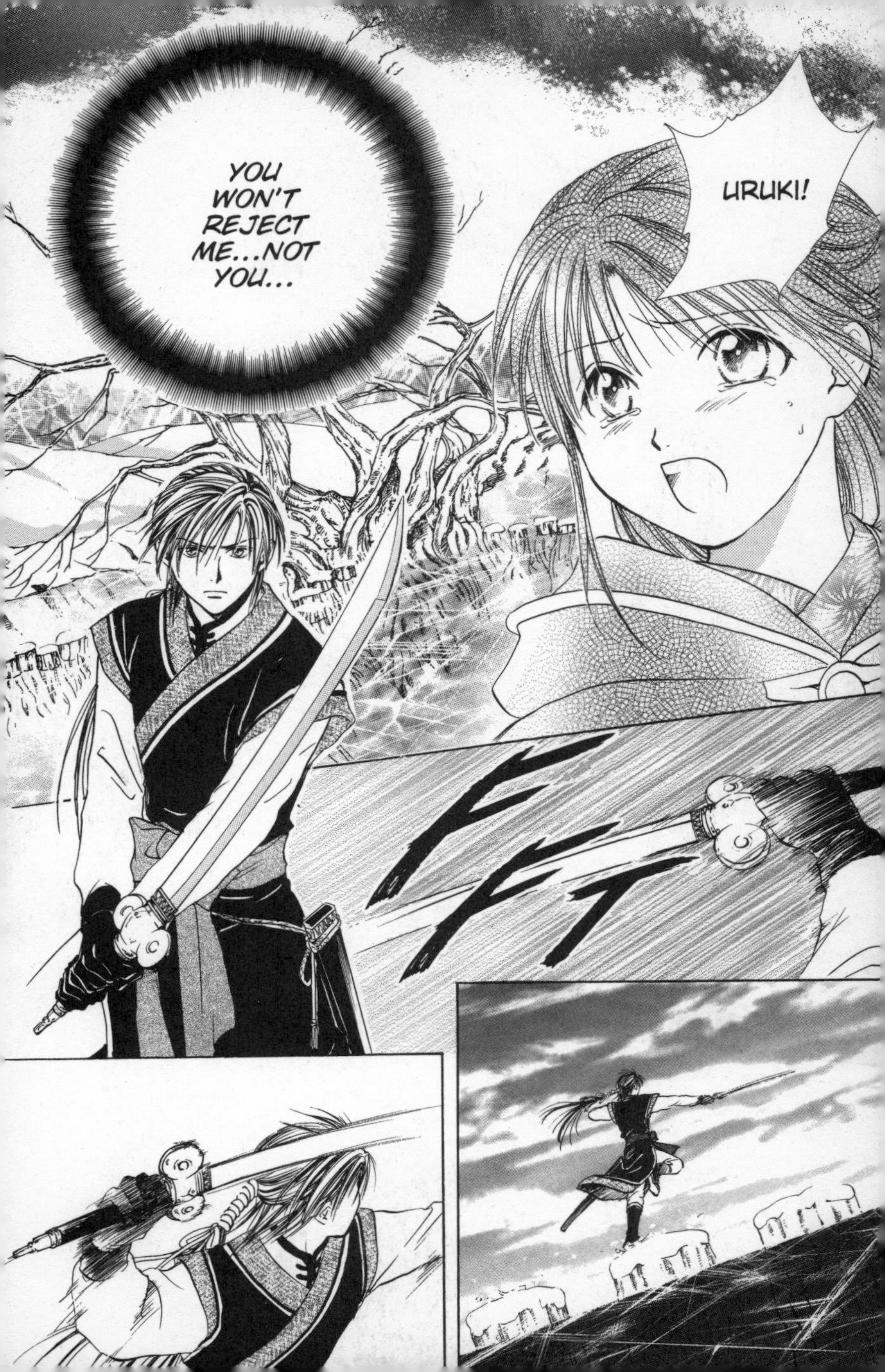
URUKI!
YOU WON'T REJECT ME...NOT YOU...

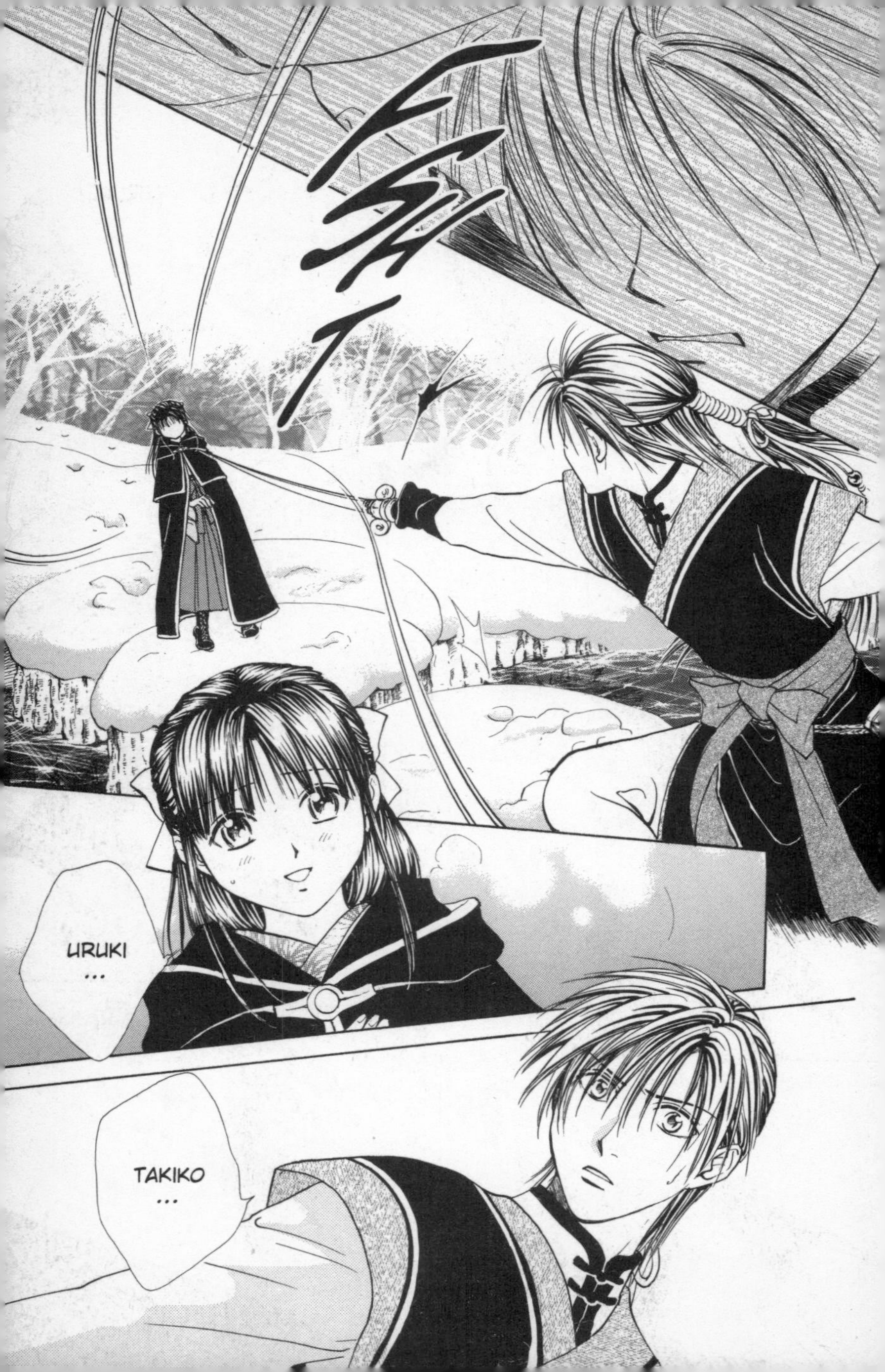
FSHHT
URUKI ...
TAKIKO ...

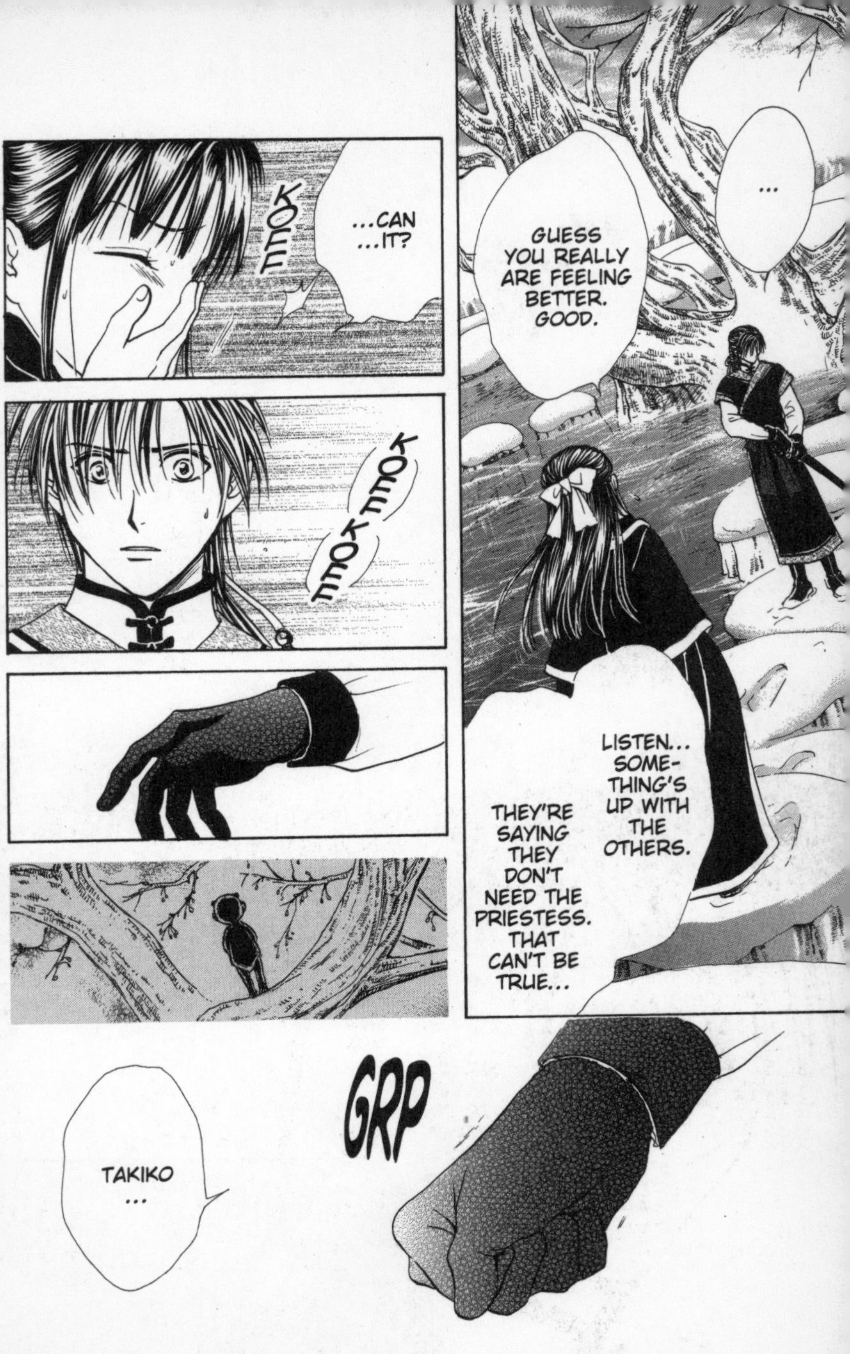
...
GUESS YOU REALLY ARE FEELING BETTER. GOOD.
LISTEN... SOMETHING'S UP WITH THE OTHERS.
THEY'RE SAYING THEY DON'T NEED THE PRIESTESS. THAT CAN'T BE TRUE...
...CAN ...IT?
KOFF
KOFF KOFF
GRP
TAKIKO ...

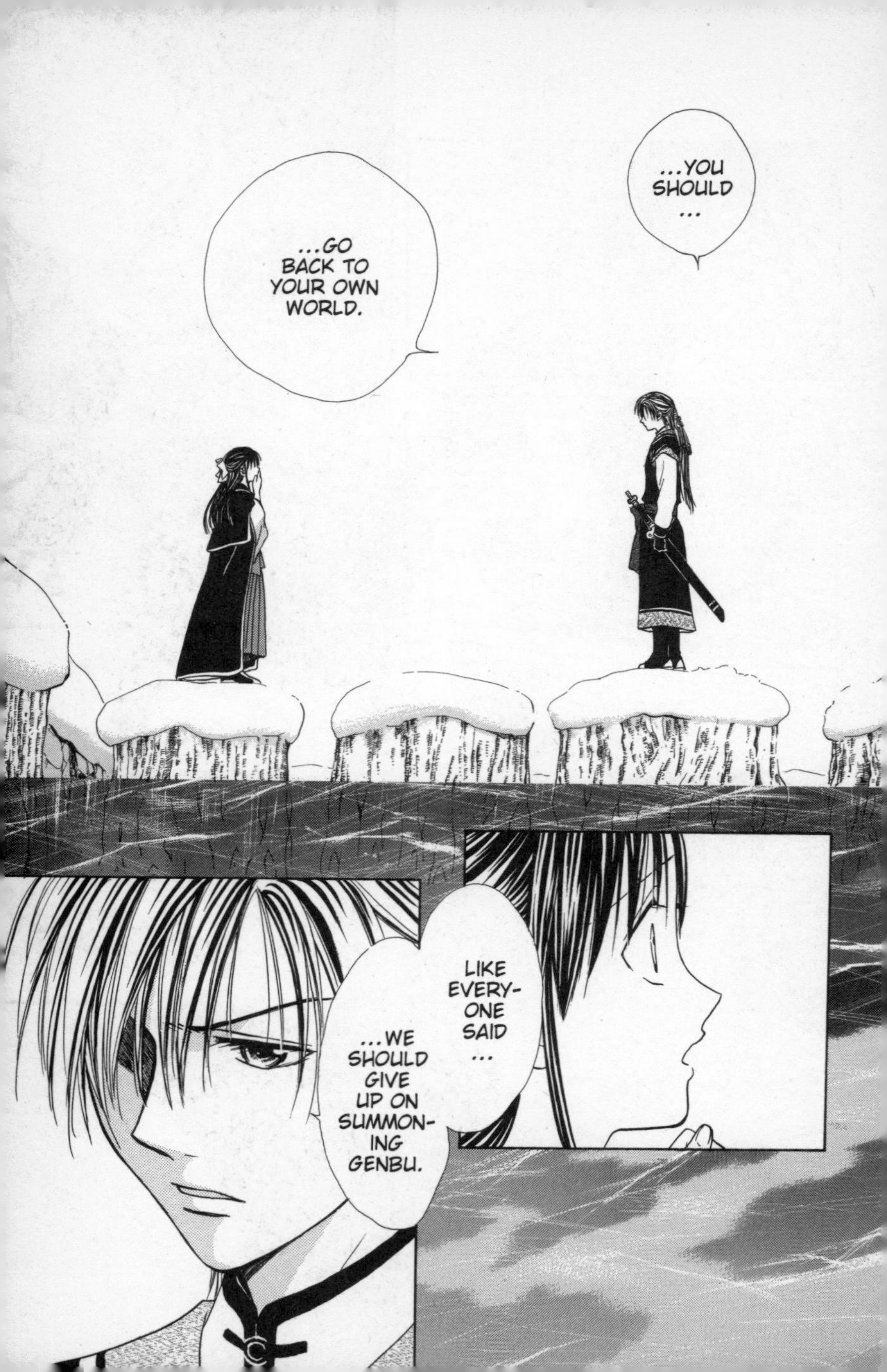
...YOU SHOULD ...
...GO BACK TO YOUR OWN WORLD.
LIKE EVERY-ONE SAID ...
...WE SHOULD GIVE UP ON SUMMON-ING GENBU.

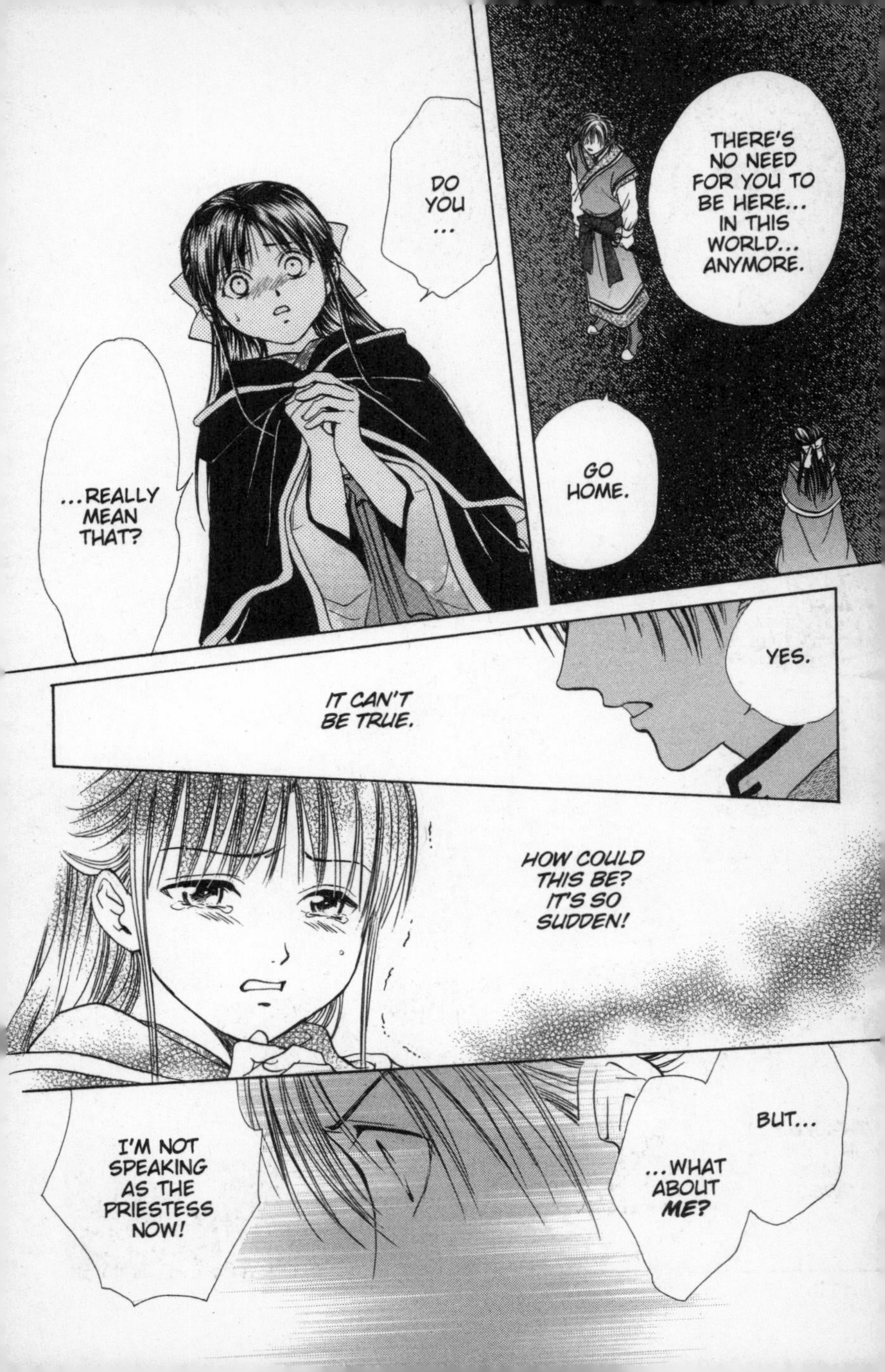
THERE'S NO NEED FOR YOU TO BE HERE... IN THIS WORLD... ANYMORE.
GO HOME.
DO YOU ...
...REALLY MEAN THAT?
YES.
IT CAN'T BE TRUE.
HOW COULD THIS BE? IT'S SO SUDDEN!
BUT...
...WHAT ABOUT ME?
I'M NOT SPEAKING AS THE PRIESTESS NOW!

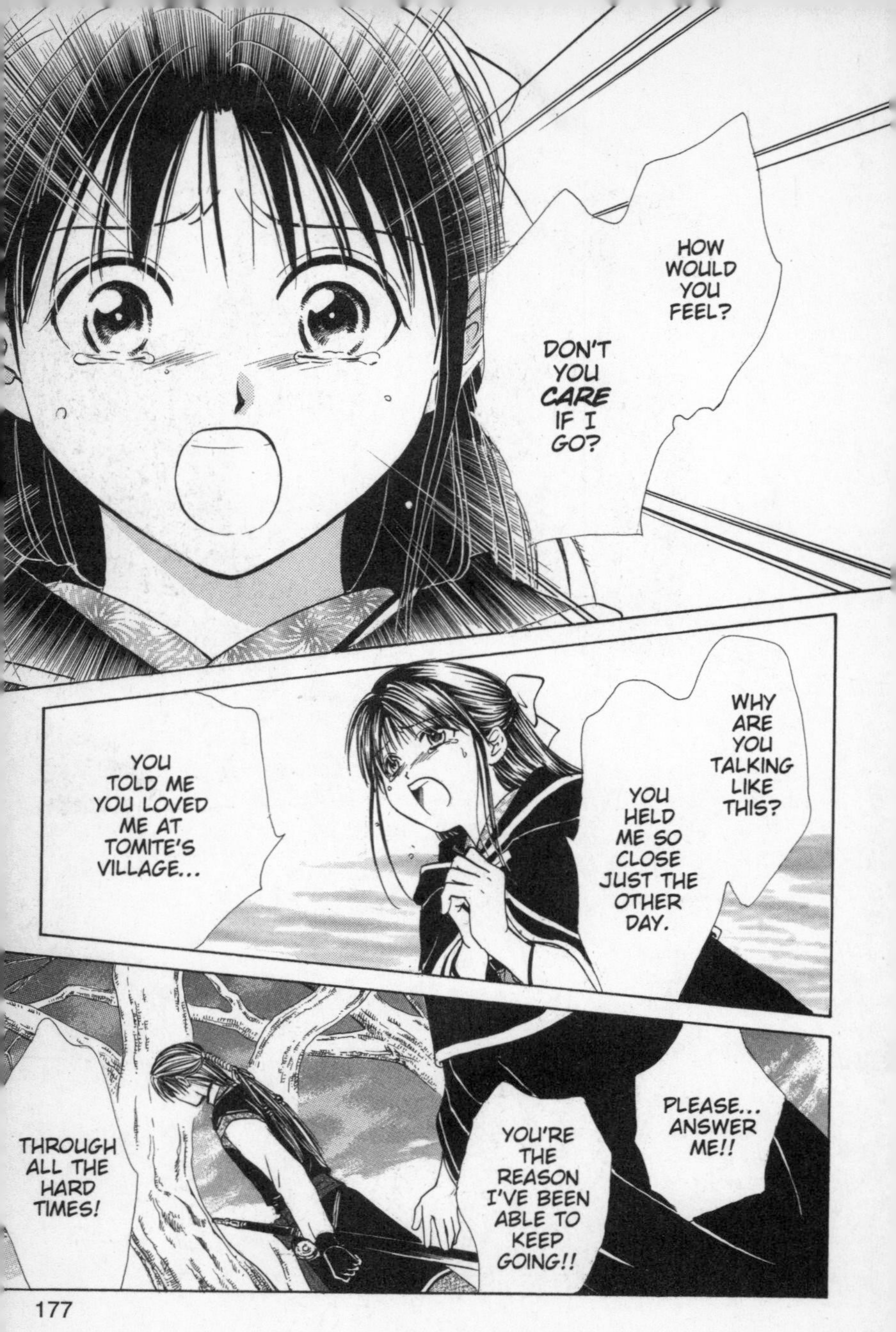
HOW WOULD YOU FEEL?
DON'T YOU *CARE* IF I GO?
WHY ARE YOU TALKING LIKE THIS?
YOU HELD ME SO CLOSE JUST THE OTHER DAY.
YOU TOLD ME YOU LOVED ME AT TOMITE'S VILLAGE...
PLEASE... ANSWER ME!!
YOU'RE THE REASON I'VE BEEN ABLE TO KEEP GOING!!
THROUGH ALL THE HARD TIMES!

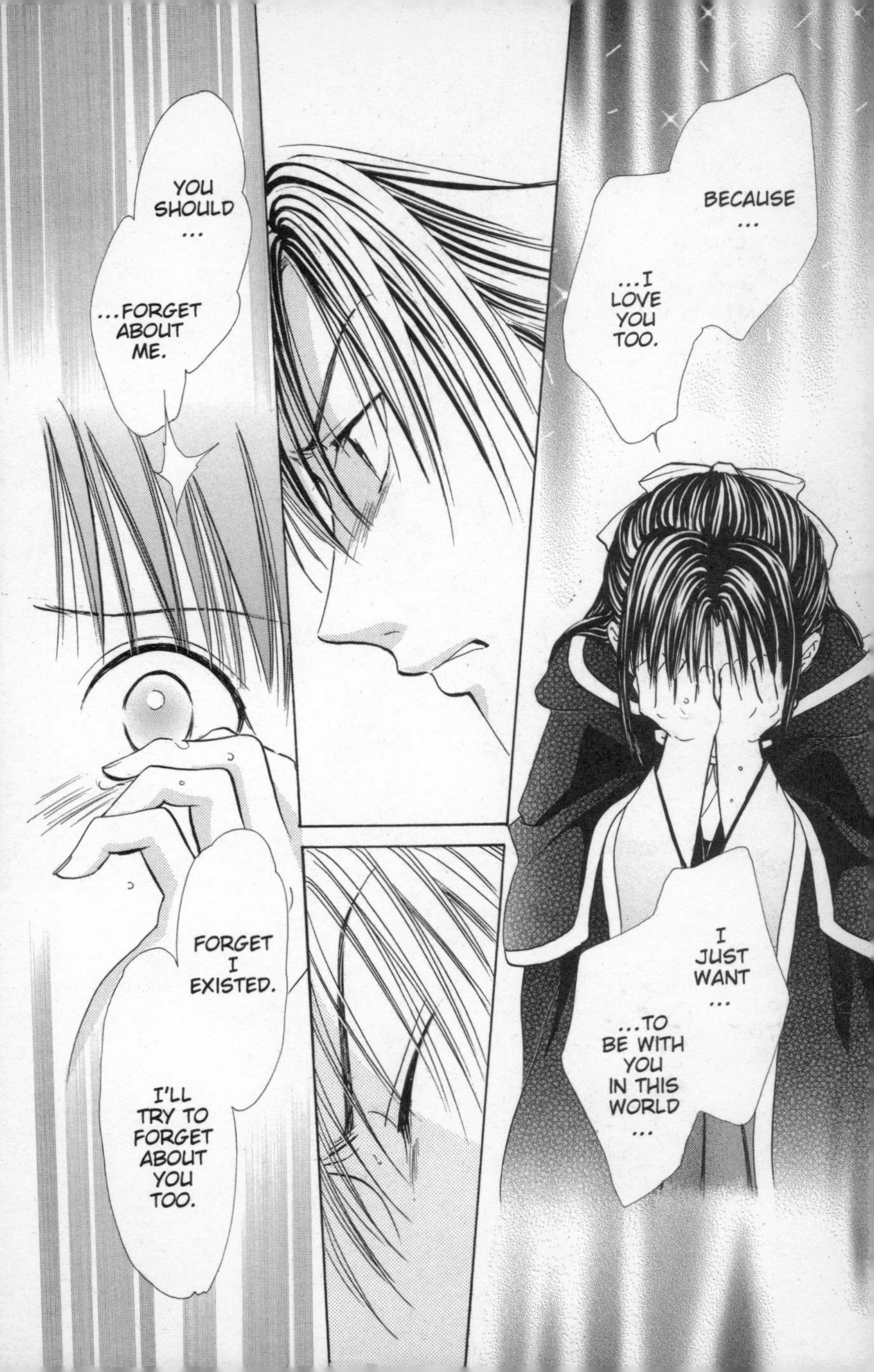
BECAUSE ...
...I LOVE YOU TOO.
I JUST WANT ...
...TO BE WITH YOU IN THIS WORLD ...
YOU SHOULD ...
...FORGET ABOUT ME.
FORGET I EXISTED.
I'LL TRY TO FORGET ABOUT YOU TOO.

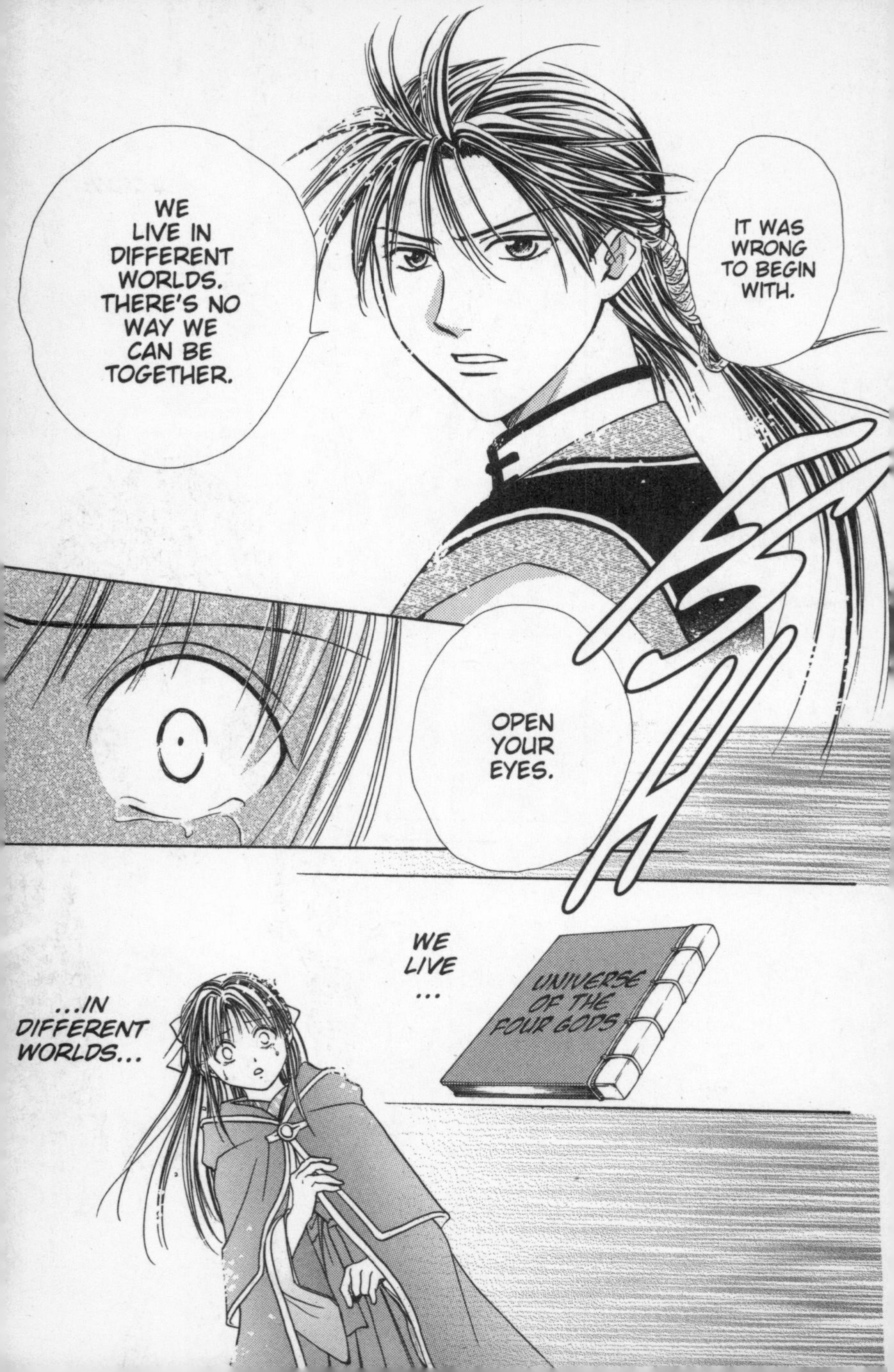
IT WAS WRONG TO BEGIN WITH.
WE LIVE IN DIFFERENT WORLDS. THERE'S NO WAY WE CAN BE TOGETHER.
OPEN YOUR EYES.
WE LIVE ...
UNIVERSE OF THE FOUR GODS
...IN DIFFERENT WORLDS...

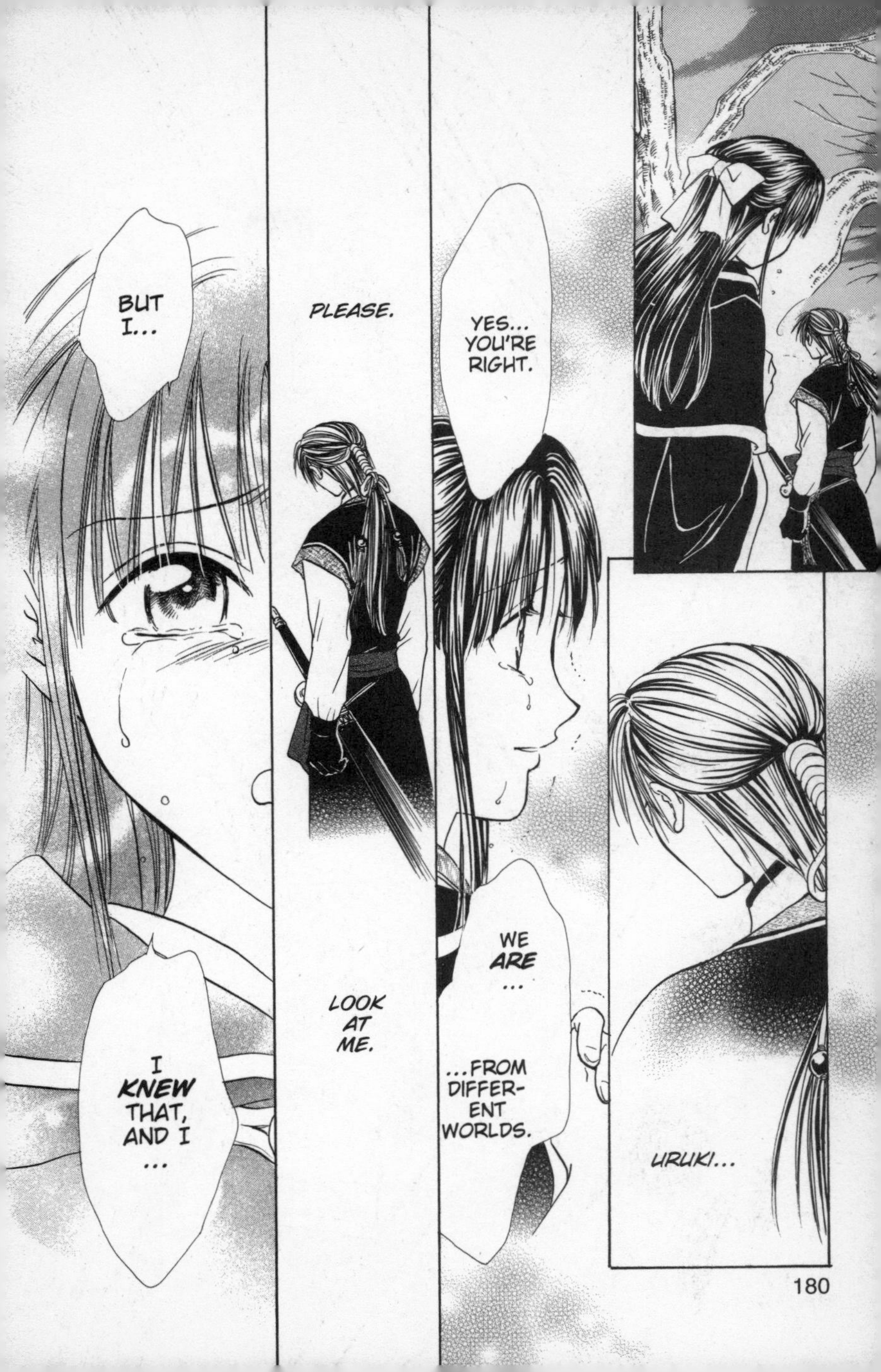
URUKI...
YES... YOU'RE RIGHT.
WE ARE...
...FROM DIFFER-ENT WORLDS.
PLEASE.
LOOK AT ME.
BUT I...
I KNEW THAT, AND I ...

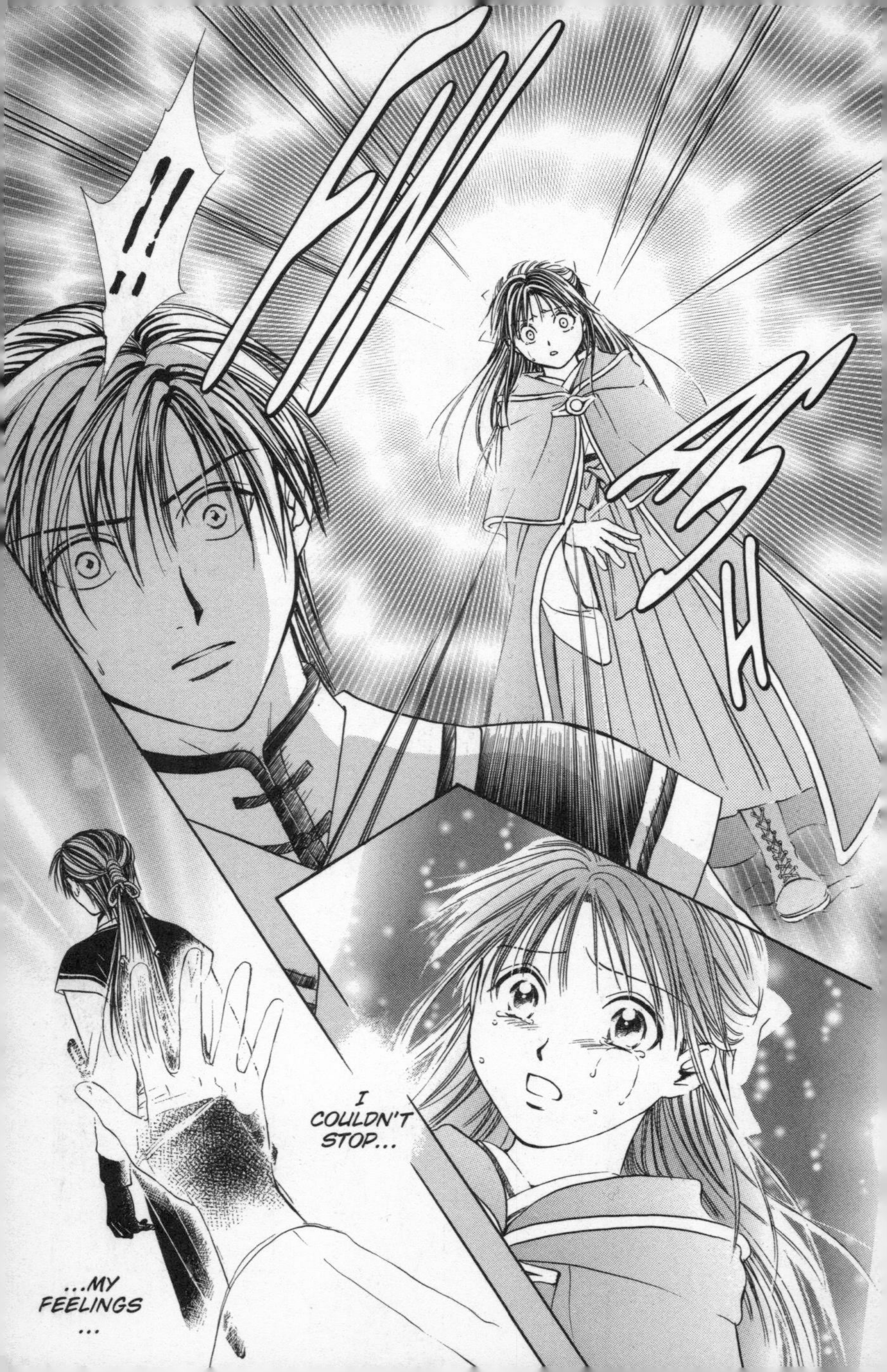
!!
FWASH
I COULDN'T STOP...
...MY FEELINGS...

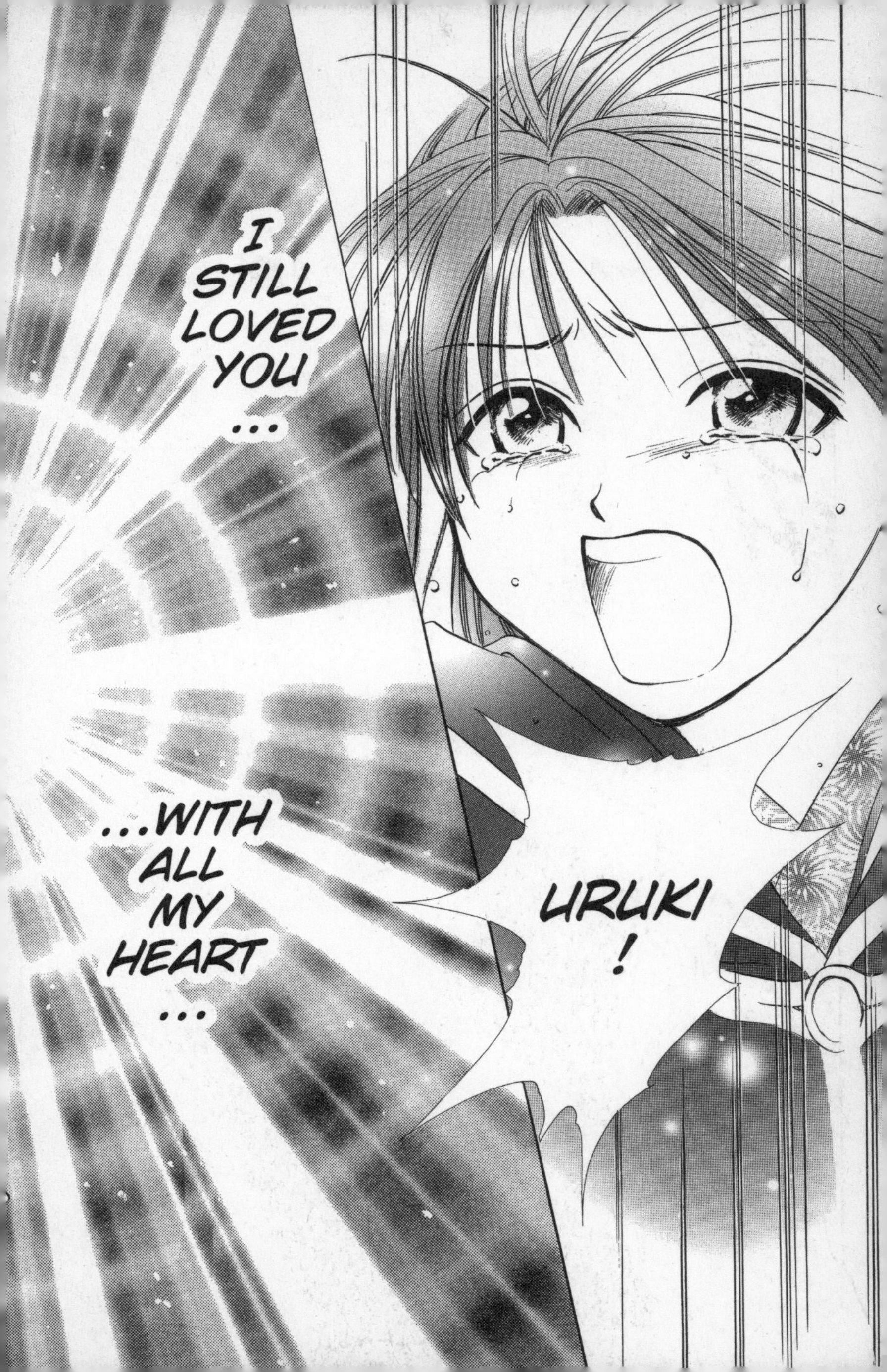
URUKI!
I STILL LOVED YOU...
...WITH ALL MY HEART...

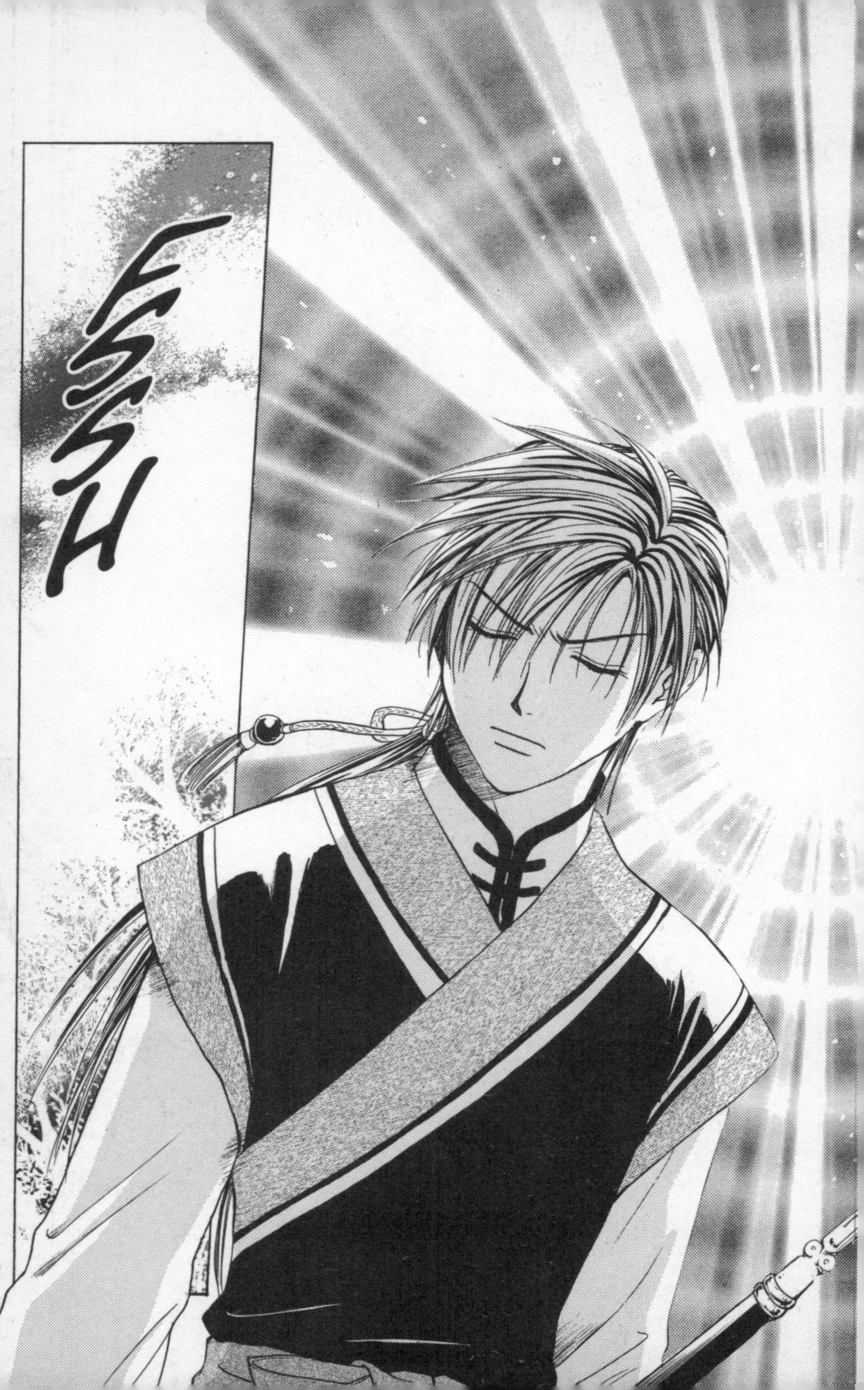
FSSSH

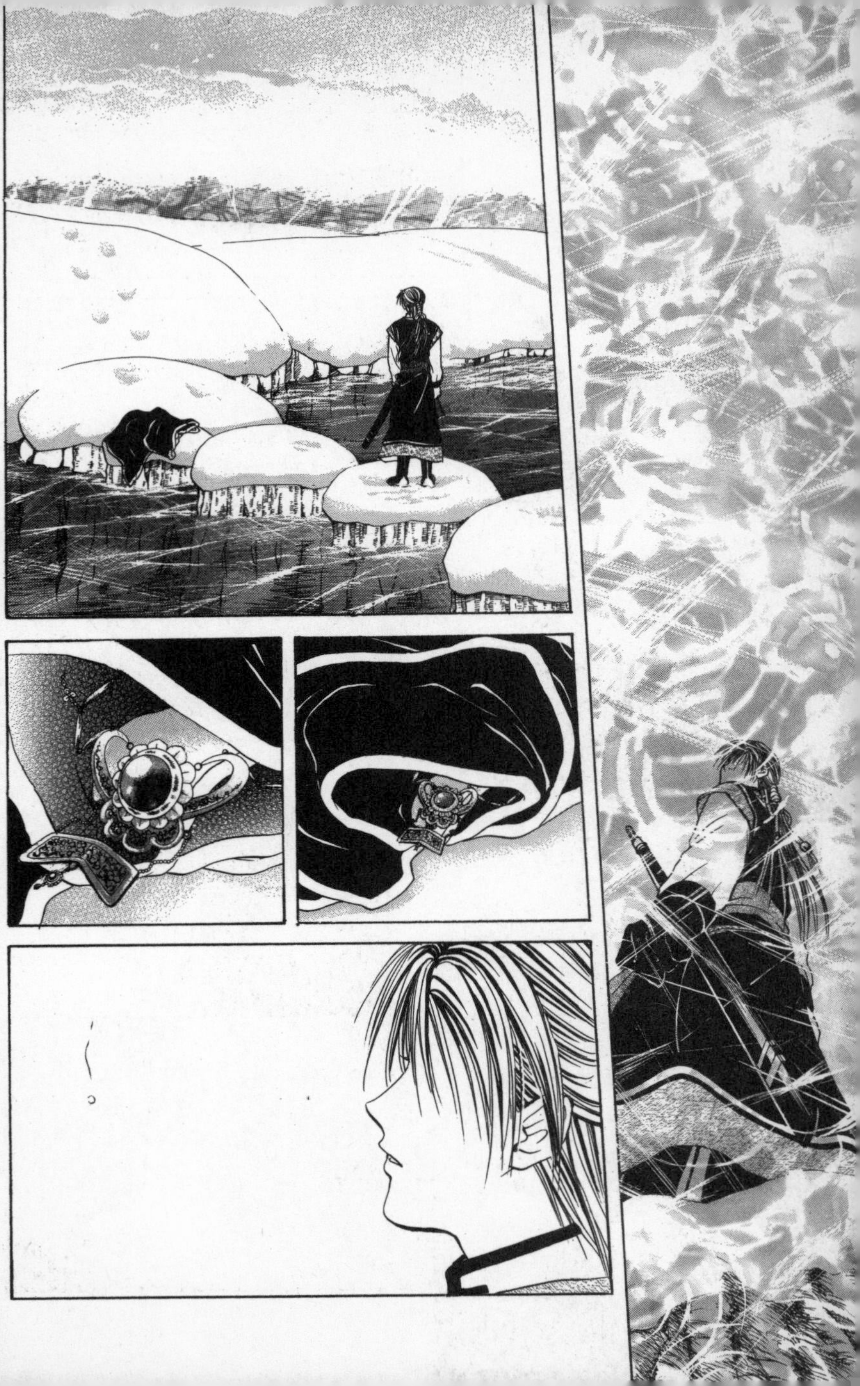

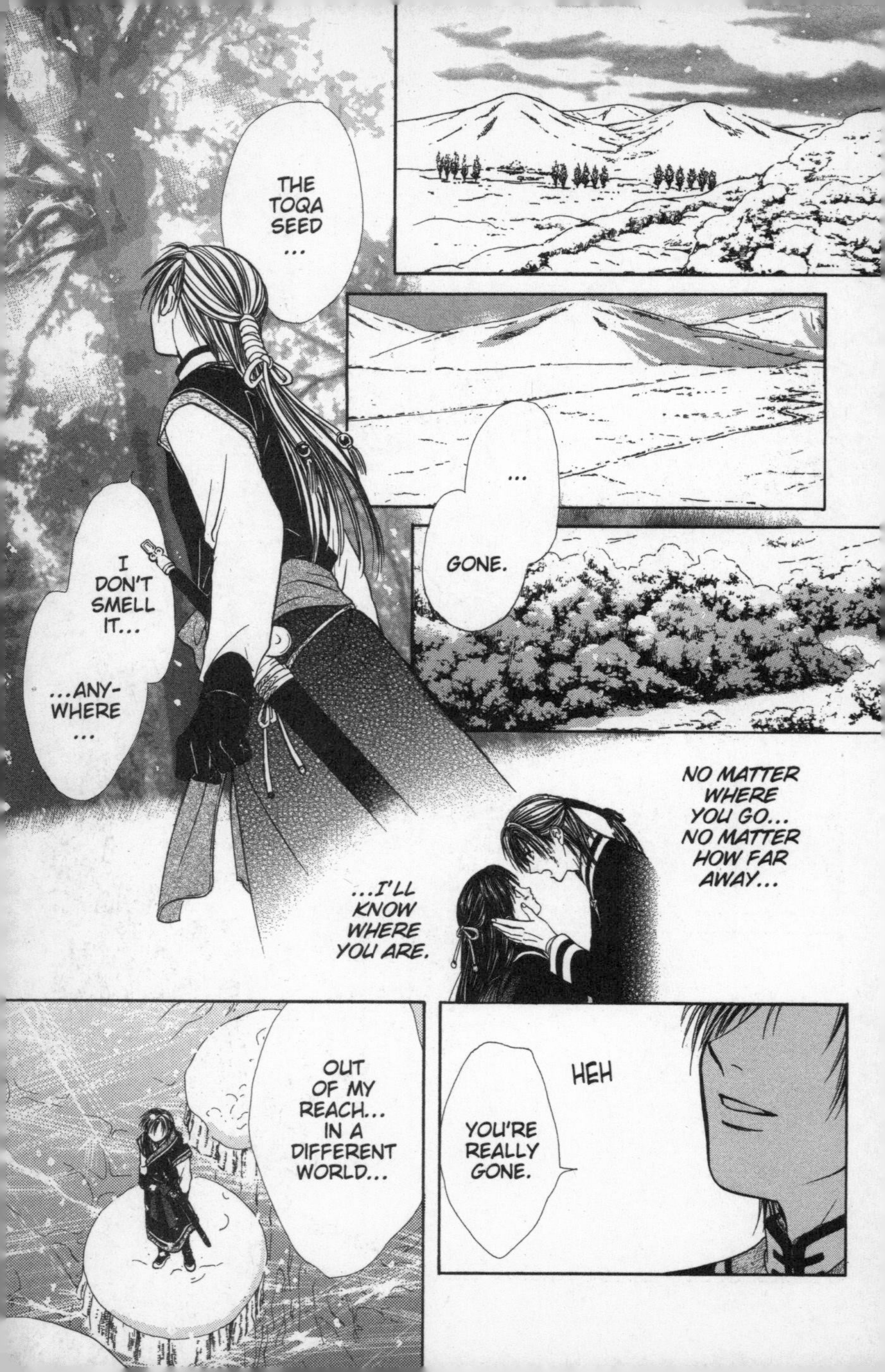
... GONE.
THE TOQA SEED ...
I DON'T SMELL IT...
...ANY-WHERE ...
NO MATTER WHERE YOU GO... NO MATTER HOW FAR AWAY...
...I'LL KNOW WHERE YOU ARE.
HEH
YOU'RE REALLY GONE.
OUT OF MY REACH... IN A DIFFERENT WORLD...

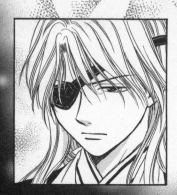

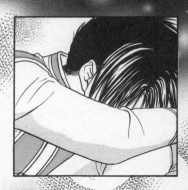

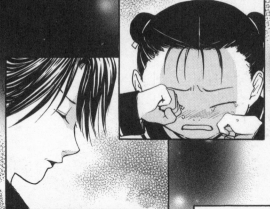

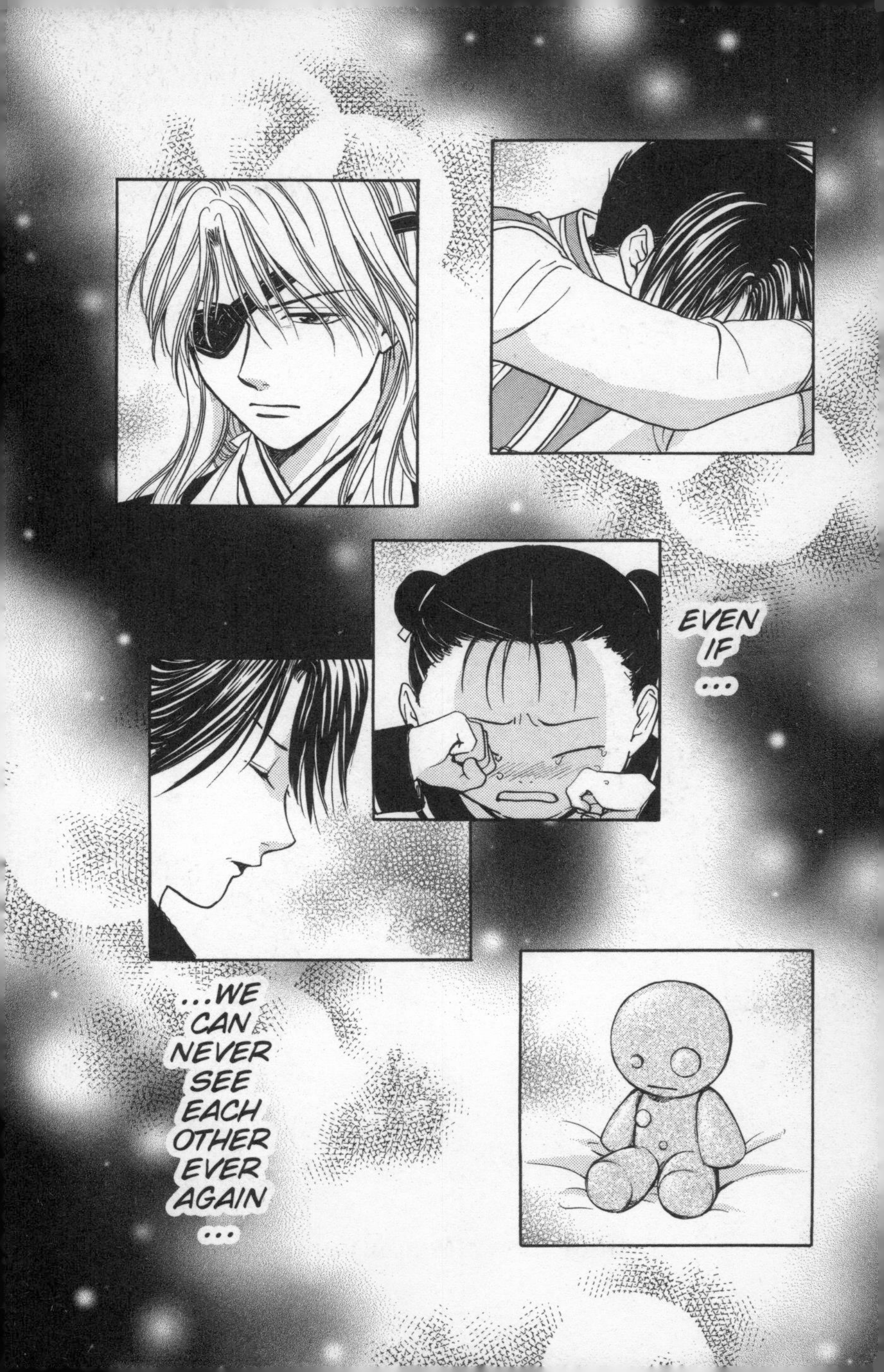

EVEN IF
...

...WE
CAN
NEVER
SEE
EACH
OTHER
EVER
AGAIN
...

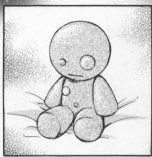

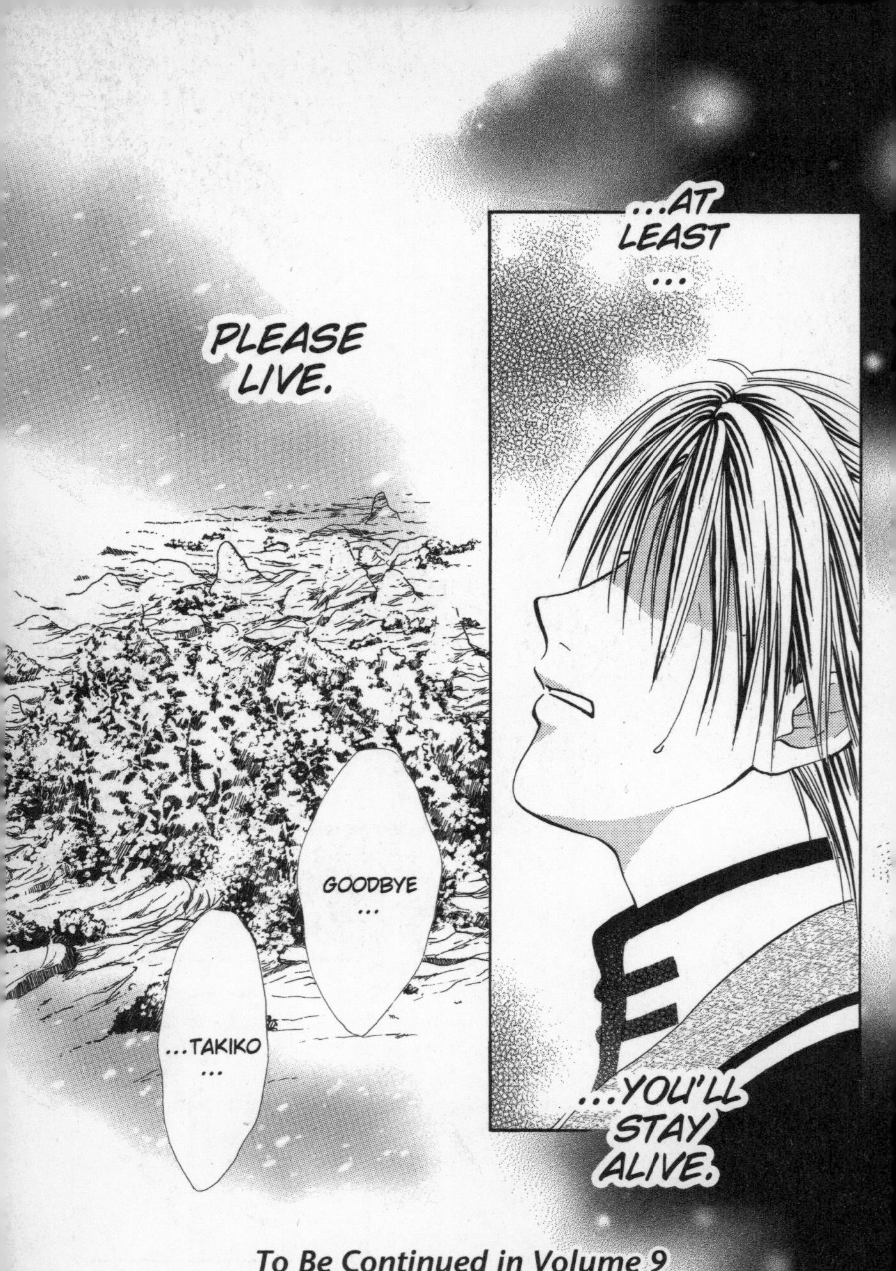
...AT LEAST ...
...YOU'LL STAY ALIVE.
PLEASE LIVE.
GOODBYE ...
...TAKIKO ...

To Be Continued in Volume 9

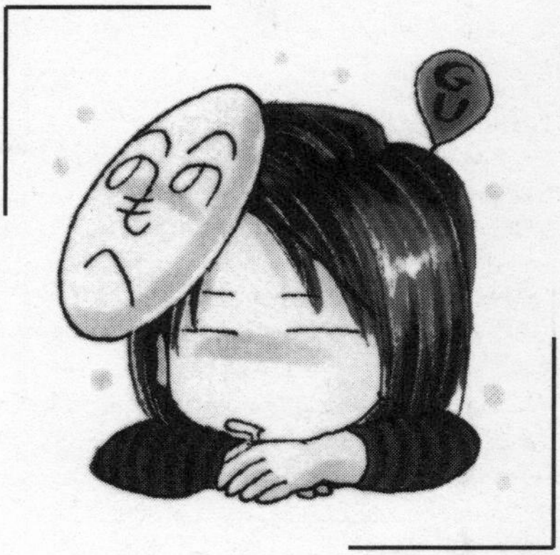
GU

Yuu Watase was born on March 5 in a town near Osaka, Japan. She was raised there before moving to Tokyo to follow her dream of creating manga. In the decade since her debut short story, *Pajama De Ojama* (An Intrusion in Pajamas), she has produced more than 50 volumes of short stories and continuing series. Her latest work, *Absolute Boyfriend*, appeared in Japan in the anthology magazine *Shôjo Comic* and is currently serialized in English in *Shojo Beat* magazine. Watase's other beloved series, *Alice 19th*, *Imadoki!*, and *Ceres: Celestial Legend*, are available in North America in English editions published by VIZ Media.

Fushigi Yûgi:
Genbu Kaiden Vol. 8

The Shojo Beat Manga Edition

STORY AND ART BY
YUU WATASE

Translation/Lillian Olsen
Touch-up Art & Lettering/Rina Mapa
Design/Hidemi Sahara
Editor/Shaenon K. Garrity

Editor in Chief, Books/Alvin Lu
Editor in Chief, Magazines/Marc Weidenbaum
VP, Publishing Licensing/Rika Inouye
VP, Sales & Product Marketing/Gonzalo Ferreyra
VP, Creative/Linda Espinosa
Publisher/Hyoe Narita

FUSHIGI YUGI GENBUKAIDEN 8 by Yuu WATASE © 2008 Yuu WATASE
All rights reserved. Original Japanese edition published in 2008 by
Shogakukan Inc., Tokyo.

The rights of the author(s) of the work(s) in this publication to be so identified
have been asserted in accordance with the Copyright, Designs and Patents Act
1988. A CIP catalogue record for this book is available from the British Library.

Printed in Canada

Published by VIZ Media, LLC
P.O. Box 77010
San Francisco, CA 94107

Shojo Beat Manga Edition
10 9 8 7 6 5 4 3 2 1
First printing, April 2009

PARENTAL ADVISORY
FUSHIGI YÛGI: GENBU KAIDEN is rated T+ for Older
Teen and is recommended for ages 16 and up.
Contains nudity, strong language, sexual themes,
and realistic and fantasy violence.
ratings.viz.com

www.viz.com

store.viz.com

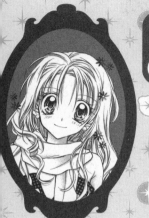
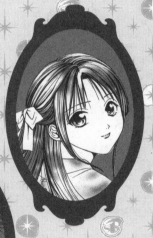

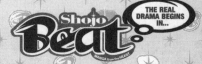

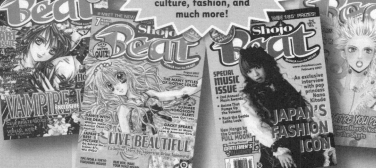

Save OVER **50%** off the

Shojo Beat
MANGA from the HEART

The Shojo Manga Authority

This monthly magazine is injected with the most **ADDICTIVE** shojo manga stories from Japan. PLUS, unique editorial coverage on the arts, music, culture, fashion, and much more!

☑ **YES!** Please enter my one-year subscription (12 GIANT issues) to **Shojo Beat** at the LOW SUBSCRIPTION RATE of **$34.99!**

Over **300 pages** per issue!

NAME

ADDRESS

CITY   STATE   ZIP

E-MAIL ADDRESS   P7GNC1

☐ MY CHECK IS ENCLOSED (PAYABLE TO Shojo Beat)   ☐ BILL ME LATER

CREDIT CARD: ☐ VISA   ☐ MASTERCARD

ACCOUNT #   EXP. DATE

SIGNATURE

CLIP AND MAIL TO ➤

SHOJO BEAT
Subscriptions Service Dept.
P.O. Box 438
Mount Morris, IL 61054-0438